A GUIDE TO THE

REPTILES
OF BELIZE

D1715494

About the Authors

Peter Stafford has been involved with herpetological field research in Belize since 1988, where much of his work has focused on the little known Maya Mountains. His principal interest concerns the natural history of reptiles, particularly snakes. He has written widely on the subject of herpetology, including several scientific papers and a recently co-authored book on Neotropical boas, and serves as a council member of the British Herpetological Society. His studies in Belize are ongoing.

John Meyer is a research herpetologist and biogeographer who has a long-standing affiliation with Central American herpetology. Among his numerous publications he is credited with having written many scientific papers on Mexican and Central American reptiles and amphibians. He co-authored the comprehensive *Snakes of Honduras,* and is co-author of a recently published *Guide to the Frogs and Toads of Belize.* He currently coordinates the Maya Forest Anuran Monitoring Project (MAYAMON) in this region.

A GUIDE TO THE
REPTILES
OF BELIZE

Peter J. Stafford
The Natural History Museum
London, United Kingdom

John R. Meyer
Navajo Natural Heritage Program,
Window Rock, Arizona

The Natural History Museum, London

ACADEMIC PRESS
San Diego   San Francisco   New York   Boston   London   Sydney   Toyko

Cover photos: Front cover, left: *Corytophanes cristatus* © Peter Stafford; right, top: *Crocodylus moreletii* © S. Von Peltz; right, bottom: *Dermatemys mawii,* © J. A. Campbell, University of Texas at Arlington.   Back cover: *Leptophis mexicanus* © Peter Stafford.

This book is printed on acid-free paper.

Academic Press
A Harcourt Science and Technology Company
525 B Street, Suite 1900, San Diego, California 92101-4495, U.S.A.
http://www.apnet.com

Academic Press
24-28 Oval Road, London NW1 7DX, UK
http://www.hbuk.co.uk/ap/

Library of Congress Catalog Card Number: 98-84371

International Standard Book Number: 0-12-662760-6

PRINTED IN CANADA
99 00 01 02 03 04 FR 9 8 7 6 5 4 3 2 1

To Marian

Peter J. Stafford

To my good friend and colleague,
Larry D. Wilson

John R. Meyer

Contents

The Environment and Reptile Fauna of Belize

Crocodilians (Order Crocodilia)

Turtles and Tortoises (Order Testudines)

Lizards (Order Squamata; Suborder Sauria)

Snakes (Order Squamata; Suborder Serpentes)

Appendix 1: Ecological Summary

Appendix 2: Distributional Summary

Preface

In publishing his inaugural account of Belize's amphibians and reptiles nearly sixty years ago, Karl P. Schmidt (1941) listed a total of 98 species noting "the prospect of still further additions is such that I now present only an annotated list." The herpetofauna of this small but biologically fascinating country is now known to be more diverse than perhaps even Schmidt suspected, comprising more than 160 species, 75% of which are reptiles. This book provides a complete guide to these animals—specifically the crocodiles, marine and freshwater turtles, lizards, and snakes—with details of their local variation, distribution, and ecology. During the various stages of its preparation we have received invaluable help from a number of individuals, to whom we owe a large debt of thanks. At The Natural History Museum, London, we are particularly grateful to Malcolm Penn and Bob Press for producing the maps,[1] Philip Hurst and Philip Crabb for photographing museum specimens on which most of the drawings are based, and the Publishing Division team for overseeing editorial matters.

We are pleased to acknowledge the help of David Warrell (Centre for Tropical Medicine, Nuffield Department of Clinical Medicine, John Radcliffe Hospital, Oxford, U.K.) for his contribution on the features and treatment of snake bites. Nicholas Brokaw (Manomet Observatory for Conservation Sciences, Massachusetts, U.S.A.) submitted helpful comments and suggestions on the description of vegetation types. Additional information on Belize and its reptile life was furnished by Paul Edgar, Tony

[1] Physical, rainfall, and district boundary maps are based on originals designed largely by the Land Information Center, Ministry of Natural Resources, Belize, published by Cubola Productions, Benque Viejo del Carmen, Belize.

Garel (Belize Zoo and Tropical Education Center), Robert Henderson (Milwaukee Public Museum, Wisconsin, U.S.A.), Julian Lee (University of Miami, Florida, U.S.A.), Jacob Marlin (Belize Foundation for Research and Environmental Education), Jan Meerman (Belize Tropical Forest Studies), Carolyn Miller (Wildlife Conservation Society, New York Zoological Society, U.S.A.), and Steven Platt (Clemson University, South Carolina, U.S.A.). For providing additional photographs, we are grateful to Jonathan Campbell, William Duellman, Peter and Donna Dutton, Paul Edgar, Carol Farneti Foster, Paul Freed, David George, John Iverson, Tony King, Jan Meerman, Alex Monro, Randy McCranie, Carolyn Miller, Stephen Von Peltz, and David Sutton. Other illustrations are by Peter Stafford unless credited differently.

We also thank the curators and collection managers of the following institutions for the loan of specimens and help in providing information: American Museum of Natural History, New York (AMNH), The Natural History Museum, London (BMNH), Carnegie Museum of Natural History, Pittsburgh (CM), Field Museum of Natural History, Chicago (FMNH), Louisiana State University Museum of Natural Science, Baton Rouge (LSUMZ), Museum of Comparative Zoology, Harvard (MCZ), Muséum National d'Histoire Naturelle, Paris (MHNH), Milwaukee Public Museum, Milwaukee, Wisconsin (MPM), University of Colorado Museum, Boulder (UCM), University of Kansas Museum of Natural History, Lawrence (UKMNH), University of Michigan Museum of Zoology, Ann Arbor (UMMZ), Smithsonian Institution National Museum of Natural History, Washington, DC (USNM), University of Texas, Arlington (UTA), and Zoologisches Museum, Berlin (ZMB).

Peter Stafford extends further thanks to Steven Blackmore and David Sutton of The Natural History Museum, London, and Alastair Rogers (Royal Marines, Reserve), for supporting his herpetological field work in the Maya Mountains and for their part in providing him with such a unique opportunity. His visits to Belize have been made even more pleasurable in the company of the various participants of the Joint Services Scientific and Raleigh International expeditions to the upper Raspaculo, and he is also appreciative of the inestimable help accorded to him by 25 Flight AAC, British Army Training Support Unit, Belize. For their assistance in providing information and issuing permits, he is grateful to the staff of the Forestry and Conservation Divisions, Ministry of Natural Resources. He also extends special thanks to John Howell, Chris Minty, and Nicodemus and Celia Bol at the Las Cuevas Research Station, and Tony Garel, Carol Farneti Foster, Sharon Matola, Jan Meerman, Carolyn Miller, and Steven Platt, who helped in a variety of different ways. At The Natural History Museum's Lower Vertebrate Division in London he is especially grateful to Colin McCarthy for his assistance with various collection-based enquiries, and Garth Underwood for useful comments on aspects of taxonomy. Finally, Peter Stafford thanks his wife, Marian, who checked the various manuscript proofs, assisted with photography, and cheerfully endured many an imposition in the cause of this book.

John R. Meyer thanks the faculty and administration of the University College of Belize for their patience and understanding during his tenure as Lecturer in Biology in 1992–1993. At Programme for Belize, he is indebted to Joy Grant and Roger Wilson, as well as the staff of La Milpa Field Station, for their support of his field studies at Rio Bravo. It has also been his pleasure to work with the staff of the Belize Audubon Society, and he is particularly grateful to Osmany Salas and the personnel of the national parks and reserves for help and companionship in the field. Also particularly helpful during his studies in Belize were Lou Nicolait and Frances Griffith of the Belize Center for Environmental Studies, and Celeste W. Moore, Jacksonville Zoo, Florida. He is also in debt to Paul Walker, Sarteneja; Sharon Matola and Tony Garel, Belize Zoo and Tropical Education Center; and Anelie Rodriguez, Belize City, for their input and field assistance. He is particularly pleased to acknowledge the assistance and friendship of his many biology students at the University College of Belize, whose persistence and cheerfulness in the field were an inspiration. Finally, John Meyer thanks his wife, Cyndi, for her patience and assistance in the preparation of this book and for her companionship in the field.

Overview

If you find yourself lost in the jungles of Belize, there are some among the Maya who believe you should stand beneath a cottonwood tree and wrap your arms around its trunk. Here, they say, you will be rescued by the *duende*, a little old man and guardian of the forest who announces himself by wrapping his arms around the other side of the tree and clasping your hands in his. He is said to carry a razor-sharp machete and if you meet him you are advised to keep your thumbs hidden, as the misfortunate character has none of his own and will try to chop them off for himself if he sees them. It is also said that his feet point backward to confuse anyone who should try to follow him.

No doubt this delightful story has been unable to escape some distortion of the facts, but among the cottonwood trees lives an equally mysterious creature that bears an odd resemblance to the fabled little denizen of the forest and, by intriguing coincidence, is known by the local name of "Old Man." Despite the goblin-like features, however, it is a type of lizard. Seldom seen and extremely well camouflaged, *Corytophanes cristatus* is usually found perched vertically on the lower trunks of forest trees and vines. If spotted and approached, it puffs out its scaly throat, taking on the appearance, some say, of a bearded old man; but the most striking feature is a spectacular crest on the back of its neck, which, if the animal feels threatened, is erected and stretched out like a sail. Should its elaborate threat display fail to intimidate, the lizard takes flight, running away upright on its long hind legs.

The Old Man lizard is just one of the many interesting and unusual reptiles found in Belize. Squeezed into a corner of the Caribbean between northern Guatemala and the Mexican states of Campeche, Quintana Roo,

and Yucatán, this republic, known as British Honduras until its indepen-
dence in 1981, is Central America's second smallest nation. In total area it
covers a modest 8867 square miles (22,965 km²), including 266 square miles
(676 km²) of islands, but it boasts some of the finest natural wonders to be
found on the entire continent. Running along the length of the coast and
sprinkled with tiny islands, the coral reef is perhaps second only to
Australia's Great Barrier Reef in its splendor and diversity of marine life.
Rolling, jungle-covered hills, remote river valleys, and pine forests provide
a haven for the endangered jaguar, scarlet macaw, Baird's tapir, and
Morelet's crocodile, while haunting relics of an ancient Mayan civilization
contribute to the mystic ambience of the country. The main population cen-
ters of modern Belize lie on the coast, or along the major waterways and
roads, and much of the interior has thus far escaped significant development.
Places like Never Delay, Go to Hell Camp, Double Head Cabbage, and
Teakettle are just a few of the more intriguingly named rural settlements,
populated by a culturally diverse mixture of humanity including Creole,
Mestizo, Garifuna, Maya, European, and Asiatic.

The herpetofauna of Central America has received devoted attention
from generations of herpetologists. Perhaps the earliest and most prolific
was E. D. Cope, whose "Contributions to the Herpetology of Tropical
America" and other works between 1860 and the turn of the century provided the first major insights into the region's herpetofauna. The first specific checklist of Belize's reptiles and amphibians was prepared by K. P.
Schmidt in 1941, who listed a total of 98 taxa, although it was not until
1965, after the publication of some 11 papers by W. T. Neill and R. Allen,
that a clearer picture of the Belizean herpetofauna began to emerge. In this
1965 paper, Neill provided supplementary information and a list of 118
species, and an extensive series of studies by R. W. Henderson and L. G.
Hoevers in early 1970s culminated in a revised distributional checklist and
key to 134 species (Henderson and Hoevers, 1975). A subsequent analysis
of species distribution in the Guatemalan region as a whole, by J. A.
Campbell and J. P. Vannini (1989), listed a new total of 28 amphibians and
99 reptiles from Belize (excluding marine turtles). As currently known, the
number of amphibians and reptiles reported from Belize stands at 161 and,
while the potential exists for a number of extralimital species to be added,
it is becoming increasingly unlikely that many more will come to light.
Further studies, however, will undoubtedly reveal fresh insights into distribution patterns, infraspecific variation, and ecology.

Herpetological investigations in northern Guatemala, the Yucatán
Peninsula states of Mexico, and other neighboring areas have done much to
close the gaps in our knowledge where information on species in Belize has
been lacking. In particular, the works published by L. C. Stuart on the herpetofauna of El Petén and Alta Verapaz, by W. E. Duellman, and more

recently by J. A. Campbell and contemporaries have provided a much clearer understanding of species composition in the region. To the west of Belize, the reptiles of Chiapas have been treated by Alvarez del Toro (1982), and the amphibians and reptiles in Honduras to the south have been documented by L. D. Wilson and J. R. Meyer (Meyer and Wilson, 1971, 1973; Wilson and Meyer, 1985). The herpetofauna of the entire Yucatán Peninsula, including Belize, has been the subject of ongoing research since the early 1970s by J. C. Lee at the University of Miami, recently culminating in a comprehensive monograph (Lee, 1996). Over many years the amphibians and reptiles of this particular area were also studied by C. J. McCoy at the Carnegie Museum, a research interest continued today by his associate, E. Censky. Guidebooks dealing with individual components of Belize's herpetofauna have been published by Weyer (1990) (snakes) and by Garel and Meyer and Farneti Foster (1996) (frogs and toads), while a regional guide to the herpetology of adjacent parts of Guatemala has recently been completed by Campbell (1998).

USING THE IDENTIFICATION KEYS

Dichotomous keys to families, genera, and species are provided for each of the four main reptile groups. These have been based largely on the keys of Meyer and Wilson (1973), Henderson and Hoevers (1975), and Wilson and Meyer (1985), using external characters where possible to facilitate application in the field. The keys are primarily intended for use in helping to ascertain the identity of small species, and those that resemble each other closely, where attention to detail is particularly important. In many cases, however, it will be possible to recognize an animal simply by comparing it with the photograph(s) provided or by reading through some of the descriptions, without the need for recourse to the identification keys.

The keys consist of pairs of alternative, constrasting statements listed in numbered steps. By selecting the most applicable statement at each step and proceeding to the next numbered step indicated, the likely identity of the animal in question is ascertained by a process of elimination. The final diagnosis should then be cross-checked by referring to the appropriate species description, paying particular attention to any alternatives listed under Similar Species, and comparing the animal with the photographs(s) or drawing where provided. In the case of snakes, it is clearly imperative that the reader be able to recognize *all* the venomous species before attempting to catch one for the purpose of examining it more closely, and it should also be borne in mind that even nonvenomous snakes, along with some of the larger lizards and turtles, can inflict a painful bite.

ORGANIZATION OF THE SPECIES ACCOUNTS

The species accounts are organized in alphabetical order within genera, and the genera are listed alphabetically within families. Higher taxonomic categories (order through family) are listed in phylogenetic sequence and follow Lee (1996). In consideration of various anomalies that exist in the subspecific demarcation of certain taxa and the need for more information regarding infraspecific variation in general, we have chosen not to list subspecies and use only the species name in the title of the account. However, anecdotal reference to subspecific forms is, in a number of cases, made under Remarks.

Each account begins with a reference to the most commonly used vernacular names: the Belizean name(s) appears first in italics, followed by the English and Spanish versions. For English and Spanish common names we have in general followed Liner (1994). Emphasis in the species descriptions is on features that characterize the animal concerned and distinguish it from all others. Details of size, physical structure, scale arrangement, color, and other identifying features are provided as they apply to individuals from Belize, although are not intended as a complete diagnosis. It may be inferred that the eye has a round pupil unless stated otherwise. Size is expressed in millimeters and represents the approximate known maximum for the species; in the case of crocodiles and snakes, the measurement given represents the overall total length; in turtles, the length of the carapace; and in lizards, which may frequently be observed with incomplete tails, the distance from snout to vent. Physical characteristics referred to in the species descriptions and identification keys are defined in the Glossary and in the introduction to each of the main reptile groups, or illustrated in the associated figures.

Habitat details are given in terms of the principal ecological formations outlined in the vegetation section of Chapter 1. This is followed by a brief description of the species' adaptive zone (i.e., terrestrial, arboreal, fossorial, aquatic) and its elevational range in Belize. Next, the general distribution of the species is given (from approximate northern to southern geographical limits), followed by its local distribution in terms of the six main political divisions (districts) of Belize (see Fig. 3). Only those districts where the occurrence of a species has been confirmed are listed, although the possibility of its existence elsewhere in the country, or at a higher or lower elevation than that given, should not be ignored; many of the reptiles found in Belize have much wider ranges in the lowlands of Central America, and some also extend into North and South America. The term "countrywide" is used as a reference to mainland Belize only and, unless otherwise stated, does not include the cayes. Precise locality records are presented in tabulated form in Appendix 2. For a more comprehensive list of locality records the reader is directed to Lee (1996).

A Similar Species section is included, with details of salient features that will distinguish the species in question from others of similar appearance. This is followed by remarks on behavior, ecology, conservation status, and taxonomy. Finally, a key reference is cited that may assist in identification of the species or group of species concerned.

Illustrations

Illustrations are included for all but 3 of the 122 species of reptiles treated in this book. Except for 6 species represented by ink drawings or monochrome photographs only, the remainder are illustrated with color photographs, and some of those shown in color have also been portrayed in ink and/or by monochromes to illustrate particular features. Most of the illustrations are of specimens from Belize; for some species, however, we have resorted to using photographs of examples from wider afield. Photographs of both adults and juveniles have been provided where possible, and for species that exhibit sexual dimorphism or variable color patterns, we have endeavoured to include a selection of photographs to illustrate the range of variation.

THE ENVIRONMENT AND REPTILE FAUNA OF BELIZE

ENVIRONMENTAL PROFILE

Physiography

Although Belize lacks the extensive montane topography that has con-
tributed to the biological complexity of adjacent Chiapas, southern
Guatemala, and other parts of Central America, environmental diversity
within the country is considerable, especially for such a relatively small
area. The dominant physical feature inland is the Maya Mountain massif,
which lies in a northeast–southwest arc across the central and southern
part of the country (Fig. 1). East of the main divide the mountain slopes rise
steeply from the coastal plain, while on the opposite side they descend
more gradually, extending to the Vaca Plateau and over the border into
Guatemala in the vicinity of Poptún. Much of the area, especially the

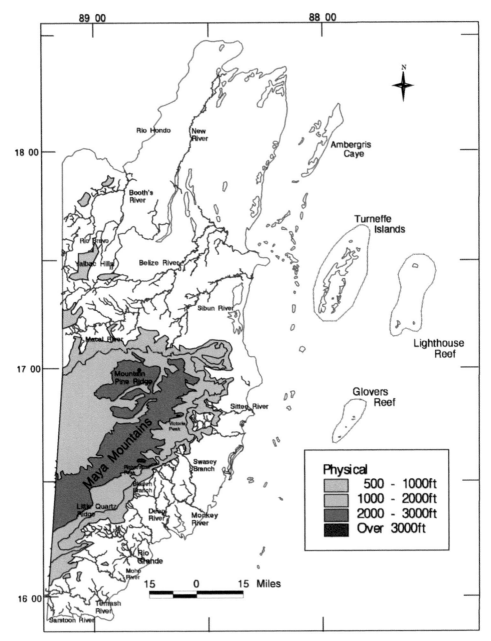

FIGURE 1 Physical map of Belize showing main lowland river systems and areas of relief. Modified from "Atlas of Belize," 19th revised edition (1994), with permission of the publisher, Cubola Productions, Benque Viejo, Belize.

Cockscomb Range to the east of the divide, is steeply sloped (often 40° of slope or more) and has only a thin soil cover. Outcropping rock is common. Peaks and ridges commonly rise to 3000 ft (914 m); Victoria Peak in the Cockscomb Range, long considered the highest peak in Belize, reaches an elevation of approximately 3650 ft (1120 m), although at 3800 ft (1160 m), a ridge-top plateau in the southern part of the Maya Mountains, known as Doyle's Delight, is actually the highest point.

The underlying rock consists of a granite core, largely overlaid by meta-morphosed Paleozoic sediments. Following the retreat of the sea, which inundated much of the country during the Cretaceous, all but the highest parts remain covered by a thick deposit of limestone. Due to the impervi-ous nature of the granite substrata, drainage is largely on the surface (except in limestone areas), and the mountains are dissected by numerous streams and rivers. Those draining the eastern slopes, such as the Swasey, Bladen, South Stann Creek, Columbia, and Rio Grande, pursue independent and relatively direct courses to the Caribbean Sea. The rivers of the leeward side, such as the Raspaculo, Chiquibul, and Macal, all flow in a winding westerly direction to meet the Belize River before emptying into the Caribbean, except for the Rio Machiquila, which joins the Rio Usumacinta in Guatemala to discharge into the Gulf of Mexico.

At both the northern and southern edges of the Maya Mountains is karst topography consisting of jagged limestone peaks, caves, sinkholes, and underground rivers. Ranges of karst hills also occur in central Belize between the Sibun and Mullins rivers, and to the south in the vicinity of Punta Gorda, though these are generally less than 300 ft (90 m) in elevation.

Between the Maya Mountains and the Caribbean is a flat coastal plain, an agriculturally fertile area overlaid by alluvial soils laid down by streams and rivers eroding the windward slopes. South of Punta Gorda the low topography of this region has encouraged the development of marshes and swamp forest, particularly along and between the Moho, Temash, and Sarstoon rivers.

Northern Belize is essentially a flat limestone shelf with little topo-graphical relief. Much of the area lies below 330 ft (100 m). Only in the west near the Guatemalan border do low hills appear, with those west of the Rio Bravo escarpment and Yalbac Hills reaching as high as 900 ft (275 m). The rivers in this area, such as the Rio Bravo, Booth's, Hondo, and the New River, generally flow in a north or northeasterly direction, and connect with several major wetlands, such as the New River Lagoon, Northern and Southern Lagoons, and Cox's Lagoon.

Climate

Belize lies in the tropics between 15° and 19° N latitude. Temperatures remain fairly uniform throughout the year, with an annual mean of 79°F

(26°C), a mean high of 86°F (30°C), and a mean low of 71°F (21.7°C), with local differences due to topography. Winds from the north bring relatively cooler temperatures December through February, while the month of May tends to be particularly hot. Generally, temperatures are highest at sea level, but they rarely fall below the mid-50s Farenheit, even in upland areas. Day length varies from slightly over 11 hr in December and January to 13 hr in June.

Although it can rain at any time of the year, the country experiences a well defined dry period between February and May, during which time it may receive only about 10% of its annual rainfall. Rainfall varies considerably from one part of the country to another (Fig. 2). It is greatest in the south, where rainfall may exceed 170 in. (432 cm) a year, and declines markedly northward to under 50 in. (127 cm) near the border with Quintana Roo. Annual rainfall in the Belize City area averages 73 in. (185 cm); at Orange Walk, 61 in. (155 cm); at Gallon Jug, 59 in. (150 cm); at Douglas D'Silva (previously Augustine, Mountain Pine Ridge), 65 in. (165 cm); while in the southern part of the Maya Mountains and along the coastal plain in the extreme south, rainfall is reputed to average about 200 in. (508 cm) per year. Rainfall is high and seasonality less severe on the eastern slopes of the Maya Mountains, while on the leeward side a rain shadow effect reduces the precipitation and seasonality is more severe.

A short period of wet weather often occurs in late April or May, known by some as the "iguana rains," so called because by moistening the ground, they reputedly allow hatching iguanas to dig their way out of their underground nests. From June to November rainfall may be heavy and accompanied by strong tropical storms. Hurricanes are a constant threat, although a severe one on the scale of Hurricane Hattie, which devastated much of the country in 1961, has not struck since. During August there is frequently a dry spell between the rains, known to the Maya as the *mawger* season (Rabinowitz, 1987).

Vegetation

Belize remains covered by substantial areas of natural vegetation. With a long-established timber industry, and history of devastating tropical storms, most of its forests are secondary in nature, although isolated pockets of old growth forest may survive in parts of the Maya Mountains.

A number of distinct vegetation types have arisen in Belize, largely influenced by the seasonal and clinal variation in rainfall from north to south. Various attempts have been made to classify them. Among the more recent, Wright et al. (1959) categorized the different types in terms of composition and function, reflecting the underlying rock formation and associated tree species (e.g., "broadleaved forest with a few lime-loving species") and sea-

4

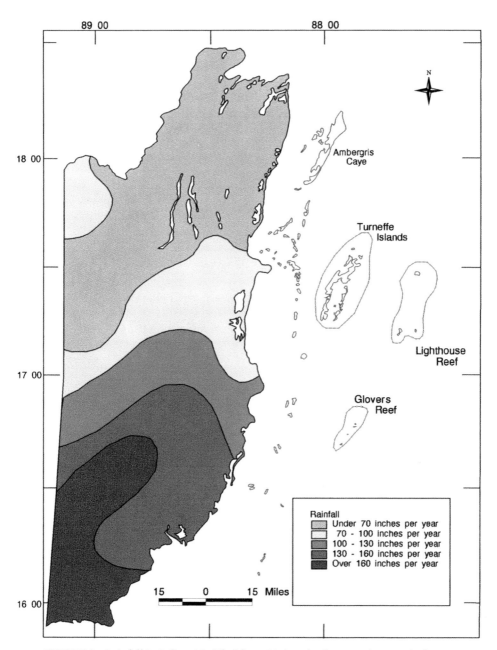

FIGURE 2 Rainfall in Belize. Modified from "Atlas of Belize," 19th revised edition (1994), with permission of the publisher, Cubola Productions, Benque Viejo, Belize.

sonality of rainfall (e.g., "semi-evergreen seasonal forest"). Hartshorn *et al.* (1984) used the life zone system (Holdridge, 1967) to classify them in the broader context of neotropical vegetation, based on the combined effects of latitude, altitude, evapotranspiration, and precipitation. Iremonger and Brokaw (1995) provided a comprehensive, hierarchical classification based at the first level on physionomic structure (*forests, scrubs, herbaceous communities*), and thereafter ranked in descending order through such further distinctions as water table influence, soil type, species composition, and additional details of structure.

While other systems have been used to reflect the distribution and ecology of birds (Russell, 1964) and the herpetofauna in general (Neill and Allen, 1959b), we follow Meyer and Farneti Foster (1996) in adopting a simplified classification of vegetation types for the purpose of understanding the distribution of the reptile fauna, attempting to reference it with Neill and Allen (1959b) and some of the other aforementioned classifications.

Evergreen Broadleaf Forest (Plates 1–3)

This vegetation type includes the *rainforest* of Neill and Allen (1959b) and the *rainforest* and *tall humid forest* of Russell (1964), and is embraced by the *tropical moist, tropical wet, subtropical wet,* and *subtropical lower montane* life zones of Hartshorn *et al.* (1984). Iremonger and Brokaw (1995)

PLATE 1　Evergreen broadleaf forest. Lower Raspaculo River, Cayo District.

PLATE 2 Evergreen broadleaf forest. Forest interior at Salamanca, Toledo District. Photograph by A.K. Monro.

PLATE 3 Evergreen broadleaf forest. Riparian vegetation with *Iguana iguana*, upper Raspaculo River, Cayo District.

refer to this vegetation type under several different groupings within the *lowland broadleaf wet forest* subcategory. It is restricted to the lower half of the country, covering the forested coastal lowlands and the lower slopes of the Maya Mountains. Although rainfall is seasonal, the forest does not take on a dry aspect; the forest leaf litter usually remains moist and the underlying soil supports at least some ground-level herbaceous plants (e.g., *Selaginella* spp.) year-round. Conspicuous in the understory are small *Chamaedorea* and *Geonoma* palms, and there may be occasional colonies of the terrestrial bromeliad, *Aechmea magdalenae*. Old growth canopy trees are generally large, often approaching 100 ft (33 m). Many possess buttress and stilt roots and are covered with epiphytes. Characteristic species include Santa María (*Calophyllum brasiliense*), cabbage palm (*Euterpe macrospadix*), banak (*Virola koschnyi*), wild akee (*Guarea grandifolia*), trumpet (*Pourouma aspera*), copal macho (*Protium schippii*), and yemeri (*Vochysia hondurensis*), as well as tree ferns (e.g., *Cyathea myosuroides*) where edaphic conditions permit. Characteristic secondary growth species, typically found in riparian habitats or previously cleared land, include cottonwood (*Ceiba pentandra*), quamwood (*Schizolobium parahybum*), salmwood (*Cordia alliodora*), trumpet (*Cecropia mexicana*), moho (*Trichospermum campbellii*), prickly yellow (*Zanthoxylum* sp.), polak (*Ochroma bicolor*), and bribrí (*Inga edulis*). Reptile life is abundant and diverse.

Semi-evergreen Seasonal Forest (Plates 4 and 5)

A drier variant of the previous vegetation type, this includes the *rainforest* (in part) and *cohune ridge* of Neill and Allen (1959b) and the *tall moist forest* of Russell (1964), and is embraced by the *subtropical moist forest* ecological formation of Hartshorn *et al.* (1984). Iremonger and Brokaw (1995) distinguish between a number of variants of semi-evergreen seasonal forest within their *lowland moist evergreen seasonal forest* subcategory. This vegetation type is distributed exclusively in the northern and western quarter of the country, and extends southward along the Guatemalan border on the leeward side of the Maya Mountains. Its character changes from the northeast corner of the country, where the dry season is severe and many trees lose their leaves, to the forests of the Rio Bravo escarpment, which exhibit a lesser degree of leaf loss. The vegetation type also appears scattered throughout the lowland savannas wherever edaphic conditions permit, as well as along most of the streams and lagoons in the north, and as isolated "islands" on limestone caps within the highland pine savanna formation. Many of the same trees that occur in evergreen broadleaf forest, including both old and secondary growth species, are also found in this formation, although they are generally neither as tall nor as rich in epiphytic growth. Due to the pronounced dry season, the forest leaf litter may become completely dried out. Conspicuous patches of liana growth may be present.

PLATE 4   Semi-evergreen seasonal forest. Dry oak forest at Guacamallo Bridge, Cayo District.

Understory vegetation is typically sparse. Characteristic tree species include mahogany (*Swietenia macrophylla*), nargusta (*Terminalia amazonica*), gombolimbo (*Bursera simaruba*), polewood (*Xylopia frutescens*), wild rubber (*Castilla elastica*), *Pouteria* spp., *Manilkara* spp., *Drypetes* spp., and cedar (*Cedrela odorata*), as well as large, sometimes nearly monotypic stands of the cohune palm (*Attalea cohune*). Reptile life is abundant and diverse.

Karst Hills Forest (Plates 6 and 7)

Although this vegetation type has much in common with the semi-evergreen seasonal forest, particularly with respect to some of the attendant tree species and seasonal leaf loss, it owes its nature more to the underlying rock porosity than to seasonal rainfall. The karst hills forest vegetation type is embraced by the *tropical moist forest* and *subtropical wet forest* ecological formations of Hartshorn *et al.* (1984), and described under the *hill forests* subcategory of Iremonger and Brokaw (1995). It is most noticeable in the region between the Sibun and Mullins rivers, but similar conditions also exist in the karst hills of Toledo District (Fig. 3), although the higher rainfall may mitigate against desiccation of the forest here. In terms of species composition, the tree flora of karst hills forest is not dissimilar to that of the semi-evergreen seasonal forest formation, although the trees do

PLATE 5 Semi-evergreen seasonal forest. Limestone cap forest with *Beaucarnea pliabilis* (Agavaceae), Mountain Pine Ridge, Cayo District. Photograph by A.K. Monro.

PLATE 6   Karst hills topography. Society Hall area, Cayo District.

PLATE 7   Karst hills forest. Gracy Rock area, Belize District.

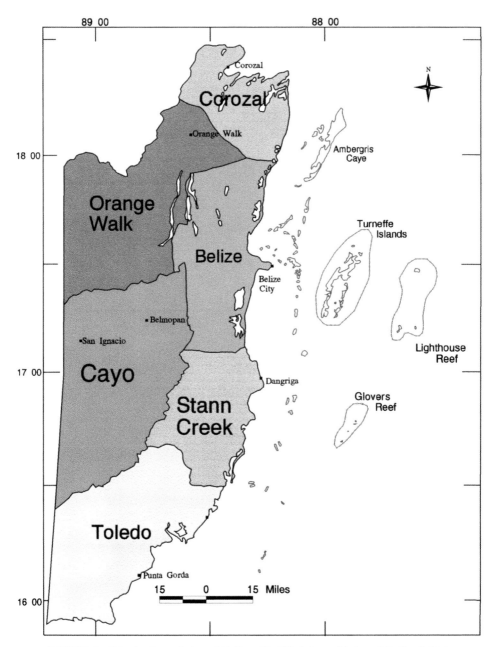

FIGURE 3 District boundaries of Belize. Modified from "Atlas of Belize," 19th revised edition (1994), with permission of the publisher, Cubola Productions, Benque Viejo, Belize.

not reach the heights encountered in the previous two vegetation types, buttress roots are less well developed, and epiphytic growth is variable. Forest floor leaf litter tends to remain dry, supporting little herbaceous growth, though abundant shelter for terrestrial reptile life abounds in the form of caves and potholes in the weathered rock base.

Subtropical Evergreen Forest (Plate 8)

This is one of the biologically least explored formations in Belize, occurring only at elevations of between 1500 and 3000 ft (460 to 914 m) on the windward slopes of the Maya Mountains. It includes the *rainforest* (in part) of Neill and Allen (1959b), the *rainforest* (in part) and *palm brake* of Russell (1964), the *subtropical lower montane wet forest* life zone of Hartshorn *et al.* (1984), and is analogous with the *montane forests and scrub forests* subcategory of Iremonger and Brokaw (1995). Because of the higher elevations, evapotranspiration is lower and moisture condensation higher, resulting in a more humid environment and a more exuberant vegetation. The effects of the dry season are minimal. Trees may be large, the canopy often reaching 100 ft (33 m), and buttress roots are common. Moss growth on tree trunks and branches is often extensive. Forest floor leaf litter is always moist, supporting a varied ground-level herbaceous vegetation and an understory layer of dwarf palms. This is the closest vegetation type in Belize to what is called cloud forest in Central America. At higher elevations the tree flora is characterized in some areas by palm brake, dominated by *Colpothrinax cookii*. Reptile life is less well known than that in the lowlands, but may comprise many of the same species.

Elfin Forest (Plates 9 and 10)

This vegetation type was termed *elfin woodland* by Russell (1964), who encountered it on the windward slopes of the Maya Mountains above 2600 ft (865 m) in elevation. Iremonger and Brokaw (1995) describe it within their *montane palm forest over volcanics* subcategory of *hill forests*. Exposed to strong winds and frequently enveloped by cloud, it is characterized by stunted trees festooned with epiphytes. Leaf litter is constantly moist. Cavities between rocks and tree roots are filled with mosses, liverworts, and other small hydrophytic plants, or hold semipermanent pools of rainwater. Characteristic tree species include *Clusia* spp. The reptile life of this vegetation type remains almost completely unknown.

Savanna (Plate 11)

This is the predominant vegetation type in northern, central, and coastal southern Belize, found extensively west of the Northern Highway, along both sides of the Western Highway in Belize District, and along the Coastal

PLATE 8   Subtropical evergreen forest. Near Palmar, Cayo District.

PLATE 9 Victoria Peak, Cockscombe Range, Stann Creek District, with elfin forest at summit.

PLATE 10 Elfin forest. Victoria Peak, Stann Creek District. Photograph by J. Hall.

PLATE 11   Savanna. Mile 34, Western Highway, Belize District.

and Southern highways between the Sibun and Deep rivers. It was termed the *palm and pine savanna* by Neill and Allen (1959b), and the *pine savanna, pine ridge,* and *broken pine ridge* by Russell (1964). It is embraced within the *subtropical moist forest* and *tropical moist forest* ecological formations of Hartshorn *et al.* (1984), and comparable with the *lowland needle-leaf moist open forests over poor soils, disturbed scrub,* and *fire-induced herbaceous vegetation* subcategories of Iremonger and Brokaw (1995). The essential nature of this vegetation type is its openness, tempered by a variety of tree and shrub associations. The predominant plants are grasses and sedges, with stands (hammocks) of pines (*Pinus caribaea*), oaks (*Quercus barbeyana* and *Q. hondurensis*), palms and palmettos, calabash (*Crescentia* sp.), and other shrubby trees in places. This formation owes its existence to edaphic factors, drying to parched, rock hardness in the dry season, and frequent flooding during the rainy season. A noticeable feature of the savanna is the occurrence of fires, both natural and human-induced, during the dry season. Temporary ponds, marshes, and streams are common, providing important refuges for turtles. The reptile fauna is characteristically different from that of broadleaf forest associations.

Highland Pine Savanna (Plates 12 and 13)

Situated on the northwestern corner of the Maya Mountains, the Mountain Pine Ridge area is somewhat of an anomaly, surrounded as it is by broadleaf forest. It was called *pine parkland* by Neill and Allen (1959b)

PLATE 12   Highland pine savanna. Mountain Pine Ridge, Cayo District.

PLATE 13   Highland pine savanna. Forest interior near Douglas D'Silva, Mountain Pine Ridge, Cayo District. Photograph by A.K. Monro.

and *pine forest* by Russell (1964), and lies within the *subtropical moist forest* zone of Hartshorn *et al.* (1984). In the system of Iremonger and Brokaw (1995) it is included within the *needle-leaf hill forests over poor soils* subcategory. This vegetation type is characterized by the predominance of pine trees (*Pinus caribaea* and *P. oocarpa*), with a dense ground cover of grasses; there are also areas of shrub understory dominated by Melastomataceae. In appearance it differs little from the pine savannas of lower elevations. To some extent, the savanna-like vegetation is determined by frequent fires, preventing the accumulation of undergrowth. The area is bisected by numerous rocky ravines and swiftly flowing streams that are bordered by narrow belts of broadleaf evergreen vegetation, in which some reptile species not usually associated with highland pine savanna may occur. The reptile fauna, although characteristically different from that of other forest vegetation types, is essentially similar to that of pine savannas found elsewhere in Belize.

Interior Wetlands (Plate 14)

This vegetation type, termed *freshwater savanna* by Russell (1964), is found throughout the lowlands of Belize. It is encompassed by the *subtropical moist forest, tropical moist forest, subtropical wet forest,* and *tropical wet forest* ecological formations of Hartshorn *et al.* (1984), and divided by Iremonger and Brokaw (1995) into a number of variants within the *saline*

PLATE 14 Interior wetlands. Chan Chen and Patchchacan area, Corozal District.

influence not significant subcategories of *scrubs* and *herbaceous communities*. Freshwater wetland habitats, varying from reed-swamps and marshes to extensive lagoons, are prominent in the northern part of the country, and a few large areas of swampland are also to be found in Toledo District. Surrounding vegetation is often dense and typically consists primarily of grasses, sedges, and rushes (*Eleocharis* spp., *Typha* spp. etc.), or may be more complex with extensive palm and hardwood forests. Reptile life is dominated largely by aquatic and semiaquatic forms and terrestrial inhabitants of waterside vegetation.

Coastal Lagoons and Marshes (Plates 15 and 16)

In certain coastal areas of Belize, this vegetation type, dominated by mangroves (*Avicennia, Conocarpus, Laguncularia,* and *Rhizophora*), forms extensive stands. It embraces the *red mangrove swamp, black mangrove forest,* and *saltmarsh* habitats of Neill and Allen (1959b), and the *red mangrove* and *brackish savanna* of Russell (1964). In the system of Iremonger and Brokaw (1995), it is split between a number of different plant associations described under the *saline influence significant* categories within *forests, scrubs,* and *herbaceous communities*. The primary influence is that of the marine environment, with extensive areas being covered by mangroves and other saltmarsh plant associations highly tolerant of varying degrees of salinity. In places the red mangrove (*Rhizophora mangle*) also extends some distance inland along the edges of major rivers and drainage channels. Submerged beds of the aquatic turtlegrass (*Thalassia testudinum*) may be present in the inshore shallows. This vegetation type is the preferred habitat of *Crocodylus acutus*, although its reptile fauna is otherwise limited to a few ubiquitous, opportunistic species.

Sand Strand and Cocotal (Plates 17 and 18)

This vegetation type, found exclusively on the coast and offshore islands, is typified by communities of dry, supratidal dune plants such as sea grape (*Coccoloba uvifera*), goat's foot (*Ipomoea pes-caprae*), and sea-oats (*Uniola paniculata*), that in places give way entirely to coconut palms (*Cocos nucifera*). The two different components were treated by Neill and Allen (1959b) as separate habitats (*sand strand* and *cocotal*). Iremonger and Brokaw (1995) refer to this vegetation association as *coastal beach sand scrubs* within the *scrubs not influenced by high water tables* subdivision of their *scrubs* category. Due to the relative scarcity of natural shelters, reptile life tends to be limited to a few lizard species that utilize the trunks or leaf bases of the palms, fallen palm fronds and other debris lying on the ground, scattered clumps of low vegetation, or holes in the sand.

PLATE 15 Coastal lagoons and marshes. *Rhizophora* mangrove vegetation, lower Belize River. Photograph by D.A. Sutton.

PLATE 16 Coastal lagoons and marshes. *Avicennia* mangrove forest, Shipstern Lagoon, Corozal District. Photograph by P. Edgar.

PLATE 17 Sand strand and cocotal. Shoreline vegetation, Glovers Reef. Photograph by David George.

PLATE 18 Sand strand and cocotal. Coconut grove, Calabash Caye, Turneffe Islands. Photograph by David George.

SPECIES DISTRIBUTION AND BIOGEOGRAPHY

While it is true that Belize has a relatively depauperate reptilian fauna when compared with neighboring Guatemala, the country is nevertheless of significant herpetological interest due to its location in a transitional region. The faunas of North and South America have historically mingled in Central America, mixing with a large autochthonous element to produce the current complex of species found in Belize. In addition, occupation of the Yucatán Peninsula by the ancient Maya for over a millennium before Europeans arrived in the region undoubtedly had some influence on reptilian distribution (Lee, 1980, 1996; Neill and Allen, 1959b). The only published information on the biogeography of Belizean reptiles is that of Lee (1980), who treated the country as part of the wider Yucatán Peninsula, and Campbell and Vannini (1989), who considered Belize to be part of their *Petén faunal area*. Other analyses of herpetofaunas in the region have been undertaken by Johnson (1989), for northwestern Nuclear Central America, and Meyer (1969) and Wilson and Meyer (1985), for Honduras. These studies have analyzed amphibian and reptilian distributions with respect to ecological formations, physiographic regions, and elevation. In Belize, the mapping of ecological formations is incomplete, and the elevational range (0–1160 m) is relatively small, leaving physiographic regions as the most meaningful units for examining reptile distribution patterns.

We have designated physiographic regions in the country (Fig. 4) to assess the similarities and differences between the reptilian faunas of different parts of Belize. This designation is limited to three regions, the Northern, the Southern Lowlands, and the Southern Uplands, although a fourth, the Marine Region, could be recognized due to the wealth of offshore cayes encompassed by Belize. These islands are poorly known faunally and in the following discussion, introduced, marine, and strictly insular species are not included, resulting in a total of 113 species of reptiles covered (Table 1).

Northern Region

This region extends from the valley of the Belize River in the south, northward to the Mexican border, and is bounded in the east by the Caribbean Sea and in the west by Guatemala. It is characterized for the most part as very low and flat terrain, with a series of higher ridges in the west approaching the Guatemalan border, up to about 900 ft (275 m) in elevation. The primary river systems flow in a more or less southwest to northeast direction, except for the Belize River, which generally courses west to east. The climate of the region is characterized by strong seasonality, with the months from January to May being dry with little rainfall. Vegetation formations

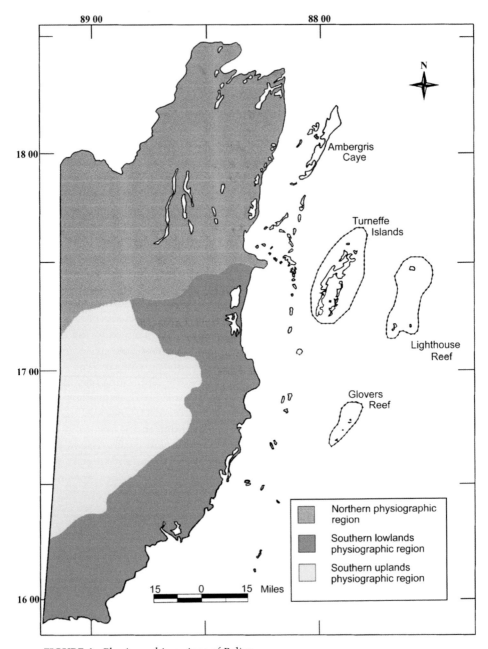

FIGURE 4 Physiographic regions of Belize.

TABLE 1 Distribution of Reptiles in Belize by Physiographic Region (Introduced, Marine, and Insular Forms Excluded)

Species	Northern	Southern lowlands	Southern uplands
Crocodylidae			
Crocodylus acutus	X	X	
Crocodylus moreletii	X	X	X
Dermatydidae			
Dermatemys mawii	X	X	X
Chelydridae			
Chelydra serpentina		X	
Kinosternidae			
Claudius angustatus	X	X	
Kinosternon acutum	X	X	X
Kinosternon leucostomum	X	X	X
Kinosternon scorpioides	X	X	X
Staurotypus triporcatus	X	X	X
Emydidae			
Rhinoclemmys areolata	X	X	X
Trachemys scripta	X	X	X
Eublepharidae			
Coleonyx elegans	X	X	X
Gekkonidae			
Aristelliger georgeensis		X	
Phyllodactylus tuberculosus	X	X	
Sphaerodactylus glaucus	X	X	X
Sphaerodactylus millepunctatus	X	X	X
Thecadactylus rapicauda	X	X	X
Corytophanidae			
Basiliscus vittatus	X	X	X
Corytophanes cristatus	X	X	X
Corytophanes hernandezii	X	X	X
Laemanctus longipes	X	X	X
Laemanctus serratus	X		
Iguanidae			
Ctenosaura similis	X	X	X
Iguana iguana	X	X	X
Phrynosomatidae			
Sceloporus chrysostictus	X		X
Sceloporus lundelli			X
Sceloporus serrifer			X
Sceloporus variabilis	X	X	X
Polychrotidae			
Norops biporcatus	X	X	X
Norops capito	X	X	X
Norops lemurinus	X	X	X
Norops pentaprion		X	X
Norops rodriguezi		X	X
Norops sagrei	X	X	
Norops sericeus	X	X	X
Norops tropidonotus	X	X	X
Norops uniformis		X	X
Scincidae			
Eumeces schwartzei	X		X
Eumeces sumichrasti		X	X

(continues)

TABLE 1 (continued)

Species	Northern	Southern lowlands	Southern uplands
Mabuya unimarginata	X	X	X
Sphenomorphus cherriei	X	X	X
Gymnophthalmidae			
Gymnophthalmus speciosus	X		
Teiidae			
Ameiva festiva		X	X
Ameiva undulata	X	X	X
Cnemidophorus angusticeps	X	X	
Cnemidophorus lemniscatus		X	
Cnemidophorus maslini	X	X	
Xantusiidae			
Lepidophyma flavimaculatum		X	X
Lepidophyma mayae			X
Anguidae			
Diploglossus rozellae		X	X
Typhlopidae			
Typhlops microstomus	X		
Leptotyphlopidae			
Leptotyphlops goudotii	X		
Boidae			
Boa constrictor	X	X	X

Species	Northern	Southern lowlands	Southern uplands
Leptodeira frenata	X	X	X
Leptodeira septentrionalis	X	X	X
Leptophis ahaetulla	X	X	X
Leptophis mexicanus	X	X	X
Masticophis mentovarius	X		X
Ninia diademata	X	X	X
Ninia sebae	X	X	X
Oxybelis aeneus	X	X	X
Oxybelis fulgidus		X	X
Oxyrhopus petola		X	X
Pseustes poecilinotus	X	X	X
Rhadinaea decorata		X	X
Scaphiodontophis annulatus	X	X	X
Senticolis triaspis	X	X	X
Sibon dimidiata		X	X
Sibon nebulata	X	X	X
Sibon sanniola	X		X
Sibon sartorii	X	X	X
Spilotes pullatus	X	X	X
Stenorthina degenhardtii			X
Stenorthina freminvillii	X		X

Species			
Colubridae			
Adelphicos quadrivirgatus	X		
Amastridium veliferum	X	X	X
Clelia clelia	X	X	X
Clelia scytalina	X		
Coluber constrictor	X	X	X
Coniophanes bipunctatus	X	X	X
Coniophanes fissidens	X	X	X
Coniophanes imperialis	X	X	X
Coniophanes schmidti	X	X	X
Conophis lineatus	X	X	X
Dendrophidion nuchale	X	X	X
Dendrophidion vinitor		X	X
Dipsas brevifacies	X		X
Dryadophis melanolomus	X	X	X
Drymarchon corais	X	X	X
Drymobius margaritiferus	X	X	X
Elaphe flavirufa	X	X	X
Ficimia publia	X		X
Imantodes cenchoa	X	X	X
Lampropeltis triangulum	X	X	X
Symphimus mayae	X		
Tantilla cuniculator	X	X	X
Tantilla schistosa	X	X	X
Tantillita canula	X		X
Tantillita lintoni			X
Thamnophis marcianus	X		
Thamnophis proximus	X	X	
Tretanorhinus nigroluteus	X	X	
Urotheca elapoides	X	X	X
Xenodon rabdocephalus	X	X	X
Elapidae			
Micrurus diastema	X	X	X
Micrurus hippocrepis		X	X
Micrurus nigrocinctus	X	X	X
Viperidae			
Agkistrodon bilineatus	X		
Atropoides nummifer		X	X
Bothriechis schlegelii	X	X	X
Bothrops asper	X	X	X
Crotalus durissus	X		X
Porthidium nasutum		X	X
Total: 113	88 (78%)	87 (77%)	92 (81%)

29

encountered in this region are the coastal lagoons and marshes, savanna, interior wetlands, semi-evergreen seasonal forest, and sand strand and cocotal.

Southern Lowlands Region

This is the smallest of the three physiographic regions, occupying the coastal plain between the Maya Mountains and the Caribbean. To the north it is bounded by the Sibun River, to the west by the Maya Mountains, to the east by the Caribbean Sea, and to the south by the Guatemalan border. It is generally a narrow coastal plain, most extensive in the south, and traversed by numerous, relatively short and swiftly flowing streams that originate in the Maya Mountains. Breaking the monotony of the lowlands in the north between the Sibun and Mullins rivers is a series of karst hills that generally are below 300 ft (90 m) in elevation; a similar situation is encountered in the south in the area inland from the town of Punta Gorda. There is a gradual change in climate from north to south, with an increase in annual rainfall and a decrease in the severity of the dry season. The vegetation formations encountered in this region are the coastal lagoons and marshes, interior wetlands, savanna, karst hills forest, evergreen broadleaf forest, and sand strand and cocotal.

Southern Uplands Region

This region basically encompasses the mountainous terrain of the southern half of Belize, ranging from about 300 ft (90 m) to over 3000 ft (914 m) in elevation. To the east and south it is bounded by the lowlands, to the north by the valley of the Belize River, and to the west by the Guatemalan border. On the eastern, northern, and southern sides the elevation rises abruptly from the lowlands, while to the west it continues as a plateau gradually sloping into Guatemala. The spine of the Maya Mountains forms an arc from near Belmopan in the north, southwestward toward the Guatemalan border west of Punta Gorda, with much of the spine reaching elevations above 2500 ft (830 m). Rivers along the windward side tend to be short, although a few extend for appreciable distances into the mountains. To the north, branches of the Belize River penetrate far into the Vaca Plateau and the leeward side of the Maya Mountains. The vegetation formations encountered in this region are the evergreen broadleaf forest, highland pine savanna, subtropical evergreen forest, and elfin forest.

Physiographic Region Analysis

The transitional nature of the Belizean herpetofauna was recognized by Lee (1980) in his analysis of the Yucatán Peninsula. Additional information that has since become available (Campbell and Vannini, 1989; Iremonger and Sayre, 1994; Lee, 1996; McCoy, 1990; McCoy *et al.*, 1986; Meerman, 1993; Meerman and Williams, 1995; Parker *et al.*, 1993; Stafford, 1991, 1994) has made it possible to more closely evaluate the distribution and relationships of the Belizean reptilian fauna. Future investigations in Belize, particularly in the poorly known Maya Mountains, are likely to reveal species that are presently unknown from Belize, but these additions to the fauna should not appreciably alter the patterns discussed herein.

The Northern Region has a total of 88 reptilian species (Table 2), comprising 78% of the total Belizean reptilian fauna. Two of these are crocodilians, 8 are turtles, 29 are lizards, and 49 are snakes. Within Belize, 69 species (78.5%) are shared with the Southern Lowlands Region, and 69 species (78.5%) are shared with the Southern Uplands Region (Table 5). In the Southern Lowlands Region, a total of 87 reptilian species are known (Table 3), comprising 77% of Belizean reptiles. This includes 2 crocodilians, 9 turtles, 32 lizards, and 44 snakes. Within Belize, 69 species (79%) are shared with the Northern Region and 76 species (87%) are shared with the Southern Uplands Region (Table 5). In the Southern Uplands Region, a total of 92 reptile species are known (Table 4), comprising 81.5% of the Belizean reptile fauna. Of this number, 1 is a crocodilian, 7 are turtles, 31 are lizards, and 53 are snakes. In Belize, 69 species (75%) are shared with the Northern Region and 76 species (82.5%) are shared with the Southern Lowlands Region (Table 5).

It appears from these data that the three physiographic regions have relatively diverse and comparable reptilian faunas. Each region has between 77 and 81.5% of the total Belizean fauna, and the major taxa are relatively evenly represented in each region: crocodilians 1–2%, turtles 8–10%, lizards 33–37%, snakes 51–58%. Lee (1980), in his analysis of herpetofaunal distributions in the Yucatán Peninsula, posited distinct faunal breaks for lizards and snakes in the region of central Belize. Our analysis shows that 73–87% of lizards and 69–73% of snakes are shared between northern and southern Belize, indicating that the reptilian fauna of Belize does not exhibit sufficient heterogeneity to warrant the designation of separate faunal areas.

Campbell and Vannini (1989) used the faunal resemblance factor (FRF) to measure faunal similarities between regions in Guatemala, and we have used this measure to examine the similarities of the three Belizean physiographic regions. The FRF is calculated as FRF = $2C/N_1 + N_2$, where N_1 = the number of species in the first region, N_2 = the number of species in the second region, and C = the number of species common to both regions. The FRF similarity coefficients for Belizean reptiles of 0.78–0.85 (Table 5) indicate that there is a relatively high degree of sharing between the three

TABLE 2 Affinities of Reptiles of Northern Physiographic Region

Species	Yucatán	Petén	Honduras
Crocodylidae			
Crocodylus acutus	X	X	X
Crocodylus moreletii	X	X	
Dermatydidae			
Dermatemys mawii		X	
Kinosternidae			
Claudius angustatus		X	
Kinosternon acutum		X	
Kinosternon leucostomum	X	X	X
Kinosternon scorpioides	X	X	X
Staurotypus triporcatus		X	X
Emydidae			
Rhinoclemmys areolata	X	X	
Trachemys scripta	X	X	X
Eublepharidae			
Coleonyx elegans	X	X	
Gekkonidae			
Aristelliger georgeensis	X		
Phyllodactylus tuberculosus	X		X
Sphaerodactylus glaucus	X	X	X
Sphaerodactylus millepunctatus		X	X
Thecadactylus rapicauda	X	X	X
Corytophanidae			
Basiliscus vittatus	X	X	X
Cortophanes cristatus		X	X
Corytophanes hernandezii	X	X	X
Laemanctus longipes		X	X
Laemanctus serratus	X		
Boidae			
Boa constrictor	X	X	X
Colubridae			
Adelphicos quadrivirgatus		X	X
Clelia scytalina		X	X
Coniophanes bipunctatus	X	X	X
Coniophanes fissidens		X	X
Coniophanes imperialis	X	X	X
Coniophanes schmidti	X	X	
Conophis lineatus	X	X	X
Dipsas brevifacies	X		
Dryadophis melanolomus	X	X	X
Drymarchon corais	X	X	X
Drymobius margaritiferus	X	X	X
Elaphe flavirufa	X	X	X
Ficimia publia	X	X	
Imantodes cenchoa	X	X	X
Lampropeltis triangulum	X	X	X
Leptodeira frenata	X	X	X
Leptodeira septentrionalis	X	X	X
Leptophis ahaetulla	X	X	X
Leptophis mexicanus	X	X	X
Masticophis mentovarius	X	X	X
Ninia sebae	X	X	X
Oxybelis aeneus	X	X	X
Oxybelis fulgidus	X	X	X

Taxon			
Iguanidae			
Ctenosaura similis	X		X
Iguana iguana		X	X
Phrynosomatidae			
Sceloporus chrysostictus	X		X
Sceloporus variabilis	X	X	X
Polychrotidae			
Norops biporcatus	X	X	X
Norops capito	X	X	X
Norops lemurinus	X	X	
Norops rodriguezii	X	X	X
Norops sagrei	X		X
Norops sericeus	X	X	X
Norops tropidonotus	X	X	X
Scincidae			
Eumeces schwartzei	X	X	X
Mabuya unimarginata	X	X	X
Sphenomorphus cherriei	X	X	X
Gymnophthalmidae			
Gymnophthalmus speciosus			X
Teiidae			
Ameiva undulata	X	X	X
Cnemidophorus angusticeps	X		X
Cnemidophorus maslini	X	X	X
Typhlopidae			
Typhlops microstomus	X	X	
Leptotyphlopidae			
Leptotyphlops goudotii	X	X	X
Pseustes poecilonotus	X	X	X
Scaphiodontophis annulatus	X	X	X
Senticolis triaspis	X	X	X
Sibon nebulata	X	X	X
Sibon sanniola	X	X	X
Sibon sartorii	X	X	X
Spilotes pullatus	X	X	X
Stenorrhina freminvillii	X	X	X
Symphimus mayae	X	X	
Tantilla cuniculator		X	X
Tantilla schistosa	X	X	X
Tantilla canula	X	X	X
Thamnophis marcianus	X	X	X
Thamnophis proximus	X	X	X
Tretanorhinus nigroluteus		X	X
Urotheca elapoides	X	X	X
Xenodon rabdocephalus	X	X	X
Elapidae			
Micrurus diastema	X	X	X
Micrurus nigrocinctus	X		X
Viperidae			
Agkistrodon bilineatus	X	X	X
Bothreichis schlegelii		X	X
Bothrops asper	X	X	X
Crotalus durissus	X	X	X
Total: 88	69 (78%)	78 (87%)	68 (77%)

33

TABLE 3 Affinities of Reptiles of Southern Lowlands Physiographic Region

Species	Yucatán	Petén	Honduras	Species	Yucatán	Petén	Honduras
Crocodylidae				Xantusiidae			
Crocodylus acutus	X	X	X	Lepidophyma flavimaculatum		X	X
Crocodylus moreletii	X	X		Anguidae			
Dermatydidae				Diploglossus rozellae		X	
Dermatemys mawii		X		Boidae			
Chelydridae				Boa constrictor	X	X	X
Chelydra serpentina		X	X	Colubridae			
Kinosternidae				Adelphicos quadrivirgatus		X	X
Claudius angustatus	X	X		Amastridium veliferum		X	X
Kinosternon acutum	X	X		Clelia clelia		X	X
Kinosternon leucostomum	X	X	X	Coniophanes bipunctatus	X	X	X
Kinosternon scorpioides	X	X	X	Coniophanes fissidens		X	X
Staurotypus triporcatus		X	X	Coniophanes imperialis	X	X	X
Emydidae				Coniophanes schmidti	X	X	
Rhinoclemmys areolata	X	X		Conophis lineatus	X	X	X
Trachemys scripta	X	X		Dendrophidion nuchale			X
Eublepharidae				Dryadophis melanolomus	X	X	X
Coleonyx elegans	X	X		Drymarchon corais	X	X	X
Gekkonidae				Drymobius margaritiferus	X	X	X
Aristelliger georgeensis	X			Elaphe flavirufa	X	X	X
Phyllodactylus tuberculosus	X		X	Imantodes cenchoa	X	X	X
Sphaerodactylus glaucus	X	X	X	Lampropeltis triangulum	X	X	X
Sphaerodactylus millepunctatus		X	X	Leptodeira frenata	X	X	
Thecadactylus rapicauda	X	X	X	Leptodeira septentrionalis		X	X
Corytophanidae				Leptophis ahaetulla	X	X	X
Basiliscus vittatus	X	X	X	Leptophis mexicanus	X	X	X
Corytophanes cristatus		X	X	Ninia diademata		X	X

34

Species			
Corytophanes hernandezii	X		X
Laemanctus longipes	X		X
Iguanidae			
Ctenosaura similis	X	X	X
Iguana iguana		X	X
Phrynosomatidae			
Sceloporus variabilis	X		X
Polychrotidae			
Norops biporcatus	X	X	
Norops capito	X	X	
Norops lemurinus	X	X	X
Norops pentaprion	X	X	
Norops rodriguezii	X	X	X
Norops sagrei	X		
Norops sericeus	X	X	X
Norops tropidonotus	X	X	X
Norops uniformis	X	X	X
Scincidae			
Eumeces sumichrasti	X	X	X
Mabuya unimarginata	X	X	X
Sphenomorphus cherriei	X	X	X
Teiidae			
Ameiva festiva	X	X	X
Ameiva undulata	X	X	X
Cnemidophorus angusticeps	X	X	X
Cnemidophorus lemniscatus			X
Cnemidophorus maslini	X	X	X

Species			
Ninia sebae	X	X	X
Oxybelis aeneus	X	X	X
Oxybelis fulgidus	X	X	X
Oxyrhopus petola		X	X
Pseustes poecilonotus	X	X	X
Rhadinaea decorata		X	
Scaphiodontophis annulatus	X	X	X
Senticolis triaspis	X	X	X
Sibon dimidiata	X	X	X
Sibon nebulata	X	X	X
Sibon sartorii	X	X	X
Spilotes pullatus	X	X	X
Thamnophis proximus	X	X	X
Tretanorhinus nigroluteus		X	X
Urotheca elapoides	X	X	X
Xenodon rabdocephalus	X	X	X
Elapidae			
Micrurus diastema	X	X	X
Micrurus hippocrepis	X	X	
Micrurus nigrocinctus	X		X
Viperidae			
Atropoides nummifer	X	X	X
Bothriechis schlegelii	X	X	X
Bothrops asper	X	X	X
Porthidium nasutum		X	X
Total: 87	54 (62%)	80 (92%)	73 (84%)

35

TABLE 4 Affinities of Reptiles of Southern Uplands Physiographic Region

Species	Yucatán	Petén	Honduras
Crocodylidae			
Crocodylus moreletii	X	X	
Dermatydidae			
Dermatemys mawii		X	X
Kinosternidae			
Kinosternon acutum		X	
Kinosternon leucostomum	X	X	X
Kinosternon scorpioides	X	X	X
Staurotypus triporcatus		X	X
Emydidae			
Rhinoclemmys areolata	X	X	
Trachemys scripta	X	X	X
Eublepharidae			
Coleonyx elegans	X	X	
Gekkonidae			
Sphaerodactylus glaucus	X	X	X
Sphaerodactylus millepunctatus		X	X
Thecadactylus rapicauda	X	X	X
Corytophanidae			
Basiliscus vittatus	X	X	X
Corytophanes cristatus		X	X
Corytophanes hernandezii	X	X	X
Laemanctus longipes		X	X
Iguanidae			
Ctenosaura similis	X	X	X
Iguana iguana		X	X
Boidae			
Boa constrictor	X	X	X
Colubridae			
Adelphicos quadrivirgatus		X	X
Amastridium veliferum		X	X
Clelia clelia		X	X
Coluber constrictor		X	X
Coniophanes bipunctatus	X	X	X
Coniophanes fissidens		X	X
Coniophanes imperialis	X	X	X
Coniophanes schmidti	X	X	X
Conophis lineatus	X	X	X
Dendrophidion nuchale			X
Dendrophidion vinitor		X	X
Dryadophis melanolomus	X	X	X
Drymarchon corais	X	X	X
Drymobius margaritiferus	X	X	X
Elaphe flavirufa	X	X	X
Ficimia publia	X	X	X
Imantodes cenchoa	X	X	X
Lampropeltis triangulum	X	X	X
Leptodeira frenata	X	X	X
Leptodeira septentrionalis	X	X	
Leptophis ahaetulla	X	X	X
Leptophis mexicanus	X	X	X
Masticophis mentovarius	X	X	X
Ninia diademata		X	X
Ninia sebae	X	X	X
Oxybelis aeneus	X	X	X

	Site 1	Site 2	Site 3
Phrynosomatidae			
Sceloporus chrysostictus	X	X	X
Sceloporus lundelli	X	X	X
Sceloporus serrifer		X	X
Sceloporus variabilis	X	X	X
Polychrotidae			
Norops biporcatus		X	X
Norops capito		X	X
Norops lemurinus	X	X	X
Norops pentaprion		X	X
Norops rodriguezii	X	X	X
Norops sericeus	X	X	X
Norops tropidonotus	X	X	X
Norops uniformis		X	X
Scincidae			
Eumeces schwartzei	X	X	X
Eumeces sumichrasti	X	X	X
Mabuya unimarginata	X	X	X
Sphenomorphus cherriei	X	X	X
Teiidae			
Ameiva festiva	X	X	X
Ameiva undulata	X	X	X
Xantusiidae			
Lepidophyma flavimaculatum	X	X	X
Lepidophyma mayae		X	X
Anguidae			
Diploglossus rozellae		X	X
Oxybelis fulgidus	X	X	X
Oxyrhopus petola		X	X
Pseustes poecilonotus	X	X	X
Rhadinaea decorata		X	X
Scaphiodontophis annulatus	X	X	X
Senticolis triaspis	X	X	X
Sibon dimidiata	X	X	X
Sibon nebulata	X	X	X
Sibon sanniola	X	X	X
Sibon sartorii	X	X	X
Spilotes pullatus	X	X	X
Stenorrhina degenhardtii		X	X
Stenorrhina freminvillii	X	X	X
Tantilla schistosa		X	X
Tantillita canula	X	X	X
Tantillita lintoni		X	X
Urotheca elapoides	X	X	X
Xenodon rabdocephalus	X	X	X
Elapidae			
Micrurus diastema	X	X	X
Micrurus hippocrepis		X	
Micrurus nigrocinctus	X		X
Viperidae			
Atropoides nummifer		X	X
Bothriechis schlegelii		X	X
Bothrops asper	X	X	X
Crotalus durissus	X	X	X
Porthidium nasutum		X	X
Total: 92	57 (62%)	89 (97%)	73 (79%)

37

TABLE 5 Comparison of Reptiles among Belizean Physiographic Regions

	Northern	Southern lowlands	Southern uplands
Northern	**88**	69	69
Southern lowlands	0.79	**87**	76
Southern uplands	0.78	0.85	**92**

Numbers on the diagonal (boldface type) indicate total faunas for each region. Numbers above the diagonal indicate proportion of shared species, and values below represent the Faunal Resemblance Factor (FRF = $2C/N_1+N_2$).

regions and supports the view that they cannot be considered to be distinct reptilian faunal areas.

In the larger northern Middle American area, herein defined as the Yucatán Peninsula, Guatemala, and Honduras, the Northern Region shares 69 species (78%) with the upper Yucatán Peninsula, 78 species (87%) with the Petén region of Guatemala, and 68 species (77%) with Honduras (Table 2). The high degree of affinity with the Petén region may be attributed to the more mesic climate there as opposed to the drier outer Yucatán Peninsula, while the lower affinity between the region and Honduras may be a reflection of the geological history of northern Middle America, which has influenced faunal movement both northward and southward in Middle America. The Southern Lowlands Region shares 54 of its species (62%) with the upper Yucatán Peninsula, 80 of its species (92%) with the Petén region, and 73 of its species (84%) with Honduras (Table 3). Considering the short distance between the southern Toledo District and northwestern Honduras, it is surprising that even 16% of the reptilian fauna is not shared, a situation that may be a reflection of the area's geologic history. Savage (1982) designated the Yucatán Peninsula as an area of herpetofaunal endemism, and Honduras lacks a number of those taxa with restricted ranges. The reptilian affinities of the Southern Uplands Region (Table 4) are greatest with the Petén region of Guatemala, with 89 of the species (97%) shared, while 73 species (79%) are shared with Honduras. The lowest affinity, not surprisingly, is with the upper Yucatán Peninsula, with which the Southern Uplands Region shares only 57 of its species (62%).

Although we have not recognized separate faunal regions in Belize, there is a noticeable difference in the degree of sharing of species between the upper Yucatán Peninsula and the northern and southern parts of Belize, respectively. As Lee (1980) has shown, a distinct herpetofaunal difference exists between the drier outer portion of the Yucatán Peninsula and the more mesic southern part, and the Belizean reptiles reflect this pattern. There is a decrease in shared species from 69 (78%) in the Northern

Region to 54–57 (62%) in the Southern Uplands and Southern Lowlands Regions.

In summary, the Belizean reptiles tend to be widely distributed throughout the area of northern Middle America, as only 22 species could be described as having restricted distributions, and none are endemic to mainland Belize. This observation is not surprising in view of the relatively low environmental heterogeneity exhibited in Belize, especially the lack of high mountain areas that might have been isolated from other similar areas of northern Central America during the region's geological history. Johnson (1989) and Wilson and Meyer (1985) have shown that the sharpest elevational change in reptile species occurs near what is essentially the upper elevational limit of the Belizean landmass.

Species of Possible Occurrence

A number of additional species occur around the periphery of Belize that may eventually become part of its herpetofauna. The smallest of the marine turtles, *Lepidochelys kempii*, is well known from the Gulf of Mexico and along the northern coast of the Yucatán Peninsula, but has not yet been found in Belizean waters. Among the terrestrial extralimital forms, *Kinosternon creaseri*, *Coniophanes meridanus*, *Coniophanes quinquevittatus*, *Imantodes gemmistratus*, *Imantodes tenuissimus*, *Sibon fasciata*, and *Porthidium yucatanicum* are known from adjacent parts of Campeche and Quintana Roo, Mexico, and may range over the northern border of Belize into Corozal and Orange Walk districts. The exotic gecko, *Hemidactylus turcicus*, occurs along the northern coast of the Yucatán Peninsula and, as a human commensal, is likely to spread southward into Belize. *Sphaerodactylus argus* from Cuba and Jamaica is also known from coastal Yucatán, and may find its way into Belize at some point. Another widely introduced species, *Rhamphotyphlops braminus*, has been recorded from various parts of Central America and, given the colonizing ability of this species and the ease with it is transported by humans, is also likely to appear in the country (there is an unconfirmed report of this species from the Turneffe Islands).

To the west of Belize in the Guatemalan region of El Petén, *Ameiva chaitzami* is known from the vicinity of Poptún, *Rhadinaea anchoreta* from parts of the southern mountain ranges (Izabal), and *Tantilla moesta* from Tikal (also central parts of Quintana Roo, Mexico). *Storeria dekayi* occurs in Alta Verapaz and probably also in El Petén near the border with Toledo District, and the boid *Corallus annulatus* has recently been reported from northeastern Izabal, only 20 km from the southern border of Belize (Smith and Acevedo, 1997). On ecological and biogeographical grounds, it is also conceivable that some of the mid- to high-elevation species known from the highlands of southeastern Guatemala, particularly the Sierra de Santa Cruz and Montaños del Mico, might occur in the subtropical evergreen and elfin forest formations of the southern Maya Mountains.

NATURAL HISTORY

Diet and Feeding

Reptiles as a group are generalists that feed on a diverse range of prey types and species, and some have adaptations for eating particular kinds of prey. The crocodiles are opportunistic carnivores that will also take carrion when available. Among the marine turtles, the loggerhead (*Caretta caretta*) is more carnivorous than most, feeding largely on crustaceans, mollusks, and fish, while the green turtle (*Chelonia mydas*) is an exclusively herbivorous species, grazing on sea grasses and algae. Most freshwater turtles are omnivorous in feeding habits, with the exception of *Dermatemys mawii*, which is strictly vegetarian.

As a group the lizards are predominantly invertebrate eaters, although some (i.e., *Norops biporcatus*) will also prey on smaller lizards if given the opportunity. *Ctenosaura* and *Iguana* are unusual in being vegetarian as adults, whereas in the juvenile stage they are chiefly insectivorous. The spiny lizards (*Sceloporus*) and whiptails (*Ameiva* and *Cnemidophorus*) are fast-moving species that actively hunt for their food, while at the other extreme, the highly camouflaged helmeted iguanas (*Corytophanes*) employ a sit-and-wait feeding strategy, ambushing unsuspecting prey that passes by.

Snakes are more specialized in their dietary habits. Those of the genera *Dipsas* and *Sibon* have specialized dentitional modifications for feeding on snails and slugs, while the teeth of *Scaphiodontophis* are modified for dealing with the hard, smooth-scaled bodies of skinks on which it largely preys. Some species have a natural predisposition for eating other snakes. Duellman (1963) describes finding a giant black-tailed indigo snake (*Drymarchon corais*) in the forests of El Petén, Guatemala, trying to engulf a 1.6-m-long boa (*Boa constrictor*); when captured, the *Drymarchon* was found to have also recently eaten an adult jumping pitviper (*Atropoides nummifer*). Another large colubrid, the mussurana (*Clelia clelia*), is well known throughout Central America as a predator of *Bothrops asper*. The kingsnake, *Lampropeltis triangulum*, will readily accept snakes as food, including the coral snakes which it mimics, and coral snakes themselves also habitually predate on small snakes. Except for *Boa constrictor*, *Tretanorhinus nigroluteus*, and the pitvipers, most snakes in Belize are active foragers. Among the most agile and fleet are the racer-like species that prey on fast-moving lizards by day, such as *Dryadophis* and *Masticophis*. Feeding relationships among species which utilize the same habitat resources are complex. Syntopic forms that coexist in this way are probably able to avoid competition by eating different kinds or size classes of prey or by foraging at different times of the day. For example, the nocturnal invertebrate-eating snakes (a number of which may occur in close association) each appear to have different feeding specializations; *Adelphicos quadrivirgatus* eats mostly worms, the two species of *Ninia* predate largely on small gastropods, while the diets of *Tantilla* and *Tantillita* spp. appear to consist largely of centipedes and beetle larvae.

Diel Activity

Most reptiles in Belize are diurnal in habit. Some turtles of the family Kinosternidae, the majority of geckos, and a number of snake genera (i.e., *Imantodes, Leptodeira, Sibon, Bothrops*) are active only by night, while a small minority, including *Boa, Atropoides*, and *Micrurus*, appear to have no clear-cut pattern of activity. Among the diurnal species, many are forest-dwelling forms that conduct their lives in relatively low light levels. Other species, such as *Sceloporus, Ameiva*, and *Cnemidophorus*, may be observed only in conditions of full sunlight, and tend to be conspicuous by their absence on days that are rainy or overcast.

The activity of nocturnal reptiles appears to be correlated to some extent with the lunar cycle. Snakes in particular tend to be more prevalent when the moon is typically less than three-quarters full, and may be observed only rarely on bright moonlit nights. The optimal time for finding nocturnal snakes on these occasions is soon after dark, and especially on warm nights during or after light rain. Diurnal snakes appear to be most frequently observed on sunny days before midday.

Seasonality

The marked contrast between wet and dry seasons in Belize is reflected in the behavior of many reptiles, especially snakes. Henderson and Hoevers (1977a) studied the seasonal incidence of snakes in the area of Orange Walk town, and found an apparent positive correlation between the amount of precipitation and the number of snakes collected, with activity peaking in the month of September. The period during which snakes were found to be least conspicuous extended from February through April, normally the driest months of the year. The authors reasoned that inactivity during this period may be induced by water loss, and that "snakes might retreat into damp microhabitat in order to keep desiccation to a minimum," adding that "snakes may be sporadically active during the dry season, but not until rain-fall becomes consistent (i.e. in June) do they remain active." Our observations reflect those of Henderson and Hoevers (1977a) in that certain species, particularly those of the genera *Dipsas, Leptodeira, Leptophis, Oxybelis,* and *Sibon,* are more abundant in the wet season, although others, including *Boa, Coniophanes fissidens,* and *Dryadophis,* appear to be equally conspicuous at the driest time of the year. Neill (1962) commented that the local dry season may not be sufficiently dry to curtail the activities of most snakes, and we have observed a number of species more commonly associated with activity in the wet season, including *Clelia clelia, Dendrophidion nuchale, Leptophis ahaetulla, Leptodeira septentrionalis,* and *Urotheca elapoides,* in mid-dry season following a short period of rainfall.

The seasonal occurrence of certain snakes appears to be directly linked with the abundance of prey. Species that feed predominantly on frogs, such as the arboreal *Leptophis* and *Leptodeira,* have been recorded with greater frequency during the wet season following large-scale emergence and breeding of anurans. Likewise, the frequency with which the specialized gastropod-feeding snakes (*Dipsas* and *Sibon*) have been recorded appears to be greatest during the wet season, possibly in accordance with increased availability of their molluskan prey. These and other species may even undergo a period of estivation during the dry season. Arboreal snakes appear to be the most closely linked with seasonal increases in precipitation, the probable reason being that these species prey chiefly on arboreal frogs, whose emergence and proliferation is directly induced by rainfall. The abundance of small mammals and lizards may to some extent also be influenced by precipitation, thus making species that feed on these prey groups similarly rainfall dependent.

Some reptiles are more conspicuous during the dry season. These include mostly aquatic and semiaquatic forms, such as the small kinosternid turtles and the colubrid snake, *Tretanorhinus nigroluteus,* which in times of drought either congregate in isolated pools and other remaining bodies of water, or retreat back to the major rivers. Once the rains return and the ponds, lakes, and rivers begin again to overflow, these species become more migratory, dispersing with the spreading flood waters.

Reproductive Cycles

The majority of reptiles in Belize are egg layers, with several live-bearers among the lizards and snakes. Reproduction in many species is cyclic and seems to be largely contingent on seasonal changes in rainfall, availability of food, and perhaps day length and temperature. Others appear to follow no particular set pattern and remain reproductively active year-round, although breeding in some may peak at times of the year when environmental conditions are most conducive.

Crocodiles

The two species of crocodile in Belize each produce a single large clutch of eggs per year. *Crocodylus moreletii* is a mound-nesting species that breeds during the wet season, while *C. acutus* typically excavates a burrow in which to deposit the eggs and breeds during the dry season. Timing of reproduction in crocodiles, especially freshwater species such as *C. moreletii*, may be partly influenced by rising water levels that help to restrict access to the nesting sites by would-be predators, although temperature, food availability, and other environmental variables may also be implicated.

Clutch size in both species is in the range 50–100.

Turtles

The marine species deposit either a single clutch or several clutches in a season and invariably return to the same beaches to nest. Most freshwater turtles appear to deposit one clutch annually, although some kinosternids may produce multiple clutches. In *Dermochelys, Claudius,* and other species that utilize exposed river banks or mud flats for clutch deposition, breeding typically occurs late in the rainy season or early in the dry season, and is perhaps timed to coincide with low water levels when nesting sites are less likely to flood.

Clutch size in turtles varies from perhaps a single egg in *Rhinoclemmys,* to approximately 200 in the larger marine species.

Lizards

Reproduction in lizards is generally timed to the onset of the wet season, and in some species, such as the anoles, is protracted over several months. In a study of *Norops sagrei* in the Belize City area, Sexton and Brown (1977) noted that while large males were always reproductively active, egg production was generally highest in the wet season, and concluded that temperature rather than moisture was the best indicator of reproductive activity in this particular species. Oviposition in *Ctenosaura* and *Iguana* occurs during the dry season, and is timed so that the young emerge after the first heavy rains, when food is most plentiful.

Clutch size in lizards ranges from 1–2 eggs in the geckos and anoles, to approximately 70 in *Iguana*. Arboreal species tend to have smaller clutches, the probable reason being that females laden with large numbers of eggs are more susceptible to predation. Small clutch size in the anoles and geckos may be compensated for by the proclivity of these lizards to reproduce more frequently. *Norops limifrons* in Panama, for example, lays only 1 egg at a time but produces a clutch on average every 8 days throughout its extensive breeding season (Andrews and Rand, 1974). In contrast, the females of *Ctenosaura* and *Iguana* invest their entire reproductive effort into producing a single large clutch in a season. Andrews and Rand (1974) reasoned that the adhesive subdigital lamellae of geckos and anoles limits the load-bearing capacity of these arboreal lizards, and consequently the number of eggs they can carry, while the strong claws of *Iguana* allow this particular species to climb relatively unimpeded by the weight of a large clutch.

Snakes

Considerable variation is exhibited in the reproductive patterns of snakes. In several species breeding is limited to a single event, either annually or bienially, and timed to coincide with seasonal changes and/or abundance of food. Neill (1962) commented that seasonal variation in temperature may be ultimately responsible for the reproductive cycle of snakes in Belize. Censky and McCoy (1988) reported that *Leptophis ahaetulla*, *L. mexicanus*, and *Oxybelis aeneus* in the Yucatán Peninsula reproduce annually in the rainy season, with oviposition occurring July through August, and that females remain sexually inactive until the following season. A virtually identical cycle is seen in the gastropod-eating *Sibon sanniola* (Kofron, 1983). *Dryadophis melanolomus*, a terrestrial, lizard-eating species, also breeds during the rainy season, but only in alternate years (Censky and McCoy, 1988). *Stenorrhina freminvillii*, a fossorial predator of spiders and scorpions, lays two clutches of eggs annually at the driest time of the year, while reproduction in *Senticolis triaspis*, a mammal specialist, is seemingly aseasonal and continuous (Censky and McCoy, 1988). The newly emerged young of many species typically appear in the early months of the rainy season (June to September). Neill (1962) concluded that egg-laying in oviparous species generally occurs after April and before the end of July, with hatching and birth taking place no earlier than July and no later than early November, mostly around August and September. As shown by Censky and McCoy (1988) however, reproduction in some oviparous species may occur at other times of the year, or at least is not constrained to the summer wet season. In at least one species, *Ninia sebae*, hatching of eggs has been reported in March (Bohuslavek, 1996), normally the driest month of the year. Courtship and mating in *Boa constrictor* in Belize have been observed in January at the end of the rainy season (P. J. Stafford, personal observation), and other viviparous species may also become reproductively active at this time of year.

Among the oviparous species, clutch size is smallest in the diminutive invertebrate feeders, such as those of the genus *Tantilla*, which produce 1, 2, or 3 relatively large eggs per clutch, and greatest in the heavy-bodied terrestrial species, such as *Clelia*, in which clutches of at least 22 eggs have been reported (Duellman, 1963). Clutch size in the long, slender arboreal forms, such as *Imantodes*, *Leptophis*, and *Oxybelis*, is limited to no more than 6 eggs, probably as an adaptation to living in trees. The largest ovarian complements are found in the terrestrial, heavy-bodied viviparous species, such as *Boa* and *Bothrops*, in which broods of 60 or more young are known.

Coloration and Defense

Most reptiles are colored and patterned in a way that conceals them in their natural habitat, reducing the risk of detection by predators and helping them to remain hidden from potential prey. Among lizards this is perhaps best seen in the sit-and-wait ambush hunters, such as the arboreal helmeted iguanas (*Corytophanes*) and certain anoles, whose background-matching coloration renders them almost invisible when perched motionless on tree trunks and vines. Cryptic coloration is also especially well developed in many of the larger, slow-moving snakes. The dorsal patterns of *Boa constrictor* and most pitvipers, for example, are extremely effective in disguising these snakes among leaf litter, while the mottled green coloration of some *Bothriechis schlegelii* is perhaps unsurpassed in concealing this species amongst lichen and moss-covered foliage. Snakes of the genus *Oxybelis* are distinctive in resembling vines, and also have the habit of moving with an irregular swaying action reminiscent of a thin vine or branch trembling in the breeze.

Aposematic (warning) coloration, as seen in the venomous red, yellow, and black banded coral snakes, is exhibited by a number of harmless species including *Dipsas brevifacies, Lampropeltis triangulum, Oxyrhopus petola, Scaphiodontophis annulatus, Sibon sartorii,* and *Urotheca elapoides. Ninia sebae* and juvenile individuals of *Clelia*, although not banded, are also conspicuously red and black. Mimicry among snakes in Belize appears to have been cultivated in one other species, *Xenodon rabdocephalus,* which bears a striking similarity to the highly venomous *Bothrops asper.*

In contrast to color patterns that serve to deceive or ward off predators, the vividly colored tails of some juvenile lizards (e.g., *Diploglossus rozellae, Eumeces sumichrasti, Ameiva* spp.) appear to solicit attention by design. In some North American skinks the tail is also held upward and purposefully wriggled while the lizard forages about on the forest floor. This adaptation is thought to function by inducing a would-be predator to target a part of the body that, as a final defense against capture, can be discarded, allowing the lizard itself to escape (Cooper and Vitt, 1985).

Caudal urotomy (the ability of a species to voluntarily cast-off its tail) as a predator avoidance adaptation is common in several families of lizards. In Belize these include the anguid *Diploglossus* and most geckos and skinks, which are also able to regrow their tails. Among snakes, tail loss has been reported in a number of genera including *Coluber, Coniophanes,*

Dendrophidion, Drymobius, Scaphiodontophis, Thamnophis, and *Urotheca,* although unlike lizards regeneration does not occur. Tail breakage in most lizards is intravertebral, known as "autotomy" (Slowinski and Savage, 1995), whereas in snakes it occurs between the vertebrae, termed "pseudautotomy" (Slowinski and Savage, 1995). In some snakes pseudautotomy is better developed than in others. Studies of *Coniophanes fissidens* show that in this species tail loss is limited to a single breakage, with no further breaks occurring after the initial severance (Mendelson, 1992). The mechanism in *Scaphiodontophis* and *Urotheca,* however, allows for multiple breaks and would seem to be more specialized. In these species it is thought that the exceptionally long, thick, fragile tail is a specific adaptation that has evolved to facilitate multiple breaks and provide the snake with more than one chance of escape (Slowinski and Savage, 1995). The effectiveness of urotomy as an antipredatory device is indicated by Stuart (1948), who found the broken tail of a false coral snake (*Urotheca elapoides*) in the stomach of a black-tailed indigo snake (*Drymarchon corais*), a species renowned for its predacious snake-eating habits.

While many species resort to biting and various other forms of defensive behavior when frightened, the startle and threat displays of certain lizards and snakes are particularly impressive. *Coleonyx elegans,* a nocturnal, terrestrial gecko, stiffens its limbs and stands upright to elevate its profile when confronted with danger. The diurnal, tree-dwelling helmeted iguanas (*Corytophanes*) compress their bodies laterally, raise the dorsal crest, inflate their throat pouches, and threaten to bite with the mouth widely agape. A number of arboreal snakes, including *Leptophis ahaetulla, Oxybelis aeneus, Pseustes poecilonotus,* and *Spilotes pullatus* respond to danger by expanding the neck and/or opening the mouth. In *Oxybelis aeneus* a contrasting color is also exposed when the mouth is opened. *Xenodon rabdocephalus* displays a conspicuous dorsoventral hood, and other terrestrial species, such as *Ninia sebae,* may flatten the body when alarmed. The threat display of the tropical rattlesnake (*Crotalus durissus*) is particularly intimidating. When threatened with danger this snake elevates its head and anterior part of the body high off the ground, facing the source of the threat with the neck coiled like a shepherd's crook. The display is accompanied by an audible warning produced by the snake shaking the rattle on the end of its tail, an appendage specially adapted for the purpose.

Parasitism

Reptiles act as hosts to a variety of parasitic organisms. Ectoparasites in the form of ticks and mites are particularly conspicuous and may be commonly found on lizards and snakes in Belize. A few lizard species have small invaginations in the skin that frequently contain tiny, orange-colored chiggers, the larvae of trombiculid mites. Those of the genus *Sceloporus* have one on each side of the neck between the ear and shoulder, and *Sceloporus variabilis* also has a postfemoral pocket directly behind the base of the hind limb (see Fig. 13). In *Anolis allisoni*, there is a deep pocket beneath the upper edge of the ear opening (see Fig. 14), and certain other anoles (*Norops tropidonotus* and *N. uniformis*) have similar pockets in the axillary region (see Plate 79). Paradoxically, these structures appear to provide a secure refuge for the mites, with shelter from solar radiation, high temperatures, and dessication, protection from being brushed off, and unimpeded access to a rich food source beneath. Research has shown that the epidermis within mite pockets is also capable of rapidly repairing damage caused by feeding chiggers (Arnold, 1986). With chigger activity concentrated in these small areas, and not spread widely over the host's body, such adaptations may substantially reduce the deleterious effects of mite infestations, and ameliorate the harm that these organisms can cause.

CROCODILIANS
(Order Crocodilia)

Crocodilians represent perhaps the best known of all reptile groups; feared, admired, or exploited, there can be hardly anyone without at least some perception of these large aquatic predators. Ranging in size from a little over 1 m to as long as 7 m, crocodiles and their relatives are characterized by a thick, leathery skin, reinforced to varying degrees with bony plates. Three families are recognized, one of which occurs in Belize, represented by two species of the genus *Crocodylus*. The crocodilian skull is massive, and the powerful jaws are equipped with numerous conical teeth that are lost and replaced continuously throughout life. A valve-like flap covers the ears and nostrils when the animal submerges. The snout is elongate and may be broad, as seen in the American alligator and caimans, or exceptionally long and narrow, as in the fish-eating gharials. The limbs of all species are well developed. There are five fingers and four toes, all of which are webbed. The long tail is laterally compressed and, with the limbs folded backward, is used to propel the body forward when swimming. All crocodilians are oviparous, with one or both parents providing care of the nest and often the hatchlings for several months. Males are typically larger. Sex determination in many species is temperature dependent, eggs incubated at the higher and lower ends of the range producing only females, and intermediate values producing all males.

KEY TO THE CROCODILES OF BELIZE

Rows of subcaudal scales regular, not interrupted by groups of small scales
. . . . *Crocodylus acutus*

Rows of subcaudal scales interrupted by groups of small scales. . . . . . .
. . . . *Crocodylus moreletii*

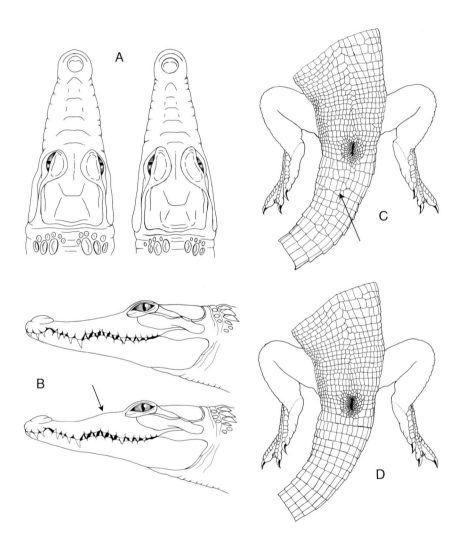

CROCODILES (FAMILY CROCODYLIDAE)

Two species of the family Crocodylidae occur in Belize, and both are protected by law. Attacks on humans by either species are rare but not unknown; a recent authenticated incident is documented by Marlin *et al.* (1995) and involved a large *Crocodylus moreletii*. In certain circumstances crocodiles may be more prone to attack; these are likely to include females defending a nest, males defending a territory during the breeding season, or perhaps an occasional individual driven by hunger. Both species in Belize have suffered at the hands of hide hunters and are also seriously threatened by habitat destruction.

Crocodylus acutus Cuvier. Fig. 5; Plates 19, 20, 23.

Vernacular Names: *Alligator, agarei,* American crocodile, cocodrilo amarillo.

Description: A large species, possibly reaching lengths of over 6 m (Pérez-Higareda *et al.,* 1990). Juveniles are light grey with dark crossbands, the pattern gradually fading with age. The adults are generally tan to olive-brown or gray-brown dorsally, with or without dark markings. The venter is whitish yellow.

Habitat: In Belize, this species is apparently restricted to the mangrove swamps on some of the cayes and brackish coastal lagoons, ponds, and rivers in the coastal lagoons and marshes formation; aquatic; sea level. The species is known to frequent the same coastal areas as *C. moreletii,* where it can be difficult to distinguish between them. Ross and Mayer (1983) have suggested that hybridization may occur between the two species, and a number of suspected intergrade specimens are presently being studied (Steven Platt, personal communication).

Distribution: Extreme southeastern United States to Colombia and Venezuela, and in the Lesser Antilles. Distribution in Belize is poorly known, but potentially to be found in suitable habitat throughout coastal areas and some cayes; the largest nesting population appears to be resident on the Turneffe group of cayes (Platt, 1995b).

Similar Species: Easily confused with *C. moreletii.* The American crocodile tends to have a narrower snout and be lighter in color with some

---

FIGURE 5 Crocodiles of Belize. (A) Dorsum of head in *C. moreletii* (left) and *C. acutus* (right); note comparative widths of mandible and tip of snout. (B) Lateral view of head; *C. moreletii* (above), and *C. acutus* (below); note presence of preorbital "hump" in *C. acutus* (large adult animals only). (C) Ventral scute pattern in lower body of *C. moreletii* (note extra scale rows in postanal region) and (D) *C. acutus.*

PLATE 19 Mature adult *Crocodylus acutus* showing prominent preorbital ridge. Canón El Sumidero, Chiapas, Mexico.

pattern visible, but this is not always obvious, particularly in subadults. The species are most positively differentiated by the condition of the subcaudal scales: the rows are regular and not interrupted by groups of small scales in *C. acutus*, while the rows of scales are interrupted by groups of small scales in *C. moreletii*. Large adult *C. acutus* may also have a more prominent preorbital ridge (located medially on the upper

PLATE 20 Subadult *Crocodylus acutus*. Costa Rica. Photograph by S. Von Peltz.

surface of the head); this may, however, be a sex-specific character restricted to either males or females.

Remarks: A wide-ranging, typically estuarine species. Occasionally found swimming at sea considerable distances from the shore, although tends to avoid open surf, preferring sheltered creeks or lagoons with little surface disturbance. Females generally deposit their eggs in a hole excavated in the sand or mud, with debris sometimes piled on top forming a low mound. Nesting in Belize probably follows the general Caribbean pattern, with clutch deposition in March and April (Platt, 1995b). The nest is guarded by the parents, which may inhabit a nearby hole. Adults appear to feed largely on fish, although carrion may also be an important food resource.

Key Reference: Ross (1989).

Crocodylus moreletii Duméril and Bibron. Fig. 5; Plates 21, 22, 23.

Vernacular Names: *Alligator, agarei,* Morelet's crocodile, cocodrilo de pantano.

Description: A moderate-sized species, possibly reaching lengths of up to 4.25 m (Pérez-Higareda *et al.,* 1990). The dorsal color is generally dark brown or olive-green to black in adults, with some evidence of spots or banding in lighter individuals; juveniles are more boldly marked with

PLATE 21   *Crocodylus moreletii.* Mature adult male. Photograph by S. Von Peltz, courtesy of the Belize Zoo.

PLATE 22   A 1-week-old hatchling *Crocodylus moreletii*. Gold Button Lagoon, Orange Walk District. Photograph by S. Von Peltz.

dark crossbands that tend to fade with age. The venter is yellowish white.

Habitat: Typically an inhabitant of deep freshwater rivers, lakes, lagoons, flooded sinkholes, and ponds, but also found in brackish water of coastal lagoons and swamps; sea level to 450 m. In Belize the species can occur in the same coastal areas frequented by *C. acutus*, where it may be difficult to distinguish between them without close examination.

Distribution: Central Mexico to Guatemala and Belize. In Belize the species probably occurs in all districts. Habitat destruction and hunting has reduced populations, but some areas, particularly in the north of Belize such as Cox's Lagoon in Belize District and Laguna Seca in Orange Walk District, still support healthy populations of this crocodilian; its distribution and status in the south is poorly documented.

Similar Species: Easily confused with *C. acutus*. Morelet's crocodile tends to have a wider snout and be darker in color with little pattern visible, but this is not always obvious, particularly in subadults. It is most positively differentiated by the condition of the subcaudal scales: the rows are regular and not interrupted by groups of small scales in *C. acutus*, while the rows of scales are interrupted by groups of small scales in *C. moreletii*. The medial preorbital ridge, although present, appears to be less well developed than in *C. acutus*. In an early account of the two species in Belize, Schmidt (1924) reported that the scales on the upper sides of the limbs are smooth in *C. moreletii* and slightly keeled in *C.*

PLATE 23   A suspected intergrade *Crocodylus acutus* × *moreletii* (Steven Platt, unpublished data). The specimen (a juvenile) has the appearance of *C. moreletii* and the subcaudal scale characters of *C. acutus*. Monkey River Town, Toledo District.

acutus; he also described *C. moreletii* as having more dorsal and nuchal scutes, although added that this character was by no means well defined.

Remarks: Eggs are deposited in a mound of vegetation constructed above ground after the beginning of the rainy season, usually during the months of June and July. During incubation only the female attends the nest site, actively defending it from predators; upon hatching she digs open the nest and carries the young to water. The diet of young crocodiles consists largely of aquatic insects and larvae, spiders, crayfish, and snails. The adult diet includes crustaceans, turtles, frogs, and other small vertebrates, with a large proportion of fish and ampullarid snails (Platt, 1996). Carrion in the form of livestock carcasses is also an important food resource when available.

Key Reference: Ross (1989).

TURTLES AND TORTOISES
(Order Testudines)

This structurally bizarre group of reptiles is unique in having expanded ribs incorporated into a bony, protective shell, and the limb girdles placed inside the rib cage, allowing the limbs to be retracted into the shell. There are approximately 290 living species, ranging in size from the 2-m-long ocean-dwelling leatherback (*Dermochelys coriacea*) and giant land tortoises of the Galapagos islands, to the small kinosternid mud turtles less than 10 cm in length.

The shell of turtles and tortoises is divided into an upper *carapace* and lower *plastron,* and is covered with large, symmetrical, epidermal scutes. The head is typically bony in character and the snout beak-like, sometimes with strongly hooked jaws. As with the limbs, the head and neck in many species are capable of being withdrawn almost completely into the shell. Tortoises are normally regarded as terrestrial animals, whereas turtles are more often associated with water and occur in almost every aquatic environment, freshwater or marine. Most species are diurnal and habitually fond of basking in the sun, although some are active only at night. A number of species have well-developed homing instincts. In many cases males may be distinguished from females by their larger size and relatively longer and thicker tails. All turtles and tortoises are oviparous.

The four marine turtles in Belize may be easily recognized by their paddle-shaped forelimbs. Of these, the leatherback is unique in being the only species with a ridged leathery hide. In the case of hard-shelled marine species, note in particular the number of pairs of *prefrontal* scales on the head and the number of *costal* (sometimes also called *pleural*) scutes on the carapace. The carapace of terrestrial and freshwater turtles (Fig. 6) may be smooth and unkeeled, with a single medial keel (*unicarinate*), or with three keels (*tricarinate*). Note also the size and shape of the plastron (broad and well developed or reduced and cross-shaped), the configuration of the bridge and proximity of the *axillary* and *inframarginal* scutes, and if the lobes are hinged or fixed and immovable. Some species have paired barbels on the chin or throat, and the skin of the neck may be strongly tuberculate. The color pattern of the carapace, plastron, and the head and neck may also provide useful clues to identification.

KEY TO THE FAMILIES OF CHELONIANS IN BELIZE

1. Limbs modified to form paddle-like structures; strictly marine turtles
. . . . 6

   Limbs not paddle-like, although feet may be fully webbed; not marine, although may be encountered in estuarine habitats 2

2. At least one scute of the carapace in contact with pectoral scute of plastron 3

   Scutes of carapace separated from pectoral scute of plastron by a ligament or one or more inframarginal scutes of bridge . . . .

   . . . . Emydidae [page 80]

3. Inframarginal scutes 4 or more . . . . Dermatydidae [page 66]

   Inframarginal scutes fewer than 4. 4

4. Plastron of 11 scutes . . . . Kinosternidae [page 70]

   Plastron of fewer than 11 scutes 5

5. Plastron of 8 or fewer scutes. . . . . Kinosternidae [page 70]

   Plastron of 10 scutes . . . . Chelydridae [page 68]

6. Shell covered by leathery skin, except in juveniles, in which the covering is a mosaic of numerous, plate-like bones; no claws on limbs . . . .
. . . . .Dermochelyidae [page 65]

   Shell covered by horny scutes; limbs with claws. . . . .
. . . . Cheloniidae [page 60]

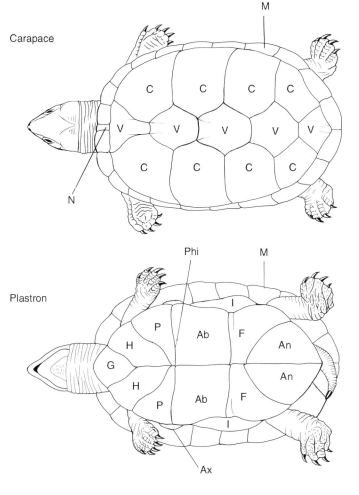

Kinosternon leucostomum

FIGURE 6 Scutellation and anatomical features of freshwater turtles: Ab, abdominals; An, anals; Ax, axillary; C, costals; F, femorals; G, gulars; H, humerals; I, inguinal; M, marginals; N, nuchal; P, pectorals; Phi, plastral hinge; V, vertebral.

HARD-SHELLED SEA TURTLES (FAMILY CHELONIIDAE)

The marine turtles of this family occur in tropical waters throughout the world, with several species ranging well into temperate seas. All six species have hard shells, and the carapace is typically heart-shaped, especially in juveniles. The limbs are modified as paddle-like flippers. Nesting invariably takes place at night on sandy beaches. The female uses her limbs to excavate a hole above the high water mark, in which she may deposit up to 200 eggs before returning to the sea. Sex determination in many species is temperature dependent; eggs incubated at higher temperatures produce all females. Due to predation by humans for their meat, shells, and eggs, all are threatened to one degree or another with extermination. The three species recorded from Belizean waters are all protected from hunting by law, and it is also illegal to collect their eggs.

Key to the Genera of the Family Cheloniidae in Belize

1. A single pair of prefrontal scales. . . . . *Chelonia*

   Two pairs of prefrontal scales 2

2. Four pairs of costal scutes. . . . . *Eretmochelys*

   Five or more pairs of costal scutes . . . . *Caretta*

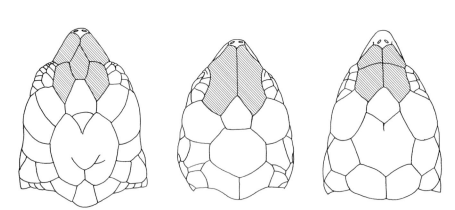

FIGURE 7 Dorsal view of head shields in *Caretta caretta* (left), *Chelonia mydas* (center), and *Eretmochelys imbricata* (right), showing configuration and appearance of prefrontals (shaded). Redrawn from Robert Bustard (1972), "Sea Turtles, Their Natural History and Conservation," with permission of the publisher, Harper Collins, London.

Caretta caretta (Linnaeus). Fig. 7; Plate 24.

Vernacular Names: Loggerhead, caguama.

Description: The largest of the living, hard-shelled turtles, reaching carapace lengths of 2300 mm and weights up to 540 kg. The carapace is weakly serrated posteriorly and has a medial keel and a pair of dorsolateral keels that are progressively lost with age. There are five or more pairs of costal scutes and three inframarginals. The head is large and broad with powerful jaws and a somewhat pointed snout. All four limbs have a pair of claws on the leading edge, and the margin of each limb is fringed with enlarged scales. Coloration of the carapace is reddish brown, sometimes tinged with olive; the plastron and undersurfaces of the limbs and tail are distinctly lighter and cream to yellowish in color. The head is typically brown above with suffusions of yellow.

Habitat: Marine; an inhabitant of open oceans as well as coastal waters.

Distribution: Throughout the tropical, subtropical, and temperate seas of the world. Potentially to be found in any of the coastal waters of Belize; recorded from the vicinity of Ambergris Caye, Lighthouse Reef, Carrie Bow Caye, Southwater Caye, Ranguana Caye (Moll, 1985), and Half Moon Caye (Smith *et al.*, 1992).

Similar Species: Distinguished from the leatherback sea turtle by the presence of horny scutes on the carapace. The presence of five or more pairs of costal scutes separates it from *Chelonia* and *Eretmochelys*, both of which have four pairs of costals.

PLATE 24   *Caretta caretta.* Honduras. Photograph by J.R. McCranie.

Remarks: This species is known to nest on certain beaches in Belize. Females always emerge at night, usually during periods of high tide, and a female may nest several times in a season at the same beach. These sea turtles are omnivorous, often feeding around coral reefs, where they consume a variety of invertebrates and plants including mollusks, crustaceans, fish, squid, and jellyfish, and perhaps marine grasses and algae. The species may bite viciously and with its large head and powerful jaws is a formidable animal.

Key Reference: Ernst and Barbour (1989).

Chelonia mydas (Linnaeus). Fig. 7; Plate 25.

Vernacular Names: *Carey*, green sea turtle, parlama.

Description: A medium-large sea turtle, reaching carapace lengths of up to 1530 mm and weights of more than 100 kg. The carapace is relatively flattened, with large, plate-like scutes and a serrated posterior edge. There are four costal scutes and four inframarginals. In juveniles there is a medial keel that disappears before adulthood. The head is large and broad with a single pair of prefrontal scales, and the cutting edge of the lower jaw is strongly serrated. The forelimbs of males have a single,

PLATE 25 Adult female *Chelonia mydas* excavating nest. Turtle Islands off Sabah, northern Borneo, Malaysia. Photograph by S. Von Peltz.

curved claw. Coloration of the carapace is olive to brownish; the plastron and undersurfaces of the limbs and tail are cream or yellowish. The head scales are yellowish brown to nearly black with paler margins.

Habitat: Marine; this turtle is known to migrate across open seas, although it is primarily an inhabitant of shallow coastal waters.

Distribution: Primarily a species of tropical seas, although may also wander into northern temperate waters. In Belize it occurs in shallow coastal waters around the beaches, cayes, and reefs; the species has been recorded from the vicinity of Ambergris Caye, Pompion Caye, South Silk Caye, and Northeast Caye (Moll, 1985).

Similar Species: Distinguished from the leatherback sea turtle by the presence of horny scutes on the carapace; the presence of four pairs of costal scutes separates it from *Caretta*, which has five or more pairs of costals. From *Eretmochelys* it differs in having only one pair of prefontal scales (two pairs in *Eretmochelys*), and in having a strongly serrated lower jaw (weakly serrated in *Eretmochelys*).

Remarks: This species nests on various beaches around the Caribbean and is reported to nest on Half Moon Caye (Smith *et al.,* 1992). Juvenile green sea turtles are primarily carnivorous, but as adults they are omnivorous, depending greatly upon eelgrass and marine algae as food. They may frequently be encountered feeding on the extensive beds of eelgrass located leeward of the reef in the shallow water. The common name comes not from the color of the shell or skin, but from the greenish color of the fat.

Key Reference: Ernst and Barbour (1989)

Eretmochelys imbricata (Linnaeus). Fig. 7; Plate 26.

Vernacular Names: Hawksbill, tortuga carey.

Description: A medium-sized sea turtle, reaching carapace lengths of approximately 900 mm, and probably not exceeding 50 kg in weight. The carapace is shield-shaped in juveniles and subadults, becoming elongate in older individuals, with a medial keel and four pairs of costal scutes. The posterior edge of the carapace is serrated. The head is relatively narrow with a pointed snout, a strongly hooked upper jaw, a weakly serrated lower jaw, and two pairs of prefrontal scales. There are two claws on each forelimb, and the margin of all four limbs is fringed with enlarged scales. Coloration of the carapace is dark greenish brown with a cream or yellowish "tortoiseshell" pattern, most conspicuous in young individuals; the plastron and undersurfaces of the chin, throat, and limbs are yellow. The head scales are dark brownish, sometimes suffused with red, and with paler margins.

PLATE 26 Adult female *Eretmochelys imbricata* at nest site. Sandy Point, St. Croix, Virgin Islands. Photograph by P. Dutton.

Habitat: Marine; generally found near coral reefs and rocky areas of the sea bed, although may also occur in mangrove-lined bays and estuaries.

Distribution: Tropical waters of the Pacific, Atlantic, and throughout the Caribbean. Potentially to be found in most of the coastal waters of Belize, particularly around the reefs and shallows; recorded from the vicinity of Belize City, Glovers Reef, Pompion Caye, Hunting Caye, Nicholas Caye, and Ranguana Caye (Moll, 1985).

Similar Species: Distinguished from the leatherback sea turtle by the presence of horny scutes on the carapace; the presence of four pairs of costal scutes separates it from *Caretta*, which has five or more pairs of costals. From *Chelonia* it differs in having two pairs of prefrontal scales (only one pair in *Chelonia*), and in having a weakly serrated lower jaw, versus a strongly serrated one in *Chelonia*.

Remarks: This species is known to nest on some of the outlying cayes of southern Belize, and also on the mainland coast (G. W. Smith, 1992). In feeding habits it is omnivorous, although it seems to prefer a diet of mollusks, sponges, and other marine invertebrates, which abound around the coral reefs. The original tortoiseshell of commerce is derived from the scutes of the carapace, for which the turtles are killed.

Key Reference: Ernst and Barbour (1989).

LEATHERBACK SEA TURTLES (FAMILY DERMOCHELYIDAE)

This is a monotypic family, and the single species is the largest living turtle in the world. The carapace and plastron are without horny scutes and are covered instead with a ridged, leathery skin. Many of the bones associated with the shells of other turtles are missing, and the species is anatomically different in a number of other respects. As with all the sea turtles, the limbs are modified as paddle-like flippers. It is strictly marine and primarily pelagic. In common with the cheloniid sea turtles, the female leaves the water only to lay her eggs.

Dermochelys coriacea (Linnaeus). Plate 27.

Vernacular Names: *Trunk-back,* leatherback, tortuga laúd.

Description: This is the largest living turtle, purportedly reaching carapace lengths in excess of 2000 mm and weighing over 800 kg. The carapace is shield-shaped with seven longitudinal ridges, and tapers to a point posteriorly; the plastron also bears ridges. The large head is devoid of scales, and the margin of the upper jaw is sharply indented with a

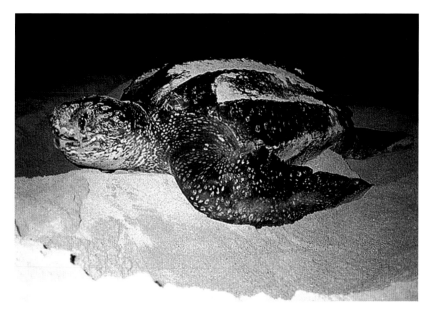

PLATE 27   Adult female *Dermochelys coriacea* at nest site. Sandy Point, St. Croix, Virgin Islands. Photograph by P. Dutton.

tooth-like cusp. There are no claws on the limbs. Coloration of the carapace is brown to blackish, sometimes with pale spots; the head is dark
above and pinkish on the throat.

Habitat: Marine; although occasionally seen in the shallower waters of
estuaries and other coastal waters, this species is primarily pelagic.

Distribution: Tropical and subtropical waters of the Atlantic, Pacific, and
Indian Oceans. Potentially to be found in any of the deep coastal waters
of Belize.

Similar Species: No other marine turtle lacks horny scutes covering the
carapace.

Remarks: As an inhabitant primarily of the open ocean, the leatherback
turtle is poorly known in Belizean waters. Although it nests in the
Caribbean region, there are no known nesting areas in Belize. The
species is omnivorous, although it appears to prefer a diet of jellyfish,
and may follow the northward migrations of jellyfish in summer.

Key Reference: Ernst and Barbour (1989).

CENTRAL AMERICAN RIVER TURTLES
(FAMILY DERMATYDIDAE)

This is a monotypic family, its single species being confined to the Gulf
and Caribbean drainages from Veracruz, Mexico, to Belize. It is almost
entirely aquatic, inhabiting rivers, alluvial lagoons, lakes, and large ponds,
where it feeds largely upon vegetation and fruit fallen from waterside
trees. Males are distinguishable from females in having a much longer,
thicker tail.

Dermatemys mawii Gray. Plates 28, 29.

Vernacular Names: *Hickety, hiccatee,* Central American river turtle, tortuga blanca.

Description: A large freshwater turtle, potentially reaching lengths of 650
mm. The head is relatively small and the snout is slightly upturned with
tubular-shaped nostrils. The adult carapace is smooth, only slightly
domed, and without keels; in juveniles there is a single medial keel that
usually disappears with age. The margins of the carapace are smooth, not
serrated. A row of inframarginal scales separate the scutes of the carapace and the large plastron. The digits are strongly webbed. Coloration
of the carapace is generally uniform olive-gray or brownish; the plastron
is cream-colored. The head is olive-gray, contrasted above in males by
tan-yellow; in juveniles there is usually a yellowish stripe in the vicinity of the eye.

PLATE 28 *Dermatemys mawii.* Izabal, Guatemala. Photograph by J. A. Cambell, courtesy of the University of Texas at Arlington.

PLATE 29 Head detail of *Dermatemys mawii.* Izabal, Guatemala. Photograph by J.A. Cambell, courtesy of the University of Texas at Arlington.

Habitat: Found primarily in freshwater lagoons, lakes, and slow-flowing rivers, although it can tolerate brackish coastal waters; sea level to 200 m.

Distribution: Southern Mexico to Guatemala and Belize. In Belize it occurs countrywide in appropriate habitat, and where not exterminated by over-hunting.

Similar Species: With its smooth shell and thoroughly aquatic habits, this turtle could only be confused with *Trachemys scripta*, from which it can be distinguished by the presence of a row of inframarginal scutes; in *Trachemys*, the marginals of the carapace are in contact with the pectorals of the plastron.

Remarks: This turtle, the only living member of the family, is considered endangered and has been virtually exterminated in Mexico. Its status in Guatemala is unknown, and only in Belize are any conservation measures in place (Polisar, 1994; Polisar and Horwich, 1994). A totally aquatic species, it is capable of remaining submerged for extended periods. Nocturnal. Herbivorous, feeding exclusively on fruits, leaves, and other plant material. The eggs are laid in the banks of rivers and other water bodies late in the rainy season; the scattered sites prevent over-exploitation by humans or other predators.

Key Reference: Ernst and Barbour (1989).

SNAPPING TURTLES (FAMILY CHELYDRIDAE)

This family of semiaquatic turtles consists of the monotypic genera *Chelydra* and *Macroclemys*, both of which are restricted to the New World. Only the genus *Chelydra* occurs in the tropics, ranging from Canada to Ecuador. These are large, aggressive turtles, inhabiting a variety of aquatic habitats, and with omnivorous feeding habits. Females lay large numbers of eggs in a flask-shaped cavity close to the water's edge.

Chelydra serpentina (Linnaeus). Plate 30.

Vernacular Names: Common snapping turtle, tortuga lagarto.

Description: A large, heavy-bodied turtle, measuring up to 470 mm in length, with a massive, tricarinate carapace; the posterior edge of the carapace is strongly serrated, and the posterior vertebral and costal scutes may bear large, knob-like protuberances, especially in old males. The small plastron is cruciform in shape and lacks hinges. The head is massive with powerful, hooked jaws. There are two prominent barbels on the chin, and the neck bears a number of projecting tubercles. The strongly clawed feet are enveloped in folds of fleshy skin, and the tail is

PLATE 30 Adult female *Chelydra serpentina* of unknown provenance. Photographed at the West Midlands Safari Park, U.K., courtesy of Mark O'Shea.

long and thick with two rows of enlarged, tooth-like scales. Coloration of the carapace varies from tan to dark brown; the plastron is yellowish to tan in color; head typically marked on the sides with dark mottling and a pale eye stripe.

Habitat: Throughout its range this species has been found in almost every type of aquatic habitat, including brackish water; sea level to 100 m.

Distribution: Southern Canada to Colombia and Ecuador. It is absent from much of the Yucatán Peninsula and in Belize is known only from the southern part of Toledo District.

Similar Species: With its tricarinate, posteriorly serrated carapace, and large head and body, this species should not be confused with any other turtle in Belize.

Remarks: A highly aquatic species of muddy rivers and ponds, although may be frequently encountered on land during rainy periods. Omnivorous, feeding on a wide variety of animal prey and plant material. Vicious in temperament; with its massive head and strong jaws it is capable of inflicting serious wounds. The reasons for its limited distribution in Belize are poorly understood, although competition with the similarly built *Staurotypus triporcatus* may restrict the spread of both species; *Staurotypus* is absent throughout most of Honduras, where *Chelydra* is more wide ranging.

Key Reference: Ernst and Barbour (1989).

MUD AND MUSK TURTLES
(FAMILY KINOSTERNIDAE)

This family of small- to medium-sized essentially semiaquatic turtles is found only in the Americas. Two of the genera, *Claudius* and *Staurotypus,* are restricted to southern Mexico and northern Central America, and are sometimes treated as a separate family, the Staurotypidae. The remaining genus, *Kinosternon,* is composed of numerous species and is found from southern Canada to South America. Three species occur in Belize; a fourth species, *K. creaseri,* is known from northern parts of the Yucatán Peninsula and may perhaps range into Corozal District.

Mud and musk turtles are typically oval-shaped in dorsal view. The plastron may be unhinged, as in *Claudius,* or bear one or two well-developed hinges. There are a number of glands beneath the outer edge of the carapace that secrete a characteristically offensive odor. All of the species are essentially carnivorous, feeding on a variety of vertebrates and invertebrates, but some are known to also feed on plant material at times. Males are larger and have a long thick tail, while that of the female is short and blunt. In the genus *Kinosternon,* the plastron is slightly concave in males and flat or slightly convex in females. The males of some species may also have patches of rough scales on their thighs that probably serve to assist in grasping the female during copulation.

Clutches are typically small, and in some species of *Kinosternon* may consist of only two or three eggs.

Key to the Genera of the Family Kinosternidae in Belize

1. Plastron of 11 scutes. . . . . *Kinosternon*

   Plastron of fewer than 11 scutes 2

2. Large axillary and inguinal scutes present on bridge; plastron with a moveable hinge. . . . . *Staurotypus*

   Axillary and inguinal scutes absent or, if present, small and not well developed; plastron lacking moveable hinge . . . . *Claudius*

Claudius angustatus Cope. Fig. 8; Plate 31.
Vernacular Names: *Toe-biter,* narrow-bridged musk turtle, chopontil.
Description: A medium-sized, largely aquatic turtle, attaining a maximum length of approximately 170 mm. The oval-shaped carapace has a smooth outline and generally bears three keels that tend to disappear

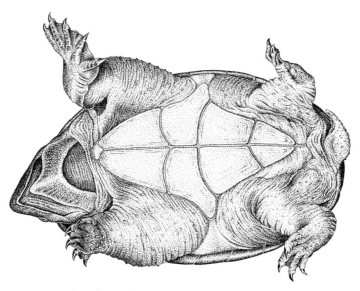

FIGURE 8 Ventral surface of *Claudius angustatus* illustrating reduced, cross-shaped plastron. Drawing based on photograph in Alvarez del Toro (1982).

PLATE 31 *Claudius angustatus.* Belize. Photograph by J. B. Iverson.

with age. The plastron is very reduced in size, cruciform in shape, and connected to the carapace by ligaments; there is no moveable hinge on the plastron. The head is relatively large and the beak moderately to strongly hooked. There is a pair of prominent barbels on the chin. The digits are strongly webbed. Coloration of the carapace is yellowish brown to blackish, usually with darker seams; the plastron is cream-colored to yellowish. The head is yellowish brown with lighter jaws.

Habitat: An inhabitant of shallow water in freshwater ponds, swamps, marshes, and small streams in lowland areas of semi-evergreen seasonal forest and savanna formations; sea level to 200 m.

Distribution: Southern Mexico to northern Guatemala and Belize. In Belize it is known from Corozal, Orange Walk, Belize, Cayo, and Stann Creek Districts. Its occurrence in Toledo District is doubtful, since it is not known from farther south in Honduras.

Similar Species: *Staurotypus triporcatus* and members of the genus *Kinosternon* can be distinguished by the presence of one or two moveable hinges on the plastron; in *Claudius* these hinges are absent. It differs from *Chelydra* in having a smooth posterior edge to the plastron (strongly serrated in *Chelydra*).

Remarks: A thoroughly aquatic species that may be found wandering away from water bodies once the rains arrive. We have found them occupying partially flooded crayfish burrows around temporary ponds in June and July in the savanna formations of Belize District. Adults may estivate in the mud of pond bottoms or in burrows during the dry season. The species appears to be carnivorous, eating a variety of vertebrates and invertebrates. It is pugnacious in habits, and prone to strike out with upward biting lunges when threatened (Dodd, 1978). Eggs are laid usually at the onset of the dry season, where they undergo prolonged incubation until the rains arrive.

Key Reference: Ernst and Barbour (1989)

Key to the Species of *Kinosternon* in Belize

1. Head brown, each side with a broad, cream to yellowish stripe, sometimes broken into a series of spots or blotches; upper lip distinctly paler than head color and unmarked . . . . *K. leucostomum*

   Head pattern not as above 2

2. Abdominal scute more than 33% of plastron length; carapace with a single dorsal keel . . . . *K. acutum*

   Abdominal scute less than 33% of plastron length; carapace with three dorsal keels in all but old individuals . . . . *K. scorpioides*

Kinosternon acutum (Gray). Fig. 9; Plate 32.

Vernacular Names: *Swanka* (?), Tabasco mud turtle, chechahua de monte.

Description: A small mud turtle, reaching lengths of approximately 120 mm. Adults usually have a single middorsal keel on the carapace. The plastron has a double hinge and almost completely covers the shell opening when closed. The head is relatively small, and the beak strongly hooked. Paired barbels are present on the chin and throat. Coloration of the carapace is dark brown to blackish with dark seams; the plastron is yellowish, also with dark seams. Head coloration varies, but is typically grayish brown with yellow or reddish marks in the temporal and neck region and dark spotting on the upper jaw. The limbs may be marked with yellow or reddish spots.

Habitat: Lagoons, streams, lakes, swamps, temporary ponds, and other bodies of freshwater in evergreen broadleaf forest, savanna, interior wetlands, and probably other formations where suitable freshwater habitats occur; aquatic; sea level to 300 m.

Distribution: Southern Mexico to northern Guatemala and Belize. In Belize it is known from Orange Walk, Belize, Cayo, and Stann Creek Districts. The species does not occur north of Belize in Yucatán and consequently its range may not include Corozal District; it is also unknown south of Belize, so may not occur in Toledo District.

Similar Species: Distinguishable from *Kinosternon leucostomum* by the head coloration, which in *K. leucostomum* is brownish with a broad cream to yellowish stripe or series of blotches or vermiculations extend-

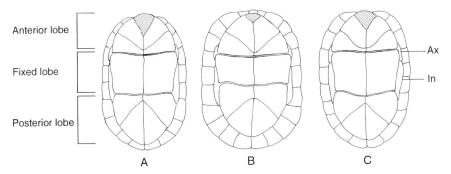

FIGURE 9 Ventral surfaces of species of *Kinosternon* in Belize. (A) *Kinosternon acutum* (note large size of gular scute [shaded] and proportionally large size of the fixed lobe of the plastron compared to the anterior and posterior lobes); (B) *K. leucostomum* (note small size of gular scute [shaded], proportionally small size of the fixed lobe of the plastron, and distance between the axillary and inguinal scutes); (C) *K. scorpioides* (note firm contact between the axillary [Ax] and inguinal [In] scutes).

PLATE 32 *Kinosternon acutum.* Provenance unknown. Photograph by J.B. Iverson.

ing from the eye to the neck, a pattern never present in *K. acutum*; the gular scute in *K. acutum* is also larger (more than half the length of the anterior lobe of the plastron) than that in *K. leucostomum* (appreciably less than one-half the length of the anterior lobe). From *K. scorpioides* it differs in having a longer abdominal scute (more than 33% of plastron length in *K. acutum* compared to less than 33% in *K. scorpioides*), and in having only a single dorsal keel, as opposed to three keels in *K. scorpioides. Claudius* and *Staurotypus* have markedly reduced, cross-shaped plastra.

Remarks: Little is known regarding the natural history of this relatively uncommon species, especially in respect of its ecological relationships with its congeners in Belize. Generally nocturnal. In savanna habitats *K. acutum* may occur in association with both *K. leucostomum* and *K. scorpioides.*

Key Reference: Iverson (1976).

Kinosternon leucostomum Duméril and Bibron. Figs. 6, 9; Plates 33, 34, 35.

Vernacular Names: *Swanka,* white-lipped mud turtle, pochitoque.

Description: A medium-sized mud turtle, reaching a length of approximately 170 mm. Compared to that in other mud turtles, the carapace is relatively flattened, and in adults the single middorsal keel of juveniles is usually absent. The plastron is relatively large and there is a single

PLATE 33 *Kinosternon leucostomum* with typical striped head pattern. Smokey River Camp, Chiquibul Forest, Cayo District.

PLATE 34 Juvenile *Kinosternon leucostomum*. Variant with mottled head pattern. Millionario, Cayo District.

LATE 35 *Kinosternon leucostomum*. An unusually pale color variant. Hidden Valley, Cayo District. Photograph by C.M. Miller.

hinge between the pectoral and abdominal scutes, allowing the turtle to completely close the shell. The axillary and inguinal scutes are usually separated. The upper jaw is strongly hooked, especially in males. There is a pair of relatively large barbels on the chin followed by one or more smaller pairs on the throat. Coloration of the carapace is dark brown; the plastron may be yellowish or red-brown, typically with darker seams. The head is typically dark brown with a broad yellowish stripe or series of vermiculations extending posteriorly from the snout over the eye to the neck; the jaws are usually pale and unmarked. In some individuals the head may be uniformly dark with little evidence of patterning, or almost completely yellow mottled with pale brown spots.

Habitat: Freshwater ponds, aguadas, cenotes, man-made livestock pools, forest streams, creeks, drainage channels, and other water bodies in the evergreen broadleaf forest, semi-evergreen seasonal forest, savanna, highland pine savanna, and interior wetland formations; aquatic; sea level to 600 m.

Distribution: Southern Mexico to Colombia and Ecuador. In Belize it occurs countrywide. Its distribution in the Maya Mountains, however, is poorly understood.

Similar Species: Distinguishable from *Kinosternon acutum* by the head pattern, which in *K. leucostomum* is brown with a broad cream stripe or series of blotches extending from the eye to the neck, a pattern not seen in *K. acutum*; the gular scute in *K. acutum* is also larger (more than half the length of the anterior lobe of the plastron) than that in *K. leucostomum* (appreciably less than one-half the length of the anterior lobe). From *K. scorpioides* it differs in the presence of a single keel, versus one keel in all but old individuals of *K. scorpioides,* and in having a broad postorbital light stripe or series of blotches (a pattern not present in *K. scorpioides*); in *K. scorpioides* the axillary and inguinal scutes of the plastron are invariably in contact (only rarely in contact and often widely separated in *K. leucostomum*). *Claudius* and *Staurotypus* have markedly reduced, cross-shaped plastra.

Remarks: A common species typically observed in quiet streams, lagoons, and ponds with accumulations of silt and leaf litter at the bottom. May be encountered traveling across dry land, especially in the rainy season; during the dry season it frequents ponds, small puddles, or even water-filled vehicle tracks, moving on as they dry out. Generally nocturnal. In other parts of its range this mud turtle is known to be omnivorous, feeding on a variety of small animals and aquatic plants. Eggs are probably deposited in a shallow nest or on the surface covered with debris.

Key Reference: Iverson (1976).

Kinosternon scorpioides (Linnaeus). Fig. 9; Plate 36.

Vernacular Names: *Swanka* (?), scorpion mud turtle, tortuga de pecho quebrado.

Description: A moderately large mud turtle, reaching lengths of approximately 270 mm. The carapace is high-domed, with three distinct longitudinal keels in all but aging individuals. The plastron bears a single moveable hinge between the pectoral and abdominal scutes, and is not always large enough to cover the shell opening. The axillary and inguinal scutes are in contact. The upper jaw is strongly hooked, especially in males. There is one anterior pair of relatively large barbels on the chin followed by two or three smaller pairs on the throat. Coloration of the carapace is pale brown to blackish; the plastron is usually brownish orange with darker seams. The head is dark brownish, often with a marbled pattern of yellow, orange, or pinkish spots in the postorbital region; the lips are usually of a similar color to the head.

Habitat: An inhabitant of lowland streams, ponds, swamps, lagoons, and other aquatic environments, primarily in the semi-evergreen seasonal forest, savanna, and interior wetland formations; sea level to 450 m. This species may be encountered on dry land during the rainy season.

Distribution: Central Mexico to northern Argentina and Brazil. In Belize it occurs countrywide, although its distribution in the Maya Mountains is poorly understood.

PLATE 36 *Kinosternon scorpioides.* Mile 24, Western Highway, Belize District.

Similar Species: From *K. acutum* it differs in having a shorter abdominal scute (more than 33% of plastron length in *K. acutum* versus less than 33% in *K. scorpioides*), and in having three dorsal keels, versus one keel in *K. acutum*. From *K. leucostomum* it differs in the presence of three keels in all but old *K. scorpioides*, versus one keel in *K. leucostomum*, and in the lack of a broad postorbital light stripe or series of blotches in *K. scorpioides* (present in *K. leucostomum*); in *K. scorpioides* the axillary and inguinal scutes are always in firm contact (usually separated in *K. leucostomum*). *Claudius* and *Staurotypus* have markedly reduced, cross-shaped plastra.

Remarks: Chiefly nocturnal, although during the rainy season may be encountered abroad during the day. Its dietary habits are omnivorous, including a wide variety of invertebrate prey, leaves, fruits, and other plant material. Turtles inhabiting water bodies that dry out seasonally may bury themselves and remain dormant until the rains return. The female excavates a shallow nest near the water's edge to deposit her eggs, and probably breeds during the dry season in Belize.

Key Reference: Iverson (1976).

Staurotypus triporcatus (Wiegmann). Plate 37.

Vernacular Names: *Loggerhead,* Mexican giant musk turtle, guao.

Description: A medium-large turtle that may reach lengths of up to 400 mm. The carapace is elongate and relatively flattened, and bears three

PLATE 37 *Staurotypus triporcatus.* El Petén, Guatemala. Photograph by J.A. Campbell, courtesy of the University of Texas at Arlington.

strongly developed keels that persist throughout life; the medial keel extends along all five vertebral scutes, and the two dorsolateral keels extend the entire length of the costal scutes. The small plastron is cross-shaped, with a moveable hinge between the pectoral and abdominal scutes; the bridge has large axillary and inguinal scutes, connected to the carapace by a bony suture. The head is large with powerful jaws and a pair of barbels on the throat. The digits are strongly webbed. Males typically have conspicuous patches of rough scales on the thighs. Coloration of the carapace is brown with yellowish seams, with or without dark reticulations and spots; the plastron is pale yellowish brown and may have dark seams. The head and neck are yellowish to olive green with numerous dark reticulations.

Habitat: An inhabitant of slow-moving waters of rivers and streams, lakes, lagoons, and swamps in semi-evergreen seasonal forest and interior wetland formations, and most other lowland habitats; sea level to 200 m.

Distribution: Southern Mexico to northern Guatemala and Belize. In Belize it occurs countrywide, although its distribution in the southern part of the country is not well known.

Similar Species: Distinguishable from all members of the genus *Kinosternon* by its relatively small, cross-shaped plastron, which consists of no more than 8 scutes (versus 11 in *Kinosternon*). From the relat-

79

ed *Claudius angustatus*, it differs in having large axillary and inguinal scutes on the bridge (absent or very small in *Claudius*), and in the presence of a moveable hinge on the plastron (absent in *Claudius*). It differs from *Chelydra serpentina* in lacking serrated marginals (strongly serrated in *Chelydra*), and in the presence of a moveable hinge on the plastron (lacking in *Chelydra*).

Remarks: With its large head and powerful, heavy-set jaws, this musk turtle is apparently strictly carnivorous, feeding on a wide variety of invertebrates and vertebrates. The species is pugnacious in temperament and capable of inflicting a serious bite. Nocturnal and diurnal; typically observed foraging at night in mud and leaf litter at the bottom of ponds and river beds (Platt, 1993). The twin barbels on the throat may assist in locating prey in murky water.

Key Reference: Ernst and Barbour (1989).

WOOD TURTLES AND SLIDERS (FAMILY EMYDIDAE)

This is the largest family of turtles, found on all continents except Australia and Antarctica, and includes the semiaquatic pond turtles and their relatives. They are in general small- to moderate-sized species, although some Old World members of the family are known to reach lengths in excess of 750 mm. The limbs are modified for swimming, with at least some webbing between the toes. Two genera, *Rhinoclemmys* and *Trachemys*, occur in Belize; a third species, *Terrapene carolina* (Linnaeus), is found in northern parts of the Yucatán Peninsula.

Key to the Genera of the Family Emydidae in Belize

Chin and throat immaculate or spotted; toes weakly separated and only slightly webbed; red markings on top and side of head . . . *Rhinoclemmys*

Chin and throat with longitudinal light and dark stripes; toes, especially those of hind feet, well separated and connected by a broad web; yellowish stripes on side of head . . . . *Trachemys*

Rhinoclemmys areolata (Duméril and Bibron). Plate 38.
Vernacular Names: *Black belly*, aragagao, furrowed wood turtle, mojina.
Description: A medium-sized turtle attaining some 200 mm in length, characterized by a high carapace with a single, weak medial keel. The head is rather small. The upper surface of the forelimbs bear enlarged,

PLATE 38 *Rhinoclemmys areolata.* Gold Button Lagoon area, Orange Walk District. Photograph by S. Von Peltz.

rugose scales and the digits are only slightly webbed. Coloration of the carapace varies from olive green with yellow mottling to brown or black, especially in older individuals; young turtles may also have a yellow to red, dark-bordered spot within the costal scutes. The plastron is yellow-ish, with a dark blotch that may occupy a large proportion of the central area, and darkened seams between the scutes. Head coloration is characterized by a bold yellow to red stripe or series of blotches extending posteriorly from the eye onto the neck; the chin and throat are spotted with black. The limbs are typically pale yellow-brown spotted with dark brown.

Habitat: Evergreen broadleaf forest, semi-evergreen seasonal forest, savanna, and highland pine savanna formations; semiaquatic, but most frequently encountered on dry land; sea level to 600 m.

Distribution: Southern Mexico to Guatemala and Honduras. In Belize it occurs countrywide in appropriate habitat.

Similar Species: Possibly confused with *Trachemys scripta,* from which it can be differentiated by the presence of an immaculate or lightly spotted chin and throat, compared to a pattern of longitudinal dark and light stripes on the chin and throat in *T. scripta;* the toes of the hind feet are no more than weakly webbed in *R. areolata,* versus broadly webbed in *T. scripta.*

Remarks: Presumed omnivorous, feeding on a variety of plant material, small invertebrates, and occasionally eggs of other turtles. Essentially a diurnal, terrestrial species, most frequently encountered roaming about the savannas or on roads, particularly during the early part of the rainy season. Males may be distinguished by their longer tail and concave plastron (flat

in females). Clutches consist of perhaps no more than a single egg layed at weekly or 5-day intervals, as observed in populations from western Tabasco, Mexico (Pérez-Higareda and Smith, 1988). In previous work this species has appeared under the generic names *Callopsis* and *Geomyda.*
Key Reference: Ernst and Barbour (1989)

Trachemys scripta (Schoepff). Plate 39.
Vernacular Names: *Bokatora, wayamu,* slider, jicotea.
Description: A large emydid turtle, which may reach 600 mm in length. The carapace is rather flattened and weakly serrated posteriorly, sometimes with an indistinct medial keel, and is attached to the unhinged plastron by a broad bridge. The head is large and the beak moderately hooked. The digits are strongly webbed. Coloration of the carapace is generally olive brown or greenish with a pattern of yellow lines or vermiculations and large, dark-centered ocelli on the costal scutes, most noticeable in young individuals; the plastron is yellowish in color, and may have dark smudges or spots present. Head coloration is essentially brownish or olive-green with a bold yellowish to orangish postorbital stripe, with finer streaks extending onto the chin and throat.
Habitat: This species frequents slow moving streams, lakes, permanent ponds and lagoons, and occasionally temporary ponds in most lowland

PLATE 39 *Trachemys scripta.* Mile 29, Western Highway, Belize District. Photograph by S. Von Peltz.

habitats, particularly in the semi-evergreen seasonal forest, savanna, and interior wetlands formations; sea level to 200 m.

Distribution: Central and eastern United States to Colombia and Venezuela. In Belize is occurs countrywide in appropriate habitat.

Similar Species: Easily distinguished from *Dermatemys mawii* by the row of inframarginal scutes in *D. mawii*, while in *T. scripta* the scutes of the plastron and carapace are in contact. It differs from *Rhinoclemmys areolata* by the presence of longitudinal dark and light stripes on the chin and throat, versus an immaculate or lightly spotted chin and throat in *R. areolata*; the toes of the hind feet are no more than weakly webbed in *R. areolata*, versus broadly webbed in *T. scripta.*

Remarks: Juveniles are highly carnivorous but change to a more omnivorous diet as adults, eating almost anything that is available. Diurnal and particularly fond of basking; several individuals may be seen sunning themselves "piled up" on emergent logs and rocks in the water. Nesting is probably coincident with the dry season; females may produce up to six clutches per season, depositing the eggs in a flask-shaped nest in the ground. The species is known to have homing instincts and is capable of returning to specific home ranges over a distance of up to 2 km (Moll and Legler, 1971). Males may be distinguished by their relatively larger and thicker tails; males may also have elongated foreclaws and/or an elongated, upturned snout. Females tend to have relatively higher-domed shells and longer plastra than males. In earlier herpetological literature this species has appeared under the generic names *Pseudemys* and *Chrysemys.*

Key Reference: Ernst and Barbour (1989).

Lizards

(Order Squamata; Suborder Sauria)

Lizards comprise the largest living group of reptiles, numbering well in excess of 4400 species. They range in size from the 3-m-long komodo dragon (*Varanus komodoensis*) to diminutive geckos no longer than a few centimeters, and are highly diverse in shape and form. Most lizards are sun-loving surface dwellers, while others are secretive and fossorial in habits, living mainly underground. A considerable number are adapted to life in the trees, and at least one arboreal form has developed the ability to take to the air and "glide." Some are semiaquatic, and one species of iguana from the Galapagos islands is adapted for living in an entirely marine environment. In feeding habits they may be carnivorous, vegetarian, or omnivorous. As quadruped animals, most lizards use all four limbs when moving about, although some are able to stand upright and employ a bipedal form of locomotion when running at speed. Legless forms typically move in a snake-like, undulating manner. The majority are diurnal and have eyes with round pupils, although many of the geckos have vertically elliptical pupils and are active only by night. Several forms are capable of caudal autotomy and tail regeneration. Sexual dimorphism is evident in many lizards,

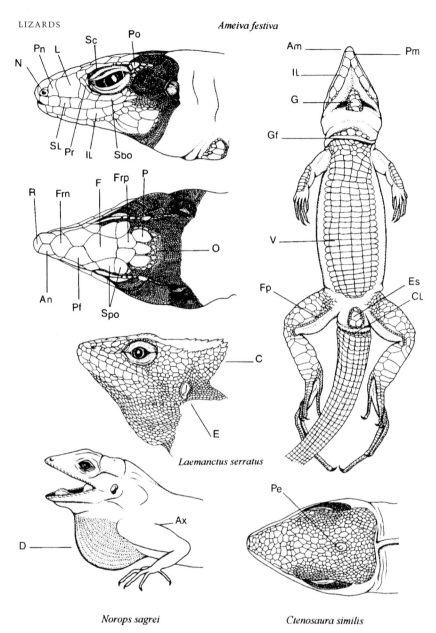

FIGURE 10 Scalation and anatomical features of lizards. Am, anterior mental; An, anterior nasal; Ax, axilla; C, cephalic casque; CL, cloaca; D, dewlap; E, ear opening; Es, escutcheon scales; F, frontal; Fp, femoral pores; Frn, frontonasal; Frp, frontoparietal; G, gulars; Gf, gular fold; IL, infralabials; L, loreal; N, nostril; O, occipitals; P, parietals; Pe, parietal eye; Pf, prefrontal; Pm, posterior mental; Pn, postnasal; Po, postoculars; Pr, preocular; R, rostral; Sbo, subocular; Sc, supercilliaries; SL, supralabials; Spo, supraocular; V, ventral scutes.

and in some is especially pronounced. The male is typically larger and more brightly colored, and in species having an extendible throat fan, head crest, or other decorative adornment, these are frequently larger and more extravagant in males. Most species are egg layers, although some are viviparous, and a number of all-female species have also evolved that reproduce by means of parthenogenesis. Only the genus *Heloderma* from the southern United States, Mexico, and northern Central America, with two species, is venomous.

The physical characteristics of lizards are many and varied (Fig. 10). The body may be flattened dorsoventrally or compressed laterally. In some the limbs are long and well developed, while in others they are much reduced or even lacking. A number of species bear conspicuous horns or bizarre, helmet-like extensions on the head. Others have a sail-like fin or crest of elongate scales on the neck, body, and tail, or a fan-like appendage (*dewlap*) suspended beneath the throat. The tail may be prehensile or not, long and whip-like or short and tapering, smooth-scaled or heavily armored with whorls of spine-like keratinized scales. Other important features to check for include the shape and form of the toes and condition of the subdigital *lamellae*, the presence or absence of movable eyelids, configuration of the pupil (round or vertically elliptical), and the number of specialized glandular scales (if present) on the underside of the thigh (*femoral pores*) or preceding the cloaca (*preanal pores*).

The size, shape, and character of the scales are especially important in distinguishing among species of similar appearance (Fig. 11). These may be small, rounded and nonoverlapping (*granular*), uniform in size, or intermixed with enlarged conical scales (*tubercles*). Alternatively they may be flat, smooth, rounded or hexagonal in shape with a lustrous surface (*cycloid*). Scales that overlap are termed *imbricate*, whereas scales that do not are said to be *juxtaposed.* Those bearing a horizontally oriented medial ridge are termed *keeled*, and some scales on the head may have a wrinkled

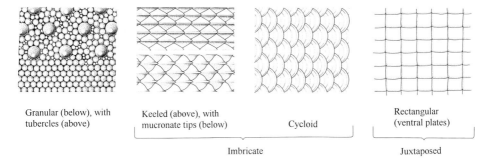

Granular (below), with tubercles (above)

Keeled (above), with mucronate tips (below)

Cycloid

Rectangular (ventral plates)

Imbricate

Juxtaposed

FIGURE 11   Scale types in lizards.

surface with a number of irregular keels (*rugose*). The character of scales may vary on different parts of the body.

KEY TO THE FAMILIES OF LIZARDS IN BELIZE

1. Hand with five digits 2

   Hand with four digits . . . . Gymnophthalmidae [page 153]

2. Abdomen covered with large, squarish, juxtaposed, plate-like scales or with large, smooth, imbricate cycloid scales. 3

   Abdomen covered with numerous small, rounded or pointed, imbricate or subimbricate scales, either smooth or keeled, or with granular scales 6

3. Frontonasal scales paired . . . . Anguidae [page 166]

   Frontonasal scale single 4

4. Scales of dorsum similar to those of venter, cycloid-like; femoral pores absent . . . . Scincidae [page 147]

   Scales of dorsum unlike those of venter, granular; femoral pores present. 5

5. Scales of dorsum uniform in size; eyelids present . . Teiidae [page 155]

   Scales of dorsum not uniform in size, some distinctly larger than others and scattered randomly or arranged linearly; eyelids absent . . . .
   . . . . Xantusiidae [page 163]

6. Upper surface of head covered with plate-like scales of variable size, never granular in appearance 8

   Upper surface of head covered with minute, granular scales 7

7. Eyelids fully developed; granular scales on upper surface of head of two distinct sizes . . . . Eublepharidae [page 89]

   Eyelids lacking; granular scales on upper surface of head more or less subequal in size, none prominently enlarged . . Gekkonidae [page 91]

8. Femoral pores absent 9

   Femoral pores present 10

9. Proximal part of digits with widened lamellae; head neither pronounced posteriorly to overhang the neck nor with a prominent crest . . . . Polychrotidae [page 126]

Proximal part of digits not widened; head either pronounced posteriorly to overhang the neck or with a prominent crest . . . .
. . . . Corytophanidae [page 105]

10. Dewlap present, well developed; dorsum with crest of short or long spine-like scales . . . . Iguanidae [page 115]

Dewlap absent; dorsum not as above . . . Phrynosomatidae [page 119]

BANDED GECKOS (FAMILY EUBLEPHARIDAE)

This family of typically ground-dwelling geckos is widely distributed in the Old World but limited to a single genus, *Coleonyx*, in Central America. They are characterized by the presence of thick, movable upper and lower eyelids and, at least in the New World forms, by their striking banded pattern. In common with other geckos, the skin is thin and fragile and covered with small granular scales. Many species appear to have the ability to vocalize. Males typically have a series of preanal pores; femoral pores are absent.

Coleonyx elegans Gray. See Fig. 12; Plates 40, 41.
Vernacular Names: *Escorpión*, Yucatán banded gecko, cuija manchado.
Description: A moderately large gecko, reaching a snout–vent length of about 100 mm, with a tail length about equal to that of the body. The limbs are long and slender, with long, clawed digits lacking widened lamellae. The large eyes have vertically elliptical pupils and eyelids, allowing the eyes to be closed. Dorsal scales are granular with scattered enlarged tubercles. Preanal pores 7–13. Coloration of the dorsum consists of a complex series of light tan to yellowish bands alternating with rich reddish to chocolate brown bands on a field of pale brown; the head is characterized by an intricate pattern of light and dark markings, with a prominent backward-pointing light and dark chevron behind the eyes. In juveniles, the dorsal pattern is more regular, consisting of triads of wide, fawn-colored bands, bordered by narrow dark brown bands and separated by narrow, buff-colored interspaces.
Habitat: Evergreen broadleaf forest, semi-evergreen seasonal forest, karst hills forest, and highland pine savanna formations; terrestrial; sea level to approximately 600 m.
Distribution: Central Mexico to Guatemala and Belize. In Belize it is found countrywide.
Similar Species: With its fully developed eyelids and bold banded pattern, this distinctive species cannot be confused with any other gecko in Belize.

PLATE 40 *Coleonyx elegans.* Las Cuevas, Chiquibul Forest, Cayo District.

PLATE 41 *Coleonyx elegans* showing erect, stiff-legged defense posture. Cuxta Bani, upper Raspaculo River, Cayo District.

Remarks: A nocturnal, terrestrial lizard. During the daytime it hides beneath leaf litter, boards, fallen palm fronds, and the bark of dead trees. Oviparous, probably depositing two to four eggs during the dry season. When alarmed may lift its body off the ground and assume an upright, stiff-legged posture. This gecko may emit high-pitched squeaking sounds when handled (Lee, 1996).

Key Reference: Klauber (1945).

GECKOS (FAMILY GEKKONIDAE)

These distinctive lizards comprise a large, cosmopolitan family, occurring throughout much of the tropics and subtropical regions of both Old and New Worlds. While some species have eyes with vertically elliptical pupils and are strictly nocturnal, a significant number have round pupils and are typically active by day. The skin is generally thin and fragile, and characterized dorsally by very small granular scales, or a mixture of granular scales and larger tubercles. There are often expanded toe pads, allowing these animals to climb on smooth, vertical surfaces. All of the Belizean species are oviparous, usually producing one or two eggs per clutch. Many species are capable of caudal autotomy and tail regeneration.

In Belize this family is represented by six genera and eight species. Two of these, *Gonatodes albogularis* and *Hemidactylus frenatus*, occur as exotic immigrants. The authors have also received alarming reports of tokay geckos (*Gecko gecko* Linnaeus), a large predatory species from southern Asia, released on South Water Caye. *Hemidactylus turcicus* (L.), a highly successful colonist from the Old World, and *Sphaerodactylus argus* Gosse from Cuba and Jamaica, have become firmly established in northern parts of the Yucatán Peninsula and may in time also be recorded from Belize.

Key to the Genera of the Family Gekkonidae in Belize

1. Eye with circular or subcircular pupil; adult snout–vent length less than 35 mm; digits with a single, expanded terminal lamella, the claw placed laterally to it, or the distal portion somewhat compressed forming an angle with more proximal parts 2

    Eye with vertically elliptic pupil; adult snout–vent length much greater than 35 mm; digits with paired terminal lamellae or, if single, not expanded 3

2. Lamellae beneath digits more or less subequal or, if different, enlarged

under basal phalanges only; claws not retractile into a sheath; color pattern of males blue-black with a yellowish head . . . . *Gonatodes*

Terminal lamellae beneath digits very much larger than other lamellae; claws retractile into a sheath; color pattern of males not as above . . . .
. . . . *Sphaerodactylus*

3. Scales of dorsum and on base of tail unequal in size, intermixed with enlarged, flattened or pointed tubercle-like scales 4

   Scales of dorsum and on tail more or less equal in size, without enlarged tubercles 5

4. Subdigital lamellae in a single row except for a distinctly expanded terminal pair; scales on base of tail not conspicuously different from those of dorsum; males without preano-femoral pores. . . . .
   . . . . *Phyllodactylus*

   Subdigital lamellae mostly in two rows without an expanded terminal pair; base of tail with rows of pointed, tubercle-like scales, distinct from those of dorsum; males with preano-femoral pores . . . . *Hemidactylus*

5. Subdigital lamellae in a single row, undivided; pupil of eye with regular margins. . . . . *Aristelliger*

   Subdigital lamellae in two rows, divided medially; pupil of eye with scalloped margins . . . . *Thecadactylus*

Aristelliger georgeensis (Bocourt). Fig. 12; Plate 42.
Vernacular Names: *Weatherman, escorpión,* Saint George Island gecko, geco de pestañas.
Description: A medium-sized, robust gecko with a maximum snout–vent length of 115 mm in males and a tail length of approximately the same. Females are considerably smaller. The eye has a vertically elliptic pupil without scalloped edges. Scales of dorsum granular, more or less homogeneous, and smooth; those of venter cycloid and imbricate. There are no femoral or preanal pores present. By night the dorsum of adults is greenish gray with rusty brown reticulations and a pattern suggestive of dark crossbanding on the tail; during daylight the lizard darkens to a uniform brownish color. Juveniles are more strikingly marked, with pale tan coloration on top of the head extending as a middorsal stripe to the base of the tail; side of head, flanks, and limbs dark brown flecked with white, and tail yellow at the distal end with four rectangular, pale blotches near the base. Ventrally the coloration is yellowish white.
Habitat: Sand strand and cocotal formation, and edificarian situations; arboreal and occasionally terrestrial; sea level.

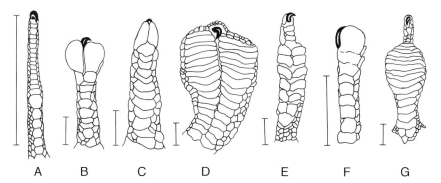

FIGURE 12 Subdigital lamellae in the genera of geckos in Belize: (A) *Gonatodes*; (B) *Phyllodactylus*; (C) *Coleonyx*; (D) *Thecadactylus*; (E) *Hemidactylus*; (F) *Sphaerodactylus*; (G) *Aristelliger*. Vertical lines = 5 mm. Adapted from Julian C. Lee (1996), "The Amphibians and Reptiles of the Yucatán Peninsula," with permission of the publisher, Cornell University Press.

Distribution: Caribbean Mexico, Belize, Honduras, and associated islands. In Belize it occurs on most of the larger island groups and many small cayes, including English Caye, Crawl Caye, and Tom Owen's Caye, as well as on the coast of Belize and Corozal Districts; its southern limit of distribution in Belize is unknown.

Similar Species: Geckos of the genus *Phyllodactylus* have the distal phalanges symmetrically dilated, with a pair of subdigital lamellae, while *Aristelliger* has no subdigital lamellae under the terminal joint. *Coleonyx elegans* has fully developed eyelids, lacking in *Aristelliger*. From the genera *Gonatodes* and *Sphaerodactylus*, *Aristelliger* differs in having eyes with vertically eilliptic pupils, and in having a single symmetrical terminal phalanx (in *Gonatodes* and *Sphaerodactylus* there is a

PLATE 42 *Aristelliger georgeensis.* Caye Caulker. Photograph by J.C. Meerman.

93

single terminal lamella with the claw lateral to it). *Thecadactylus* and *Hemidactylus* have subdigital lamellae arranged in two rows, versus a single, undivided row in *Aristelliger*. In male *Hemidactylus* there is also a series of preano-femoral pores.

Remarks: Strictly an insular and coastal species. May be observed basking during the day but primarily crepuscular and nocturnal in habits, hiding under fallen palm fronds and in rotting palm trunks during the daylight hours. Chiefly arboreal; at night these geckos are active on coconut palm trunks, scrub trees, and buildings, where they have been heard to emit a "low chirping sound" (Duellman, 1965) or a "screech" (Schwartz and Henderson, 1991). In places, *Aristelliger* may be abundant; Lee (1996) remarks that virtually every house on Caye Caulker has at least one, and they are common at night on the sides of buildings near lights. The diet consists largely of invertebrates, but the species has been known to prey on anoline lizards (Schwartz and Henderson, 1991). *Aristelliger* produces only a single egg per clutch. The type locality for the species is St. George's Caye off the coast of Belize City.

Key Reference: Bauer and Russell (1993).

Gonatodes albogularis (Duméril and Bibron). Fig. 12; Plate 43.

Vernacular Names: Yellow-headed gecko, geco cabeza-amarilla.

Description: A medium-small gecko with a maximum snout–vent length of approximately 45 mm and a tail length of 50 mm. Head relatively short; eye with circular pupil. Tail swollen and cylindrical. No femoral or preanal pores present, but escutcheon area, underside of thighs, and base of tail in males with a large number of specialized glandular scales. The dorsum is covered with small conical, more or less uniformly sized granules; ventrally the scales are smooth, rounded, and imbricate. In coloration the sexes are strikingly dimorphic. Males are bluish black dorsally with a dark yellow to orange-brown head and purplish-brown venter. Females are pale grey or brownish grey with a horseshoe-shaped dark mark behind the eyes, a pair of dark spots on the sides of the neck, and rows of indefinite dark spots on the back; the toes are banded with light and dark and the limbs and tail have light and dark spots.

Habitat: Restricted to edificarian situations.

Distribution: Native to South and Central America and widely introduced in the West Indies. In Belize it is currently known only from Belize City, although is likely to become more widespread.

Similar Species: Geckos of the genera *Coleonyx*, *Aristelliger*, *Hemidactylus*, *Phyllodactylus*, and *Thecadactylus* have eyes with vertically elliptic pupils (circular in *Gonatodes*). It differs from *Sphaerodactylus* in having more or less subequal lamellae beneath the

PLATE 43   Male (above) and female (below) *Gonatodes albogularis,* showing characteristic sexual dimorphism. Volcán Santa Maria, Cordillera de Guanacaste, Costa Rica.

digits (terminal lamellae conspicuously larger than other lamellae in *Sphaerodactylus*), a nonretractile claw, and a distinctive male color pattern.

Remarks: An introduced species, recently discovered in Belize City (Tony Garel, personal communication). Diurnal; typically seen perched about a meter above the ground on the walls of wooden houses and side buildings, taking refuge in holes and crevices between the timbers when alarmed. The species is also known to inhabit the bark of trees, even in semi-urban areas. There is no voice mechanism present. Females lay a single egg.

Key Reference: Taylor (1956).

Hemidactylus frenatus Schlegel. Fig. 12; Plate 44.

Vernacular Names: Common house gecko, besucona.

Description: A medium-sized gecko with a maximum snout–vent length of 60 mm and a tail length of 65 mm. The eye has a vertically elliptic pupil with scalloped edges. Tail swollen and cylindrical with rows of pointed tubercles at base. Males have a continuous series of 24–36 femoral pores across the underside of the thighs and preanal region. The dorsum is covered with small granules, among which are scattered flat,

PLATE 44 *Hemidactylus frenatus.* Corozal Town, Corozal District.

smooth tubercles, arranged in 2–8 irregular longitudinal rows; ventrally
the scales are smooth, rounded, and imbricate. Dorsal coloration is gray
or pinkish brown, uniform or variegated with dark markings, and usually paler by night. Head sometimes variegated with brown and labials
mottled with light and dark markings; a dark line runs from the nostril
posteriorly through the eye and onto the flank. Venter whitish.

Habitat: Restricted to edificarian situations along the coast.

Distribution: Widely distributed through the tropical and subtropical
regions of the Old World; introduced into Central America. In Belize it
is currently known from Corozal, Belize, Cayo, and Stann Creek
Districts, and may eventually be found in coastal areas of Toledo.

Similar Species: *Hemidactylus frenatus* is the only gecko in Belize in
which males have a series of preano-femoral pores. Rudimentary pores
may also be present in females. Geckos of the genera *Gonatodes* and
Sphaerodactylus may be further distinguished by their circular pupils
(eyes with vertically elliptic pupils in *Hemidactylus*). In *Phyllodactylus*
and *Sphaerodactylus* the distal phalanges of the digits are dilated, while
Hemidactylus has no dilation of the terminal joint. Members of the
genus *Coleonyx* have fully developed eyelids, lacking in *Hemidactylus*.
Aristelliger differs in having a single row of subdigital lamellae, as
opposed to a divided row in *Hemidactylus*. *Hemidactylus frenatus* differs from the much larger *Thecadactylus* in having enlarged scales scattered throughout the granular dorsal scales and rows of pointed tubercles
on the base of the tail, versus a dorsum and tail with granular scales of
about equal size in *Thecadactylus*.

Remarks: An introduced species, recently discovered on the walls of buildings at night in Dangriga (Jan Meerman, personal communication), and now common along much of the coast. Originally from Asia, this small nocturnal gecko has also become firmly established in coastal Mexico and Guatemala. Its vocalizations have been likened to the barking of a small dog (Marcellini, 1974). *Hemidactylus turcicus*, a related species native to the Mediterranean region and Middle East, occurs as an exotic in northern parts of the Yucatán Peninsula and, although not yet reported from Belize, its appearance is expected.

Key Reference: Loveridge (1947).

Key to the Species of *Phyllodactylus* in Belize

Tubercles from axilla to groin 26 or more; paravertebral tubercles 46 or more . . . . *P. insularis*

Tubercles from axilla to groin 26 or fewer; paravertebral tubercles 44 or fewer. . . . . *P. tuberculosus*

Phyllodactylus insularis Dixon. Fig. 12; Plate 45.

Vernacular Names: *Escorpión* (?), island leaf-toed gecko, salamanquesa de isla.

Description: A moderate-sized gecko with a snout–vent length of some 58 mm and a complete tail equal to or a little longer than the head and

PLATE 45 *Phyllodactylus insularis.* Half Moon Caye, Lighthouse Reef. Photograph by J.C. Meerman.

body. The eye has a vertically elliptic pupil with slightly scalloped edges. Terminal pads of fingers and toes twice as long as wide, extending beyond the insertion of the claws. There are no femoral or preanal pores present. Dorsum characterized by small granules intermixed with 16–18 longitudinal rows of enlarged tubercle-like scales; scales of venter imbricate and abruptly differentiated from the lateral scales. Dorsal coloration is typically brownish with indistinct undulating cross bands or spots of grayish white. Side of head with a distinct whitish spot beneath the eye, and a whitish loreal stripe. The ventral surface is yellowish brown.

Habitat: Sand strand and cocotal formations; arboreal and occasionally terrestrial; sea level.

Distribution: Endemic to Belize, where it is known with certainty only from Half Moon Caye in Lighthouse Reef and Long Caye in Glovers Reef; it may eventually prove to be more widespread in the cayes.

Similar Species: Differs from *P. tuberculosus* in having 26 or more tubercles between the axilla and groin (fewer than 26 in *P. tuberculosus*) and 46 or more paravertebral tubercles (44 or fewer in *P. tuberculosus*). It may be distinguished from *Aristelliger*, *Thecadactylus*, and *Hemidactylus* by the dilation of the terminal phalanges (no dilation of this joint in *Aristelliger*, *Thecadactylus*, or *Hemidactylus*). In male *Hemidactylus* there is also a series of preano-femoral pores (absent in *Phyllodactylus*). Species of the genera *Gonatodes* and *Sphaerodactylus* have eyes with circular pupils (vertically elliptic in *Phyllodactylus*), and a single terminal lamella (terminal subdigital lamellae paired in *Phyllodactylus*). It differs from *Coleonyx* in lacking an eyelid.

Remarks: An insular species, currently known in Belize from only two small outlying islands. Nocturnal; usually observed foraging at night on low vegetation. Juveniles are typically found beneath fallen palm fronds and other surface debris, whereas adults are more often observed on the trunks of palm trees. Vocalization in *P. insularis* has not been described, although the species may produce sounds similar to those of *P. tuberculosus*. There is a need for a more detailed analysis of specimens representing the caye and mainland populations of *Phyllodactylus* in Belize. Neill and Allen (1962) commented on the variability of mainland populations of *P. tuberculosus*, and recently, J. C. Meerman (in litt.) has indicated to the authors that specimens he collected from Caye Caulker resemble supposed *P. insularis*, although *P. tuberculosus* is to be expected there.

Key Reference: Dixon (1960).

Phyllodactylus tuberculosus Wiegmann. Fig. 12; Plate 46.

Vernacular Names: *Escorpión*, yellow-bellied leaf-toed gecko, geco tuberculoso.

PLATE 46   *Phyllodactylus tuberculosus.* Volcán Orosí, Cordillera de Guanacaste, Costa Rica.

Description: A moderate-sized gecko with a snout–vent length of approximately 60 mm and a complete tail equal to or a little longer than the head and body. The eye has a vertically elliptic pupil with slightly scalloped edges. Terminal pads of fingers and toes twice as long as wide, extending beyond the insertion of the claws. There are no femoral or preanal pores present. Dorsum characterized by small granules intermixed with 13–16 rows of enlarged tubercle-like scales; scales of venter imbricate and abruptly differentiated from the lateral scales. Dorsal coloration is typically brownish, dull gray, or a pale shade of lavender with small, darker spots arranged in 10–12 transverse rows. Posterior half of unbroken tail with about 7 dark transverse bands. Other dark markings are present on the sides, limbs, and head; there may or may not be a distinct whitish spot beneath the eye or a whitish loreal stripe. At night the darker pigment disappears and the body becomes uniformly pale pinkish gray. Ventrally the coloration is yellowish.

Habitat: Coastal lagoons and marshes and sand strand and cocotal formations, and edificarian situations; arboreal and occasionally terrestrial; sea level.

Distribution: Pacific versant of north-central Mexico to Costa Rica, and Caribbean coast of the Yucatán Peninsula. In Belize it occurs throughout the entire coastal region and on many cayes.

Similar Species: Differs from *P. insularis* in having fewer than 26 tubercles between the axilla and groin (26 or more in *P. insularis*) and 44 or fewer paravertebral tubercles (46 or more in *P. insularis*). It may be distinguished from *Aristelliger*, *Thecadactylus*, and *Hemidactylus* by the dilation of the terminal phalanges (no dilation of this joint in *Aristelliger, Thecadactylus,* or *Hemidactylus*). In male *Hemidactylus* there is also a series of preano-femoral pores (absent in *Phyllodactylus*). Species of the genera *Gonatodes* and *Sphaerodactylus* have eyes with circular pupils (vertically elliptic in *Phyllodactylus*), and a single terminal lamella (terminal subdigital lamellae paired in *Phyllodactylus*). It differs from *Coleonyx* in lacking an eyelid.

Remarks: Mainland populations of this species are generally found on the Pacific slopes of Central America, Belize being an exception. In Belize it occurs only on the coast and several cayes of the barrier reef, where it inhabits loose bark of trees, decaying tree trunks, and similar hiding places during the day. Strictly nocturnal. Its vocalization has been described as sounding like a kiss (Alvarez del Toro, 1982). Relationships of Belizean *P. tuberculosus* to *P. insularis,* and to the other Central American populations of *P. tuberculosus,* would benefit from further investigation.

Key Reference: Dixon (1964).

Key to the Species of *Sphaerodactylus* in Belize

Dorsal scales keeled . . . . *S. millepunctatus*

Dorsal scales smooth . . . . *S. glaucus*

Sphaerodactylus glaucus Cope. Fig. 12; Plates 47, 48.

Vernacular Names: *Escorpión,* dwarf gecko, gequillo collarejo.

Description: A small gecko, with a maximum snout–vent length of 30 mm and a tail of approximately equal length. Eye with rounded pupil. No femoral or preanal pores present, but the escutcheon area and underside of the thighs in males have specialized glandular scales. The dorsal scales are minuscule, homogeneous, and smooth. The pattern is highly variable in juveniles and adults, but Belizean individuals generally have a light middorsal area that may form a broad longitudinal band with scalloped edges and/or a series of light spots or stripes that cross the dorsum. There is typically a dark nuchal spot and frequently either a paired series of dark spots or a transverse band at the base of the tail. A pale, dark-bordered spot is often present at the elbow joint of the forearm, and/or on the hind leg. Venter whitish.

Habitat: Evergreen broadleaf forest, semi-evergreen seasonal forest, karst hills forest, savanna, highland pine savanna, and sand strand and cocotal formations, edificarian situations, banana groves, and other fruit plantations; arboreal and terrestrial; sea level to 600 m.

Distribution: Southern Mexico to western Honduras. In Belize it is found countrywide and on many cayes.

PLATE 47 *Sphaerodactylus glaucus.* Sarteneja, Corozal District. Photograph by P. Edgar.

Similar Species: From *Gonatodes albogularis,* the only other gekkonid genus in Belize that has eyes with circular pupils, *Sphaerodactylus* may be distinguished by its enlarged subdigital lamellae and retractile claw. Male *Gonatodes* also have a distinctive color pattern. Its asymmetrical, single, terminal subdigital lamellae and rounded eye pupil distinguish this gecko from *Coleonyx, Aristelliger, Hemidactylus, Phyllodactylus,* and *Thecadactylus.* It may be separated from

PLATE 48 *Sphaerodactylus glaucus.* Fallen Stones, Toledo District. Photograph by S. Von Peltz.

101

S. millepunctatus by its smooth dorsal scales, versus keeled dorsals in *S. millepunctatus.*

Remarks: This small gecko has been found in a wide variety of situations, from the inside of houses in towns to undisturbed rainforest; generally active during the daytime and usually seen running about on tree trunks, walls, or among leaf litter foraging for insect prey. There is no voice mechanism present. A single egg is produced in each clutch.

Key Reference: Harris and Kluge (1984).

Sphaerodactylus millepunctatus Hallowell. Fig. 12; Plate 49.

Vernacular Names: *Escorpión* (?), spotted gecko, gequillo cabeciamarillo.

Description: A small gecko, with a snout–vent length of 30 mm and a tail of about equal length. Eye with round pupil. No femoral or preanal pores present, but escutcheon area and underside of thighs have specialized glandular scales in males. The dorsal scales are essentially homogeneous and keeled. Juveniles are light brown in color with dark bands or paired crescent-shaped markings dorsally near the forelimbs, and a dark spot over the pelvic region. In adults, the dark juvenile pattern changes into minute dark and light dorsal spots, arranged more or less in irregular rows. There are usually a pair of postorbital longitudinal dark lines or reticulations on the head. The venter is generally pale and peppered with small dark spots, most densely under the chin and throat.

Habitat: Evergreen broadleaf forest, semi-evergreen seasonal forest, karst hills forest, subtropical evergreen forest, savanna, and highland pine

PLATE 49 *Sphaerodactylus millepunctatus.* Honduras. Photograph by J.R. McCranie.

savanna formation, banana groves, and fruit orchards; arboreal and terrestrial; sea level to 1000 m.

Distribution: Southern Mexico to northern Costa Rica. In Belize it is found countrywide, possibly including some cayes.

Similar Species: From *Gonatodes albogularis*, the only other gekkonid genus in Belize that has eyes with circular pupils, *Sphaerodactylus* may be distinguished by its enlarged subdigital lamellae and retractile claw. Male *Gonatodes* also have a distinctive color pattern. Its asymmetrical, single, terminal subdigital lamellae and rounded eye pupil distinguish this gecko from *Coleonyx, Aristelliger, Hemidactylus, Phyllodactylus,* and *Thecadactylus*. It differs from *S. glaucus* in having keeled dorsal scales (all completely smooth in *S. glaucus*).

Remarks: A small terrestrial and arboreal gecko. Diurnal in habits; typically found among bunches of bananas, secreted beneath dead tree bark and palm fronds, or among forest floor debris. There is no voice mechanism present. In previous herpetological literature on Belize, this species has gone under the name *S. lineolatus.*

Key Reference: Harris and Kluge (1984).

Thecadactylus rapicauda (Houttuyn). Fig. 12; Plates 50, 51.

Vernacular Names: *Escorpión,* turnip-tailed gecko, geco patudo.

Description: A large gecko, reaching a snout–vent length of up to 120 mm, with a tail length of approximately 80 mm. Head triangular and very dis-

PLATE 50 *Thecadactylus rapicauda.* Fallen Stones, Toledo District. Photograph by S. Von Peltz.

PLATE 51 *Thecadactylus rapicauda* showing well-developed turnip-shaped tail. Shipstern Nature Reserve, Corozal District. Photograph by J.C. Meerman.

tinct from neck; the large eye has a vertically elliptic pupil with scalloped edges. The legs are stout with flanges of loose skin along the posterior edges, and the fingers and toes are heavily webbed with greatly expanded lamellae beneath the digits. There are no femoral or preanal pores present. The tail is somewhat flattened dorsoventrally and constricted at the base; in some specimens it is markedly swollen to accommodate stored fat, giving rise to one of the common names, turnip-tailed gecko. Scales of dorsum granular; those of the venter cycloid-like and imbricate. Dorsal coloration pale gray or brownish lavender to beige with a complex pattern of dark brown bars, spots, and lines implicative of transverse bands but broken except for one broad, complete band near the end of the tail. Head usually with a blackish stripe extending from behind the eye to the shoulder, bordered above by a paler stripe. The venter is pale lavender brown or gray with small speckles of darker pigment.

Habitat: Evergreen broadleaf forest, semi-evergreen seasonal forest, karst hills forest, subtropical evergreen forest, and highland pine savanna formations, and perhaps fruit orchards; arboreal and occasionally terrestrial; sea level to 750 m.

Distribution: Yucatán Peninsula region of southern Mexico to northern South America and the Lesser Antilles. In Belize it occurs countrywide, in forested areas.

Similar Species: *Thecadactylus* differs from *Coleonyx* in lacking eyelids (an unmodified, fringe-like "eyelid" is present but does not completely surround the eye). It may be distinguished from *Sphaerodactylus* by the presence of a single, widened terminal subdigital lamella in *Sphaerodactylus*, versus no widened terminal lamellae in *Thecadactylus*. Geckos of the genera *Gonatodes* and *Sphaerodactylus* have eyes with circular pupils (vertically elliptic in *Thecadactylus*). *Phyllodactylus* species have a pair of widened terminal subdigital lamellae, a character lacking in *Thecadactylus*. It differs from *Aristelliger* in having two rows of subdigital lamellae, versus a single row in *Aristelliger*. It may be distinguished from *Hemidactylus* by the absence of enlarged scales scattered throughout the granular dorsal scales and rows of pointed tubercles on the base of the tail (dorsum and tail with granular scales of more or less equal size in *Thecadactylus*). In male *Hemidactylus* there is also a series of preano-femoral pores (absent in *Thecadactylus*).

Remarks: A nocturnal forest gecko; during the daytime it can be found under tree bark and the basal sheaths of palm fronds, in tree hollows and deep recesses of buttress roots, and in drainage pipes and caves. The vocalization has been described as a high-pitched, rapidly repeated "chick-chick-chick" or "chack-chack-chack" (Beebe, 1944). When disturbed, the species has been known to jump from considerable heights in trees and "parachute" to lower branches (Vitt and Zani, 1997). A single egg is produced at intervals of a few days and deposited in rotting logs or under loose bark.

Key Reference: Taylor (1956).

CASQUE-HEADED LIZARDS (FAMILY CORYTOPHANIDAE)

This is a relatively small family of neotropical lizards, consisting of three genera, all of which occur in Belize. They characteristically have some type of head and/or body crest, a light-weight body frame with well-developed slender legs and a long tail, and are of moderate to large size. All are essentially arboreal in habits; when running at speed on the ground, locomotion is bipedal. Femoral pores, characteristic of the family Iguanidae in which these lizards were until fairly recently included (Frost and Etheridge, 1989), are lacking in the Corytophanidae. The species in Belize are all oviparous.

Key to the Genera of the Family Corytophanidae

1. Head crest flattened laterally, fin-like and semierect. 2

   Head crest flat-topped, broadly triangular and helmet-like, projecting more or less horizontally . . . . *Laemanctus*

2. Marginal fringe of head crest and gular pouch serrated; scales of venter between axilla and groin 35 or fewer . . . . *Corytophanes*

   Marginal fringe of head crest smooth, not serrated; scales of venter between axilla and groin 40 or more . . . . *Basiliscus*

Basiliscus vittatus Wiegmann. Plate 52.

Vernacular Names: *Maklakka, cock lizard, cock maklaka,* striped basilisk, basilisco rayada.

Description: A moderately large lizard with a laterally compressed body, males reach a snout–vent length of approximately 225 mm, with a tail of up to almost three times as long; females are considerably smaller. Males have a prominent head crest that projects backward and continues as a less conspicuous fin-like crest along the dorsum, supported by short bony spines; in females, the head crest is not as well developed. The hind limbs are large and muscular, with long, well-developed toes, and the tail is somewhat laterally compressed. Scales of dorsum and venter imbricate and keeled, those on the limbs larger and more conspicuously keeled. Dorsum olive to yellowish brown and usually with a pale middorsal stripe, a pair of yellowish dorsolateral stripes, and series of dark transverse bands that continue on to the tail; the dorsal pattern in juveniles is generally brighter and more distinct. The ventral surface is dull purplish gray.

Habitat: Evergreen broadleaf forest, semi-evergreen seasonal forest, karst hills forest, savanna, highland pine savanna, interior wetlands, and coastal lagoons and marshes formations, and edificarian situations; arboreal and terrestrial; sea level to 600 m.

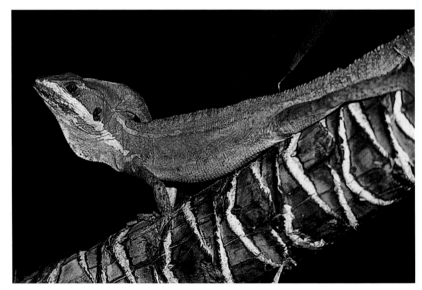

PLATE 52 Adult male *Basiliscus vittatus* showing characteristic fin-like head crest. Santa Elena, Cayo District.

Distribution: South-central Mexico to northern South America. In Belize it is found countrywide.

Similar Species: Differs from species of *Laemanctus* in having a dorsal crest that extends from the head onto the body; it may be distinguished from *Corytophanes* by its smaller ventral scales, at least 40 between the axilla and groin, versus fewer than 35 in *Corytophanes*. Juvenile *Basiliscus* may be distinguished from long-legged anoles, such as *Norops capito*, by the lack of widened subdigital lamellae in *Basiliscus*.

Remarks: An abundant lizard in Belize, occurring in a wide variety of habitats. Diurnal, climbing into low bushes to sleep at night; during the daytime it is frequently observed on the ground, although is chiefly arboreal. Most commonly encountered in the vicinity of aquatic habitats and will occasionally run for short distances across the surface of the water, using its hind legs in bipedal locomotion. The species may breed year-round; in southern parts the most common period for egg deposition appears to be during August and September.

Key Reference: Fitch (1973).

Key to the species of *Corytophanes* in Belize

Head crest continuous with dorsal body crest . . . . *C. cristatus*

Head crest not continuous with dorsal body crest, broken over shoulders. . .
. . . . *C. hernandezii*

Corytophanes cristatus (Merrem). Plate 53, front cover.

Vernacular Names: *Old man*, smooth-headed helmeted basilisk, turipache selvatico.

Description: A medium-sized lizard, with a snout–vent length of approximately 125 mm and a tail length of 265 mm. The body and head are laterally compressed, and the limbs are long and thin. The head bears a conspicuous occipital crest that projects caudally and is continuous with a low crest on the body; in the gular region there is a coarsely scaled pouch with a serrated free edge that may be expanded as a threat gesture. Dorsal coloration varies from tan to greenish or reddish brown, with darker crossbanding resembling the pattern of leaves; the tail, arms, and legs may also be marked with dark, broad, sometimes indistinct transverse bands. The side of the head is often characterized by a series of dark lines that radiate more or less from the eye, sometimes extending on to the gular pouch; the chin is typically brownish black. There may be one or more prominent white spots at the elbow, and the posterior surface of the thighs may be distinctly marked with small, irregular whitish spots.

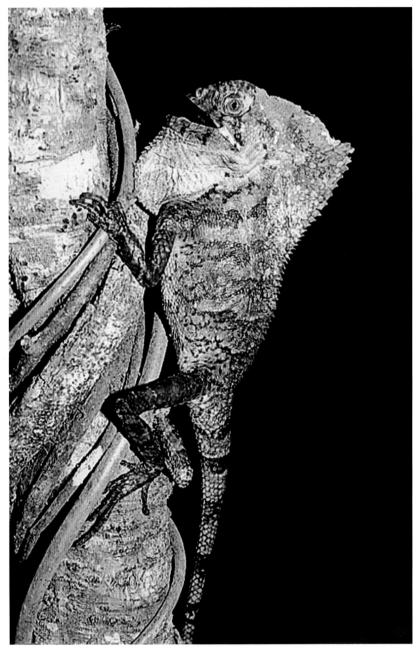

PLATE 53 *Corytophanes cristatus* demonstrating typical defense posture. Cuxta Bani, upper Raspaculo River, Cayo District.

Habitat: Evergreen broadleaf forest, semi-evergreen seasonal forest, and karst hills forest formations. The species may also occur in the narrow belts of broadleaf woodland along some of the streams bordering Mountain Pine Ridge (highland pine savanna formation); arboreal; sea level to 600 m.

Distribution: Southern Mexico to Colombia. In Belize it is known from Orange Walk, Cayo, Stann Creek, and Toledo Districts.

Similar Species: Differs from species of *Laemanctus* in having a dorsal crest that extends from the head onto the body; it may be distinguished from *Basiliscus* by its larger ventral scales, fewer than 35 between the axilla and groin in *C. cristatus,* versus at least 40 in *Basiliscus.* Juveniles may be distinguished from long-legged anoles, such as *Norops capito,* by the lack of widened subdigital lamellae. From *C. hernandezii* it can be distinguished by the nature of the head and dorsal body crest, which is regular and continuous, and not sharply interrupted on the neck.

Remarks: A highly arboreal, strictly forest inhabitant, typically encountered perched upright on the trunks of small trees or vines. Its cryptic coloration makes this lizard difficult to detect, even at close range, and its reluctance to move enhances its hiding ability. In response to danger the species will erect its head and body crest, puff out its throat, and open its mouth. Diurnal. Primarily insectivorous in feeding habits, although has also been known to consume small anoline lizards. Eggs are deposited in the ground between May and September. Observations documented by Bock (1987) and by Lazcano-Barrero and Gongóra-Arones (1993) suggest that the female may use her head as an earth-moving tool in excavating the nest. Lazcano-Barrero and Gongóro-Arones (1993) also indicated that females may prefer to nest in clear, open areas devoid of leaf litter to reduce detection by predators, and detection of the buried eggs by terrestrial, leaf litter, and fossorial predators.

Key Reference: Taylor (1956).

Corytophanes hernandezii (Wiegmann). Plates 54, 55.

Vernacular Names: *Old man,* Hernandez's helmeted basilisk, turipache de montana.

Description: Like its congener, this is a medium-sized lizard, with a snout–vent length of approximately 120 mm and a tail length of 250 mm. The body and head are laterally compressed, and the limbs are long and thin. The head bears a conspicuous occipital crest that projects caudally, but unlike *C. cristatus,* is not continuous with a low crest on the body; in the gular region there is a coarsely scaled pouch with a serrated free edge that may be expanded as a threat gesture. In some specimens a short bony outgrowth projects laterally from the side of the head. Dorsal coloration varies from yellowish tan to greenish or reddish brown, often with a promi-

PLATE 54 *Corytophanes hernandezii.* Sibun Hills area, Belize District. Photograph by C. Farneti Foster.

PLATE 55 Head detail of *Corytophanes hernandezii.* Sibun Hills area, Belize District. Photograph by C. Farneti Foster.

nent, dark mask-like stripe on the side of the head enclosing the eye, a similar dark marking over the shoulder, and with darker crossbanding that tends to mimic the patterns of leaves; the tail, arms, and legs may also be marked with dark, broad, sometimes indistinct transverse bands.

Habitat: Evergreen broadleaf forest, semi-evergreen seasonal forest, and karst hills forest formations; arboreal; sea level to 300 m.

Distribution: Southeastern Mexico to northern Guatemala and Belize. In Belize it is known from Corozal, Orange Walk, Cayo, Stann Creek, and Toledo Districts, and probably occurs countrywide.

Similar Species: Differs from species of *Laemanctus* in having a dorsal crest that extends from the head onto the body; it may be distinguished from *Basiliscus* by its larger ventral scales, fewer than 35 between the axilla and groin in *C. hernandezii,* versus at least 40 in *Basiliscus.* Juveniles may be distinguished from long-legged anoles, such as *Norops capito,* by the lack of widened subdigital lamellae in *Corytophanes.* From *C. cristatus* it can be distinguished by the nature of the head and dorsal body crest, which in *C. hernandezii* is sharply bisected on the neck and not regular and continuous.

Remarks: An essentially arboreal species of high forests. Similar in habits to *C. cristatus* and generally encountered on the sides of small trees and vines. It appears to be more tolerant of xeric conditions than *C. cristatus,* and in the semi-evergreen seasonal forest formation, where both

111

species may occur sympatrically, *C. hernandezii* is often the more abundant of the two.

Key Reference: Lee (1996).

Key to the Species of *Laemanctus* in Belize

Posterior contour of head casque serrated with a series of projecting spine-like scales. . . . . *L. serratus*

Posterior contour of head casque smooth and regular, not serrated . . . . .
. . . . *L. longipes*

Laemanctus longipes Wiegmann. Plate 56.

Vernacular Names: *Old man* (?), eastern casque-headed iguana, lemacto coludo oriental.

Description: A medium-sized lizard, with a snout–vent length of 130 mm and a long tail in relation to its body size, measuring up to approximately 450 mm. The body is laterally compressed and the limbs are exceptionally long and slender. The head bears a conspicuous flat-topped casque that projects backward and has a fringe of more or less undifferentiated, regular scales lining the posterior edge. Scales of dorsum and venter large, keeled, and imbricate. Dorsum bright green, crossed by five or six bars of darker green that may be outlined in black; the tail is also

PLATE 56 *Laemanctus longipes.* Cuxta Bani, upper Raspaculo River, Cayo District.

green and marked with regular dark bands. Top of head yellow-green, the edge of the casque normally outlined in black, and side of the head with a yellow-white stripe extending posteriorly from the supralabials to the groin. The venter is uniformly pale green.

Habitat: Evergreen broadleaf forest, semi-evergreen seasonal forest, and karst hills forest formations; arboreal and terrestrial; sea level to 600 m.

Distribution: Southern Mexico to northern Honduras. In Belize it probably occurs countrywide, except perhaps in northern Corozal District.

Similar Species: Differs from species of *Basiliscus* and *Corytophanes* in the character of its cephalic crest, which is flat-topped and does not extend onto the body. Juveniles may be distinguished from long-legged anoles, such as *Norops capito*, by the lack of widened subdigital lamellae (present in *Laemanctus*). It may be distinguished from *L. serratus* by the presence of a series of projecting triangular, spine-like scales on the posterior contour of the head (absent in *L. longipes*).

Remarks: A typically arboreal, forest lizard, diurnal in habits and usually encountered in understory trees; juveniles may be somewhat more terrestrial. Its background-matching coloration and habit of remaining still make this lizard extremely difficult to detect in vegetation. Capable of rapid bipedal locomotion. A small number of relatively large-sized eggs are deposited in a hole dug by the female under tree roots or on the forest floor; egg-laying in Belize has been observed by the authors in late April, and also in early August (McCarthy, 1982). In the semi-evergreen seasonal forest formations of northern Belize *L. longipes* appears to be ecologically replaced by its congener, *L. serratus*.

Key Reference: McCoy (1968).

Laemanctus serratus Cope. See Fig. 10; Plate 57.

Vernacular Names: *Old man* (?), serrated casque-headed iguana, lemacto coludo.

Description: A medium-sized lizard, with a snout–vent length of some 125 mm and a long tail in relation to its body size, measuring up to approximately 430 mm. The body is laterally compressed, with a row of enlarged, serrated middorsal scales, and the limbs are exceptionally long and slender. The head bears a conspicuous flat-topped casque that projects caudally and has a fringe of enlarged conical scales lining the posterior edge. Scales of dorsum and venter large, keeled, and imbricate. Ordinarily the dorsum is lime green crossed by five to seven transverse black bars separated by interspaces of approximately twice the width of the bars, although the lizard is capable of changing to a brownish ground color. The tail is marked with regular brownish bands, sometimes arranged in pairs. Top of head gray-green, the edge of the casque normally outlined in black;

PLATE 57 Head of *Laemanctus serratus* showing characteristic head casque edged with enlarged spines. Sarteneja, Corozal District. Photograph by J.C. Meerman.

side of head with a white stripe extending posteriorly from the supralabials to the groin, and a darker green, sometimes black-edged lateral stripe extending from the orbit posteriorly over the shoulder and along the dorsolateral part of the body. The venter is clear light green.

Habitat: Semi-evergreen seasonal forest formation; arboreal and terrestrial; sea level to 100 m.

Distribution: East-central Mexico to northern Belize. In Belize it is known only from Corozal District.

Similar Species: Differs from species of *Basiliscus* and *Corytophanes* in the character of its cephalic crest, which is flat-topped and does not extend onto the body. Juveniles may be distinguished from long-legged anoles, such as *Norops capito,* by the lack of widened subdigital lamellae in *Laemanctus.* It may be distinguished from *L. longipes* by the presence of a series of projecting triangular scales on the posterior contour of the head (absent in *L. longipes*).

Remarks: A diurnal and essentially forest-dwelling species. Adults are both arboreal and terrestrial in habits; juveniles may be somewhat more terrestrial. Its cryptic coloration and habit of remaining still make detection of this lizard among leaves and branches extremely difficult. Capable of rapid, bipedal locomotion. The eggs are deposited in a hole dug in the ground by the female, probably at the end of the dry season in June. Food consists mainly of insects, although Martin (1958) also reported finding snails and lizards among the stomach contents of specimens in Mexico. In the southern, wetter broadleaf forest formations *L. serratus* appears to be ecologically replaced by its congener, *L. longipes.*

Key Reference: McCoy (1968).

IGUANAS (FAMILY IGUANIDAE)

This family, once considered to contain numerous genera and a very large number of species, was recently redefined to include only a small number of closely related, primarily New World genera (Frost and Etheridge, 1989). Two of these, *Ctenosaura* and *Iguana,* occur in Central America, and contain the largest lizards to be found in the region. The two species in Belize are conspicuous and heavy-set in form, with moderately long, well-developed limbs. Both animals are sometimes exploited as food by humans, especially *Iguana iguana,* although not to the extent as elsewhere in Central America. Members of this family are all oviparous.

Key to the Genera of the Family Iguanidae in Belize

Dorsal and lateral surfaces of tail with whorls of enlarged scales separated by smaller granular scales. . . . . *Ctenosaura*

Scales of tail more or less uniform in size, never in conspicuous whorls . . . . *Iguana*

Ctenosaura similis (Gray). See Fig. 10; Plates 58, 59.

Vernacular Names: *Wish-willy,* black iguana, iguana negra.

Description: A large species, with a snout–vent length of approximately 350 mm and a tail length of 700 mm; males are larger than females. The tail is armored with transverse whorls of heavily keeled, spinose scales, separated dorsally by two rows of smaller scales. A gular pouch and transverse gular fold are present. Undersurface of hind limbs with four or five femoral pores on each side. Scales on the dorsum are granular in form, with a middorsal crest of erect, short, spine-like scales. In adults, the flattened, stocky body is generally a dull grey, blackish or dark

PLATE 58 Adult male *Ctenosaura similis.* Sarteneja, Corozal District. Photograph by P. Edgar.

brownish coloration with variable markings, usually tan to greenish in color; juveniles are bright green with dark transverse markings. The coloration can change rapidly, especially in adults.

Habitat: Semi-evergreen seasonal forest, savanna, highland pine savanna, coastal lagoons and marshes, and sand strand and cocotal formations, agricultural land, and edificarian situations; arboreal and terrestrial; sea level to 600 m.

Distribution: Southern Mexico to Panama. In Belize it occurs country-wide, including many cayes.

Similar Species: Adults can be distinguished from large green iguanas by their dark color and/or the whorls of enlarged scales on the tail; green

PLATE 59 Hatchling *Ctenosaura similis.* Belize District. Photograph by S. Von Peltz.

iguanas have essentially smooth tails. Differences in tail scalation may also be used to differentiate between small *Ctenosaura* and *Iguana*, both of which are green. Juveniles may be distinguished from long-legged anoles, such as *Norops capito*, and members of the genera *Corytophanes* and *Laemanctus*, by the presence of femoral pores, a character lacking in these other genera.

Remarks: A gregarious and common inhabitant of open and cleared habitats, where adults may be frequently observed sunning themselves on rocks, trees, and fence posts; juveniles are less conspicuous, their green color helping them to remain concealed among vegetation. Adults are omnivorous, although the bulk of the diet consists of fruits, leaves, seeds, and other vegetable matter; juveniles appear to be primarily insectivorous. Adult activity is largely centered around the nesting area, which may be a tree cavity, rock crevice, or burrow excavated by the lizard. Eggs are deposited during the dry season in burrows dug by the females, and more than one female may utilize the same burrow system. The ecology of this species in Belize has been documented by Henderson (1973).

Key Reference: Fitch (1973).

Iguana iguana (Linnaeus). Plates 60, 61.

Vernacular Names: *Iguana, bamboo chicken, bayamaga, hu,* green iguana, iguana de ribera.

Description: This is the largest, and in the adult stage, the most readily identifiable lizard in Belize. Adults may reach a maximum snout–vent length of 500 mm with a tail approaching almost three times this length. The tail is long and whip-like, without whorls of enlarged scales. Males are larger than females with a more massive head. There is a middorsal crest of greatly enlarged spine-like scales extending from the neck to the tail, most prominent in males. The sides of the head have a large circular scale at the angle of the jaw, and there is a pendulous gular flap, especially well developed in males. Undersurface of hind limbs with approximately 15 femoral pores on each side. Dorsal coloration is essentially green, with a variable number of dark, irregular transverse bands on the body and tail. In old males the green coloration may be lost and replaced by an orange or orange-tan coloration, especially prominent during the breeding season. Juvenile coloration is significantly brighter.

Habitat: Evergreen broadleaf forest, semi-evergreen seasonal forest, highland pine savanna, coastal lagoons and marshes, and sand strand and cocotal (on cayes only) formations; arboreal and terrestrial; sea level to 600 m.

Distribution: Southern Mexico to tropical South America, including

PLATE 60 Adult male *Iguana iguana*. Belize. Photograph by C. Farneti Foster.

PLATE 61 A 2-year-old juvenile male *Iguana iguana*. Photographed at the Belize Zoo, courtesy of Sharon Matola and Tony Garel.

many Caribbean islands. In Belize it is found countrywide and on some cayes (introduced?).

Similar Species: Adults can be distinguished from large black iguanas by their green color and/or the lack of whorls of enlarged scales on the tail; the tails of green iguanas are, in comparison, essentially smooth; this tail scalation may also be used to differentiate between small *Ctenosaura* and *Iguana*, both of which are green and similar in form. Juveniles may be distinguished from long-legged anoles, such as *Norops capito*, and members of the genera *Corytophanes* and *Laemanctus*, by the presence of femoral pores, a character lacking in these other genera.

Remarks: Primarily arboreal, inhabiting riverside trees, although occasionally terrestrial. Juveniles tend to be encountered more on the ground or among reeds and the lower branches of riparian vegetation; the height at which the lizards perch has been found to be correlated with their size (Henderson, 1974b). Adults readily climb to great heights in trees, from which they will launch themselves spectacularly into the water when alarmed or to escape predation. The adult diet is almost exclusively herbivorous, while juveniles are omnivorous, feeding upon insects and vegetation. Eggs are laid during the dry season in holes dug in the sand along river banks. Both the adults and eggs are esteemed as food by humans, and in some areas of Belize this lizard has disappeared due to persistent hunting.

Key Reference: Fitch (1973).

SPINY LIZARDS (FAMILY PHRYNOSOMATIDAE)

This large family of lizards reaches its greatest diversity in the American southwest and is of limited distribution in the tropics. Only one genus, *Sceloporus*, is represented in Central America, with four species occurring in Belize. These are characteristically spiny-scaled, rather stout, flat-bodied lizards, with a behavioral repertoire that aids in species recognition and includes head-bobbing, nodding, and push-ups to declare territory. The dorsal scales of most species are strongly keeled, the keels often forming straight lines that converge at the middle of the dorsum; ventrally the scales are smooth and, in most species, conspicuously smaller. Femoral pores are present in both sexes. All are diurnal, and spend much of their time basking. Oviparous and viviparous species occur in Belize.

Key to the Species of *Sceloporus* in Belize

1. Postfemoral dermal pocket present . . . . *S. variabilis*

   Postfemoral dermal pocket absent 2

119

2. Dorsal pattern such as to give impression of a dorsolateral light stripe on either side . . . . *S. chrysostictus*

Dorsal pattern variable, but never giving impression of dorsolateral light stripe on either side 3

3. Parietals and frequently frontoparietals separated from posterior supraorbital by row of small scales . . . . *S. serrifer*

Parietals in contact with posterior supraorbitals . . . . *S. lundelli*

Sceloporus chrysostictus Cope. Plates 62, 63.

Vernacular Names: Yellow-spotted spiny lizard, lagartija de pintas amarillas.

Description: A small species, reaching a snout–vent length of 60 mm and a tail length of approximately 90 mm. Dorsal body scales are moderately keeled and pointed or mucronate, those on the upper surface of the tail and hind limbs more prominently. Femoral pores 12–17 on each side. The general dorsal color of the male is brown, with a pair of yellow lines extending from the eyes posteriorly to the base of the tail and bordered beneath by a pair of dark brown bands; in females, the yellow lines are indistinct or absent. The middorsal brown area is marked with approximately 9 or 10 pairs of dark brown spots, often in the shape of posterior-

PLATE 62 Male *Sceloporus chrysostictus.* Altun Ha, Belize District.

PLATE 63 Female *Sceloporus chrysostictus.* Shipstern Nature Reserve, Corozal District. Photograph by P. Edgar.

ly directed chevrons. A conspicuous dark, elongate blotch is usually present where the foreleg joins the body. In subadults and some adult females the sides of the body are barred. Head brownish; in males, the lower lips are reddish brown speckled with black, while in reproductively active females the lips are bright red. Tail cinnamon brown usually with irregular bands. Ventral coloration is uniformly yellowish white. There are no blue flank patches in males, nor are postfemoral dermal pockets present.

Habitat: Semi-evergreen seasonal forest, savanna, and highland pine savanna formations; terrestrial; sea level to 600 m.

Distribution: Yucatán Peninsula region of Mexico, northern Guatemala, and Belize. In Belize it is known from Corozal, Orange Walk, Cayo, and Belize Districts.

Similar Species: Readily distinguished from *S. variabilis* by the lack of a postfemoral dermal pocket (present in *S. variabilis*); male *S. variabilis* also have brightly colored flashes on the abdomen. It may be further defined by the character of the scales on the posterior surface of the thigh, which are imbricate (not granular, as in *S. variabilis*). The presence of dorsolateral pale lines in *S. chrysostictus* distinguish it from *S. serrifer* and *S. lundelli,* neither of which have a dorsal pattern that includes stripes or lines.

Remarks: An alert, keen-eyed lizard that seems to prefer open and cleared areas with scattered bush vegetation, rocks, fences, and log piles. Habitually fond of basking and thrives in high temperatures. The species is primarily insectivorous, although cannibalism has been reported (Smith and Fritts, 1969). Oviparous; gravid females have been found in May and early June, and newly formed young have been observed in mid-May following the first heavy rains of the year.

Key Reference: Maslin (1963).

Sceloporus lundelli Smith. Plate 64.

Vernacular Names: Lundell's spiny lizard, lagartija espinosa de Lundell.

Description: A medium-sized spiny lizard, with a maximum snout–vent length of approximately 85 mm and a tail length of 120 mm. Dorsal body scales large, strongly keeled, and mucronate. Femoral pores 8–10 on each side. There are no postfemoral dermal pockets present. The dorsal ground color of males is uniformly olive-gray, with a pair of black spots in front of the forelegs that may connect to form a narrow neck band, a black shoulder spot, sometimes connecting in a narrow band across the neck, and indistinct dark markings on the sides of the body. The throat region is orange anteriorly, followed by an iridescent greenish blue to dark blue posteriorly. Sides of abdomen lavender; middle of ventral surface dark blue and with lateral blue patches continuous across the chest. Top of head sometimes with light spots in males. In females the dorsal ground color is lighter with about four narrow, undulating dark gray bands across the back; there are no black shoulder spots although a narrow dark neck band may be present; ventrally the throat and abdomen are pale whitish and lack the metallic color patches of males. Both sexes may have narrow dark bars on the limbs.

Habitat: Semi-evergreen seasonal forest and highland pine savanna formations; arboreal; sea level to 600 m.

Distribution: Yucatán Peninsula region of Mexico, northern Guatemala, and Belize. In Belize it is known from Corozal, Orange Walk, and Cayo Districts.

PLATE 64 Juvenile *Sceloporus lundelli*. Near Caracol, Cayo district.

Similar Species: The smaller *S. variabilis* possesses postfemoral dermal pockets, while *S. chrysostictus* has a pair of dorsolateral pale lines, lacking in *S. lundelli*. In *S. serrifer* the parietals are separated from the posterior supraorbitals by a row of small scales, whereas in *S. lundelli* the parietals are in contact with the posterior supraorbitals.

Remarks: An uncommon species in Belize, apparently restricted to forested areas. Habitually fond of basking, although wary and elusive by nature. Aboreal in habits, being found as high as 20 m above ground in trees; has also been observed on rock walls, fences, and the sides of old wooden buildings (Julian Lee, personal communication). *S. lundelli* is thought to reproduce viviparously (Fitch, 1973). Cohune Ridge, in Cayo District, is the type locality for this species.

Key Reference: Smith (1939).

Sceloporus serrifer Cope. Plate 65.

Vernacular Names: Blue spiny lizard, lagartija espinosa azul.

Description: A medium-sized species, with a snout–vent length of approximately 85 mm and a tail length of 120 mm. Dorsal body scales keeled and mucronate. Femoral pores 6–11 on each side. Dorsal ground coloration is essentially light gray-brown in both sexes, more or less uniform in males but crossed by about four broad, transverse bands in

PLATE 65 Male *Sceloporus serrifer* from the United States (Starr County, Texas). This northern form may represent a different species, *S. cyanogenys*; specimens from Belize are less brightly colored. Photograph by P. Freed.

123

females. The head is boldly marked with light yellow and black, especially prominent in juveniles, with a conspicuous, pale, crescent-shaped mark on the side; there is also a black nuchal collar, occasionally interrupted medially and bordered on both sides by a white line. The scales of the posterior dorsum and tail may be marked with blue, and the tail is patterned with light and dark banding, most conspicuous in females. In males the throat is bluish anteriorly, and black posteriorly, forming a ventral extension of the nuchal collar, and there are pale blue flank marks, broadly bordered with black medially and separated by white.

Habitat: Semi-evergreen seasonal forest and highland pine savanna formations; terrestrial; sea level to 600 m.

Distribution: Southern Mexico and Yucatán Peninsula region, including northern Guatemala and Belize. In Belize it is known only from Cayo District, but possibly also occurs in Corozal and Orange Walk Districts.

Similar Species: The smaller *S. variabilis* possesses postfemoral dermal pockets, while *S. chrysostictus* has a pair of dorsolateral light lines, lacking in *S. serrifer*. It may be distinguished from *S. lundelli* by the presence of a row of small scales between the parietals and the posterior supraorbitals (parietals in contact with the posterior supraorbitals in *S. lundelli*).

Remarks: Primarily a ground-dwelling species, although it will readily climb the trunks of large trees, rock walls, and other structures. *S. serrifer* is presumed to be viviparous. Its distribution and ecology in Belize are poorly known; early records of the species in Belize, however, may have been mistakenly based on specimens of *S. lundelli* (McCoy, 1990).

Key Reference: Maslin (1963).

Sceloporus variabilis Wiegmann. Fig. 13; Plate 66.

Vernacular Names: Rose-bellied lizard, lagartija escamoso variable.

Description: A relatively small lizard, with a maximum snout–vent length of approximately 70 mm and a tail length of 100 mm. Head scales somewhat rugose; dorsal body scales keeled and mucronate, most strongly on the tail, the keels often forming straight lines converging at the middle of the dorsum. Postfemoral dermal pockets present in both sexes. Femoral pores 9–13 on each side. The ground color is reddish brown to olive-tan, with an indistinct middorsal line and a pale dorsolateral stripe on each side extending from behind the eye onto the tail, more conspicuous in males; between the light-colored middorsal and dorsolateral lines there is a series of about 10 dark brown to black, typically chevron-shaped spots, usually more prominent in females. A black spot behind the forearm continues posteriorly as a stripe, bordered above

FIGURE 13 Detail of lower abdomen in *Sceloporus variabilis,* showing position of postfemoral dermal pocket. Scale bar = 1 cm. Photograph by P. Hurst.

PLATE 66 Male *Sceloporus variabilis*. San Luis, Cayo District.

by the pale dorsolateral line and beneath by reddish brown. Males have prominent blue-bordered, metallic pink or lavender areas on the lower sides of the abdomen extending between the axilla and groin. Nearly all females exhibit a bright orange-red coloration on the lips.

Habitat: Semi-evergreen seasonal forest, savanna, and highland pine savanna formations, edificarian situations, and agricultural land; terrestrial; sea level to 600 m.

Distribution: Extreme southern United States to Costa Rica. In Belize it is found countrywide.

Similar Species: Readily separated from the other species of *Sceloporus* by the presence of the postfemoral dermal pocket, lacking in the other three Belizean species. It can be further distinguished from *S. chrysostictus* by the granular-like scales on the posterior surface of the thigh (imbricate in *S. chrysostictus*); male *S. chrysostictus* also lack brightly colored flashes on the abdomen.

Remarks: Typically a species of open, sunny places with little ground vegetation, especially in forested areas. It is primarily terrestrial, although will climb into the lower parts of trees and bushes on occasion, and may be commonly observed on stone walls among Maya ruins, even in the heat of midday. Oviparous; eggs are probably deposited in loose soil toward the end of the dry season or at the start of the wet season. The species is also occasionally reported from Belize under the name *S. teapensis.*

Key Reference: Sites and Dixon (1982).

ANOLES (FAMILY POLYCHROTIDAE)

This family, essentially restricted to the New World tropics and subtropics, is composed of a very large number of species. Most are of the typical anole body type: slender, long-limbed, small- to medium-sized lizards with a conspicuous throat fan, or dewlap, that functions as a signaling device. In males this is especially prominent and often brightly colored; the females of some species also have a small dewlap. Anoles are generally active, swift-moving lizards and may be terrestrial or arboreal in habits. All are diurnal. Many species occur in relatively high population densities. Infraspecific coloration is typically variable, and often expressed as two discrete forms, involving either a pattern of blotches or stripes; while the blotched pattern may be associated with both males and females, the striped pattern seems to be restricted to females only. Most species are also capable of lightening or darkening their coloration in chameleon fashion so that markings may become indistinct or disappear altogether. Some species have the ability to vocalize. All are oviparous; females typically produce multiple clutches at regular intervals, each consisting of one or two eggs.

Following Guyer and Savage (1986), the anoline lizards in Belize may be divided among the genera *Anolis,* represented by two insular forms, and *Norops,* which includes nine species found principally on the mainland. The taxonomy of this large, historically ill-defined group, however, remains under debate.

Key to the Species of *Anolis* and *Norops* in Belize

1. Tail strongly laterally compressed . . . . *N. sagrei*

   Tail cylindrical or ovoid in cross section 2

2. Lower leg length greatly exceeding distance from tip of snout to ear opening . . . . *N. capito*

   Lower leg length not or only slightly exceeding distance from tip of snout to ear opening. 3

3. Midventral scales at midbody very weakly keeled, subconical, or smooth and flat 4

   Midventral scales at midbody distinctly and often strongly keeled. . 6

4. Lower leg length shorter than distance from tip of snout to posterior border of eye 5

   Lower leg length longer than distance from tip of snout to posterior border of eye. . . . . *N. rodriguezii*

5. Ventrals weakly keeled; tail never with a crest; head with an elongated snout . . . . *A. carolinensis*

   Ventrals smooth; tail sometimes with a crest; snout not noticeably pronounced . . . . *N. pentaprion*

6. Six to 12 rows of enlarged dorsal scales strongly and abruptly differentiated from lateral scales; axillary pocket present 7

   Enlarged dorsal scales, if present, grading into laterals; axillary pocket absent 8

7. Length of lower leg as long as distance from tip of snout to ear opening; dewlap in males canary yellow to orange with a burnt orange central spot . . . . *N. tropidonotus*

Length of lower leg shorter than distance from tip of snout to ear opening; dewlap in males bright red with blue to purple central spot . . . .
. . . . *N. uniformis*

8. Lower leg length shorter than distance from tip of snout to posterior border of eye. . . . . *A. allisoni*

   Lower leg equal to or greater than distance from tip of snout to posterior border of eye. 9

9. Lower leg equal to or slightly exceeding distance from tip of snout to posterior border of eye 10

   Lower leg greatly exceeding distance from tip of snout to posterior border of eye . . . . *N. lemurinus*

10. Approximately 10–15 rows of dorsal scales differentiated from laterals; 18 or fewer lamellae beneath phalanges ii and iii of fourth toe; head–body length in adults approximately 50 mm . . . . . *N. sericeus*

    No more than 2–4 rows of dorsal scales differentiated from laterals; more than 20 lamellae beneath phalanges i and ii of fourth toe; head–body length in adults exceeding 75 mm . . . . . . *N. biporcatus*

Anolis allisoni Barbour. Fig. 14; Plate 67.
Vernacular Names: Giant caye anole, Allison's anole, abiniquillo de Allison.

PLATE 67 Adult male *Anolis allisoni* from Islas de Bahia, Honduras. Specimens from Belize lack the dark shoulder spot. Photograph by J.R. McCranie.

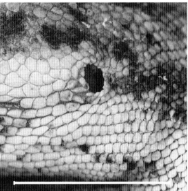

FIGURE 14 Detail of the ear openings in *Anolis allisoni* [left] (BMNH 1985.1099; Roatau, Islas de la Bahia) and *A. carolinensis* [right] (BMNH 1957.1.5.66; Florida, U.S.A.), showing differences in shape and appearance. Scale bar = 5 mm. Photographs by P. Crabb.

Description: A large anole, with a snout–vent length of 100 mm and a cylindrical tail of approximately 110 mm. The snout is long and prominent, with the nostrils medial to the canthal ridge. Scales of dorsum granular and slightly keeled, those of venter imbricate, more or less equal in size to dorsal scales and strongly keeled. Males are larger with a prominent nuchal crest and enlarged postcloacal scales. In both sexes the body color is normally green, although the species is capable of rapid change to a dull brown color. A darker, indeterminate reticulate pattern may sometimes be present. The head may be marked with a whitish stripe below the eye that fades posteriorly in the temporal area. The top of the head and the forelegs in males from Belize are bluish, the chin is white, and the dewlap is bright pink or pale blue; in females, the top of the head is brownish, the forelegs are not blue, and the dewlap is inconspicuous. Ventral coloration is suffused with blue, and there may be fine dark streaking on the throat in males.

Habitat: Sand strand and cocotal formation; arboreal; sea level.

Distribution: Cuba, Bay Islands of Honduras, and Lighthouse Reef islands of Belize. Within Lighthouse Reef it is known from Half Moon Caye, Long Caye, Northern Caye, and Sandbore Caye; it may also occur on other cayes.

Similar Species: This species can be distinguished from the green iguanids by the presence of femoral pores in the latter, versus their absence in *Anolis*. It differs from the green *A. carolinensis* in having more strongly keeled ventrals (smooth to weakly keeled ventral scales in *A. carolinensis*), and from the green *N. biporcatus* by its shorter lower leg (length of

LIZARDS

lower leg shorter than distance from tip of snout to posterior border of eye in *A. allisoni*, versus length of lower leg equal to or slightly exceeding this distance in *N. biporcatus*). From *A. carolinensis* it may be further distinguished by its horizontal, linear-shaped ear opening (ear opening subcircular or vertically elliptic in *A. carolinensis*); male *A. carolinensis* also lack a prominent nuchal crest and bluish coloration on the head and forelegs (present in male *A. allisoni*).

Remarks: Little has been published on this species in Belize, but on the Bay Islands of Honduras it is diurnal and found on banana trees, houses along the beach, coconut trees, mango trees, and wooden fences (Wilson and Hahn, 1973). Recently, Meerman (1996b) reported that on Half Moon Caye the species inhabits the upper trunks and crowns of the coconut palm, but that the saltwater palmetto (*Thrinax radiata*) may have been the preferred habitat before it was exterminated in the 1960s. The giant caye anole is thought to have naturally dispersed to the Belizean cayes from Cuba. Small individuals can be difficult to distinguish from the related, but smaller, *A. carolinensis*.

Key Reference: Ruibal and Williams (1961).

Anolis carolinensis Voigt. Fig. 14.

Vernacular Names: Green anole, abaniquillo verde.

Description: A medium-sized anole, with a maximum head–body length of 75 mm and cylindrical tail up to twice as long. The snout is long, sharp, and prominent, with the nostrils medial to the canthal ridge. Scales of dorsum granular and slightly keeled, those of venter equal in size or slightly smaller than dorsal scales, imbricate, and smooth to weakly keeled. Males are larger with enlarged postcloacal scales but without a conspicuous nuchal crest. Dorsal coloration is normally bright green although can change rapidly to olive green or gray-brown. The prominent throat fan in males is pinkish; in females the dewlap is small and inconspicuous. Ventral coloration is whitish or very pale blue, sometimes with fine brownish-gray mottling on the throat in males.

Habitat: Sand strand and cocotal formation; arboreal and semiterrestrial; sea level.

Distribution: Southeastern United States and Cuba. In Belize it is known only from Half Moon Caye and Lighthouse Reef (introduced ?); it may occur on other offshore cayes.

Similar Species: This anole can be distinguished from the green iguanid species by the presence of femoral pores in the latter, versus their absence in *Anolis*. It differs from the green *A. allisoni* in having smooth or only very weekly keeled ventral scales (ventrals more strongly keeled in *A. allisoni*) and in having a rounded or vertically elliptic ear opening

130

(ear opening of *A. allisoni* horizontal with sharply tapered posterior edge). Males may be further distinguished from male *A. allisoni* by the lack of bluish coloration on the head or forelegs, and absence of a prominent nuchal crest (present in male *A. allisoni*). From the mainland-dwelling *Norops biporcatus* it differs in having smooth or only very weakly keeled ventral scales (ventrals more strongly keeled in *N. biporcatus*).

Remarks: An exotic species thought to have been introduced to Half Moon Caye from Cuba or the southeastern United States. Its occurrence on the island is based on the discovery of a single specimen in 1966, and the species may no longer be present there. However, Meerman (1996b) reports on a population of small, green-colored *Anolis* from the western half of the island that may represent this taxon.

Key Reference: Conant and Collins (1991).

Norops biporcatus (Wiegmann). Plate 68.

Vernacular Names: Central American green anole, toloque.

Description: A large, robust anole, reaching a snout–vent length of 111 mm and having an unbroken tail length of approximately 150 mm. Head

PLATE 68   *Norops biporcatus.* Costa Rica. Photograph by S. Von Peltz.

elongate. The legs are short and stocky, with well-developed pads under the toes. Scales of dorsum small, granular, slightly keeled, and more or less homogenous; those of venter larger, imbricate, and strongly keeled. The changeable coloration of this species can range from bright yellow-green to purplish brown, sometimes with darker chain-like reticulations and pale spots; the tail may be faintly banded with light brown. In males, the dewlap is relatively small and pale orange in color with a pinkish or bluish central spot. Ventral coloration is yellowish white.

Habitat: Evergreen broadleaf forest, semi-evergreen seasonal forest, karst hills forest, and highland pine savanna formations; arboreal; sea level to 600 m.

Distribution: Southern Mexico to northern South America. In Belize it occurs countrywide in appropriate habitat.

Similar Species: This large green anole can be distinguished from young green *Iguana* and *Ctenosaura* by the lack of femoral pores. The only other green-colored anoles, *Anolis allisoni* and *A. carolinensis,* are insular forms.

Remarks: An arboreal, forest-dwelling species capable of rapid color change, from bright green to gray or purple-brown. Typically encountered on the sides of small trees and branches, sometimes at considerable heights, where it preys chiefly on insects and occasionally other anoline lizards. This anole is reported to produce a squeak-like vocalization when handled (Myers, 1971).

Key Reference: Taylor (1956).

Norops capito (Peters). Plates 69, 70.

Vernacular Names: Big-headed anole, abaniquillo jaspeado.

Description: A large, long-legged anole, reaching snout–vent lengths of 90 mm and tail lengths of 170 mm. Head short and deep with snub-nosed appearance. Scales of dorsum smooth, granular, and more or less homogenous; those of venter larger, imbricate, and strongly keeled. Coloration of this species in Belize may take either of two main forms: ground color tan to olive-brown, with two or three broad, darker, more or less hourglass-shaped crossbands on the body and a dark chevron-shaped head band in the supraocular region that may continue laterally through the eye to the angle of the jaw; or, dorsum of some females with a broad, yellowish or cream-colored medial stripe and a blackish brown dorsolateral stripe, extending the length of the body onto the tail and intermixed with contrasting, narrower, and sometimes broken dark and light streaks. In both forms the hind limbs may be streaked with lines of dark brown. Females lack a dewlap; in males it is pale olive-brown or whitish yellow and relatively small. Ventral

PLATE 69   Male *Norops capito*. Las Cuevas, Chiquibul Forest, Cayo District.

PLATE 70   Female *Norops capito*. Striped variant. Las Cuevas, Chiquibul Forest, Cayo District.

133

coloration is cream to yellowish-white, sometimes mottled with gray in the gular region.

Habitat: Evergreen broadleaf forest, semi-evergreen seasonal forest, and karst hills forest formations; may also occur in pockets of broadleaf forest in highland pine savanna formation; arboreal; sea level to 600 m.

Distribution: Extreme southern Mexico to Panama. In Belize it is known from appropriate habitat in all districts except Corozal.

Similar Species: With its stubby head and long legs, this large anole should not be confused with any other member of the genera *Anolis* or *Norops*. Its lack of green coloration and absence of femoral pores distinguish it from juvenile *Ctenosaura* and *Iguana*.

Remarks: An arboreal, forest-dwelling species, generally encountered from near ground level up to 10 m on tree trunks and fallen limbs. Its background-matching coloration, resembling the pattern of bark, and habit of pressing its body against the trunks of trees, makes observation of this lizard extremely difficult. The diet consists largely of insects, although may occasionally include other anoles.

Key Reference: Taylor (1956).

Norops lemurinus (Cope). Plates 71, 72, 73.

Vernacular Names: Ghost anole, abaniquillo lemurino.

Description: A medium-sized anole, with a snout–vent length of 65 mm and an unbroken tail length of approximately 120 mm. Head relatively short. The legs are moderately long and slim. Scales of dorsum smooth and granular with the middle 20 or so rows slightly enlarged; those of venter larger, imbricate, and strongly keeled. Coloration variable; in Belize the species is typically tan to pale pinkish gray dorsally with one of three main patterns, the most common of which is a series of five or six dark, hourglass-like crossbars, usually marked with a small black X in the center, that may connect with a similarly colored lateral stripe originating on the snout and extending through the eye to the groin; alternatively in some females there may be a pale, straight-edged vertebral stripe, or a golden brown vertebral stripe with deeply scalloped, cream-colored edges outlined with dark brown. The head is typically marked with a dark crossband extending between the eyes, and another band in the occipital region. The dewlap in males appears to be variable, ranging from reddish to light orange with a deep orange border, typically with scales of pure white. Ventral coloration is pinkish white and usually immaculate.

Habitat: Evergreen broadleaf forest, semi-evergreen seasonal forest, karst hills forest, highland pine savanna, coastal lagoons and marshes, and sand strand and cocotal formations; terrestrial and arboreal; sea level to 600 m.

PLATE 71   Male *Norops lemurinus*. Fallen Stones, Toledo District. Photograph by S. Von Peltz.

Distribution: Southern Mexico to Colombia. In Belize it is found countrywide; not reported from any cayes.

Similar Species: This species can be distinguished from *N. sagrei* by the strongly laterally compressed tail in *N. sagrei*; it differs from *N. tropidonotus* and *N. uniformis* in lacking the axillary pocket present in these two species. *Norops pentaprion* and *N. rodriguezii* have smooth or weakly keeled midventral scales, while those of *N. lemurinus* are

PLATE 72   Female *Norops lemurinus*. Diamond-backed variant. Cuxta Bani, upper Raspaculo River, Cayo District.

PLATE 73 Female *Norops lemurinus*. Striped variant. Fallen Stones, Toledo District. Photograph by S. Von Peltz.

strongly keeled. In *N. capito*, the lower leg greatly exceeds the distance from tip of snout to the ear opening, whereas in *N. lemurinus* this distance is no more than slightly exceeded; *N. capito* also has smooth dorsal scales (keeled in *N. lemurinus* and all other anoles from Belize). The distance from tip of snout to posterior border of the eye is greatly exceeded by the lower leg length in *N. lemurinus*, while this distance is no more than slightly exceeded in *N. sericeus*.

Remarks: A medium-sized anole generally encountered in lower understory vegetation and on the forest floor. Most commonly observed perched face downward on vertical stems, tree trunks and buttress roots up to 2 m or so above ground, rarely higher. Its cryptic color pattern is changeable from light to dark according to environmental and/or behavioral stimuli; at night a pale pinkish or lavender-gray coloration is adopted, giving rise to the name ghost anole. Two eggs are probably laid at regular intervals between May and December. In previous literature concerning Belize this species has sometimes been reported under the name *Anolis bourgaei*.

Key Reference: Taylor (1956).

Norops pentaprion (Cope). Plate 74.

Vernacular Names: Lichen anole, albaniquillo liquen.

Description: A medium-sized anole, with a total snout–vent length of approximately 75 mm and an unbroken tail length of 100 mm. Head relatively long with a small nuchal crest in males. The legs are short and muscular-appearing. All body scales smooth and unkeeled; those of dorsum with two vertebral rows slightly enlarged; those of venter very slightly larger than on dorsum. Coloration is typically grayish with lighter and darker lichen-like flecks and streaks on the dorsum, sides, and upper surface of limbs, and with indefinite banding on the tail. There may be an indistinct pale line above the shoulder, a dark blotch on the nape, and smaller dark areas on the posterior dorsum. The dewlap in males is deep red with orange-colored scales; females also have a fairly well-developed dewlap, not as brightly colored as in the males. Ventral coloration is yellowish suffused with gray on the chin.

Habitat: Evergreen broadleaf forest and semi-evergreen seasonal forest formations; arboreal; sea level to 300 m.

Distribution: Southern Mexico to northwestern Colombia. In Belize it is known with certainty only from Cayo District, but probably occurs in all districts, except possibly Corozal.

Similar Species: *Norops sagrei* has a strongly laterally compressed tail,

PLATE 74   *Norops pentaprion.* Xunantunich, Cayo District. Photograph by J.R. Meyer.

versus a rounded or ovoid one in *N. pentaprion*; it differs from *N. tropidonotus* and *N. uniformis* in lacking the axillary pocket present in these two species. It may be distinguished from *N. lemurinus, N. biporcatus,* and *N. sericeus* by the presence of distinctly keeled midventral scales in these three species, versus smooth or weakly keeled midventral scales in *N. pentaprion.* In *N. pentaprion,* the lower leg length is shorter than the distance from the tip of the snout to the posterior border of the eye, while in *N. rodriguezii* the lower leg length is longer. *Norops capito* has a lower leg length that greatly exceeds the distance from tip of snout to the ear opening, while this distance is not exceeded in *N. pentaprion.* *N. capito* also has smooth dorsal scales (keeled in all other Belizean anoles).

Remarks: An apparently arboreal species, infrequently encountered throughout its range and currently known from only two localities in Belize. May be observed on the sides of trees adjacent to areas of forest. A female containing two eggs was found in August (J. R. Meyer, personal observation); hatching of the eggs took place during October and November, 40 days after separate deposition in September and October. In many earlier herpetological references concerning Belize this species has been reported under the name *Anolis beckeri.*

Key Reference: Taylor (1956).

Norops rodriguezii (Bocourt). Plate 75.

Vernacular Names: Smooth anole, slender anole, abaniquillo chipojo.

Description: A small, slender-bodied anole, with a maximum snout–vent length of 50 mm and an unbroken tail length of approximately 120 mm. Head relatively narrow and elongate. The legs are relatively long and very slender. Scales of dorsum minute, more or less homogenous, and smooth; those of venter subconical to smooth or weakly keeled. Coloration variable; in Belize the species is typically tan to gray with a dorsal pattern of small, dark, middorsal spots or, in some females, a broad, cream or yellowish medial band that may be boldly outlined with black. In males, the relatively large dewlap is pastel yellowish orange; in females the dewlap is lacking or present only as a reduced gular fold. Ventral coloration is cream or whitish green, usually paler on the chin and throat.

Habitat: Evergreen broadleaf forest, semi-evergreen seasonal forest, karst hills forest, subtropical evergreen forest, savanna, highland pine savanna, and sand strand and cocotal formations, agricultural land, and edificarian situations; arboreal and terrestrial; sea level to 1000 m.

Distribution: Southern Mexico to northern Honduras. In Belize it is found countrywide, including some cayes.

PLATE 75   Male *Norops rodriguezii*. Cuxta Bani, upper Raspaculo River, Cayo District.

Similar Species: *Norops sagrei* has a strongly laterally compressed tail, as opposed to a round or ovoid one in *N. rodriguezii*. In *N. capito*, the lower leg length greatly exceeds the distance from the tip of the snout to the ear opening, while in *N. rodriguezii* this distance is no more than slightly exceeded; *N. capito* also has smooth dorsal scales (keeled in *N. rodriguezii* and all other Belizean anoles). It differs from all other Belizean anoles, except *A. carolinensis* and *N. pentaprion*, in having smooth or weakly keeled midventral scales at midbody, as opposed to distinctly keeled midventrals in these species. In *A. carolinensis* and *N. pentaprion*, the lower leg length is shorter than the distance from the tip of the snout to the posterior border of the eye, while in *N. rodriguezii* this distance is exceeded.

Remarks: A relatively common species found in a variety of situations, ranging from cocotal on the cayes to the mountain rainforests. Arboreal and terrestrial; generally observed near ground level in tall grass or perched vertically face downward on the lower parts of trees and bushes, but may also be seen in trees as high as 5 m above the ground. Two eggs are probably laid at regular intervals between May and December. In previous herpetological literature on Belize, this species has frequently been referred to as a subspecific form of *Anolis limifrons*, or under the name *Anolis aureolus*.

Key Reference: Stuart (1955).

Norops sagrei (Duméril and Bibron). See Fig. 10; Plate 76.

Vernacular Names: *Cock maklaka, hu wa,* brown anole, abaniquillo pardo.

Description: A medium-sized anole with a snout–vent length of approximately 70 mm and an unbroken tail length in excess of 130 mm. There is a moderately distinct nuchal, dorsal, and caudal crest in males, and the tail is strongly laterally compressed. Scales of dorsum small, granular, and weakly keeled; those of venter larger, imbricate, and more strongly keeled. Coloration variable; in Belize the most common coloration is dark brown with inconspicuous, small white-centered occelli and dark-outlined, pale vertical lines on the sides, but in some individuals the dorsum is marked with a lighter, straight or scalloped-edged mid-dorsal stripe. In males, the relatively large dewlap is dark orange-red. Ventral coloration is brownish white.

Habitat: Coastal lagoon and marshes and sand strand and cocotal formations, and edificarian situations; arboreal; sea level to 75 m.

Distribution: Southeastern United States, western Caribbean islands, northern Bahamas, and from southern Mexico to northern Honduras. In Belize it is generally restricted to coastal areas and the cayes; it occurs on all of the larger island groups and most of the smaller outlying cayes (i.e., Crawl Caye, Rendezvous Caye, Caye Caulker). It has also been recorded at several inland localities (Lee, 1996), where it was presumably transported by humans.

Similar Species: Differs from all the other Belizean *Anolis* and *Norops* in possessing a strongly laterally compressed tail.

Remarks: A ubiquitous and commonly seen reptile in coastal areas and on the cayes, particularly in edificarian situations. May be frequently observed perched vertically with head pointing downward on fence posts and trunks of coconut palms. *N. sagrei* appears to be an accomplished

PLATE 76 Male *Norops sagrei* showing extended dewlap. Belize City, Belize District.

colonizing animal in Central America and may have been brought accidentally to these shores from the West Indies by humans, probably in pre-Columbian times. Reproductive activity is believed to be largely dependent on temperature; egg production in the Belize City area is reported as being highest in the wet season from May through August (Sexton and Brown, 1977).

Key Reference: Neill (1965).

Norops sericeus (Hallowell). Plates 77, 78.

Vernacular Names: Silky anole, abaniquillo yanki.

Description: A small, slender anole, with a snout–vent length of 50 mm and an unbroken tail length of at least twice as much. The legs are moderately long and of medium build. Scales of body granular with approximately 10–15 medial rows differentiated from laterals; those of ventral surface larger, imbricate, and more heavily keeled. Coloration variable; dorsum typically tan to gray, often silky in appearance with either a series of six or seven dark middorsal spots that may extend onto the tail as faint rings or, in some females, a broad, light middorsal stripe sometimes outlined with darker pigment. In males, the relatively large dewlap is yellowish orange with a large deep blue central spot; females have a well-developed dewlap with little coloration. Ventral coloration is yellowish white, usually with some dark stippling.

Habitat: Evergreen broadleaf forest, semi-evergreen seasonal forest, karst hills forest, savanna, and highland pine savanna formations; arboreal and terrestrial; sea level to 600 m.

Distribution: Central Mexico to northern Costa Rica. In Belize it is found countrywide.

Similar Species: *Norops sagrei* has a strongly laterally compressed tail, as opposed to a round or ovoid one in *N. sericeus*, with which it is perhaps most likely to be confused. The axillary pocket present in *N. tropidonotus* and *N. uniformis* is absent in *N. sericeus*. In *N. capito*, the lower leg length greatly exceeds the distance from the tip of snout to the ear opening, while in *N. sericeus* this distance is never more than slightly exceeded. *Norops pentaprion* and *N. rodriguezii* have only weakly keeled or smooth midventral scales at midbody, while in *N. sericeus* these scales are strongly keeled. In *N. lemurinus*, the lower leg length greatly exceeds the distance from the tip of the snout to the posterior border of the eye, while in *N. sericeus* this distance is no more than slightly exceeded. The green-colored *Norops biporcatus* has only 2 to 4 rows of dorsal scales differentiated from the laterals, while in *N. sericeus* there are 10 to 15 rows of scales differentiated.

Remarks: An agile, semiarboreal species generally encountered in open

PLATE 77 *Norops sericeus.* Sarteneja, Corozal District. Photograph by P. Edgar.

PLATE 78 Male *Norops sericeus* with dewlap extended to show characteristic color pattern. Escuintla, Guatemala. Photograph by J.A. Campbell, courtesy of the University of Texas at Arlington.

forest or woodland edge situations, where it frequents bushes and the lower branches of small trees. It may not occur in areas inhabited by anoles with similar ecological requirements, such as *N. rodriguezii,* although the interspecific relationships of these species in Belize is unknown. In earlier literature concerning Belize this species has sometimes gone under the name *Anolis ustus.*
Key Reference: Fitch (1973).

Norops tropidonotus (Peters). Plates 79, 80.
Vernacular Names: Greater scaly anole, chipojo escamudo.
Description: A medium-sized anole, with a snout–vent length of approximately 65 mm and a tail length of at least 100 mm. The legs are relatively long and of medium build. A deep axillary pocket is present. Scales of dorsum granular with approximately 12 enlarged, heavily keeled, and abruptly differentiated medial rows; those of venter equal in size or slightly larger than medial dorsal rows, imbricate, and strongly keeled. Coloration variable; in Belize the species is essentially a medium to dark shade of brown with either a series of dark and light chevron markings or, in some females, a broad, slightly lighter, brown to orange-brown dark-outlined middorsal stripe. In males, the relatively large dewlap is bright yellow with a burnt orange central spot. Ventral coloration is creamish white and usually immaculate.
Habitat: Evergreen broadleaf forest, semi-evergreen seasonal forest, karst hills forest, and highland pine savanna formations; arboreal and terrestrial; sea level to 600 m.
Distribution: Southern Mexico to Nicaragua. In Belize it is currently known from Orange Walk, Cayo, and Belize Districts, but may also occur in Stann Creek District.

PLATE 79 Male *Norops tropidonotus*. Chevron-patterned variant. Las Cuevas, Chiquibul Forest, Cayo District. An accumulation of small, orange mite larvae can be seen at the edge of the axillary pocket.

PLATE 80 Female *Norops tropidonotus*. Striped variant. Las Cuevas, Chiquibul Forest, Cayo District.

144

Similar Species: This medium-sized forest anole differs from all other Belizean anoles, except *N. uniformis,* in possessing distinct axillary pockets. In *N. uniformis,* the lower leg length is shorter than the distance from the tip of the snout to the ear opening, while in *N. tropidonotus,* this distance is equal; additionally, the dewlap in male *N. uniformis* is bright red with a blue or purple spot, versus a yellow dewlap with a burnt orange spot in male *N. tropidonotus,* and the enlarged medial dorsal scales in *N. humilis* are substantially larger than the ventrals (of almost equal size in *N. tropidonotus*).

Remarks: This species is the common anole of the semi-evergreen limestone forests of Orange Walk and northern Cayo Districts, where it may be encountered either on the ground or on the lower parts of tree trunks. It appears to be ecologically replaced by the smaller *N. uniformis* in the wetter evergreen broadleaf forests of southern Cayo, Stann Creek, and Toledo Districts, although there is a record of the species from the latter (Lee, 1996). In males the chevron-shaped dorsal markings may all but disappear under conditions of stress.

Key Reference: Stuart (1955).

Norops uniformis (Cope). Plates 81, 82.

Vernacular Names: Lesser scaly anole, abaniquillo de selva.

Description: A small species, with a snout–vent length of approximately 40 mm and a tail length in the region of twice as long. The head is relatively elongate and the limbs are moderately long to short. A deep axillary pocket is present. Scales of dorsum granular, minute with approximately 10 enlarged, heavily keeled, and abruptly differentiated medial rows; those of venter smaller than enlarged medial dorsal rows, imbricate, and strongly keeled. Dorsum invariably medium to dark brown in coloration, patternless or with a slightly paler, typically broken middorsal stripe that may continue onto the tail as a series of diamond-shaped markings. There may be occasional whitish flecks and/or vertical lines on the sides. The large dewlap in males is red with a dark blue to purple central spot. Ventral coloration is brownish white.

Habitat: Evergreen broadleaf forest, semi-evergreen seasonal forest, karst hills forest, and subtropical evergreen forest formations; arboreal and terrestrial; sea level to 1000 m.

Distribution: Southern Mexico to northern Honduras. In Belize it is known from Cayo, Stann Creek, and Toledo Districts, and possibly occurs in Orange Walk District.

Similar Species: This small forest anole differs from all other Belizean anoles, except *N. tropidonotus,* in possessing distinct axillary pockets. In *N. tropidonotus,* the lower leg length is equal to the distance from the tip

PLATE 81 Male *Norops uniformis*. Cuxta Bani, upper Raspaculo River, Cayo District.

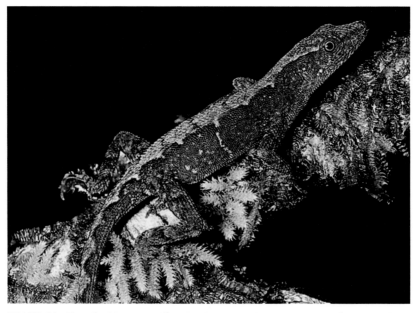

PLATE 82 Female *Norops uniformis*. Cuxta Bani, upper Raspaculo River, Cayo District.

146

of the snout to the ear opening, while in *uniformis*, this distance is shorter; additionally, the dewlap in male *N. uniformis* is bright red with a blue or purple spot, versus a yellow to orange dewlap with a burnt orange spot in male *N. tropidonotus*, and the enlarged medial dorsal scales are substantially larger than the ventrals (of almost equal size in *N. tropidonotus*).

Remarks: This is the characteristic anole of the wetter forests of southern Belize, where it appears to replace *N. tropidonotus*, the common forest-dwelling species of northern parts. It is an active, diurnal lizard, generally encountered on the forest floor, on the branches of small sapling trees and fronds of dwarf palms, or on the lower boles of tree trunks. In much of the older herpetological literature pertaining to Belize this species was either listed as a subspecies of *Anolis humilis* or under the name *Anolis ruthveni*.

Key Reference: Stuart (1955).

SKINKS (FAMILY SCINCIDAE)

This is a large and cosmopolitan family, with New World species ranging from small to medium size. The three genera and five species found in Belize have smooth, polished, cycloid-type scales (those on the dorsal surface often distinctly hexagonal in shape) and small limbs that give them a characteristically sleek, streamlined appearance. All are essentially terrestrial in habits, wary, and fast-moving, resulting in lizards that are difficult to observe for long and even harder to capture. They are all diurnal, although somewhat secretive, and feed largely on arthropods and other invertebrate prey. In common with most other species, the Belizean forms have the power of caudal autotomy, and the tail may be frequently observed in a broken or regenerating state. Femoral pores are absent.

Key to the Genera of the Family Scincidae in Belize

1. Supranasals absent . . . . *Sphenomorphus*

   Supranasals present 2

2. Scales of temporal region enlarged and well differentiated . . . *Eumeces*

   Scales of temporal region not enlarged or well differentiated . . *Mabuya*

Key to the Species of *Eumeces* in Belize

Middorsal scales much broader than those of paravertebral region . . . . *E. schwartzei*

Middorsal scales not conspicuously larger than those of paravertebral region . . . . *E. sumichrasti*

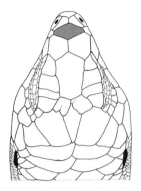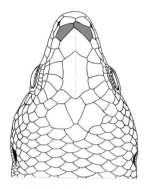

FIGURE 15   Dorsal view of head scalation in [left] a skink, *Eumeces sumichrasti* (USNM 6601; Potrero, Mexico), redrawn from an illustration by D. Cochran in E.H. Taylor (1935), showing a single frontonasal scale (shaded), and [right], the anguid, *Diploglossus rozellae* (BMNH 973.2753; Bokawina, Stann Creek), showing paired frontonasals (shaded).

Eumeces schwartzei Fischer. Plate 83.

Vernacular Names: Schwartze's skink, lincer de Schwartze.

Description: A large species with an elongate body of rather heavy, broad proportions, and short though well-developed limbs that scarcely meet

PLATE 83   *Eumeces schwartzei.* Sarteneja, Corozal District. Photograph by P. Edgar.

148

when adressed in adults; maximum snout–vent length approximately 120 mm, and a tail of at least equal length when entire. Scales smooth, cycloid-like, and dorsally somewhat hexagonal in shape, usually in 19–21 rows around midbody, the middle row distinctly enlarged. Dorsum cream, yellow, or orange-tan, paler anteriorly, with a broad, dark medial stripe beginning on the snout and continuing over the shoulder where it breaks up into a series of square-shaped blotches, most prominent on the tail; there is also a dark lateral band on each side, originating on the head and terminating in a series of spots near the hind legs. In juveniles the dorsum may be suffused with pale rose, and the tail coloration is bluish green, becoming less distinctive with age. Venter uniform greenish or dirty cream.

Habitat: Evergreen broadleaf forest, semi-evergreen seasonal forest, and karst hills forest formations; terrestrial; sea level to 200 m.

Distribution: Yucatán Peninsula region of Mexico, northern Guatemala, and Belize. In Belize is has been recorded from Corozal, Orange Walk, Cayo, and Stann Creek Districts; probably also occurs in Belize District.

Similar Species: This skink may be separated from its congener, *E. sumichrasti,* by its enlarged middorsal scales. It differs from skinks of the genus *Sphenomorphus* in having supranasal scales and from *Mabuya* in having enlarged scales in the temporal region. It may be distinguished from the smooth-scaled anguid *Diploglossus* in having a single frontonasal scale, versus paired frontonasals in *Diploglossus.*

Remarks: A generally secretive species, usually encountered beneath boards, in and under rotting logs, and under leaf and palm frond debris at the bases of trees. The limits of its distribution and ecological relationships with *E. sumichrasti* in Belize are poorly known. The species is oviparous, with the female probably depositing eggs in rotting logs and forest floor debris in April through June.

Key Reference: Taylor (1935).

Eumeces sumichrasti (Cope). Fig. 15; Plate 84.

Vernacular Names: Sumichrast's skink, lincer listado.

Description: A relatively large species with an elongate body of rather heavy, broad proportions, and short though well-developed limbs that broadly overlap when adressed in both young and adults; snout–vent length up to 96 mm, and a tail of at least equal length when entire. Scales smooth, cycloid-like, and dorsally somewhat hexagonal in appearance, usually in 28–30 rows around midbody. Dorsum of young and subadults blackish with a narrow medial cream or yellowish stripe that

PLATE 84 A hatchling *Eumeces sumichrasti* showing the striking color pattern characteristic of the young of this species. Cuxta Bani, upper Raspaculo River, Cayo District.

bifurcates on the head and extends the length of the body onto the tail. A similarly colored dorsolateral stripe and a third, narrower, lateral stripe extend from the head to the side of the tail; the tail is vivid blue, fading to the same bronze-brown or grayish black body color of aging specimens. In older adults (length greater than approximately 50 mm) the dorsal color tends to grow lighter and more uniform, especially in males, and the head may become spotted with light and dark brown. Venter bluish gray with yellowish white coloring on the chin, throat, and chest area.

Habitat: Evergreen broadleaf forest, semi-evergreen seasonal forest, and karst hills forest formations, possibly also highland pine savanna formation; terrestrial; sea level to 600 m.

Distribution: Southern Mexico to Honduras. In Belize it is known from Corozal, Cayo, and Toledo Districts although probably to be found in the other districts.

Similar Species: This skink may be separated from its congener, *E. schwartzei*, by its lack of enlarged middorsal scales. It differs from skinks of the genus *Sphenomorphus* in having supranasal scales and from *Mabuya* in having enlarged scales in the temporal region. It may be distinguished from the smooth-scaled anguid *Diploglossus* in having a single frontonasal scale, versus paired frontonasals in *Diploglossus*.

Remarks: Like *E. schwartzei*, this diurnal species is generally secretive, although it may be encountered basking in forest clearings or along open stream banks in undisturbed forest. Its distribution and ecological rela-

tionships with *E. schwartzei* in Belize are poorly known. Primarily insectivorous although it has been known to predate on small lizards (Alvarez del Toro, 1982). Oviparous; eggs are probably buried in rotting logs and other forest floor debris, although a female has been observed to deposit her eggs some 20 m above ground in the fork of a tree (C. Miller, in litt.).
Key Reference: Taylor (1935).

Mabuya unimarginata (Cope). Plate 85.
Vernacular Names: *Snake waiting boy,* Central American mabuya, sabandija de rayas.
Description: A medium-sized, elongate, rather broad-bodied skink with reduced limbs that when adpressed in adults fail to meet by an appreciable margin; maximum snout–vent length approximately 90 mm, with a tail length exceeding this when unbroken. Scales smooth, cycloid-like and dorsally somewhat hexagonal in appearance, usually in 30 rows around midbody. Head and dorsum brown to olive brown with a few scattered dark spots on the rump and tail base; a dark dorsolateral stripe extends from the orbit posteriorly to the groin and is bordered beneath by a bluish or greenish white line, below which there may be an additional line of black, often triangular-shaped dots. Venter whitish and more or less immaculate.
Habitat: Evergreen broadleaf forest, semi-evergreen seasonal forest, karst hills forest, savanna, highland pine savanna, and sand strand and cocotal formations, agricultural land, and edificarian situations; terrestrial and arboreal; sea level to 600 m.
Distribution: Central Mexico through Panama. In Belize it is found countrywide.
Similar Species: May be distinguished from members of the genus *Eumeces* by the lack of enlarged scales in the temporal region (enlarged

PLATE 85 *Mabuya unimarginata.* La Milpa, Orange Walk District.

151

in *Eumeces*). From the much smaller *Sphenomorphus*, it may be differentiated by the presence of supranasal scales (lacking in *Sphenomorphus*). From the anguid *Diploglossus*, it may be distinguished by its single frontonasal scale (paired in *Diploglossus*).

Remarks: A fairly common although inconspicuous species, occasionally to be found around human habitation, especially in rural areas where it will enter houses in search of insect prey. In natural situations it is semi-secretive, hiding under logs and boards and among leaf litter, although it may be sighted basking in open areas and will often climb tree trunks. Unlike other members of the family in Belize, this skink gives birth to live young, possibly in March and April.

Key Reference: Fitch (1973).

Sphenomorphus cherriei (Cope). Plate 86.

Vernacular Names: *Galliwasp,* brown forest skink, escincela parda.

Description: A small, elongate skink with reduced limbs that overlap broadly when adpressed in juveniles but barely or not at all in adults; total length approximately 60 mm from snout to vent, with a tail length greatly exceeding this when unbroken. Scales smooth, cycloid-like, and dorsally somewhat hexagonal in shape, usually in 32 rows around midbody. Dorsum brown or bronze-colored with obscure dorsolateral dark

PLATE 86 *Sphenomorphus cherriei.* Sarteneja, Corozal District. Photograph by P. Edgar.

lines and darker sides with scattered black spotting, sometimes giving the impression of faint, pale banding across body. An irregular dark stripe extends from behind the eye along the neck, breaking up posteriorly and bordered beneath by a pale line terminating over the shoulder. Side of head and neck with dark spots, and usually a dark line at angle of jaw. In juveniles the tail is bluish, but this color tends to disappear early in life. Ventral surface whitish, with pale gray beneath the tail, and dark lines on the chin.

Habitat: Evergreen broadleaf forest, semi-evergreen seasonal forest, karst hills forest, subtropical evergreen forest, savanna, and highland pine savanna formations; terrestrial; sea level to 1000 m.

Distribution: Southeastern Mexico to northern Guatemala and Belize, and from Nicaragua to Panama. In Belize it occurs countrywide.

Similar Species: May be distinguished from members of the genus *Eumeces* and *Mabuya* by the lack of supranasal scales in the temporal region (present in *Eumeces* and *Mabuya*). From the anguid *Diploglossus*, it may be distinguished by its single frontonasal scale (frontonasals paired in *Diploglossus*). It may be differentiated from the similarly sized *Gymnophthalmus* by the presence of eyelids (absent in *Gymnophthalmus*) and in having five digits on the hand (four digits in *Gymnophthalmus*).

Remarks: A relatively common but secretive inhabitant of forested areas. Diurnal; activity appears to be limited to short periods when humidity is high and the temperature moderate. Most frequently encountered in leaf litter, where it may briefly be seen basking in the sun or scampering from under one leaf to another. Oviparous, with clutch deposition probably occurring from May through September. In earlier literature on Belize this species has appeared under the names *Scincella cherriei*, *Leiolopisma assatum*, and *Lygosoma assatum.*

Key Reference: Fitch (1973).

SPECTACLED LIZARDS
(FAMILY GYMNOPHTHALMIDAE)

This is a New World family, restricted to the tropics, principally in lower Central America and South America. Only one genus, *Gymnophthalmus*, occurs in northern Central America. Also known as the microteiids, the gymnophthalmids were, until recently, included in the family Teiidae. The species are characteristically slender and short-legged, with only four digits on the hands, and have an elongate, cylindrical tail. The eye is covered with a transparent, spectacle-like membrane.

Gymnophthalmus speciosus (Hallowell). Plate 87.

Vernacular Names: Golden spectacled lizard, lisa dorada.

Description: A small, slender, skink-like lizard, with a maximum snout–vent length of approximately 45 mm and a tail length of 120 mm. Head small and covered with regular, smooth scales; eyelids absent. The tongue is elongate with a bifurcate tip. Small femoral pores are present in males. Scales of body imbricate, cycloid-like, and uniformly smooth, except for a few keeled rows at end of tail; those of the dorsum are arranged in three longitudinal rows, the medial smallest (scales around middle of body 13–15 rows in total). Dorsal coloration is generally gray to brownish gray, with the color sharply demarcated on the middle of the second lateral scale row; each scale of this series bears a light spot, giving the appearance of a pale line. The sides of the body are black; the venter is typically dark-colored and the tail pinkish orange, with or without a moderately distinct lateral stripe extending nearly to end.

Habitat: Semi-evergreen seasonal forest and savanna formations; terrestrial; sea level to 100 m.

Distribution: Southwestern Mexico, and from central Guatemala to northern South America, including the Lesser Antilles. In Belize it is known only from Orange Walk District, but may also occur in Belize and Cayo Districts.

Similar Species: Might be confused only with the skinks, from which *Gymnophthalmus* can be differentiated by the absence of eyelids (pre-

PLATE 87 *Gymnophthalmus speciosus.* Honduras. Photograph by J.R. McCranie.

sent in the skinks), and in having a hand with only four digits (five digits present in all other lizard genera in Belize).

Remarks: In Belize, this small, skink-like lizard is only known from a single specimen collected near Carmelita in Orange Walk District. Elsewhere in its range the species is known to be highly secretive in habits, usually encountered under logs, boards, and leaves in drier, semi-open situations, or burrowing in loose earth. It is capable of a surprising turn of speed for such a slender, short-legged lizard. Oviparous.

Key Reference: Taylor (1956).

WHIP-TAILED LIZARDS (FAMILY TEIIDAE)

This is strictly a New World family, represented in Belize by five species of the genera *Ameiva* and *Cnemidophorus*. Lizards of these genera are similar in form with moderately stout bodies, long tails, and muscular legs. They tend to run about in a characteristically rapid, agitated manner, giving rise to the name "racerunner," by which a number of species are alternatively known. The head is elongate and the snout somewhat pointed. All are active during the daytime and given to frequent basking. They have an elongate, snake-like tongue with a bifurcate tip, which may be protruded and withdrawn constantly while foraging. The Belizean species are terrestrial and chiefly insectivorous; some of the larger South American representatives of the family are also carnivorous, feeding on a range of small vertebrates and eggs. All are oviparous, and in the genus *Cnemidophorus* a number of unisexual, all-female species have developed through hybridization of bisexual species.

Key to the Genera of the Family Teiidae in Belize

Enlarged scales on anterior surface of upper arm in a single row; usually a sheath between larynx and scaly part of tongue . . . . *Ameiva*

Enlarged scales on anterior and dorsal surfaces of upper arm in three or more rows; tongue not sheathed . . . . *Cnemidophorus*

Key to the Species of *Ameiva* in Belize

Enlarged gular scales larger than mental; dorsum usually marked with a well-defined, light-colored medial stripe . . . . *A. festiva*

Enlarged gular scales much smaller than mental; dorsum never marked with a light-colored medial stripe . . . . *A. undulata*

Ameiva festiva (Lichtenstein and von Mertens). See Fig. 10; Plate 88.

Vernacular Names: Middle American ameiva, ameiva parda.

Description: A medium-sized lizard, with a maximum snout–vent length of approximately 120 mm and a tail length if unbroken up to 200 mm. The dorsal and lateral scales are fine and granular; ventrally the scales are enlarged, smooth, and rectangular in form. The scales of the tail are large, heavily keeled, and form regular whorls, the keels tending to form continuous ridged lines. Femoral pores number approximately 20. Dorsal coloration is typically dark brown to olive with a sinuous, yellow to grayish blue, middorsal stripe extending from the rostrum onto the tail, a dorsolateral light stripe broken into dashes, and a lower lateral pale stripe. In the axillary region there are a few small, upright bluish bars. Venter dull white, sometimes with a reddish or greenish suffusion of the throat in males. In juveniles the dorsal pattern is more distinct, with a yellow-colored middorsal stripe, bold lateral markings, and a pale blue tail.

Habitat: Evergreen broadleaf forest, semi-evergreen seasonal forest, karst hills forest, subtropical evergreen forest, and highland pine savanna formations; terrestrial; sea level to 800 m.

PLATE 88 Juvenile *Ameiva festiva*. Cuxta Bani, upper Raspaculo River, Cayo District.

Distribution: Southern Mexico to Colombia. In Belize it has been record-ed from Belize, Cayo, Stann Creek, and Toledo Districts.

Similar Species: The members of the genus *Cnemidophorus* have three or more rows of enlarged scales on the anterior and dorsal surfaces of the upper arm versus a single row in *Ameiva*. In *Ameiva undulata* the enlarged gular scales are much smaller than the mental, and there is never a light medial stripe on the dorsum, while in *A. festiva* the enlarged gulars are larger than the mental and there is generally a dis-tinct light middorsal stripe.

Remarks: This is the typical teiid lizard of the wetter, undisturbed forests of central and southern Belize. Strictly diurnal, and most frequently encountered along trails, stream banks, and edges of forest clearings. Typically runs about with rapid, jerky movements, stopping periodical-ly to bask in the sun, or dig for invertebrate prey buried in loose earth or secreted in holes and crevices. Eggs are probably laid late in the wet sea-son, with young hatching in January and February.

Key Reference: Echternacht (1971).

Ameiva undulata (Wiegmann). Plates 89, 90.

Vernacular Names: Rainbow ameiva, ameiva metalica.

Description: A medium-sized species, with a maximum snout–vent length of 115 mm and an unbroken tail length of at least 180 mm. As with the other Belizean teiids, this is a long-nosed species, with stout, muscular legs and a long tail. The dorsal and lateral scales are granu-lar; ventrally the scales are large, smooth, and rectangular in form. The scales of the tail are large, heavily keeled, and form regular whorls, the keels tending to form continuous ridged lines. Femoral

PLATE 89 Adult male *Ameiva undulata*. Mile 30, Western Highway, Belize District.

PLATE 90 Juvenile *Ameiva undulata*. Belize. Photograph by C.M. Miller.

pores number approximately 18. Dorsal coloration in adults is green-ish to bronze, changing laterally to dark brown with a series of light blue bars. Venter and underside of limbs whitish to pale blue; the chin, throat, and chest area may be suffused with pink, crimson, reddish orange, or lemon yellow in males. Juveniles are marked with a bold pattern of longitudinal light and dark stripes on the body, with blue tail coloration.

Habitat: Evergreen broadleaf forest, semi-evergreen seasonal forest, karst hills forest, savanna, highland pine savanna, and sand strand and cocotal formations, agricultural land, and edificarian situations; terrestrial; sea level to 600 m.

Distribution: Central Mexico to northwestern Costa Rica. In Belize it occurs countrywide, including some cayes.

Similar Species: The members of the genus *Cnemidophorus* have three or more rows of enlarged scales on the anterior and dorsal sur-faces of the upper arm versus a single row in *Ameiva*. In *Ameiva undulata* the enlarged gular scales are much smaller than the men-tal, and there is never a light medial stripe on the dorsum, while in *A. festiva* the enlarged gulars are larger than the mental and there is generally a distinct light middorsal stripe. A similar but smaller species, *A. chaitzami*, occurs nearby in the pine savannas around

Poptún, Guatemala, although it has not been reported from within Belize.

Remarks: This species is the common teiid lizard of the forested areas of northern Belize; in the central and southern forests, where *A. festiva* occurs, *A. undulata* is encountered only in more open, disturbed areas. Apparently much more adaptable than *A. festiva*, the rainbow ameiva occupies a wide variety of habitats in Belize, including coastal beaches and some cayes. Females carrying eggs ready for deposition have been reported in mid-July (Neill and Allen, 1959b).

Key Reference: Echternacht (1971).

Key to the Species of *Cnemidophorus* in Belize

1. Interparietal bordered by four parietals . . . . *C. lemniscatus*

   Interparietal bordered by two parietals 2

2. Dorsum with pale vertebral stripe; four supraoculars . . *C. angusticeps*

   Dorsum without a vertebral stripe; usually three supraoculars . . . . . .
   . . . .*C. maslini*

Cnemidophorus angusticeps Cope. Fig. 16.

Vernacular Names: Yucatán whiptail, black-bellied racerunner, huico Yucateco.

Description: A medium-sized lizard; maximum snout–vent length of males approximately 110 mm with an unbroken tail in excess of 160 mm. The dorsal and lateral scales are granular; ventrally the scales are large, smooth, and rectangular in form. Total number of femoral pores in the range 31–40. Dorsum of adults brownish with a pale, broad medial stripe and pattern of six cream to whitish, longitudinal lines, three on each side of the body and extending from the head to the hind legs; the lateral surfaces may be finely spotted with blue. Ventral surface posterior to the gular fold bluish black in adult males, sharply contrasted with pinkish buff on the chin and throat; in young males and females the ventral coloration is pale blue to whitish.

Habitat: Savanna formation; terrestrial; sea level to 50 m.

Distribution: Northern Yucatán Peninsula region, Mexico. In Belize it has been recorded only from Belize and Stann Creek Districts.

Similar Species: The members of the genus *Ameiva* have only a single row of enlarged scales on the anterior and dorsal surfaces of the upper

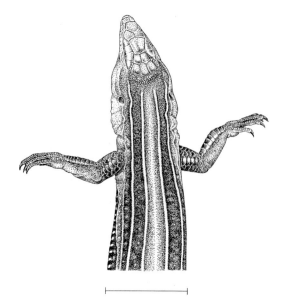

FIGURE 16 Head and fore-body of *Cnemidophorus angusticeps* (BMNH 1973.2785; Tekom, Yucatán, Mexico) in dorsal view. Scale bar = 2 cm.

arm versus three or more rows in *Cnemidophorus*. In *C. maslini* the pale gray-brown medial coloration on the dorsum is diffuse at the edges, while in *C. angusticeps* there is usually a distinct, well-defined light middorsal stripe or band. The ventral coloration of adult male *C. angusticeps* is black, compared to whitish in *C. maslini. Cnemidophorus lemniscatus* has a green dorsal coloration and also four interparietal scales, versus only two in *C. angusticeps*.

Remarks: A whiptail species of flat, open savanna, and ruderal situations, thriving on the bright sunlight and high temperatures associated with these habitats, although usually found within close proximity of cover afforded by scattered clumps of grass and low vegetation. Eggs are probably deposited late in the dry season, with young hatching well into the rainy season. In past literature on Belize, this species has sometimes gone under the name *Cnemidophorus gularis.*

Key Reference: Beargie and McCoy (1964).

Cnemidophorus lemniscatus (Linnaeus). Plate 91.

Vernacular Names: *Shake hand, shake paw,* beach racerunner, huico de playa.

Description: A medium-sized teiid lizard, with a snout–vent length of approximately 80 mm and a tail length that greatly exceeds this. The dorsal and lateral scales are granular; ventrally the scales are large,

PLATE 91   Male *Cnemidophorus lemniscatus*. Monkey River Town, Toledo District. Photograph by J.C. Meerman.

smooth, and rectangular in form. Femoral pores 15–29 in total. Dorsal coloration is yellowish green medially and bluish, grayish tan, or oliveaceous on the lower flanks, with a pattern of darker green middorsal longitudinal stripes bordered by narrower yellow stripes; females usually have eight or nine stripes that persist into adulthood, while only four or five medial stripes are retained in adult males. Males also have additional rows of lateral yellow or whitish spots extending from the head onto the tail. The top of the head is green, grading to bluish green on the sides, and the tail is bright green. Venter whitish gray to pale blue with blue-green coloration on the chin and throat.

Habitat: Sand strand and cocotal formation; terrestrial; sea level.

Distribution: Southern Belize and Guatemala to northern Brazil. In Belize it is known only from Toledo District; may also occur on some of the cayes.

Similar Species: The members of the genus *Ameiva* have only a single row of enlarged scales on the anterior and dorsal surfaces of the upper arm versus three or more rows in *Cnemidophorus*. It differs from the other Belizean *Cnemidophorus* in possessing four interparietal scales as opposed to two interparietals.

Remarks: A strikingly colored species recently discovered in Belize at Monkey River Town, Toledo District (J. C. Meerman, in litt.). It is unlikely that it occurs further north than southern Stann Creek District, but it may inhabit some of the unexplored southern cayes. Essentially an open beach and coastal grassland inhabitant throughout its range, and

undoubtedly restricted to these situations in Belize. The Belizean vernacular name shake-hand alludes to the lizard's habit of running a short
distance, stopping, and waving a front limb in the air.
Key Reference: Echternacht (1968).

Cnemidophorus maslini Fritts.
Vernacular Names: Maslin's racerunner, huico de Maslin.
Description: A small- to medium-sized lizard, with a maximum
snout–vent length of approximately 75 mm and a tail, if unbroken, measuring greatly in excess of this. The dorsal and lateral scales are granular; ventrally the scales are large, smooth, and rectangular in form.
Femoral pores 33–39 in total. Coloration of this parthenogenetic, all-
female species is pale dorsally, with a longitudinal, broad, gray-brown
medial band on the back, extending onto the tail and bordered laterally
by a series of eight pale, often undulating stripes separated by interspaces
of russet brown; the stripes are retained into adulthood. Venter whitish,
except for the tail, which is pinkish below. The dorsal pattern of juveniles is essentially the same, although significantly bolder.
Habitat: Semi-evergreen seasonal forest and savanna formations; terrestrial; sea level to 30 m.
Distribution: Yucatán Peninsula region of Mexico and Belize. In Belize it is
found in Corozal, Orange Walk, and Belize Districts, and on some cayes.
Similar Species: The members of the genus *Ameiva* have only a single
row of enlarged scales on the anterior and dorsal surfaces of the upper
arm versus three or more rows in *Cnemidophorus*. In *C. maslini* the pale
gray-brown medial coloration on the dorsum is diffuse at the edges,
while in *C. angusticeps* there is usually a distinct, well-defined light
middorsal stripe or band. The ventral coloration of adult male *C. angusticeps* is black, compared to whitish in *C. maslini*. *Cnemidophorus lemniscatus* has a green dorsal coloration and also four interparietal scales,
versus only two in *C. angusticeps*.
Remarks: An interesting whiptail species that appears to occur in more
vegetated areas than *C. angusticeps*, although the ecological relationship
of the two species in Belize is unknown; in the upper part of the Yucatán
Peninsula it is an inhabitant of open beach and cleared roadsides, using
crab burrows for refuge (Fritts, 1969). Maslin's racerunner is a parthenogenetic species, the totally female population reproducing asexually. It is
thought that the species is the result of hybridization between *C. angusticeps* and *C. deppii*, with recent DNA analysis indicating that *C. angusticeps* is the maternal ancestor (Moritz et al., 1992). *C. maslini* has been
listed in earlier literature on Belize as *C. deppei cozumelus* and *C.
cozumela*, now considered to be a parthenogenetic species restricted to
Cozumel Island in Mexico.
Key Reference: Taylor and Cooley (1995a,b).

NIGHT LIZARDS (FAMILY XANTUSIIDAE)

This is a small family, primarily restricted to North and Central America. The species are relatively elongate in form with short limbs. The scales are typically small and granular on the dorsum, with large, polished, plate-like scutes on the head. Ventrally, the scales are large and rectangular. Most species are nocturnal or crepuscular, lack eyelids, and are highly secretive in habits. Femoral pores are present. The Central American forms are inhabitants of forested areas, and as a group all give birth to fully formed live young.

Key to the Species of *Lepidophyma* in Belize

Tubercles on side of body in 24–32 vertical rows . . . . *L. flavimaculatum*

Tubercles on side of body in 33–46 vertical rows. . . . . *L. mayae*

Lepidophyma flavimaculatum A. Duméril. Plates 92, 93.

Vernacular Names: Yellow-spotted night lizard, lepidofima.

Description: A small- to medium-sized, round-bodied lizard, with a maximum snout–vent length of 95 mm and a tail length, when unbroken, of approximately 125 mm. The head is robust and covered with large, plate-

PLATE 92 Adult *Lepidophyma flavimaculatum*. Caracol, Cayo District. Photograph by C.M. Miller.

PLATE 93 Juvenile *Lepidophyma flavimaculatum*. Volcán Santa Maria, Cordillera de Guanacaste, Costa Rica.

like scales; the large eye has a circular pupil and is protected by a transparent spectacle. Dorsum covered with small, granular scales intermixed with prominent tubercles forming two longitudinal rows and 24–32 transverse rows between the axilla and groin; ventrally the scales are rectangular and plate-like. The tail bears whorls of enlarged, conical-shaped tubercles. There are 12–16 femoral pores on the underside of each thigh (rudimentary in females). Dorsal coloration is dark brown or blackish medially punctuated with relatively large, conspicuous light spots, sometimes arranged in 6 longitudinal rows. The head is dark brown (blackish in juveniles) and the labial scales have bold dark and light-colored bars. Ventrally, the color is paler, with brownish mottling on a yellowish or creamy ground color; the throat may be marked with a bold reticulate pattern enclosing pale cream spots.

Habitat: Evergreen broadleaf forest, semi-evergreen seasonal forest, karst hills forest, and highland pine savanna formations; terrestrial; sea level to 600 m.

Distribution: Atlantic versant of southern Mexico to northern Honduras, and in lower Central America from southern Nicaragua to Panama. In Belize it has been confirmed from Cayo, Stann Creek, and Toledo Districts; possibly also occurs in Orange Walk District.

Similar Species: With its dark color, tuberculate dorsum, and plate-like head scales, there is no other lizard genus in Belize with which *Lepidophyma* should be confused. From its sympatric congener, *L. mayae*, it differs in having larger and fewer pale dorsal spots, fewer lateral tubercle rows (24–32 versus 33–46 in *L. mayae*), and a paler venter, as well as a different postorbital scale pattern.

Remarks: This distinctive, forest-dwelling lizard is not only active at night, as its common name suggests, but principally during the daytime, although it tends to lead a highly secretive existence. It is typically found in leaf litter between the darkened buttress roots of large trees, under bark, in caves, under logs and tree stumps, and among the stones of Maya ruins. The species is chiefly terrestrial, and rather slow in its mannerisms, although when alarmed it may react with sudden speed. *Lepidophyma flavimaculatum* in Belize reproduces viviparously; in lower parts of Central America, some populations are parthenogenetic (Bezy, 1989).

Key Reference: Smith (1973).

Lepidophyma mayae Bezy. Plate 94.

Vernacular Names: Maya night lizard, lepidofima.

Description: A small- to medium-sized, round-bodied lizard, with a maximum snout–vent length of at least 65 mm and a tail length, when unbroken, in excess of 90 mm. The head is robust and covered with large, plate-like scales; the large eye has a circular pupil and is protected

PLATE 94 *Lepidophyma mayae.* Izabal, Montañas del Mico, Guatemala. Photograph by J.A. Campbell, courtesy of the University of Texas at Arlington.

by a transparent spectacle. Dorsum covered with small, granular scales intermixed with prominent tubercles forming two longitudinal rows and 33–46 irregular transverse rows between the axilla and groin; ventrally the scales are rectangular and plate-like. The tail bears whorls of enlarged, conical-shaped tubercles. There are 14–18 femoral pores on the underside of each thigh (rudimentary in females). Dorsal coloration is dark brown or blackish medially punctuated with numerous pale spots. The head is blackish brown, darkest in the interorbital and parietal area; the labial scales are also dark, outlined with pale bars. The ventral surface is dark yellow spotted with brown; the throat may be mottled with pale yellow-tan and dark brown.

Habitat: Evergreen broadleaf forest and subtropical evergreen forest formations; terrestrial; recorded only from approximately 700 to 800 m.

Distribution: Guatemala (border region of Alta Verapaz and El Petén) and Belize. In Belize the species has been recorded from a single locality in Toledo District.

Similar Species: With its dark color, tuberculate dorsum, and plate-like head scales, there is no other lizard genus in Belize with which *Lepidophyma* should be confused. From its sympatric congener, *L. flavimaculatum*, it differs in having smaller and more numerous pale dorsal spots, more numerous lateral tubercles (33–46 versus 24–32 in *L. flavimaculatum*) arranged in less discrete rows, and a darker, more punctate venter, as well as a different postorbital scale pattern.

Remarks: A little known species, recently recorded for the first time in Belize from the Little Quartz Ridge area, Toledo District (Julian Lee and Jan Meerman, in litt.). Individuals of the type series described by Bezy (1973) were found active during the day, and hiding under logs and rocks on the forest floor. In common with other night lizards, the species is probably viviparous.

Key Reference: Bezy (1973).

ALLIGATOR LIZARDS (FAMILY ANGUIDAE)

Although a relatively small family, there are representatives in both New and Old Worlds. In the American tropics, they are found well into South America, as well as in the Antilles. Alligator lizards are elongate and shiny-scaled, generally with small limbs or without limbs in several species. Their bodies and tails are stiff, due to the presence of osteoderms in the skin, and many species have a lengthwise, flexible groove along the side to allow expansion of the body when breathing. Anguids have moveable eyelids, and femoral pores are absent in all species. Only one genus, *Diploglossus,* occurs in Belize.

Diploglossus rozellae (Smith). Figs. 15, 17; Plate 95.

Vernacular Names: Rozella's lesser galliwasp, celesto panza verde.

Description: A small- to medium-sized lizard, with a relatively elongate, flattened snout, and a maximum snout–vent length of approximately 100 mm. There is a single, large medial prefrontal scale and 31–33 rows of cycloid-like scales around the body. Juveniles are dark above with copper-colored dorsolateral stripes, an orange tail, and black vertical bars laterally; in adults the orange tail disappears, and the dorsum is copper-colored with scattered dark spots and black vertical bars laterally. The venter is bluish or greenish white with a metallic sheen.

Habitat: Evergreen broadleaf forest and highland pine savanna formations; arboreal; 100 to 600 m.

Distribution: Southern Mexico to northern Guatemala and Belize. In Belize it is known from Cayo and Stann Creek Districts, and may also occur in Toledo District.

Similar Species: There are no other members of the family known from the region with which this species could be confused. From the families Scincidae, Gymnophthalmidae, Teiidae, and Xantusiidae it differs in having a pair of frontonasal scales, versus a single frontonasal in these families. From the remaining lizard families, it differs in having large, squarish, juxtaposed ventral scales, compared to numerous small, rounded or pointed, imbricate, subimbricate, or granular ventral scales in these other families.

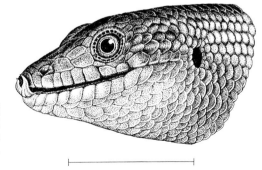

FIGURE   17 Head   of *Diploglossus rozellae* (BMNH 1973.2753; Bokawina, Stann Creek District) in lateral view. Scale bar = 1 cm.

PLATE 95 *Diploglossus rozellae.* Izabal, Guatemala. Photograph by J.A. Campbell, courtesy of the University of Texas at Arlington.

Remarks: This skink like species has usually been reported under the name *Celestus rozellae* and was only recently included in the genus *Diploglossus* (Campbell and Camarillo, 1994). Henderson and Hoevers (1975) reported it as being terrestrial, but Campbell and Camarillo (1994) indicated that this was probably in error and that the species is at least partially arboreal; the holotype, described by Smith (1942), was found climbing rapidly up a small tree. Viviparous. Its distribution and habits are very poorly known in Belize.

Key Reference: Campbell and Camarillo (1994).

5

𝕾NAKES

(Order Squamata; Suborder Serpentes)

Snakes are distinctive in having an elongated body without limbs, external ear openings, or eyelids. There are approximately 2900 extant species. In size they range from the giant reticulated python (*Python reticulatus*), which grows to lengths of almost 10 m, to the tiny blind snakes (families Typhlopidae and Leptotyphlopidae) measuring little more than 10 cm. Snakes have evolved to take advantage of the same diverse range of habitats and adaptive zones as occupied by lizards. The majority are terrestrial, although there are a large number of arboreal, fossorial, and semiaquatic forms. One group, the sea snakes, is strictly marine. All snakes feed only on living prey. Most species move with lateral undulations of the body, and some are surprisingly rapid. Larger species employ a rectilinear form of loco-motion, using the muscles on the underside of the body to creep forward in a caterpillar-like fashion. A few desert-dwelling species advance in a side-winding manner for ease of movement across loose sand. Snakes may be diurnal in habits, exclusively nocturnal, or active at any time of the day or night. A few are capable of caudal autotomy, but none have powers of

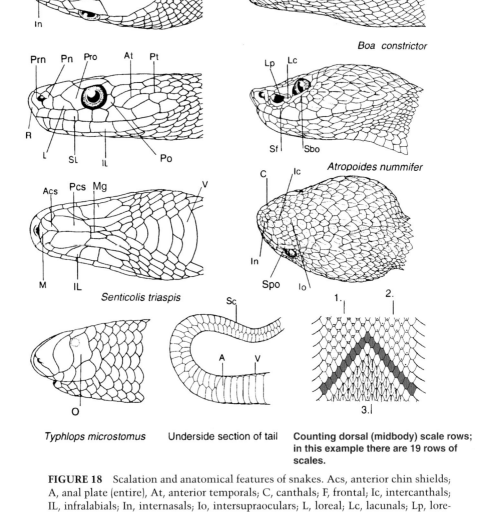

Boa constrictor

Atropoides nummifer

Senticolis triaspis

Typhlops microstomus   Underside section of tail   Counting dorsal (midbody) scale rows; in this example there are 19 rows of scales.

FIGURE 18 Scalation and anatomical features of snakes. Acs, anterior chin shields; A, anal plate (entire); At, anterior temporals; C, canthals; F, frontal; Ic, intercanthals; IL, infralabials; In, internasals; Io, intersupraoculars; L, loreal; Lc, lacunals; Lp, loreal pit; M, mental; Mg, mental groove; O, ocular; P, parietals; Pcs, posterior chin shields; Pf, prefrontals; Pn, postnasal; Po, postoculars; Prn, prenasal; Pro, preoculars; Pt, posterior temporals; R, rostral; Sbo, subocular; SL, supralabials; Spo, supraocular; Sc, subcaudals (divided); Sf, subfoveals; V, ventrals; 1, scales with paired apical pits; 2, scales with single apical pit; 3, keeled scales.

tail regeneration. Sexual dimorphism is typically limited to differences in tail length, and the number of scales on the underside of the abdomen and tail, although a few species are also dichromatic. While most snakes are egg layers, some are viviparous, and at least one is known to be parthenogenetic.

As animals that all share the same basic elongate shape, snakes tend to resemble one another fairly closely. Body shape, however, is not restricted to a single unvarying form; some species are long and thin while others are short and stout. Important features to check for include the presence or absence of a deep pit on the side of the head between the eye and naris (*loreal pit*), which in Belize indicates a venomous species of the pitviper family, and relative size of the eye and configuration of the pupil (round, subcircular, or vertically elliptic). Some have prehensile tails while others do not. One species, the common boa (*Boa constrictor*), is unique in Belize in having a pair of small horny projections either side of the vent (*cloacal spurs*).

While many have distinctive color patterns, the number and configuration of scales provide the most reliable means of identification (Fig. 18). As seen in lizards, those of the dorsum may be *keeled*, with a medial ridge, or smooth and polished, and individual scales may have a single or paired series of microscopic pits (*apical pits*) near the outer edge. The number of dorsal scale rows is particularly diagnostic. These may remain constant throughout the length of the body, or be reduced in number anteriorly and posteriorly. The scales on the upper surface of the head may be large, plate-like, and arranged symmetrically, or small, irregular, and nonsymmetrical. Note in particular the condition of the *nasal* scale (divided or entire) and, on the side of the head, the number of scales lining the upper jaw (*supralabials*), the number of scales in front of and behind the eye (*preoculars* and *postoculars*), and presence or absence of the *loreal* scale. Scales on the abdomen (*ventrals*) typically extend crosswise as large, overlapping, rectangular plates, although in a few species they may be the same or of similar size to the dorsals. The scale covering the cloaca (*anal plate*) may be divided or entire, and those beneath the tail (*subcaudals*) arranged either in a single row or in pairs. In many snakes, the number of dorsal scale rows, ventral and subcaudal scales, and the condition of the anal plate, are especially useful as a set of distinguishing characters.

KEY TO THE FAMILIES OF SNAKES IN BELIZE

1. Ventral scales not enlarged, same size as those of dorsum 2

   Ventral scales enlarged, much wider than those of dorsum 3

2. Dorsal scales in 14 rows around body . . . Leptotyphlopidae [page 173]

   Dorsal scales in 18 rows around body . . . . . . Typhlopidae [page 173]

3. A pit present between the eye and nostril . . . . . . Viperidae [page 269]

   No pit between the eye and nostril 4

4. Dorsum of head with enlarged, plate-like scales; midbody dorsal scale rows fewer than 40; spur-like vestiges of hind limbs absent 5

   Dorsum of head with numerous small, irregular scales; midbody scale rows more than 60; vestiges of hind limbs present as a pair of horny spurs either side of vent . . . . Boidae [page 174]

5. A pair of nonerectile, grooved fangs present in the front of the mouth; loreal scale never present . . . . Elapidae [page 261]

   Fangs absent or, if present, located in the back of the mouth; loreal scale present or absent . . . . Colubridae [page 176]

BLINDSNAKES (FAMILIES TYPHLOPIDAE AND LEPTOTYPHLOPIDAE)

These are small, slender, worm-like snakes comprising some 200 species distributed in Africa, southern Asia, Australasia, tropical America, and the West Indies. Two species occur in Belize; there are unconfirmed reports of an unidentified species, possibly the widely introduced *Rhamphotyphlops braminus* (Daudin), from the Turneffe Islands. The body is cylindrical and of more or less the same diameter throughout, with an inconspicuous, round, blunt head, and a short tail that terminates in a spine. The smooth body scales are all of the same size and not enlarged ventrally. Commonly called blind snakes, most are indeed blind with tiny vestigial eyes that appear like black dots, usually beneath an enlarged ocular scale.

These cryptozoic burrowing snakes are usually only seen when unearthed, but may crawl around on the surface at night. They are most frequently found in termite nests, in loose earth, or beneath decaying logs on the forest floor. The diet consists largely of ants, termites, and their eggs, but other small, soft-bodied invertebrates may be eaten. The jaws of Leptotyphlopidae species are highly modified for their specialized feeding habits, and they are unique among snakes in having teeth only in the lower jaw (List, 1966). Most blindsnakes are oviparous, although several are viviparous, and *Rhamphotyphlops braminus* is believed be an all-female species, reproducing by means of parthenogenesis.

Typhlops microstomus Cope. Fig. 18.

Vernacular Names: Yucatán blindsnake, culebra ciega de Yucatán.

Description: A small, thin (approximately 3 mm in diameter), elongate snake, slightly stouter posteriorly than anteriorly; total length approximately 360 mm. Tail very short (approximately 8.5% of head and body length). Scales smooth and close fitting, in 18 rows throughout; middorsal scales from rostral to tail spine 487–566; subcaudals 5–10. Body and head uniform white to pinkish tan.

Habitat: Savanna formation and possibly also semi-evergreen seasonal forest; fossorial; sea level to 50 m.

Distribution: Yucatán Peninsula region of Mexico, northern Guatemala, and Belize. In Belize it is known from Belize and Corozal Districts; probably also occurs in Cayo District.

Similar Species: *Leptotyphlops goudotii* has 14 scale rows around the body, fewer than 300 middorsal scales from the rostral to the tail spine, a darker, spotted dorsal pattern, and a longer tail. Other small, smooth-scaled, semifossorial species such as those of the genera *Adelphicos*, *Tantilla*, and *Tantillita* have distinct eyes and a tapering head. *Typhlops* also bears a superficial resemblance to the caecilian, *Gymnopis syntrema*.

Remarks: A small, blind, burrowing snake, also occasionally found active above ground at night, especially when soil becomes waterlogged following heavy rain. Found in loose earth, leaf litter, ant and termite nests, or beneath rotten logs, principally in grassland areas. Meerman (1992) described finding a specimen at a depth of 1.6 m while digging a well, although indicated that the animal might have been living nearer the surface and fallen into the pit. Oviparous.

Key Reference: Dixon and Hendricks (1979).

Leptotyphlops goudotii (Duméril and Bibron). Plate 96.

Vernacular Names: Black blindsnake, slender blindsnake, agujilla.

Description: A small, thin, elongate snake with an extremely short tail; total length 185 mm (tail approximately 7% of head and body length); body cylindrical and of uniform diameter throughout. Scales smooth, close-fitting, in 14 rows throughout and without apical pits; middorsal scales from rostral to tail spine 220–265; subcaudals 13–22. Dorsal color pattern of small dark spots arranged in longitudinal lines, with or without a pale spot on the snout and another at the tip of the tail.

Habitat: Semi-evergreen seasonal forest and possibly also savanna formation; fossorial; sea level to 50 m.

Distribution: Southern Mexico to Colombia and Venezuela. In Belize it has been confirmed only from Corozal District.

PLATE 96 *Leptotyphlops goudotii.* Baja Verapaz, Guatemala. Photograph by J.A. Campbell, courtesy of the University of Texas at Arlington.

Similar Species: *Typhlops microstomus* has 18 scale rows around the body, considerably more than 265 middorsal scales from the rostral to the tail spine, a proportionately shorter tail, and lacks any discernible color pattern. Other small, smooth-scaled, semifossorial species such as those of the genera *Adelphicos, Tantilla,* and *Tantillita* have distinct eyes and a tapering head. *Leptotyphlops* may also be confused with the caecilian, *Gymnopis syntrema*, which bears a superficial resemblance.

Remarks: A small, blind, burrowing snake, occasionally active above ground at night, especially when the soil becomes waterlogged following heavy rain. Typically found in loose earth, leaf litter, ant and termite nests, or beneath rotten logs on the forest floor. The species may be able to live unmolested in ant nests by adopting a behavior pattern similar to that observed in *L. dulcis* from North America; this species is known to repel attacking ants by elevating the tips of its body scales and producing a distasteful secretion (Gehlbach *et al.,* 1968). Oviparous.

Key Reference: Wilson and Meyer (1985).

BOAS (FAMILY BOIDAE)

This primitive family of approximately 90 species includes the giants of the snake world. The common boa (*Boa constrictor*) belongs to the subfamily Boinae and is the only representative of this group in Belize. *Boa constrictor* is highly variable and widely distributed. Eleven subspecies have been defined ranging from central Mexico through Central America and northern South America to Argentina, although the true extent of geographic variation is not satisfactorily represented by these forms alone. Dorsal scales are small, smooth, and present in numerous rows; ventral scales are greatly enlarged and form transverse plates. Many boines (excluding *Boa constrictor*) possess heat-sensitive pits in the labial scales. The eye has a vertically elliptic pupil. Snakes of this family possess vestiges of hind limbs, present as a pair of horny spurs either side of the vent.

Boa constrictor (Linnaeus). Fig. 18; Plates 97, 98.

Vernacular Names: *Wowla, wowler, owla,* Mexican boa constrictor, imperial boa, mazacouatl.

Description: A very large, stoutly proportioned snake with a short tail; total length up to approximately 5500 mm but generally less than 3000 mm. Head broad and distinctly wider than neck with no enlarged plates on the crown. Vestigial remains of hind limbs present as a pair of small horny spurs either side of the vent. Naris scale placed laterally; supralabials 17–22; infralabials 20–26; dorsal scales smooth, in 61–79 rows at midbody; ventrals 225–259; anal plate entire; subcaudals 48–70, undivided. Dorsum gray, yellowish gray, brown, or pinkish brown with 22–30 darker, saddle-like blotches, contrasting particularly on the tail; a series of dark circular or rhomboidal lateral blotches is arranged opposite or between the dorsal ones. Head sometimes with a dark cruciform marking or medial stripe extending from the snout to the nape and a dark temporal stripe. Venter white, yellow, or gray with variously sized, irregular dark markings, often more conspicuous posteriorly.

Habitat: Evergreen broadleaf forest, semi-evergreen seasonal forest, karst hills forest, subtropical evergreen forest, savanna, highland pine savanna, and coastal lagoons and marshes formations; terrestrial and arboreal; sea level to 700 m.

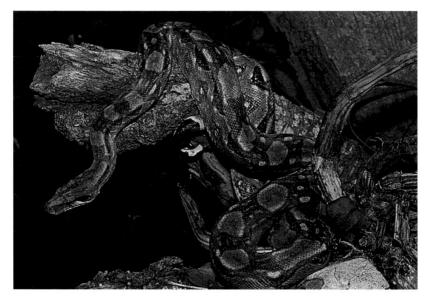

PLATE 97 *Boa constrictor.* Sarteneja, Corozal District. Photograph by P. Edgar.

PLATE 98 *Boa constrictor.* Las Cuevas, Chiquibul Forest, Cayo District.

Distribution: Central Mexico to Argentina. Also found in the Lesser Antilles. In Belize it is found countrywide, including most of the larger island groups and some smaller cayes (i.e., Crawl Caye, Caye Caulker).

Similar Species: Size alone will distinguish adult boas from all other snakes in Belize. The only other snakes with a vertically elliptic pupil and similar body form are the pitvipers, but these all have a loreal pit, keeled scales, and substantially fewer dorsal scale rows.

Remarks: A large although rather sluggish snake. Nocturnal and diurnal; often takes refuge underground beneath tree roots during the day. Typically observed basking on banks or fallen logs along rivers, but also found in dry upland forest and pine grassland. Boas feed on a wide range of vertebrate prey, including iguanas and other lizards, birds, and various mammals. If intimidated they may emit a loud, guttural hiss, audible for up to 20 m. Viviparous. Snakes from Belize and mainland Central America in general have been traditionally assigned to the subspecies *B. c. imperator* Daudin. On the cayes the species tends to be appreciably smaller with a paler color pattern.

Key Reference: Wilson and Meyer (1985).

COLUBRID SNAKES (FAMILY COLUBRIDAE)

Largest of all snake families, the Colubridae comprises 75% of the world's 2500 or so known species. They are found on all continents except Antarctica, ranging latitudinally from the Arctic Circle in the Northern

Hemisphere to the Cape of Good Hope in the Southern Hemisphere. Adaptive radiation has produced a wide range of specialized forms. In Belize these include diminutive invertebrate-eating species *(Ninia, Tantilla, Tantillita)*, several representatives of the subfamily Dipsadinae (gastropod eaters), an aquatic fish specialist *(Tretanorhinus)*, elongate arboreal forms that prey largely on frogs and lizards *(Imantodes, Leptophis, Oxybelis)*, and highly agile, terrestrial hunters *(Coluber, Dendrophidion, Dryadophis, Masticophis)*. Some of the larger generalists (e.g., *Clelia, Drymarchon,* and *Lampropeltis*) are noted for their habit of regularly predating on other snakes. Most are harmless, though some have fixed, enlarged, grooved (opisthoglyphous) or unmodified (aglyphous) maxillary fangs toward the back of the upper jaw, usually connected to a poison-producing salivary gland (Duvernoy's gland). With the exception of four Old World genera, the venom of rear-fanged species is not dangerous to humans and is lethal only to the animals that the snakes feed upon. The bite of certain species, however, including several in Belize (genera *Coniophanes, Conophis, Leptophis, Oxybelis, Urotheca,* and perhaps others), may cause severe local pain and other symptoms of poisoning in man.

The colubrid head is usually as wide or wider than the neck, with enlarged, symmetrically arranged plates on the top. In most forms the eye is well developed with a round, subcircular, or vertically elliptic pupil. A few genera, including several in Belize, have the ability to discard their tails as an antipredator defense measure, but none have powers of caudal regeneration as seen in some lizards. The dorsal scales may be smooth or keeled, and with or without apical pits. Ventral scales are as wide as the body, and the subcaudals are usually divided into pairs.

Key to the Genera of Colubridae in Belize

1. Dorsal scales in an even number of rows . . . . . . *Spilotes* [page 241]

   Dorsal scales in an odd number of rows 2

2. Mental groove present. 3

   Mental groove absent . . . . *Dipsas* [page 201]

3. Anal plate entire 4

   Anal plate divided 14

4. Number of dorsal scale rows constant between about midbody and level of vent 5

   Number of dorsal scale rows at midbody more than at level of vent . .
   7

5. Dorsal scales in 15 or 17 rows; dorsal body pattern with light and dark bands . . . . *Sibon* [page 235]

   Dorsal scales in 17 or 19 rows; dorsum unicolor, spotted, or with a collar behind the head. 6

6. Dorsal scales smooth; ventrals more than 190 . . . .
   . . . . *Clelia (part)* [page 184]

   Dorsal scales keeled; ventrals fewer than 190 . . . . . *Ninia* [page 222]

7. Dorsal scales keeled over all or part of body 8

   Dorsal scales all smooth. 10

8. Maximum number of dorsal scale rows fewer than 21 9

   Maximum number of dorsal scale rows more than 21 . . . .
   . . . . *Pseustes* [page 229]

9. Dorsal scales in 17 rows at midbody. . . . . *Dendrophidion* [page 196]

   Dorsal scales in 19 rows at midbody . . . . . . *Thamnophis* [page 254]

10. Dorsal scales in 17 rows at midbody; nasal scale entire . . . .
    . . . . *Drymarchon* [page 204]

    Dorsal scales in generally greater than 17 rows at midbody; nasal scale divided 11

11. Dorsal scales in generally greater than 21 rows at midbody . . . .
    . . . . *Lampropeltis* [page 211]

    Dorsal scales in 19 or fewer rows at midbody 12

12. Ventrals fewer than 150 . . . . *Xenodon* [page 260]

    Ventrals more than 150 13

13. Dorsal body pattern of light and dark annuli or bands . . . .
    . . . . *Oxyrhopus* [page 228]

    Dorsum unicolor, spotted, or with a collar behind the head . . . .
    . . . . *Clelia (part)* [page 184]

14. Number of dorsal scale rows greater at about midbody than at level of vent 15

    Number of dorsal scale rows constant between about midbody and level of vent. 28

15. Some or all of dorsal scales keeled, sometimes very weakly 16

    All dorsal body scales smooth 21

16. Dorsal scales in 15 rows at midbody . . . . *Leptophis* [page 217]

Dorsal scales in more than 15 rows at midbody 17

17. Head elongate with pointed snout; loreal scale absent . . . .
. . . . *Oxybelis* [page 225]

Head not as above; loreal scale present 18

18. Dorsal scales in 17 rows at midbody. 19

Dorsal scales in more than 17 rows at midbody 20

19. Dorsal pattern of longitudinal stripes; number of dorsal scale rows constant between midbody and level of vent . . . . *Rhadinaea* [page 231]

Dorsal pattern not as above; number of dorsal scale rows reduced between midbody and level of vent. . . . . *Drymobius* [page 205]

20. Dorsal scales in 19 rows at midbody . . . . . *Tretanorhinus* [page 257]

Dorsal scale exceeding 19 rows at midbody. 21

21. Eye with conspicuously small pupil; dorsal scales in 35 rows at midbody; supralabials usually 9. . . . . *Elaphe* [page 207]

Eye not as above; dorsal scales exceeding 35 rows at midbody; supralabials usually 8 . . . . *Senticolis* [page 234]

22. Dorsal scales not exceeding 17 rows at midbody. 23

Dorsal scales exceeding 17 rows at midbody 26

23. Number of dorsal scale rows at midbody more than at level of vent; nasal divided; supralabials usually 7 or more; infralabials 8–11 . . . 24

Number of dorsal scale rows constant between about midbody and level of vent; nasal single; supralabials usually 6; infralabials usually 7
. . . . *Symphimus* [page 247]

24. A single small subocular scale below preocular 25

No subocular below preocular . . . . *Dryadophis* [page 202]

25. Ventrals more than 180; supralabials usually 7 . . . .
. . . . *Masticophis* [page 221]

Ventrals fewer than 170; supralabials usually 8. . . *Coluber* [page 187]

26. Dorsal body pattern either unicolor or striped 27

Dorsum with spots, blotches, or saddles . . . . . *Leptodeira* [page 213]

27. A single anterior temporal scale . . . . *Coniophanes* [page 188]

Two or three anterior temporal scales . . . . *Conophis* [page 195]

28. Maximum number of dorsal scale rows 15 29

  Maximum number of dorsal scale rows 17 or more 31

29. Third or second and third infralabial scales reduced in width, narrow, and confined to lip border . . . . *Adelphicos* [page 180]

  No infralabials reduced in width, all regular in shape and size . . . 30

30. Pale nuchal collar present; ventrals 117–154 . . . . *Tantilla* [page 248]

  Nuchal collar absent; ventrals 103–115 . . . . . . *Tantillita* [page 248]

31. Rostral scale upturned anteriorly with a sharp, free edge and in contact with frontal. . . . . *Ficimia* [page 208]

  Rostral not as above 32

32. Dorsum with light and dark bands, at least anteriorly 33

  Dorsum unicolor or with spots, blotches, stripes, or saddles, never banded 34

33. Bands confined to anterior part of body; posteriorly small spots arranged in longitudinal rows . . . . *Scaphiodontophis* [page 232]

  Bands present throughout entire length of body. . . *Urotheca* [page 258]

34. Head much broader than neck; ventrals generally more than 215; subcaudals more than 120 . . . . *Imantodes* [page 210]

  Head not greatly broadened; ventrals fewer than 215; subcaudals fewer than 120 35

35. Tail very short; subcaudals fewer than 50. . . . *Stenorrhina* [page 243]

  Tail elongate; subcaudals more than 50 . . . . *Amastridium* [page 182]

Adelphicos quadrivirgatus Jan. Fig. 19; Plate 99.
Vernacular Names: Middle American earth snake, zacatera.
Description: A small snake with a relatively short tail; total length approximately 320 mm. Head small and conical, not or only slightly discernible from neck. Nasal scale divided; loreal single, elongate, and entering orbit; no preoculars; postoculars usually 2; supralabials usually 7 with third and fourth entering orbit; infralabials 6–8; anterior chin shields greatly enlarged; dorsal scales smooth without apical pits, in 15 rows throughout; ventrals 117–155; anal plate divided; subcaudals 29–50. Dorsum pale brownish gray to reddish with one to five darker longitudinal stripes; the lowermost lateral stripe extends forward to the eye and is sharply contrasted below by white on the supralabials. Venter

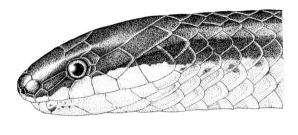

FIGURE 19 Head of *Adelphicos quadrivirgatus* (BMNH 1967.23; Baléu, San Cristóbal, Alta Verapaz, Guatemala) in lateral view. Scale bar = 5 mm.

white, cream or yellowish, frequently heavily marked with darker pigment.

Habitat: Evergreen broadleaf forest formation, and possibly highland pine savanna formation; fossorial and leaf litter; 50 to 600 m.

Distribution: Southern Mexico to northern Honduras. In Belize is has been confirmed from Belize, Stann Creek, and Cayo Districts; probably also occurs in Toledo District.

Similar Species: Other small fossorial species. *Tantilla* and *Tantillita* lack a loreal scale and may be further distinguished by the presence of a nuchal band, and/or an immaculate, unpigmented venter; the dorsal

PLATE 99 A juvenile *Adelphicos quadrivirgatus.* The pallid appearance is a symptom of the skin shedding process. Cuxta Bani, upper Raspaculo River, Cayo District.

181

pattern is essentially uniform in *Tantilla* and *Tantillita* and not striped as in *Adelphicos. Ninia* has keeled dorsal scales and a uniform, spotted, or banded dorsal pattern, never striped. The greatly enlarged chin scales will also distinguish *Adelphicos* from other similarly sized snakes.

Remarks: A burrowing snake usually found beneath decaying logs or vegetation on the forest floor and among large stones. Secretive, usually remaining below ground, but may venture onto the surface at night to forage. Feeds on earthworms and other invertebrates. Oviparous; Pérez-Higareda and Smith (1989) reported on termite nest incubation of the eggs.

Key Reference: Wilson and Meyer (1985).

Amastridium veliferum Cope. Fig. 20; Plate 100.

Vernacular Names: Rusty-headed snake, ridge-nosed snake, culebra zacatera.

Description: A medium-small snake; total length approximately 720 mm. Head viper-like; eye with round pupil. Top of head with an overhanging, shelf-like supraocular scale, and sharply angled canthus; nasal divided; loreal usually present; preoculars 1; postoculars 2; supralabials usually 7 with third and fourth entering orbit; infralabials 9, the fifth being largest; dorsal scales smooth, or keeled above vent and anterior one-third of tail only, in 17 rows throughout; apical pits present on dorsal scales of neck region only; ventrals 119–170; anal plate divided; subcaudals 68–86; males with supraanal tubercles. Dorsum dark gray with a line of white dots on the fifth scale row, each longitudinally separated by 3–4 scales; snout and anterior dorsum of head dark gray with thin, wavy black lines; supralabials black with red-brown flecking; pale blotch present on nape, bounded below by a black line extending from posterior edge of eye

FIGURE 20 Head of *Amastridium veliferum* (MPM 6734; Medina Bank, Toledo District) in lateral view. Scale bar = 1 cm.

PLATE 100 *Amastridium veliferum.* Izabal, Guatemala. Photograph by J.A. Campbell, courtesy of the University of Texas at Arlington.

almost to angle of jaw. Venter grayish brown, paler anteriorly and sometimes with fine blue spots on chin.

Habitat: Riparian forest and citrus grove in evergreen broadleaf forest formation; terrestrial; 100 to 500 m.

Distribution: Central Mexico to Panama. In Belize it is known from Cayo, Stann Creek, and Toledo Districts.

Similar Species: Some potential exists for confusion with juvenile pit-vipers (*Atropoides, Bothrops,* or *Porthidium*), although the species can be distinguished by its more or less unicolor dorsum (patterned in Belizean viperid species), smooth dorsal scales, and eye with round pupil (pupil vertically elliptic in viperids).

Remarks: By most accounts a rare snake throughout its range. Predominantly diurnal and crepuscular. Most likely to be observed foraging among leaf litter on the forest floor or at the sides of streams. Diet largely unknown although stomach contents of preserved specimens have included small frogs (Blaney and Blaney, 1978; Martin, 1955). Nothing is known about its reproductive biology.

Key Reference: Wilson and Meyer (1985).

Key to the Species of *Clelia* in Belize

Dorsal scales in 19 rows at midbody . . . . *C. clelia*

Dorsal scales in 17 rows at midbody . . . . *C. scytalina*

Clelia clelia (Daudin). Plates 101, 102, 103.

Vernacular Names: *Bejucilla,* mussurana, sumbadora, zopilota, culebra de sangre.

Description: A very large, robust snake; maximum total length exceeding 2470 mm. Head not significantly wider than neck; eye black with vertically oriented subcircular pupil. Nasal scale divided; loreal usually present; preoculars 1; postoculars 2; supralabials 7 or 8 with third and fourth entering orbit; infralabials 7–9; dorsal scales smooth with 2 apical pits, usually in 19 rows at midbody, the middorsal row slightly enlarged; ventrals 198–247; anal plate entire; subcaudals 57–93. The coloration of adult and juvenile snakes is strikingly different. Dorsum of adult uniform shiny bluish black or dark grey. Juveniles have a bright red or dull reddish dorsum, each dorsal scale usually tipped with dark red, and a whitish nuchal collar covering the parietals and bordered posteriorly by a black band (not extending onto ventrals); head black above

PLATE 101   Adult *Clelia clelia.* Smokey River Camp, Chiquibul Forest, Cayo District.

PLATE 102 Head detail of an adult *Clelia clelia*. Cuxta Bani, upper Raspaculo River, Cayo District.

PLATE 103 Juvenile *Clelia clelia* illustrating the strikingly disparate color pattern of the young of this species. Southern Ecuador. Photograph by P. Freed.

(extending from snout to postoculars). Venter immaculate white or cream.

Habitat: Evergreen broadleaf forest, karst hills forest, semi-evergreen seasonal forest, subtropical evergreen forest formations; terrestrial; sea level to 1000 m.

Distribution: Extreme southern Mexico to Uruguay and Argentina. In Belize it is known from Cayo, Stann Creek, and Toledo Districts.

Similar Species: *Clelia scytalina*; juveniles and adults alike are almost identical in form and coloration, but usually have 17 scale rows along the full length of the body (usually 19 on the neck and at midbody in *C. clelia*, falling to 17 posteriorly). The red dorsal scales of juvenile *C. scytalina* may be more heavily tipped with dark red or black.

Remarks: Opisthoglyphous, although the venom has little effect on humans. Habitually ophiophagous in feeding habits; the species frequently predates on venomous snakes and is immune to the highly toxic venom of *Bothrops* and other pitvipers. Also known to feed on small mammals and lizards, which are killed by envenomation; snake prey is normally constricted. *Clelia clelia* and its congener, *C. scytalina*, undergo a striking color change with age; juveniles are bright red with a black head and pale nuchal collar, changing to uniform black or dark bluish grey as adults. Chiefly crepuscular and nocturnal in habits; the snake illustrated (Plate 101) was found at night in a small forest pool during heavy rain. Oviparous.

Key Reference: Zaher (1996).

Clelia scytalina (Cope). Fig. 21.

Vernacular Names: *Bejucilla* (?), Mexican snake eater, culebrera mexicana.

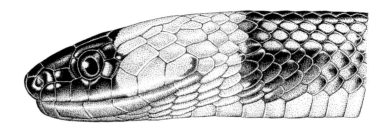

FIGURE 21   Head of juvenile *Clelia scytalina* (BMNH 68.4.7.8; City of Mexico) in lateral view. Scale bar = 1 cm.

Description: A medium-large, robust snake; total length approximately 1500 mm. Head not significantly wider than neck; eye black with vertically oriented subcircular pupil. Scales: nasal divided; loreal single; preoculars 1; postoculars 2; supralabials 7–8, with third and fourth entering orbit; infralabials usually 8; dorsal scales smooth, with 2 apical pits, in 17 rows throughout (rarely 19 on the neck), the middorsal row slightly enlarged posteriorly; ventrals 202–228; anal plate entire; subcaudals 70–92. Coloration of adult and juvenile snakes strikingly different. Dorsum of adult uniform shiny bluish black or dark grey. Juveniles with a bright red or dull reddish dorsum, each scale usually tipped with black, and a yellowish nuchal collar covering the parietals, bordered posteriorly by a black band (not extending onto ventrals); head yellowish above with black extending from the snout to postoculars. Venter immaculate white or cream.

Habitat: Semi-evergreen seasonal forest formation and cleared land; terrestrial; sea level to 100 m.

Distribution: Discontinuously distributed from central Mexico to Costa Rica. In Belize it is known from Corozal and northeastern Orange Walk Districts.

Similar Species: *Clelia clelia*; juveniles and adults alike are almost identical in form and coloration, but usually have 19 scale rows at midbody, falling to 17 rows posteriorly (usually 17 throughout, or 19 on the neck and 17 at midbody in *C. scytalina*). The scale row pattern of *C. clelia*, however, is known to be variable; Underwood (1993) cites examples of this species that have 17 and 21 rows of scales on the neck. The red dorsal scales of juvenile *C. scytalina* may be more heavily tipped with dark red or black.

Remarks: Opisthoglyphous. A poorly known species with a disjunct geographic distribution. In other parts of its range *C. scytalina* is typically associated with more mesic habitats at higher elevations than *C. clelia*, but in Belize it is known only from the seasonally dry lowlands. Hoevers and Henderson (1974) reported on a specimen found at night on the bank of the New River (Orange Walk District).

Key Reference: Zaher (1996).

Coluber constrictor Linnaeus. Fig. 22.

Vernacular Names: Racer, corredora.

Description: A medium-sized, slender snake; average total length approximately 600 mm. Nasal scale divided; loreal single; preoculars 2, the lower most (sometimes referred to as a subocular) very small; postoculars 2; supralabials 7 or 8, with fourth and fifth entering orbit; infralabials 8–10; dorsal scales smooth, usually in 15 rows at midbody and with

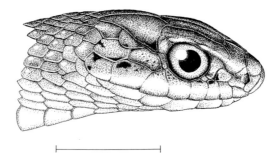

FIGURE 22 Head of *Coluber constrictor* (MPM 8186; Augustine, Cayo District) in lateral view. Scale bar = 1 cm.

apical pits; ventrals 150–172; anal plate divided; subcaudals 78–108. Dorsum uniformly olive brown to gray or brown above, grading to yellowish, greenish brown or bluish laterally; juveniles usually with a series of narrow dark blotches or crossbands on the anterior one-third of the dorsal surface. Venter pale yellow or yellowish green, immaculate.

Habitat: Savanna and highland pine savanna formations; terrestrial; 100–600 m.

Distribution: Southern Canada to Guatemala and Belize. In Belize it has been confirmed only from Cayo District; possibly also occurs in Stann Creek District.

Similar Species: *Dryadophis* is similar in form, but has a dark or copperbrown dorsum, and lacks a small subocular scale below the preoculars. May also be confused with immature *Masticophis*, which has 17 midbody dorsal rows (typically 15 rows in *Coluber*) and a higher ventral count (166–205).

Remarks: An alert, fast-moving and highly agile snake. Principally terrestrial but climbs well. May lift its head and anterior part of the body when hunting or disturbed. Diurnal. Oviparous. Relationships of the many different geographical forms of this snake are poorly known; populations in Belize and Guatemala, where the species is smallest and reaches its southernmost limit, have been assigned to the subspecific race *C. c. oaxaca* (Jan). Contrary to its scientific name, the species is not a constrictor; prey is immobilized by swallowing.

Key Reference: Wilson (1978).

Key to the Species of *Coniophanes* in Belize

1. Dorsal scales in 23 to 25 rows at midbody . . . . *C. schmidti*

   Dorsal scales in 19 to 21 rows at midbody. 2

2. Dorsal scales in maximum of 19 rows at midbody . . . . . *C. imperialis*

   Dorsal scales in 21 rows at midbody 3

3. Venter usually with a paired row of large, dark rounded spots on the outer edge of each scale; middorsal stripe conspicuously differentiated from lighter paravertebral area . . . . *C. bipunctatus*

   Venter immaculate, irregularly speckled, or with a single row of very small dark spots on the outer edge of each scale; middorsal stripe not conspicuously differentiated from paravertebral area, vertebral line often marked with a row of small dark dots . . . . *C. fissidens*

Coniophanes bipunctatus (Günther). Plate 104.

Vernacular Names: *Garden snake* (?), two-spotted snake, culebra dos-manchas, tabaquilla.

Description: A medium-sized snake; average total length between 500 and 550 mm. Nasal scale divided; loreal single; preoculars 1; postoculars 2; supralabials 7–9 with fourth and fifth entering orbit; infralabials 7–10, usually 9 or 10; dorsal scales smooth without apical pits, usually in 21 rows at midbody; ventrals 124–142; anal plate divided; subcaudals 78–96. Dorsum pale or dark brown, reddish brown or copper with dark lat-

PLATE 104   *Coniophanes bipunctatus.* Leguna Seca, Orange Walk District.

eral stripes present usually on scale rows 3, 4, and 5, and a diffuse, dark stripe coursing the length of the middorsal line. Venter yellowish grading to pinkish orange posteriorly, with conspicuous dark brown to blackish rounded spots, usually one pair to each abdominal scale; chin and throat usually with dark mottling and longitudinal streaks.

Habitat: Near water in evergreen broadleaf forest, semi-evergreen seasonal forest, and interior wetlands formations, and citrus grove; terrestrial and semiaquatic; sea level to 300 m.

Distribution: Southern Mexico to Panama. In Belize it is known from most districts and probably occurs countrywide.

Similar Species: Other *Coniophanes: C. fissidens* has numerous small pale brown spots or a small spot on the outer edges of each ventral scale, compared to a pair of large, rounded blackish spots in *C. bipunctatus* (one on each side); *C. imperialis* has 19 scale rows at midbody; *C. schmidti* has 23 to 25 scale rows at midbody and has a more boldly striped dorsal pattern. Another *Coniophanes* with a similar ventral pattern of paired dark spots, *C. quinquevittatus*, is known from El Petén and the extreme north of the Yucatán Peninsula, and may conceivably range into Belize; this species is distinguished by having more than 150 ventral scales (fewer than 150 in *C. bipunctatus*), and the chin is more boldly marked with dark spots rather than streaks.

Remarks: Opisthoglyphous, although harmless to humans. Invariably found in the vicinity of water and is presumed to feed mainly on frogs. Diurnal and nocturnal. A secretive, terrestrial and semiaquatic species; the authors have observed these snakes foraging through wet leaf litter in marginal forest at the edge of freshwater lagoons. Oviparous.

Key Reference: Bailey (1939).

Coniophanes fissidens (Günther). Plate 105.

Vernacular Names: *Garden snake* (?), yellow-bellied snake, culebra de panza-amarilla, tabaquilla.

Description: A small to medium-small snake with a long tail; total length approximately 790 mm (tail 26–41% of total length), although average size is appreciably smaller. Nasal scale divided; loreal single; preoculars 1 or 2, usually 1; postoculars 1 or 2, usually 2; supralabials 7–8; infralabials 9–10; dorsal scales smooth without apical pits, in 19–21 rows at midbody; ventrals 115–132; anal plate divided; subcaudals 63–88. Dorsum copper or rust brown with a narrow dark stripe (sometimes indistinct) extending the length of the fifth scale row and a row of dots coursing the length of the middorsal line; sometimes a secondary dark stripe on scale row 8; head with a faint, broken temporal stripe, and a black-margined pale stripe along the upper border of the supralabials,

PLATE 105 *Coniophanes fissidens.* Cuxta Bani, upper Raspaculo River, Cayo District.

extending for a short distance on the neck; supralabials uniformly stippled with gray. Venter cream medially grading to orange-tan laterally, lightly stippled with a row of darker spots on each side, usually one pair to a each abdominal scale.

Habitat: Evergreen broadleaf forest, subtropical evergreen forest, and broadleaf woodland along streams in highland pine savanna formations; terrestrial; 100 to 700 m.

Distribution: Southern Mexico to Colombia and Ecuador. In Belize it is known from Belize, Cayo, Stann Creek, and Toledo Districts; probably also occurs in Orange Walk District.

Similar Species: Other *Coniophanes: C. bipunctatus* has one or a double row of large dark, rounded spots on the outer edge of each ventral scale; *C. imperialis* and *C. schmidti* have a more boldly striped dorsal pattern with 19 and 23–25 midbody scale rows, respectively. *Dryadophis melanolomus* is similar in color but is a larger, more slender snake, with 17 dorsal scale rows at midbody and a pattern (absent or faint in adults) of crossbands rather than longitudinal stripes.

Remarks: Opisthoglyphous, although harmless to humans. A common snake of upland broadleaf forests, typically found along streams. The diet consists largely of frogs, although this species has also been known to consume salamanders, lizards, small snakes, reptile eggs and various invertebrates. Diurnal. Docile and not inclined to bite when handled. Caudal urotomy is common; tail breakage is non-specialized and limited to a single occurrence only. Oviparous.

Key Reference: Bailey (1939).

Coniophanes imperialis (Baird and Girard). Plate 106.

Vernacular Names: *Garden snake,* black-striped snake, culebra de raya-negra.

Description: A medium-small snake; total length approximately 550 mm. Nasal scale divided; loreal single; preoculars 1 or 2, usually 1; postoculars 2; supralabials 7 or 8 with the fourth and fifth entering the orbit; infralabials 8–10; dorsal scales smooth, without apical pits, in 19 rows at midbody; ventrals 114–121; anal plate divided; subcaudals 62–94. Dorsum brown, yellow-brown, or gray-brown with a continuous or broken, broad middorsal stripe, and a darker lateral band occupying three to five of the lowermost dorsal scale rows and the lateral edge of the venter. On the head there is a pale stripe extending from the tip of the snout to the temporal region that may be continuous with the light dorsolateral stripe on the body (separating the dark middorsal and lateral stripes),

PLATE 106   *Coniophanes imperialis.* Lamanai, Orange Walk District. Photograph by S. Von Peltz.

or more frequently, interrupted by a pale occipital spot. Venter pale anteriorly, grading to pinkish orange posteriorly.

Habitat: Evergreen broadleaf forest, semi-evergreen seasonal forest, karst hills forest, savanna highland pine savanna formations, gardens, and agricultural pasture; fossorial; sea level to 600 m.

Distribution: Southern United States to northern Honduras. In Belize it is found countrywide.

Similar Species: Other *Coniophanes: C. bipunctatus* and *C. fissidens* usually have 21 scale rows at midbody; *C. schmidti* has 23 to 25 scale rows at midbody. Another *Coniophanes* with an almost identical color pattern, *C. meridanus,* is known from more northern parts of the Yucatán Peninsula, and possibly occurs in the extreme north of Belize; this species is primarily distinguished in having 17 rows of dorsal scales at midbody (19 in *C. imperialis*). *Conophis lineatus* is a similarly striped snake but is larger and usually paler in coloration, with a higher ventral count (155–178) and dorsal scales usually in 17 rows at midbody. *Rhadinaea* is distinguished by having weakly keeled dorsal scales in 17 rows at midbody.

Remarks: Opisthoglyphous; generally harmless to humans, although bite may cause itching, burning, swelling, red discoloration, and muscular stiffness (Lee, 1996). A common species, frequently found among leaf litter, beneath or inside rotting tree trunks, in gardens, and occasionally on derelict ground in semi-urban areas. The diet includes insects, frogs, and lizards. Oviparous.

Key Reference: Bailey (1939).

Coniophanes schmidti Bailey. Plates 107, 108.

Vernacular Names: *Garden snake* (?), faded black-striped snake, culebra de rayas negras palida.

Description: A small- to medium-sized snake; total length approximately 570 mm. Scales: Nasal scale divided; loreal single; preoculars 1 or 2, usually 2; postoculars 2; supralabials 7–8, with third and fourth or fourth and fifth entering orbit; infralabials 9–10; dorsal scales smooth, without apical pits, in 23–25 rows at midbody; adult males with anal ridges; ventrals 153–174; anal plate divided; subcaudals 78–115. Dorsum cream with a broad blackish brown to black medial band (approximately 5 scales wide) and narrower (1/2 to 1 1/2 scale rows wide) lateral stripe that may fade posteriorly into the ground color, and below which the brown-shaded sides become lighter toward the venter; the pale dorsolateral stripes either side of the dark medial stripe may terminate anteriorly in a pale nape spot. Venter cream to pale orange-brown, lightly spotted or not with brown.

PLATE 107 *Coniophanes schmidti.* Sarteneja, Corozal District. Photograph by P. Edgar.

PLATE 108 *Coniophanes schmidti.* Fallen Stones, Toledo District. Photograph by S. Von Peltz.

Habitat: Open clearings in evergreen broadleaf forest, and highland pine savanna formations; terrestrial; sea level to 600 m.

Distribution: Southeastern Mexico to northern Guatemala and Belize. In Belize it has been confirmed from Cayo and Toledo Districts; probably also occurs in Stann Creek District.

Similar Species: Other *Coniophanes: C. bipunctatus* and *C. fissidens* usually have 21 scale rows at midbody and a less conspicuous pattern of stripes; *C. imperialis* has 19 scale rows at midbody. The striped form of *Conophis lineatus* is similar in appearance but is larger with dorsal scales usually in 17 rows at midbody.

Remarks: Opisthoglyphous, although presumed to be harmless to humans. A little known species in Belize. Purportedly nocturnal in habits. Oviparous. Neill and Allen (1960) reported on a specimen from Augustine (Douglas D'Silva), Cayo District, that exhibited features intermediate with *C. piceivittis* Cope, of which *C. schmidti* has sometimes been treated as a subspecific form.

Key Reference: Harrison (1993).

Conophis lineatus (Duméril, Bibron & Duméril). Plate 109.
Vernacular Names: Road guarder, many-lined snake, guardia camino.

PLATE 109 *Conophis lineatus.* Striped variant. Volcán Orosí, Cordillera de Guanacaste, Costa Rica.

Description: A medium-sized snake with a moderately long tail; total length approximately 1170 mm (tail more than 20% of body length). Head not distinctly wider than neck. Nasal scale divided; loreal single; preoculars 1; postoculars 2 or 3, usually 2; supralabials 7 or 8, with third and fourth, or fourth and fifth, entering orbit; infralabials 8–11, usually 9 or 10; dorsal scales smooth, without apical pits, in 19 rows at midbody; ventrals 155–178; anal plate divided; subcaudals 56–80. In Belize the species occurs in two color forms: dorsum pale brown, pale olive, or grayish white with 8–13 (usually 8–10) dark brown or black dorsal and lateral stripes; head with 3 dark stripes, 1 medially, and 1 on each side, passing through the eye and continuing posteriorly as a lateral stripe on scale rows 3 and 4; venter white or pale yellow with dark spots on the lateral edges; or dorsum uniformly pale brown or yellowish gray, sometimes with a longitudinal series of small dark spots on the scale tips of rows 4 or 7; head stripes extending only onto neck; venter immaculate.

Habitat: Semi-evergreen seasonal forest, savanna, and highland pine savanna formations; terrestrial; sea level to 600 m.

Distribution: Southern Mexico to Costa Rica. In Belize it is known from Corozal, Belize, and Cayo Districts; possibly also occurs in northern parts of Orange Walk District.

Similar Species: *Coniophanes imperialis* is a similarly striped snake but is smaller and usually darker in coloration, with a lower ventral count (114–121); *Coniophanes schmidti* has significantly fewer stripes, a conspicuous broad medial band, and dorsal scales in 23–25 rows at midbody.

Remarks: Opisthoglyphous, with relatively large rear fangs; venom may produce burning pain, bleeding, swelling, and other symptoms of poisoning in humans. Aggressive and bites constantly when handled. Alert and fast-moving. Prey consists mostly of lizards, especially *Cnemidophorus* spp., and small snakes. The popular vernacular name "road guarder" alludes to the snake's habit of patrolling roadside verges in search of prey. Diurnal. Oviparous. Pale, unicolor snakes with stripes only on the head and neck occur mostly in the north of Belize and, if the subspecies system is applied, may be referred to *C. l. concolor* Cope; snakes with a pattern of regular stripes extending the length of the body, typically found in the Mountain Pine Ridge area, are assignable to *C. l. dunni* Smith.

Key Reference: Wellman (1963).

Key to the Species of *Dendrophidion* in Belize

Dorsum brownish and conspicuously banded, at least anteriorly; subcaudal scales 111–128; anal plate entire . . . . *D. vinitor*

Dorsum not as above; subcaudal scales 140–160; anal plate usually divided . . . . *D. nuchale*

Dendrophidion nuchale (W. Peters). Plates 110, 111, 112.

Vernacular Names: Pink-tailed forest racer.

Description: A medium-large, slender snake; maximum total length approximately 1650 mm. The eyes are conspicuously large with round pupils. Nasal scale divided; loreal single; preoculars 1; postoculars 2 or 3; supralabials 9 or 10; infralabials 9–12, usually 10; dorsal scales strongly keeled (outer row more weakly keeled), with 2 apical pits, in 17 rows at midbody; ventrals 160–175; anal plate entire or indistinctly divided; subcaudals 140–160. Dorsum olive green, gray-green, or leaf green anteriorly (interstitial skin pale blue) with a series of inconspicuous dark-edged, pale crossbands, changing posteriorly to velvety black or grayish brown with black crossbands enclosing pale ocelli; head rust brown or reddish with pale upper lip; tail coral red to dark purplish brown. Venter white, grading to pinkish posteriorly and usually with darker pigment on the medial edge of the posterior ventral scales.

Habitat: Evergreen broadleaf forest formation, possibly also subtropical evergreen forest formation, citrus orchard; terrestrial; 200 to 700 m.

Distribution: Guatemala, Belize, and northern Honduras, and from Costa Rica to Colombia, Ecuador, and Venezuela. In Belize it is known from Cayo, Stann Creek, and Toledo Districts.

Similar Species: *Dendrophidion vinitor* is a smaller species with a brownish dorsum that is more conspicuously banded, at least anteriorly. The tail is also shorter than in *D. nuchale,* with fewer subcaudal scales

PLATE 110   Adult *Dendrophidion nuchale.* Cuxta Bani, upper Raspaculo River, Cayo District.

197

PLATE 111 Head of adult *Dendrophidion nuchale,* showing detail of scalation. Cuxta Bani, upper Raspaculo River, Cayo District.

PLATE 112 Juvenile *Dendrophidion nuchale.* Cuxta Bani, upper Raspaculo River, Cayo District.

(111–128 vs. 140–160), and bears a narrow, dark lateral stripe. In *D. vinitor* the anal plate is almost always entire (usually divided in *D. nuchale*) and the outer row of dorsal scales is smooth (keeled in *D. nuchale*). *Drymobius* is similar in form and also has keeled dorsal scales in 17 rows at midbody, but may be distinguished by its greenish head, yellow-spotted dorsal pattern, and fewer number of ventral scales (137–158 vs. 160–175) and subcaudals (103–138 vs. 140–160).

Remarks: An agile, strikingly colored species. Specimens found by the authors have been observed basking on fallen vines and in patches of sunlight among leaves on the forest floor, especially in the morning following a night of rain. When hunting or alarmed, the head and forebody may be lifted high off the ground. Stomach contents of preserved specimens have included frogs. Diurnal. Oviparous. In some previous herpetological literature on Belize this species has appeared under the name *Dendrophidion clarki.*

Key Reference: Lieb (1988).

Dendrophidion vinitor Smith. Fig. 23; Plate 113.

Vernacular Names: Barred forest racer, sabanerita.

Description: A medium-sized, slender snake; maximum total length approximately 1100 mm. The eyes are conspicuously large with round pupils. Nasal scale divided; loreal single; preoculars 1; postoculars 2; supralabials 9 or 10; infralabials 9–11; dorsal scales strongly keeled (except outer row), with 2 apical pits, in 17 rows at midbody; ventrals 148–165; anal plate entire; subcaudals 111–128. Dorsal surface of body and tail reddish brown or gray with multiple narrow (1–2 scales wide), dark-edged pale crossbands that gradually become indistinct posteriorly

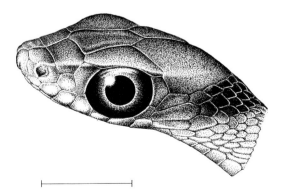

FIGURE 23 Head of juvenile *Dendrophidion vinitor* in dorsolateral view. Volcán Orosí, Cordillera de Guanacaste, Costa Rica. Scale bar = 1 cm.

PLATE 113 Juvenile *Dendrophidion vinitor*. Volcán Orosí, Cordillera de Guanacaste, Costa Rica.

(most pronounced in adults); head brownish gray, contrasting with white supralabials; on the tail there is a narrow lateral stripe of dark brown involving the upper edges of the subcaudals and lower half of the outer scale rows. Venter yellowish white, the lateral margins suffused with darker pigment posteriorly.

Habitat: Subtropical evergreen forest formation; possibly also evergreen broadleaf forest formation; terrestrial; recorded only from approximately 700 to 800 m.

Distribution: Southern Mexico to eastern Panama and adjacent Colombia. In Belize it is known only from Toledo District.

Similar Species: *Dendrophidion nuchale* is a larger species with a rust brown head that contrasts sharply with the greenish neck and blackish color of the lower dorsum. The tail is also longer than in *D. vinitor*, with more numerous subcaudal scales (140–160 vs. 111–128), and is uniform dark pink without a lateral stripe. In *D. nuchale* the anal plate is usually divided and the outer row of dorsal scales is usually keeled. *Dryadophis* and *Drymobius* are similar in form and also have dorsal scales in 17 rows at midbody; in *Dryadophis* the dorsal scales are smooth and the anal plate is divided; *Drymobius* also has keeled dorsal scales but may be distinguished by its greenish, yellow-spotted dorsal pattern and divided anal plate.

Remarks: An agile, little known species recently recorded in the Little Quartz Ridge area (Julian Lee and Jan Meerman, in litt.); earlier re-

ports of *D. vinitor* in Belize were based on specimens later confirmed to be *D. nuchale* by Lieb (1988). When hunting or alarmed, the head and forebody may be lifted high off the ground. Diurnal. Oviparous.
Key Reference: Smith (1941b).

Dipsas brevifacies (Cope). Plate 114.
Vernacular Names: Snail-eating thirst snake, culebra de sed.
Description: A small to very small snake with a strongly laterally compressed body; maximum total length approximately 510 mm. Head short and blunt, without a mental groove, distinctly wider than neck; eye with vertical pupil and completely black. Nasal scale divided; loreal single, entering orbit; preoculars 0–3; postoculars 3; supralabials 9–10, usually 9, with fourth and fifth entering orbit; infralabials 9–14; dorsal scales smooth, without apical pits, in 15 rows at midbody; ventrals 166–176; anal plate entire; subcaudals 69–100. Dorsum and venter white, yellowish, or pinkish orange with 10–16 dark brown to glossy black, complete rings around the body, and 5–11 on the tail. Head black with a pale yellowish or reddish nuchal band and a black chin.

PLATE 114 Juvenile *Dipsas brevifacies*. Sarteneja, Corozal District. Photograph by P. Edgar.

201

Habitat: Oak hammocks in savanna formation and possibly semi-evergreen seasonal forest formation; arboreal; sea level to 100 m.

Distribution: Yucatán Peninsula region of Mexico and Belize. In Belize it is known from Corozal and Belize Districts, and also possibly occurs in Orange Walk District.

Similar Species: Arboreal *Sibon* species (*S. dimidiata, S. nebulata, S. sanniola*) are similar in form but none have markings that completely encircle the body; these species also have a distinct mental groove. *Sibon sartorii* has a similar color pattern of alternating dark and light bands, but is a terrestrial species with dorsal scales in 17 rows at midbody. *Imantodes* has a mental groove and is considerably more elongate with a higher ventral count (228–261).

Remarks: A small snake with specially adapted teeth for extracting snails from their shells. Prey is chiefly molluskan but may also feed on other soft-bodied invertebrates. Usually observed foraging in understory vegetation and may also be found in bromeliads and other epiphytic growth. Neill and Allen (1960) reported a specimen found beneath an orchid growing on the bark of an oak about a foot off the ground. Nocturnal. Oviparous.

Key Reference: Peters (1960).

Dryadophis melanolomus (Cope). Plates 115, 116.

Vernacular Names: Lizard eater, dryad snake, lagartijera.

Description: A slender, medium-sized snake; total length approximately 1100 mm. The head is moderately distinct from the neck and the eyes are large. Nasal scale divided; loreal single; preoculars 1 or 2, usually 1; postoculars 2; supralabials 8–10, with fourth, fifth, and sixth entering orbit; infralabials 8–11; dorsal scales smooth, with 2 apical pits, in 17 rows at midbody; ventrals 163–195; anal plate divided; subcaudals 85–136. Coloration variable. Dorsum of adults dark brown, olive brown, or copper brown, with a suggestion of narrow pale crossbands anteriorly, replaced by a pattern of faint, darker stripes posteriorly; in juveniles the banding patterning is appreciably bolder and more extensive. Venter whitish yellow anteriorly grading to orange-tan or pinkish posteriorly, immaculate or with heavy black mottling on the infralabials, chin, and throat.

Habitat: Evergreen broadleaf forest, semi-evergreen seasonal forest, karst hills forest, savanna, and highland pine savanna formations; terrestrial; 50 to 800 m.

Distribution: Central Mexico to Panama. In Belize it is found countrywide.

Similar Species: *Coluber constrictor* is a similar racer-like species but has an olive brown, grayish, greenish brown, or bluish gray dorsum and a

PLATE 115 *Dryadophis melanolomus.* Las Cuevas, Chiquibul Forest, Cayo District.

PLATE 116 *Dryadophis melanolomus.* Slate Creek, Cayo District.

small subocular scale below the preocular. *Dendrophidion vinitor* is also similar in form and color pattern but may be distinguished by its keeled dorsal scales and entire anal plate. *Coniophanes fissidens* bears a superficial resemblance but is stouter with 19–21 scale rows at midbody and a pattern of continuous longitudinal stripes rather than faint crossbands anteriorly.

Remarks: An alert, fast-moving, and highly agile snake. Diurnal. Often observed basking in patches of sunlight on the forest floor or at the edge of jungle trails. In many upland forested areas *Dryadophis* is the most commonly seen snake during the dry season. Largely saurophagus in feeding habits. May lift its head and anterior part of the body when hunting or alarmed. Harmless although may bite when handled. Oviparous. This species is also known under the generic name of *Mastigodryas*.

Key Reference: Stuart (1939).

Drymarchon corais (Boie). Plate 117.

Vernacular Names: *Black tail,* cribo, black-tailed indigo snake, culebra arroyera, palancacoate.

Description: A very large, robust snake, potentially reaching lengths in excess of 2950 mm. Nasal scale single; loreal single; preoculars 1; pos-

PLATE 117   Adult *Drymarchon corais*. Hidden Valley, Cayo District. Photograph by C.M. Miller.

toculars 2; supralabials 7–9; infralabials 8; dorsal scales smooth with 2 apical pits, in 17 rows at midbody; ventrals 182–217; anal plate entire; subcaudals 55–88. Dorsum pale brown, olive brown, or grayish, grading posteriorly to dark gray or black on the tail, typically with a dark diagonal stripe on the side of the neck and upper body; the sutures of the posterior supralabials and corresponding infralabials are outlined with dark pigment. Venter pale yellow and dark gray beneath the tail.

Habitat: Evergreen broadleaf forest, semi-evergreen seasonal forest, karst hills forest, savanna, highland pine savanna, and coastal lagoons and marshes formations; terrestrial; sea level to 700 m.

Distribution: Southeastern United States to northern Argentina. In Belize it occurs countrywide.

Similar Species: *Dryadophis* is similar in color but is a smaller, more slender species with little or no trace of dark pigment on the labial sutures. *Dryadophis* also has a divided anal scale (entire in *Drymarchon*).

Remarks: A large, agile, opportunistic snake, feeding on a wide variety of animals though habitually ophiophagous, predating on other snakes often as large as itself. Once captured, prey is rapidly subdued by swallowing. Chiefly diurnal. Males are known to engage in ritual combat dances, battling for supremacy by rearing up and pushing against each other until the weaker contestant is forced to the ground. Snakes from northern Central America, including Belize, have been assigned to the subspecies *D. c. melanurus* (Duméril, Bibron, and Duméril).

Key Reference: Smith (1941a).

Drymobius margaritiferus (Schlegel). Plate 118.

Vernacular Names: *Guinea hen snake, blue tail,* speckled racer, petatilla.

Description: A medium-large snake; total length approximately 1340 mm. The head is moderately distinct from the neck and the eyes are large. Nasal scale divided; loreal single; preoculars 1; postoculars 2; supralabials 8–10, with fourth, fifth, and sixth entering orbit; infralabials 9–12; dorsal scales keeled with 2 apical pits, in 17 rows at midbody; ventrals 137–158; anal plate divided; subcaudals 103–138. Dorsum green to bluish green changing to orange-brown posteriorly, each scale with a pale yellow or orange spot edged posteriorly with black; head greenish brown above with a black temporal stripe extending from the posterior supralabials and forming an inverted V-shaped mark on the nape. Venter pale green with black edging on the lateral edge of the ventral and subcaudal scales.

Habitat: Near water in evergreen broadleaf forest, semi-evergreen seasonal forest, karst hills forest, savanna, highland pine savanna, and possibly

PLATE 118 *Drymobius margaritiferus*. Cuxta Bani, upper Raspaculo River, Cayo District.

subtropical evergreen forest formations; also interior wetlands and coastal lagoons and marshes formations, and agricultural pasture; terrestrial and semiaquatic; sea level to 600 m.

Distribution: Southern United States to northern Colombia. In Belize it occurs countrywide.

Similar Species: The two species of *Dendrophidion* are similar in form and also have keeled dorsal scales in 17 rows at midbody; *D. nuchale* may be distinguished by its rust-colored head and pinkish tail, and in having a higher number of ventral scales (160–175 vs. 137–158) and subcaudals (140–160 vs. 103–138); *D. vinitor* has a distinctive pattern of dark-edged, pale crossbands, at least anteriorly, and a brown head with contrasting white supralabial scales.

Remarks: A colorful and ornately patterned snake, which may appear uniformly brown when moving at speed. Opisthoglyphous, although bite appears toxic only to frogs, its principal food; bites in humans, however, may bleed excessively due to the presence of an anticoagulant in the saliva. Agile and fast-moving; when hunting or alarmed may lift the head and forebody off the ground. Diurnal. A rather common species typically observed in or near water. Oviparous.

Key Reference: Wilson and Meyer (1985).

Elaphe flavirufa (Cope). Plates 119, 120.

Vernacular Names: Night snake, tropical rat snake, ratonera tropical.

Description: A medium-large snake; total length approximately 1650 mm. Head distinctly wider than neck; eye with conspicuously small pupil. Nasal scale divided; loreal single; preoculars 1 or 2; postoculars 2; supralabials 8–10, usually 9, with fourth, fifth, and sixth entering orbit; infralabials 12–15, usually 12 or 13; dorsal scales smooth to about row 7, the remainder lightly keeled, in 27–34 rows at midbody; ventrals 245–269; anal plate divided; subcaudals 96–122. Dorsum yellowish tan to gray with 29–46 brick red or reddish brown middorsal blotches, each outlined with dark brown or black and yellowish cream, sometimes fused posteriorly into a zig–zag-like stripe; a series of smaller lateral and ventrolateral blotches is also present. Head light olive-brown or yellowish above with dark medial blotches on the frontal and parietal scales, and additional dark spotting. Venter creamish with occasional gray or pale brown square-shaped blotches.

Habitat: Evergreen broadleaf forest, semi-evergreen seasonal forest, and highland pine savanna formations; terrestrial and arboreal; sea level to 600.

Distribution: Southern Mexico to northern Honduras. Also occurs on the Corn Islands, Nicaragua. In Belize it is known from Corozal, Orange

PLATE 119   Adult *Elaphe flavirufa*. Chichén Itzá, Yucatán, Mexico. Photograph by J.R. McCranie.

PLATE 120 Juvenile *Elaphe flavirufa*. Izabal, Guatemala. Photograph by J.A. Campbell, courtesy of the University of Texas at Arlington.

Walk, Cayo, Stann Creek, and Toledo Districts, and probably occurs countrywide.

Similar Species: Juvenile specimens of *Senticolis* are similar in color pattern, but may be distinguished by their more elongate head, and in having smaller eyes.

Remarks: An uncommon and elusive snake, most likely to be observed foraging on the forest floor, although it also inhabits trees and bushes. The diet consists largely of small mammals and perhaps birds. Nocturnal; the species is an active forager and predates largely on small mammals, nestling birds, and perhaps lizards sleeping in vegetation at night. Oviparous.

Key Reference: Dowling (1952).

Ficimia publia Cope. Plate 121.

Vernacular Names: *Barber pole,* blotched hook-nosed snake, culebra de naricilla manchada.

PLATE 121 *Ficimia publia.* Gallon Jug, Orange Walk District. Photograph by C.M. Miller.

Description: A small, moderately stout, cylindrical snake; total length approximately 460 mm. Head not distinct from neck and with a projecting, upturned, pointed snout; eye small. Rostral scale large, upturned and in contact with frontal; nasal divided or entire; loreal absent; preoculars 1; postoculars 1; supralabials 7, with third and fourth entering orbit; infralabials 5–8, usually 7 or 8; dorsal scales smooth, with a single apical pit, in 17 rows at midbody; ventrals 127–157; anal plate divided; subcaudals 26–44. Dorsum yellowish, pale brown, or grayish, with a series of 28–46 transverse, light-centered blotches (2–4 scales wide), disintegrating on the sides into smaller, angular spots that reach the edge of the ventrals. Head light brown or grayish above with symmetrical darker spots on parietals, frontal and rostral, and often a dark spot below the eye. Venter whitish.

Habitat: Evergreen broadleaf forest and semi-evergreen seasonal forest formations, and agricultural land; terrestrial and fossorial; sea level to 200 m.

Distribution: Southern Mexico to Guatemala and Honduras. In Belize it is known from Corozal, Orange Walk, Cayo, Stann Creek, and Toledo Districts, and probably occurs countrywide.

Similar Species: *Porthidium nasutum* has a similar projecting, upturned snout, but has a vertically elliptic pupil, keeled dorsal scales, and a markedly different color pattern.

209

Remarks: A burrowing, little-known invertebrate-eating snake with a docile temperament. Usually encountered at night foraging for spiders and centipedes on the forest floor, especially after rain, although it may occasionally be observed by day. The species appears to be most common in the drier forests of northern Belize, and may not occur in the wetter forests of southern parts. Oviparous.

Key Reference: Hardy (1975).

Imantodes cenchoa (Linnaeus). Plate 122.

Vernacular Names: Blunt-headed tree snake, cordelilla manchada.

Description: A medium-sized, exceedingly slender snake with a laterally compressed body and long tail; maximum total length approximately 1110 mm, although usually less than 800 mm. Head swollen and rounded, distinctly wider than neck; eye large and bulging with a vertical pupil. Nasal scale divided below naris; loreal single; preoculars 1 or 2,

PLATE 122 *Imantodes cenchoa.* Fallen Stones, Toledo District. Photograph by S. Von Peltz.

usually 1; postoculars 1–3, usually 2; supralabials 7–9 with 2 or 3 entering orbit; infralabials 9–12; dorsal scales smooth without apical pits,
usually in 17 rows throughout with vertebral row conspicuously
enlarged; ventrals 228–261; anal plate divided; subcaudals 134–178. The
dorsum is pale brown or grayish with approximately 30–45 dark brown
crossbands; ventrally the coloration is dull white with brownish flecks.

Habitat: Evergreen broadleaf forest, semi-evergreen seasonal forest, karst
hills forest, subtropical evergreen forest, and highland pine savanna formations, and fruit orchards; arboreal; sea level to 700 m.

Distribution: Central Mexico to Argentina and Paraguay. In Belize it
occurs countrywide.

Similar Species: The snail-eating species *Dipsas brevifacies, Sibon
dimidiata, S. nebulata,* and *S. sanniola* are superficially similar in form
and color pattern, but have dorsal scales generally in 15 rows and are less
elongate with fewer ventrals (maximum of 200). *Dipsas* also lacks a
mental groove. The two species of *Leptodeira* have 21 or 23 rows of dorsal scales at midbody and appreciably fewer ventrals and subcaudals.
Two other species of blunt-headed tree snakes, *I. gemmistratus* and *I.
tenuissimus,* known from wider afield in the Yucatán Peninsula, are
potentially to be found in Belize; neither of these have an enlarged vertebral scale row.

Remarks: Opisthoglyphous, although docile by nature and harmless to
humans. Nocturnal. A slow-moving snake, typically observed at night
draped over low vegetation, although may occasionally be found on the
ground. The diet includes small lizards, frogs, and occasionally reptile
eggs. Oviparous.

Key Reference: Wilson and Meyer (1985).

Lampropeltis triangulum (Lacépède). Plate 123.

Vernacular Names: *Coral, bead-and-coral,* tropical kingsnake, milk snake,
and probably other local names applied generally to coral snake look-a-
likes; falsa corallila.

Description: A medium to large snake; total length approximately 1490
mm. Head not distinctly wider than neck. Nasal scale divided; loreal single; preoculars normally 1; postoculars 1–2; supralabials 7–8, usually 7;
infralabials 8–9, usually 9; dorsal scales smooth, with apical pits, in 21
or 23 rows; ventrals 215–235; anal plate entire; subcaudals 50–65.
Dorsum and venter (including tail) patterned with alternating tricolored
rings, involving the following sequence (posteriorly from nape): whitish
or yellow, black, bright red, black, all more or less complete ventrally;
red body rings typically 16–22, ranging from 2 to 11 scales in length
(except first ring), scales of red areas usually darkened toward the tip;

211

SNAKES

PLATE 123 *Lampropeltis triangulum.* Sarteneja, Corozal District. Photograph by P. Edgar.

black rings ranging from 1 1/2 to 4 scales in length (except first ring), normally expanded middorsally; whitish rings ranging from 1/2 to 2 scales in length, often obscured by black pigment. Head black with a transverse, narrow white band crossing the snout; chin and mental region black.

Habitat: Evergreen broadleaf forest, semi-evergreen seasonal forest, karst hills forest, possibly subtropical evergreen forest, savanna, and highland pine savanna formations, also agricultural land; terrestrial; sea level to 600 m.

Distribution: Southern Canada to Colombia, Ecuador, and Venezuela. In Belize it occurs countrywide.

Similar Species: The true coral snakes (genus *Micrurus*) have fewer dorsal rows (15 vs 21 or 23 in *Lampropeltis*), and the colored rings are arranged in a different sequence (red next to yellow as opposed to red next to black). *Lampropeltis* also has red pigmentation on the tail (tails of *Micrurus* spp. in Belize are banded with black and yellow only) and a loreal scale. *Urotheca elapoides* is a similar tricolored species but with red bands next to yellow (as in *Micrurus*) rather than red next to black; *Urotheca* also has 17 rows of dorsal scales throughout. *Oxyrhopus petola* is a red and black banded snake (no yellow bands except for a pale nuchal collar) with dorsal scales in 19 rows at midbody; in *Oxyrhopus* the pupil of the eye is also vertically elliptic (circular in *Lampropeltis*).

Sibon sartorii is also banded with red and black only, and has dorsal scales that are weakly keeled in 17 rows throughout.

Remarks: A wide-ranging, highly variable species occurring in some 25 subspecific forms; adult size varies geographically from 500 mm in southeastern United States to almost 2000 mm in Central America. Nocturnal and diurnal. When alarmed typically seeks refuge underground in holes or rodent burrows. Diet consists largely of other snakes, as well as amphibians, lizards, and small mammals. Oviparous.

Key Reference: Williams (1988).

Key to the Species of *Leptodeira* in Belize

A distinct dark postorbital stripe connecting with the first dark body blotch; body blotches moderately large, extending nearly to venter; nape usually without short longitudinal stripe . . . . *L. frenata*

No postorbital stripe; body blotches small, not extending below scale row 7; nape stripe usually present . . . . *L. septentrionalis*

Leptodeira frenata (Cope). Plates 124, 125.

Vernacular Names: *Cohune ridge tommygoff,* rain forest cat-eyed snake, escombrera de selva.

PLATE 124 *Leptodeira frenata.* Shipstern Nature Reserve, Corozal District. Photograph by P. Edgar.

PLATE 125 *Leptodeira frenata.* Belize District. Photograph by C.M. Miller.

Description: A medium-small, slender snake; total length approximately 720 mm. Head broad and flat, distinctly wider than neck; eye with vertical pupil. Nasal scale divided; loreal single; preoculars 2; postoculars 1–3, usually 2; supralabials 8, with fourth and fifth entering orbit; infralabials 9–11; dorsal scales smooth, with 2 apical pits, in 21 or 23 rows at midbody; ventrals 170–192; anal plate divided; subcaudals 61–86. Dorsum cream, pinkish, or light tan to gray-brown with 26–39 dark to medium brown vertebral blotches that are typically outlined with darker brown or black and extend nearly to venter. A series of dark brown lateral intercalary spots extend from the ventrals onto the second or third scale rows, and a further row of irregular small brown dots may be present along the ventral edge. Head grayish brown with one or two dark blotches on parietals, a short nape stripe and a postorbital stripe extending to and connecting with the first body blotch. Venter cream, light tan, or rosy pink.

Habitat: Evergreen broadleaf forest, semi-evergreen seasonal forest, and oak hammocks in savanna formations, agricultural land, and edificarian; terrestrial and arboreal; sea level to 300 m.

Distribution: Southern Mexico to northern Guatemala and Belize. In Belize it occurs in all districts, although may be absent from southern Toledo.

Similar Species: *L. septentrionalis* has generally more than 190 ventral scales, lacks an extended postorbital stripe, and also differs in its smaller and more numerous dorsal spots. *Imantodes cenchoa* is a longer, more slender snake with dorsal scales in 17 rows throughout and more numerous ventrals (228–261) and subcaudals (134–178).

Remarks: Opisthoglyphous but harmless to humans. Placid by nature and seldom attempts to bite, although may flatten the head and body if alarmed. Nocturnal. The species is particularly common in the savannas and broadleaf forests of northern Belize (Edgar, 1997), and is frequently found in bromeliads, beneath bark, and near water; Lee (1996) reports finding a specimen beneath driftwood on a beach. Oviparous.

Key Reference: Duellman (1958).

Leptodeira septentrionalis (Kennicott). Plates 126, 127.

Vernacular Names: *Cohune ridge tommygoff,* Central American cat-eyed snake, culebra desteñida Centro Americana.

Description: A medium-sized, slightly laterally compressed, slender snake; total length in the region of 1055 mm. Head broad and flat, distinctly wider than neck; eye with vertical pupil. Nasal scale divided; loreal single; preoculars 1–3; postoculars 1–3, usually 2; supralabials 7–9

PLATE 126   *Leptodeira septentrionalis.* Belize District. Photograph by S. Von Peltz.

PLATE 127 *Leptodeira septentrionalis.* Smokey River Camp, Chiquibul Forest, Cayo District.

with fourth and fifth entering orbit; infralabials 9–12, usually 10; dorsal scales smooth, in 21–23 rows at midbody, with 2 apical pits; vertebral and paravertebral scale rows sometimes slightly enlarged; ventrals 170–211; anal plate divided; subcaudals 60–107. Dorsum pale yellowish or reddish tan to grayish brown with a series of 20–70 small dark brown or black vertebral blotches extending laterally to scale rows 5 or 7; small lateral intercalary spots present or not. Head brown with irregular spotting on the frontal and parietals, a short nape stripe and a faint postorbital stripe that does not connect with the first body blotch. Venter cream to pale orange with darker flecking.

Habitat: Evergreen broadleaf forest, semi-evergreen seasonal forest, karst hills forest, and highland pine savanna formations, possibly interior wetlands formation, citrus orchards, and edificarian; arboreal and semiterrestrial; sea level to 650 m.

Distribution: Southern United States to Brazil and Peru. In Belize it occurs countrywide.

Similar Species: *L. frenata* has generally fewer than 190 ventral scales, a bold postorbital stripe extending to the first dark body blotch, and is also distinguished by its larger, less numerous body blotches that extend nearly to the venter. *Imantodes cenchoa* is a longer, more slender snake with dorsal scales in 17 rows throughout and more numerous ventrals (228–261) and subcaudals (134–178).

Remarks: Opisthoglyphous but harmless to humans. A rather delicate and inoffensive snake, though may flatten its head in a threatening manner if molested. Often found in the leaf bases of banana, plantain and palm trees, in bromeliads, or foraging at the edges of ponds. Diet includes small lizards and frogs. The species is known to feed on the egg masses of leaf-breeding frogs such as those of the genus *Agalychnis,* and may also be attracted by the breeding choruses of frogs. Nocturnal. Oviparous.

Key Reference: Duellman (1958).

Key to the Species of *Leptophis* in Belize

Loreal scale absent. . . . . *L. ahaetulla*

Loreal scale present . . . . *L. mexicanus*

Leptophis ahaetulla (Linnaeus). Plate 128.
Vernacular Names: *Tamagas,* green parrot snake, ranera verde.

PLATE 128 Adult *Leptophis ahaetulla.* Smokey River Camp, Chiquibul Forest, Cayo District.

Description: A long, slender snake; total length exceeding 2240 mm. Head distinctly wider then neck. Nasal scale divided; loreal absent; preoculars 1–2, usually 1; postoculars 1–4, usually 2; supralabials 7–10, usually 8, with the fourth and fifth entering orbit; infralabials 7–12, usually 10; dorsal scales keeled (except outermost and middorsal rows) with a single apical pit, in 15 rows at midbody; ventrals 147–183; anal plate divided; subcaudals 137–185. Dorsum bright green (interstitial skin yellowish), uniform or with the keels of some scale rows on the posterior part of the body marked with black forming distinct paravertebral and less distinct lateral stripes; head same color as the body with or without a dark postocular stripe; iris of eye yellow. Venter pale green, immaculate.

Habitat: River banks and clearings in evergreen broadleaf forest, semi-evergreen seasonal forest, karst hills forest, possibly subtropical evergreen forest, highland pine savanna formations, oak hammocks in savanna formation, fruit orchards, and banana groves; arboreal; sea level to 600 m.

Distribution: Southern Mexico to Brazil and Argentina. In Belize it is known from Orange Walk, Belize, Cayo, Stann Creek, and Toledo Districts, and possibly occurs countrywide.

Similar Species: *Leptophis mexicanus* has a loreal scale (absent in *L. ahaetulla*), and mainland populations have a distinct bronze-colored medial stripe on the dorsum. *Oxybelis fulgidus* is a similar green-colored tree snake, but can be readily distinguished by its elongate head and sharply pointed snout (blunt and square-shaped in *Leptophis*).

Remarks: Opisthoglyphous; envenomation may produce local pain and other symptoms of mild poisoning in humans. Temperamental and inclined to bite. Strikes repeatedly and holds mouth agape in an intimidating threat display when provoked. Unlikely to be found in dark, closed canopy forest, preferring woodland edge or riparian habitats. Diurnal. Feeds largely on frogs. Oviparous.

Key Reference: Wilson and Meyer (1985).

Leptophis mexicanus Duméril, Bibron, and Duméril. Plates 129, 130, 131.

Vernacular Names: *Green head,* Mexican parrot snake, ranera bronceada.

Description: A medium to large, slender snake; maximum total length approximately 1720 mm. Head distinctly wider than neck. Nasal scale divided; loreal single; preoculars 1 or 2; postoculars 1–3, usually 2; supralabials 8 or 9, usually 8, with fourth and fifth entering orbit; infralabials 9–11, usually 10; dorsal scales keeled (except for outermost row), with a single apical pit, usually in 15 rows at midbody; ventrals 145–183; anal plate divided; subcaudals 140–177. Two distinct color forms are known from Belize. An isolated population found only on the Turneffe

PLATE 129 *Leptophis mexicanus.* Fallen Stones, Toledo District. Photograph by S. Von Peltz.

PLATE 130 *Leptophis mexicanus.* Calabash Caye, Turneffe Islands.

PLATE 131   An axanthic blue *Leptophis mexicanus* from Calabash Caye, Turneffe Islands.

island group is uniformly bright emerald green or bluish, with a faint indication of a dark stripe on the head extending from behind the eye to the temporal region. Snakes from the mainland are also green but with a bronze medial stripe, a dark lateral stripe on rows 2 through 5 or 6, and with each dorsal scale outlined in black; the head is green above (often bluish in snakes from northern parts) with whitish supralabials tinged with yellow; venter white anteriorly grading to light grayish tan.

Habitat: Evergreen broadleaf forest, semi-evergreen seasonal forest, karst hills forest, oak hammocks in savanna formation, highland pine savanna, coastal lagoons and marshes, and sand strand and cocotal formations, citrus orchard, banana groves, gardens, and edificarian situations; arboreal and terrestrial; sea level to 700 m.

Distribution: Central Mexico to Costa Rica. In Belize it occurs countrywide, including Ambergris Caye and the Turneffe Islands.

Similar Species: *L. ahaetulla* is similar in form and color pattern to the uniformly green population of *L. mexicanus* on the Turneffe group of islands, but lacks a loreal scale (present in *L. mexicanus*).

Remarks: Opisthoglyphous; envenomation may produce local pain and other symptoms of mild poisoning in humans. On mainland Belize the species feeds largely on frogs; the Turneffe population has been

observed actively pursuing *Norops sagrei* on the beaches of Caye Bokel [Hoevers and Henderson (1974) as *Leptophis modestus*] and is presumed to subsist chiefly on a diet of these lizards. Diurnal. Oviparous. The unicolor snakes of Turneffe have been distinguished as an endemic subspecies, *L. m. hoeversi* (Henderson, 1976b); the mainland form is assignable to the nominate subspecies, *L. m. mexicanus* (Duméril, Bibron, and Duméril).
Key Reference: Wilson and Meyer (1985).

Masticophis mentovarius (Duméril, Bibron, and Duméril). Plate 132.
Vernacular Names: Central American coachwhip, tropical whipsnake, chirrionera sabanera.
Description: A very large snake; total length exceeding 2000 mm. Nasal scale divided or entire (usually divided); loreal single; preoculars 2; postoculars 2; supralabials 6–8 (usually 7) with fourth or fourth and fifth entering orbit; infralabials 8–11; dorsal scales smooth, with 2 apical pits, in 17 rows at midbody; ventrals 166–205; anal plate divided; subcaudals 95–126. Dorsum usually some shade of brown to bluish gray, with or without longitudinal lines of small dark spots. Juveniles have a pattern of narrow, pale stripes or narrow transverse bands on the neck. Venter pale yellow anteriorly, with or without orange spotting, and a richer yellow or orange-red posteriorly.
Habitat: Semi-evergreen seasonal forest, savanna, highland pine savanna formations, and among mangroves in the coastal lagoons and marshes formation, and agricultural land; terrestrial; sea level to 600 m.

PLATE 132   *Masticophis mentovarius.* Escuintla, Guatemala. Photograph by J.A. Campbell, courtesy of the University of Texas at Arlington.

Distribution: Northern Mexico to Costa Rica. In Belize it is known from Corozal, Orange Walk, Belize, and Cayo Districts.

Similar Species: *Coluber* at the same size is almost identical in form, but has 15 rows of dorsal scales at midbody, a lower ventral count (150–172) and usually 8 supralabials. *Dryadophis* is also similar in form but smaller and lacks a subocular scale below the preocular.

Remarks: A large, swift-moving, and highly agile species of open savanna, grassy sand dunes, and cleared land. Diurnal. Principally terrestrial, although may climb into small bushes in pursuit of prey. Lizards and small mammals constitute a large proportion of the diet, although the species is also known to eat other snakes; Guyer and Laska (1996) reported on an adult specimen from Costa Rica attempting to engulf a juvenile *Boa constrictor*. When hunting, often holds its head high off the ground. In Belize the species is a frequent casualty of road traffic in the latter part of the wet season (Weyer, 1990). Oviparous.

Key Reference: Johnson (1977).

Key to the Species of *Ninia* in Belize

Dorsum uniform black; venter boldly spotted. . . . . *N. diademata*

Dorsum red or red-brown, uniform or with black crossbars; venter immaculate. . . . . *N. sebae*

Ninia diademata Baird and Girard. Plate 133.
Vernacular Names: Ring-necked coffee snake, dormilona de collar.
Description: A very small snake; total length approximately 420 mm but usually less than 300 mm. Body somewhat triangular in cross section with a moderately prominent spinal ridge. Nasal scale divided; loreal single, longer than high and entering orbit; preoculars usually absent; postoculars 1 or 2, usually 2; supralabials 5 or 6 with third and fourth entering orbit; infralabials 5–7; dorsal scales strongly keeled, in 19 rows throughout; ventrals 123–159; anal plate entire; subcaudals 73–106. Dorsum black or dark gray with a pale spot in the center of each scale of the lowermost 3 dorsal scale rows, forming diffuse lines. Head black with a pale collar immediately behind the parietals, usually bisected medially. Venter cream with dark lateral edges and midventral series of dark spots.
Habitat: Evergreen broadleaf forest and perhaps subtropical evergreen forest formations; terrestrial and fossorial; 50–500 m.
Distribution: Central Mexico to northern Honduras. In Belize it is known from Cayo and Toledo Districts.
Similar Species: *Ninia sebae* is a reddish colored snake, usually with a dor-

PLATE 133   *Ninia diademata.* Honduras. Photograph by J.R. McCranie.

sal pattern of transverse bands. Other small, fossorial species, such as *Adelphicos, Tantilla,* and *Tantillita,* have smooth, unkeeled dorsal scales.

Remarks: A diminutive, invertebrate-eating species, usually found in leaf litter or beneath decaying logs and other forest floor debris. Completely innocuous, although may flatten its body and twist the tail upward in a spiral when disturbed (Greene, 1975). Nocturnal. Oviparous.

Key Reference: Wilson and Meyer (1985).

Ninia sebae (Duméril, Bibron, and Duméril). Plates 134, 135.

Vernacular Names: *Bead-and-coral,* red coffee snake, dormilona.

Description: A very small snake; total length approximately 390 mm. Body more or less triangular in cross section with a moderately prominent spinal ridge. Nasal scale divided; loreal single, elongate, and entering orbit; preoculars usually absent; postoculars 1–3, usually 2; supralabials 6–8, usually 7, with third and fourth entering orbit; infralabials 5–8, usually 7; dorsal scales keeled, in 19 rows throughout; ventrals 130–156; anal plate usually entire; subcaudals 40–74. Dorsum reddish to reddish brown, with or without dark, laterally alternating crossbars or spots outlined with pale yellow; head black above, with a yellow collar followed by a broad black nuchal band. Venter creamish, usually immaculate.

PLATE 134 *Ninia sebae.* Sarteneja, Corozal District. Photograph by P. Edgar.

PLATE 135 *Ninia sebae* with head and forebody elevated in threat posture. Mile 29, Western Highway, Belize District. Photograph by C. Farneti Foster.

Habitat: Evergreen broadleaf forest, semi-evergreen seasonal forest, karst hills forest, savanna, and highland pine savanna formations, agricultural land, and edificarian situations; fossorial and leaf litter; sea level to 600 m.

Distribution: Southern Mexico to Costa Rica. In Belize it occurs country-wide.

Similar Species: *Ninia diademata* is a darker colored species and lacks a dorsal pattern of transverse bands. Other small fossorial snakes such as *Adelphicos, Tantilla,* and *Tantillita* have smooth scales.

Remarks: A diminutive, invertebrate-eating inhabitant of leaf litter that may occasionally be observed above ground, especially when forced to the surface after heavy rain. Commonly found in agricultural pasture, cleared land, and suburban gardens. Nocturnal. Oviparous, Inoffensive, although may flatten the body if intimidated and coil the tail upward in a fashion similar to that seen in the venomous coral snakes (Greene, 1973).

Key Reference: Wilson and Meyer (1985).

Key to the species of *Oxybelis* in Belize

Dorsum green or yellow-green; venter with two longitudinal pale stripes . . . . *O. fulgidus*

Dorsum pale brown to gray; venter without longitudinal stripes . . . . *O. aeneus*

Oxybelis aeneus (Wagler). Plate 136.

Vernacular Names: *Tie-tie snake,* Neotropical vine snake, bejuquilla parda.

Description: A medium-large, exceedingly slender snake with an elongate, pointed head and a long tail; total length approximately 1450 mm. Nasal scale entire, elongate; loreal absent; preoculars 1; postoculars 2; prefrontal in contact with 2 or 3 supralabials; supralabials 6–10, usually 8, with 3 entering orbit; infralabials 6–11, usually 9; dorsal scales smooth or weakly keeled without apical pits, in 17 rows at midbody; ventrals 173–205; anal plate usually divided; subcaudals 137–203. Dorsum pale brown to grayish with darker flecks. Head brown or reddish brown above with a blackish eye stripe; supralabials and lower jaw cream or yellowish; mouth black inside. Venter pale brown, orange-tan, or yellowish.

Habitat: Evergreen broadleaf forest, semi-evergreen seasonal forest, karst hills forest, oak hammocks in savanna, highland pine savanna, and mangrove thickets in coastal lagoons and marshes formations, and fruit plantations; arboreal; sea level to 600 m.

PLATE 136   *Oxybelis aeneus.* Las Cuevas, Chiquibul Forest, Cayo District.

Distribution: Southern United States to southern Brazil and central Bolivia. In Belize it occurs countrywide.

Similar Species: *Oxybelis fulgidus* is similar in form and in having a pointed snout, but is never brown.

Remarks: Opisthoglyphous; generally harmless, but envenomation may cause irritation, local pain, and other mild poisoning symptoms in humans. When provoked this vine-like snake draws the body into an extended S-shaped coil and lunges forward, holding the mouth agape to expose the black interior. Diurnal. Feeds largely on lizards and frogs. Oviparous. The ecology of this species in Belize has been documented by Henderson (1974a).

Key Reference: Keiser (1974).

Oxybelis fulgidus (Daudin). Plate 137.

Vernacular Names: Green vine snake, bejuquilla verde.

Description: A large, slender snake with an elongate, pointed head; total length in excess of 1560 mm. Nasal scale entire; loreal absent; preoculars 1; postoculars 1 or 2, usually 2; prefrontal in contact with 2 or 3 supralabials; supralabials 9–12, usually 9 or 10 with 3 entering orbit; infralabials 9–12, usually 10; dorsal scales weakly keeled, without api-

PLATE 137   *Oxybelis fulgidus.* Chaa Creek, Cayo District.

cal pits, in 17 rows at midbody; ventrals 198–217; anal plate usually divided; subcaudals 139–186. Dorsum uniform bright green. Head green above with a dark green or blackish eye stripe; supralabials and lower jaw yellowish green; tongue also yellowish green. Venter yellowish green with a pale line along each side near the ventrolateral edge.

Habitat: Evergreen broadleaf forest, semi-evergreen seasonal forest, karst hills forest, and highland pine savanna formations, and fruit orchards; arboreal; sea level to 600 m.

Distribution: Southern Mexico to Argentina. In Belize it occurs country-wide.

Similar Species: *Leptophis ahaetulla* is similar in body proportions and color, but has a much broader head with a blunt snout, and dorsal scales in 15 rows at midbody (17 rows in *Oxybelis*). Its congener, *Oxybelis aeneus,* is a gray or brown-colored species.

Remarks: Opisthoglyphous; envenomation may cause local pain and other symptoms of mild poisoning in humans. Temperamental and inclined to bite. Diet includes arboreal lizards, small birds, and frogs. Although this species may be found in closed canopy forest, it is more commonly associated with woodland edge habitats. Diurnal. Oviparous.

Key Reference: Wilson and Meyer (1985).

Oxyrhopus petola (Linnaeus). Plate 138.

Vernacular Names: *Coral, bead-and-coral,* red-banded snake, Calico false coral snake, falsa corals de Calico; probably other local names applied generally to coral snake look-a-likes.

Description: A very large snake; maximum total length approximately 2200 mm, although usually less than 1000 mm. Head moderately distinct from neck; eye with vertically elliptic pupil. Nasal scale divided; loreal single; preoculars 1 or 2, usually 2; postoculars 2; supralabials 7–9 with fourth and fifth entering orbit; infralabials 9–11; dorsal scales smooth, with 2 apical pits, in 19 rows at midbody; ventrals 193–244; anal plate entire; subcaudals 79–117. Dorsum red or orange (yellowish in juveniles) with a series of approximately 20–26 broad black bands or blotches, none of which encircle the body completely; red scales sometimes marked with black. Head darker with pale nape blotch. Venter cream or yellowish, immaculate.

Habitat: Evergreen broadleaf forest, semi-evergreen seasonal forest, karst hills forest, highland pine savanna, and possibly subtropical evergreen forest formations; terrestrial; sea level to 600 m.

Distribution: Southern Mexico to Ecuador, Veracruz, Bolivia, and northern Brazil. In Belize it is known from Orange Walk, Belize, Cayo, Stann Creek, and Toledo Districts.

Similar Species: *Oxyrhopus* is distinguishable from coral snakes (genus

PLATE 138   *Oxyrhopus petola.* Izabal, Guatemala. Photograph by J.A. Campbell, courtesy of the University of Texas at Arlington.

Micrurus) in having only red and black bands (not triads), none of which encircle the body completely; *Oxyrhopus* also has 19 rows of dorsal scales at midbody (15 throughout in *Micrurus*), and a loreal scale. *Lampropeltis* has 21 or 23 rows of dorsal scales at midbody, and *Urotheca* has 17 rows throughout. *Sibon sartorii* has weakly keeled dorsal scales (smooth in *Oxyrhopus*), also in 17 rows throughout.

Remarks: An opisthoglyphous, strikingly marked snake. Effects of venom on man unknown although unlikely to be dangerous. *Oxyrhopus* appears to be an uncommon species in Belize. Small mammals and lizards constitute a large part of the diet. Predominantly terrestrial but occasionally found in low bushes. Generally nocturnal, although may occasionally be seen during the day; an adult specimen preparing to shed its skin was found by the authors at mid-day, coiled clearly visible amongst leaf litter. Oviparous.

Key Reference: Wilson and Meyer (1985).

Pseustes poecilonotus (Günther). Plates 139, 140, 141.

Vernacular Names: *Puffer,* puffing snake, pajarera.

Description: A very large snake; total length approximately 2000 mm. Nasal scale entire; loreal single; preoculars 1; postoculars 2–3, usually 2; supralabials 6–10, usually 7–9; infralabials 11–14; dorsal scales keeled on

PLATE 139 *Pseustes poecilonotus.* Dark color variant. Caracol, Cayo District. Photograph by C.M. Miller.

PLATE 140 *Pseustes poecilonotus.* Pale color variant. Chan Chich, Orange Walk District. Photograph by C.M. Miller.

PLATE 141 *Pseustes poecilonotus.* Cockscombe Jaguar Preserve, Stann Creek District. Photograph by C.M. Miller.

middorsal 3–4 rows in females and 7–13 rows in males, with 2 apical pits, and in 19–25 (usually 23) rows at midbody; ventrals 181–220; anal plate usually entire; subcaudals 95–145. Coloration variable; dorsum brown, olive-brown or grayish, uniform or with variously sized pale or dark spots, irregular crossbands, or dark paravertebral lines; upper surface of head often darker than body with an indistinct postorbital stripe and yellow on the supralabials and chin; juveniles generally grayish brown with a series of transverse crescent-shaped darker blotches. Venter yellowish grading to greenish gray posteriorly.

Habitat: Evergreen broadleaf forest, semi-evergreen seasonal forest, karst hills forest, wooded hammocks in savanna, and highland pine savanna formations; terrestrial and arboreal; sea level to 600 m.

Distribution: Central Mexico to Bolivia and Brazil. In Belize it occurs countrywide.

Similar Species: *Spilotes pullatus* is similar in form but has dorsal scales that are all keeled and in an even number of rows at midbody (14–18).

Remarks: An aggressive snake that typically reacts to danger by flattening its head, inflating the throat, and striking repeatedly with mouth agape, a defensive behavior that may increase its resemblance to a pitviper (Rand and Ortleb, 1969). Frequently observed in small trees and low bushes, although equally at home on the ground. The diet consists largely of birds. Diurnal. Oviparous.

Key Reference: Wilson and Meyer (1985).

Rhadinaea decorata (Günther). Fig. 24.

Vernacular Names: Adorned graceful brown snake, culebra de hojarasca.

Description: A medium-small snake with a long tail; total length approximately 470 mm (tail 35–47% of body length), although typically less

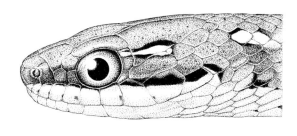

FIGURE 24 Head of *Rhadinaea decorata* (BMNH 94.10.1.27.8; Chontales Mines, Nicaragua) in lateral view. Scale bar = 5 mm.

than 300 mm. Head narrow and only slightly wider than neck; eye relatively large. Nasal scale divided; loreal single; preoculars 1 or 2, frequently with a small subpreocular between the third and fourth supralabials; postoculars usually 2; supralabials 7–9, usually 8; infralabials 9–11, usually 10; dorsal scales weakly keeled, those of the neck with either 1 or 2 apical pits, in 17 rows throughout; ventrals 110–134; anal plate divided; subcaudals 67–122. Dorsum brown, the sides darker and demarcated anteriorly by a conspicuous pale stripe, bordered below by a black lateral line that extends along the lower edge of scale row 5. Head brown, darker on the sides, and marked with a pair of vivid white, black-edged occelli, one directly behind the eye and another on the side of the neck; supralabials white, with or without fine dark spotting, and sharply delimited above by a black stripe. Venter uniformly whitish, or chin and throat white, turning pale orange under the neck and darker orange posteriorly.

Habitat: Evergreen broadleaf forest formation; terrestrial; sea level to 100 m.

Distribution: South-central Mexico to Colombia and Ecuador. In Belize it is known only from Toledo District, although probably also occurs in southern Cayo District.

Similar Species: Most likely to be confused with *Coniophanes imperialis,* which has a similar striped color pattern, but distinguished by having weakly keeled dorsal scales in 17 rows at midbody (dorsal scales smooth and in 19 midbody rows in *Coniophanes imperialis*). Although not yet reported from Belize, *Rhadinaea anachoreta* is also very similar. This smaller snake, currently known from a few localities just across the border in eastern Guatemala (Smith and Campbell, 1994), differs primarily in having a pale nuchal collar (broken middorsally) and more than 135 ventrals.

Remarks: A little known and rare snake in Belize. In Panama the species is a diurnal inhabitant of the forest floor, and has been observed prowling in leaf litter in late morning and at midday "when the maximum amount of sunlight was filtering through the trees" (Myers, 1974). The diet is thought to consist largely of amphibians. Oviparous.

Key Reference: Myers (1974).

Scaphiodontophis annulatus (Duméril, Bibron, and Duméril). Plate 142.

Vernacular Names: *Double snake,* shovel-toothed snake, neck-banded snake, culebra añadida; probably other names applied to coral snakes and their imitators.

Description: A medium-small snake with an exceptionally long tail; maximum total length approximately 790 mm (unbroken tail up to 50% of

PLATE 142 *Scaphiodontophis annulatus.* Upper Macal River, Cayo District.

total length), although usually less than 400 mm. Nasal scale divided; loreal single; preoculars 1; postoculars 2; supralabials 9 or 10 with fourth, fifth, and sixth entering orbit; infralabials 9–11; dorsal scales smooth, without apical pits, in 17 rows throughout; ventrals 132–160; anal plate divided; subcaudals 121–149. Dorsum with red, black, and yellow, gray or whitish bands anteriorly, changing abruptly on the neck or midbody to brown with three longitudinal stripes of black dots. Head dark brown or gray, uniform or broken into blotches, with a pale band across the snout and a reddish nuchal band; chin and lower jaw cream or yellowish. Venter pale cream or yellowish anteriorly, suffused with brown posteriorly.

Habitat: Evergreen broadleaf forest, semi-evergreen seasonal forest, karst hills forest, savanna, and highland pine savanna formations, and fruit orchards; terrestrial and fossorial; 50 to 600 m.

Distribution: South-central Mexico to Colombia. In Belize it is found countrywide.

Similar Species: Superficially resembles coral snakes and other red and black banded species, but distinct in having bands only on the anterior portion of the body.

Remarks: An unusual snake with specially adapted teeth for feeding on skinks, its principal food. Tail loss is common and well developed; the

233

very long and fragile tail may serve to facilitate multiple tail breaks (Slowinski and Savage, 1995) allowing the possibility of successive escape attempts from predators. Diurnal. A strictly terrestrial species, although will occasionally take to water; the snake illustrated (Plate 142) was found in midstream crossing a wide stretch of the Macal River. Oviparous.

Key Reference: Savage and Slowinski (1996).

Senticolis triaspis (Cope). See Fig. 18; Plate 143.

Vernacular Names: Green rat snake, culebra ratonera oliva.

Description: A medium-large snake with a long tail; maximum total length approximately 1220 mm (tail from 23 to 35% of body length). Head narrow and elongate, moderately distinct from the neck; eyes relatively small. Nasal scale divided; loreal single, occasionally broken into 3; preoculars usually 1 (or 2); postoculars usually 2 (or 3); 3 elongate and downwardly pointing primary temporals; supralabials 8–10, usually 8, with fourth and fifth entering orbit; infralabials 10–12, usually 11; dorsal scales smooth with faint keeling posteriorly (medial rows at midbody may also be lightly keeled), in 27–39 rows at midbody; ventrals 241–282; anal plate divided; subcaudals 87–126. Two principal color forms occur in Belize: dorsum of adult olive-green, grayish, or pale tan, unicolor or with a series of 42–57 body blotches. Head unmarked or with a unique

PLATE 143 Juvenile *Senticolis triaspis*. Costa Rica. Photograph by S. Von Peltz.

blotched pattern consisting of a transverse band on the snout, a postorbital bar, and a broad medial stripe extending from the center of the frontal scale posteriorly across the interparietal suture. Juveniles with 42–57 body blotches; medial stripe of head pale and irregularly broken, or dark and entire with small rounded opening at the interparietal suture. In both unicolor and patterned forms the venter is immaculate white, cream, or yellowish.

Habitat: Evergreen broadleaf forest, semi-evergreen seasonal forest, karst hills forest, and probably subtropical evergreen forest formations; terrestrial; 50 to 500 m.

Distribution: Southern United States to Costa Rica. In Belize it is known from Belize, Cayo, and Toledo Districts, and probably occurs countrywide.

Similar Species: Juveniles may be confused with young *Elaphe flavirufa*, from which they can be distinguished by their long, narrow head, and the size and arrangement of the primary temporal scales (elongate and downwardly pointing in *Senticolis*).

Remarks: A rarely seen and little known snake in Belize. Purportedly nocturnal. Chiefly terrestrial in habits but also an excellent climber; occasionally found in caves. The diet consists largely of small mammals, including bats (Meyer, 1966), and also birds. Oviparous. Snakes from northern Belize are typically unicolor and are assignable to the subspecies *S. t. mutabilis* (Dowling); the patterned color variant recorded from southern parts has been referred to the nominate form, *S. t. triaspis* (Cope). This species originally appeared under the generic name *Elaphe*.

Key Reference: Dowling (1960).

Key to the Species of *Sibon* in Belize

1. Dorsal scales in 17 rows throughout; dorsum with 12 to 28 black bands separated by white, yellow, or reddish interspaces . . . . *S. sartorii*

   Dorsal scales in 15 rows throughout; dorsum blotched, or if banded, with 50 to 60 dark brown bands separated by tan interspaces. 2

2. Loreal scale entering orbit 3

   Loreal not entering orbit . . . . *S. sanniola*

3. No infralabials in contact behind mental; venter usually with a series of alternating pale-centered blotches on the lateral edge . . . *S. dimidiata*

   One pair of infralabials in contact behind mental; venter usually immaculate. . . . . *S. nebulata*

Sibon dimidiata (Güther). Plate 144.

Vernacular Names: Slender snail sucker, culebra cordel negro.

Description: A medium-small, exceedingly slender snake with a laterally compressed body and a long tail; total length approximately 660 mm (tail approximately 50% of head and body length). Head short, blunt, and distinct from neck; eye with a vertically oriented subcircular pupil. Nasal scale entire or semidivided; loreal single, entering orbit; preoculars usually absent; postoculars 2; supralabials 7 or 8, with fourth and fifth, fifth and sixth, or sixth and seventh entering orbit; infralabials 7–10, none in contact behind mental; dorsal scales smooth without apical pits, in 15 rows throughout; ventrals 178–199; anal plate entire; subcaudals 106–126. Dorsum bright orange medially and dull red-brown, olive-brown, or silver-gray on the sides, with 36 to 57 dark dorsal blotches that extend onto the tail; in juveniles the color pattern is more pronounced. Venter cream with a series of alternating, pale-centered blotches on the lateral edge.

Habitat: Evergreen broadleaf forest formation; arboreal; recorded only from 100 m in Belize.

Distribution: Southern Mexico to Costa Rica. In Belize it is known only from Toledo District.

PLATE 144 *Sibon dimidiata.* Izabal, Guatemala. Photograph by J.A. Campbell, courtesy of the University of Texas at Arlington.

Similar Species: *S. sartorii* is a stouter, more distinctly banded species and has dorsal scales in 17 rows. *Dipsas* lacks a mental groove. *Imantodes* is very similar in form and color pattern but has dorsal scales usually in 17 rows and is more elongate with a higher ventral count (228–261).

Remarks: A small, rather slow-moving snake with specially adapted teeth for extracting snails from their shells. Feeds almost exclusively on gastropods. Nocturnal. During the day this species may take refuge in bromeliads and beneath the loose bark of trees. Oviparous.

Key Reference: Peters (1960).

Sibon nebulata (Linnaeus). Plate 145.

Vernacular Names: Cloudy snail sucker, speckled snail sucker, culebra jaspeada.

Description: A medium-small snake; total length approximately 830 mm. Head short, blunt, and distinct from neck; eye with vertically oriented subcircular pupil. Nasal scale divided; loreal single, entering orbit; pre-

PLATE 145   *Sibon nebulata.* Orange Walk District. Photograph by C.M. Miller.

oculars usually absent; postoculars 1–4, usually 2; supralabials 5–9 (usually 7 or 8), with fourth and fifth or fifth and sixth entering orbit; infralabials 6–10 (usually 8 or 9); dorsal scales smooth, without apical pits, in 15 rows throughout with vertebral row slightly enlarged; ventrals 159–200; anal plate usually entire; subcaudals 64–114. Dorsum pale brown or brownish gray to dark gray with 36 to 44 darker blotches; blotches irregularly elongate and narrowly outlined with pink or white, oriented diagonally, and extending to the venter. Head with large black spots on labial scales and chin. Venter cream, sometimes tinged with pink laterally.

Habitat: Evergreen broadleaf forest and semi-evergreen seasonal forest formations, and fruit orchards; arboreal and terrestrial; 100–700 m.

Distribution: Central Mexico to northern South America. In Belize it occurs countrywide.

Similar Species: *S. sartorii* is stouter, more distinctly banded, and has dorsal scales in 17 rows. *Dipsas* lacks a mental groove. *Imantodes* is similar in form and color pattern but has dorsal scales usually in 17 rows, and is more elongate with a higher ventral count (228–261).

Remarks: A secretive, rather slow-moving, innocuous little snake. Typically arboreal although has been found beneath leaflitter and fallen logs. Feeds largely on gastropods. Nocturnal. Oviparous. At Tikal in El Petén, Guatemala, recently hatched young have been found between mid-March and mid-April (Stuart, 1958).

Key Reference: Peters (1960).

Sibon sanniola (Cope). Plate 146.
Vernacular Names: Pigmy snail sucker, caracolera pigméa.

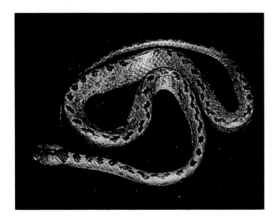

PLATE 146 *Sibon sanniola*. Chichén Itzá, Yucatán, Mexico. Photograph by W.E. Duellman.

Description: A small snake; total length approximately 400 mm. Head short and blunt; eye large with vertically elliptic pupil. Scales: Nasal scale divided or semidivided; loreal single, not entering orbit; preoculars 2–3; postoculars 2; supralabials 8–10, with fourth, fifth, and sixth entering orbit; infralabials 9–10; dorsal scales smooth, in 15 rows throughout; ventrals 143–170; anal plate entire; subcaudals 58–89. In Belize the species is typically light brown or tan above with either a single middorsal row of 35–67 small, darker brown, light-centered spots, frequently fused to form an irregular zig–zag line, or a pattern of approximately 50–60 dark brown bands extending to the ventrals. Head pale tan above with dark brown stippling and a dark brown nuchal band extending anteriorly onto the parietals and frontal. Venter of snakes with middorsal spots or zig–zag line, light cream to pale tan with heavy stippling or irregular, broken stripes along edges of ventrals. Venter of snakes with pattern of crossbands, squarish brown blotches on all ventrals except anteriormost.

Habitat: Evergreen broadleaf forest, semi-evergreen seasonal forest, and highland pine savanna formations; arboreal and terrestrial; sea level to 600 m.

Distribution: Yucatán Peninsula region of Mexico, northern Guatemala, and Belize. In Belize it is known from Corozal, Orange Walk, Belize, Cayo, and Toledo Districts, and probably occurs countrywide.

Similar Species: Other *Sibon* spp. (except *S. sartorii*) differ in having the loreal entering the orbit. *S. sartorii* is stouter, more distinctly banded, and has dorsal scales in 17 rows. *Dipsas* is distinguished by having the loreal enter the orbit and in lacking a mental groove. *Imantodes* has dorsal scales usually in 17 rows and is more elongate with a higher ventral count (228–261).

Remarks: A secretive and little known, rather slow-moving snake. Feeds exclusively on gastropods and has specially adapted teeth for extracting snails from their shells. Nocturnal. Oviparous. Snakes with a middorsal row of spots or zig–zag-like line are representative of the nominate form, *S.s. sanniola* Cope; the banded form in Belize has been distinguished as a separate subspecies, *S.s. neilli* (Henderson, Hoevers, and Wilson, 1977).

Key Reference: McCoy (1986).

Sibon sartorii (Cope). Plates 147, 148.

Vernacular Names: *Bead-and-coral,* and probably other local names applied to coral snakes and their mimics; terrestrial snail sucker, caracolera negrinaranja.

Description: A medium-small snake; maximum total length approximately 590 mm, although generally less than 400 mm. Head moderate-

PLATE 147   Juvenile *Sibon sartorii*. Quezaltenango, Guatemala. Photograph by J.A. Campbell, courtesy of the University of Texas at Arlington.

PLATE 148   Adult *Sibon sartorii*. Gallon Jug, Orange Walk District. Photograph by C.M. Miller.

ly short and blunt; eye with vertically oriented subcircular pupil. Nasal scale divided; loreal single, not or only sometimes entering orbit below a single small preocular; preoculars 1–3; postoculars 2; supralabials 6–8, with fourth and fifth entering orbit; infralabials 8–10; dorsal scales smooth to lightly keeled, with or without 2 apical pits, in 17 rows throughout; ventrals 167–199; anal plate entire; subcaudals 51–73. Dorsum and venter whitish, yellow, orange, or red with 12 to 28 black bands; bands may fuse beneath so that the midventral region is entirely black.

Habitat: Evergreen broadleaf forest and semi-evergreen seasonal forest formations, and citrus grove; terrestrial; sea level to 200 m.

Distribution: South-central Mexico through Guatemala and Belize. In Belize it has been recorded from Corozal, Orange Walk, Cayo, Stann Creek, and Toledo Districts, and probably occurs countrywide.

Similar Species: Coral snakes and their mimics; the true coral snakes have rings of red, yellow, and black almost invariably arranged in triads. *Oxyrhopus* is the only snake with a vertically elliptic pupil and a comparable color pattern of red and black bands, but is a larger species and also differs in having a pale nape blotch and 19 midbody dorsal scale rows (17 rows throughout in *Sibon sartorii*). The color pattern of *Dipsas* is very similar but this is an arboreal, more slender species that has smooth dorsal scales in 15 rows at midbody. Although presently unknown from Belize, *Sibon fasciata* is a similar banded species that occurs just across the Corozal District/Mexico (Quintana Roo) border; in this snake the pale bands are invariably white or grayish and the nuchal band does not extend as far forward beneath the eyes.

Remarks: A secretive, inoffensive snake that has faster movements and reactions than other *Sibon* species. The teeth are specially adapted for extracting snails from their shells, and the species appears to feed exclusively on gastropods. Occasionally found in caves. Males develop breeding tubercles seasonally, covering the chin and snout. Nocturnal. Oviparous. This species was previously known under the generic name *Tropidodipsas.*

Key Reference: Wilson and Meyer (1985).

Spilotes pullatus (Linnaeus). Plates 149, 150.

Vernacular Names: *Bocotora clapansaya,* tiger ratsnake, thunder and lightning snake, culebra mica.

Description: A very large, rather slender snake, commonly reaching lengths of up to 2600 mm. The body is somewhat laterally compressed with a moderately prominent spinal ridge, more conspicuous anteriorly. The head is distinct from the neck and the eyes are large. Nasal scale

PLATE 149   Juvenile *Spilotes pullatus*. Sarteneja, Corozal District. Photograph by P. Edgar.

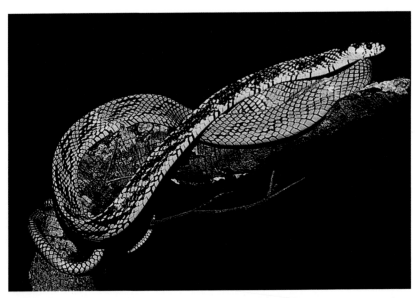

PLATE 150   Adult *Spilotes pullatus* with neck expanded in threat posture. Volcán Orosí, Cordillera de Guanacaste, Costa Rica. Adults of this species in Belize are more heavily marked with black.

entire; loreal present or absent; preoculars usually 1; postoculars 1 or 2, usually 2; supralabials 6–9, with third and fourth to fifth and sixth entering orbit; infralabials 6–10; dorsal scales keeled, with two apical pits, in an even number (14–18) rows at midbody; ventrals 198–241; anal plate entire; subcaudals 100–142. Coloration variable; snakes from Belize are generally black with irregular, diagonally oriented yellow bands, bars, or spots, or with a reticulate black and yellow pattern. In some specimens the color sequence may appear reversed, with yellow predominating on the dorsum. The coloration and markings in juveniles are more clearly defined.

Habitat: Typically near water in evergreen broadleaf forest, semi-evergreen seasonal forest, karst hills forest, savanna, highland pine savanna, and coastal lagoons and marshes formations, agricultural, and edificarian situations; terrestrial and arboreal; sea level to 600 m.

Distribution: Central Mexico to Peru, Bolivia, and Brazil. In Belize it occurs countrywide.

Similar Species: Dark-colored individuals of *Pseustes poecilonotus* may be strikingly similar in color pattern (see Plate 139), but this species has dorsal scales in an odd number of rows at midbody (19–25) and keeling present on the upper rows only.

Remarks: A large, agile, strikingly marked snake. If alarmed will inflate its throat and may bite. Commonly found near water, and also in ruderal areas around human habitations, milpas, and farm buildings, preying on vermin and domestic fowl and their eggs. Also known to frequent ant nests, using the underground tunnels as bolt holes, and palm-thatched roofs of buildings. Diurnal. Oviparous.

Key Reference: Wilson and Meyer (1985).

Key to the Species of *Stenorrhina* in Belize

Dorsum striped or unicolor, if unicolor usually reddish or pale yellow-brown; ventrals generally more than 160. . . . . *S. freminvillii*

Dorsum blotched, mottled, or unicolor, if unicolor usually olive-brown; ventrals generally fewer than 160 . . . . *S. degenhardtii*

Stenorrhina degenhardtii (Berthold). Plates 151, 152.
Vernacular Names: Degenhardt's scorpion-eating snake, alacranera de Degenhardt.
Description: A medium-sized, moderately stout snake with a short tail; total length approximately 750 mm. Head not distinctly wider than neck; eye relatively small. Rostral scale especially prominent; frontal

243

PLATE 151   Adult *Stenorrhina degenhardtii*. Las Cuevas, Chiquibul Forest, Cayo District.

PLATE 152   Hatchling *Stenorrhina degenhardtii*. Volcán Orosí, Cordillera de Guanacaste, Costa Rica.

much enlarged; nasal divided below naris, the anterior segment fused to the internasals and the posterior broadly in contact with the preocular and prefrontal; loreal absent; preoculars 1; postoculars 2; supralabials 7, with third and fourth entering orbit; infralabials 7–9, usually 7; dorsal scales smooth without apical pits, in 17 rows throughout; ventrals 136–159; anal plate divided; subcaudals 31–48. Snakes from Belize are typically unicolor with an olive-brown dorsum, sometimes marked with occasional dark-colored scales and/or a faint suggestion of a pale stripe extending the length of the body on scale row 5; the head is usually without a dark temporal stripe. Juveniles are paler with approximately 30 dark irregular crossbands on the dorsum and a series of smaller dark blotches on the lower sides; the sutures of the upper head scales are often darkened. Venter in adults cream or dull white, usually with a midventral series of dark spots or suffusion of dark pigment, most prominent beneath the tail, and/or a row of small dots along each side near the lateral edge.

Habitat: Evergreen broadleaf forest and probably subtropical evergreen forest formations; terrestrial and semifossorial; 450 to 700 m.

Distribution: Southern Mexico to Venezuela and Ecuador. In Belize it is known only from Cayo District, although probably occurs in Toledo District.

Similar Species: *Stenorrhina freminvillii* is a more slender snake, usually has a striped rather than blotched dorsal pattern, and has a higher ventral scale count (160–182 compared to fewer than 160 in *S. degenhardtii*); the dorsum of unicolor *S. freminvillii* in Belize is usually reddish or straw-colored (typically olive-brown in *S. degenhardtii*).

Remarks: Opisthoglyphous, although inoffensive and not inclined to bite. The diet consists largely of spiders, including tarantulas. Scorpions and other invertebrates may also be eaten. Oviparous. Coloration of this variable species is poorly known in Belize, although similarly colored individuals are known from the Sierra de Santa Cruz and Montañas del Mico, Guatemala (Jonathan Campbell, personal communication). Three specimens from the Maya Mountains (Stafford, 1996; also personal observation) were observed during the day following rain, although the species is thought to be chiefly nocturnal in habits.

Key Reference: Wilson and Meyer (1985).

Stenorrhina freminvillii (Duméril, Bibron, and Duméril). Plate 153.

Vernacular Names: Blood snake, alacranera.

Description: A medium-small snake; total length approximately 670 mm. Head not distinctly wider than neck; eye relatively small. Rostral scale prominent; nasal divided below naris; loreal present or absent; preocu-

PLATE 153 *Stenorrhina freminvillii.* Striped variant. Guatemala. Photograph by J.A. Campbell, courtesy of the University of Texas at Arlington.

lars 1; postoculars 1 or 2, usually 2; supralabials 6–7 with third and fourth entering orbit; infralabials 6–8; dorsal scales smooth without apical pits, in 17 rows throughout (with few exceptions); ventrals 160–182; anal plate divided; subcaudals 25–42. Two distinct color forms of this variable species occur in Belize; dorsum uniform reddish, orange, or yellowish brown, occasionally with black pigment at the base of each scale, or dorsum brown, olive-brown, gray-brown, or straw-colored, with a contrasting pattern of five dark longitudinal stripes. Venter cream, typically devoid of markings or with a dark, diffuse subcaudal stripe.

Habitat: Semi-evergreen seasonal forest, savanna, and highland pine savanna formations; terrestrial and fossorial; sea level to 600 m.

Distribution: Southern Mexico through Costa Rica. In Belize it has been recorded from Corozal, Orange Walk, Belize, Cayo, and Stann Creek Districts; probably also occurs in Toledo District.

Similar Species: *S. degenhardtii* is proportionally stouter with a uniform olive-brown dorsum, or possibly a pattern of blotches, and has fewer ventral scales (136–159 compared to usually more than 160 in *S. freminvillii*); the dorsum of unicolor *S. freminvillii* in Belize is typically reddish or straw-colored (olive-brown in *S. degenhardtii*), or otherwise with a pattern of longitudinal stripes.

Remarks: Opisthoglyphous, although inoffensive and not inclined to bite. Diurnal and crepuscular. Usually observed foraging for spiders, scorpions, and other invertebrates among leaf litter. *S. freminvilli* is not uncommon in the drier forests and savannas of northern Belize; in the wetter broadleaf forest formations the species appears to be ecologically replaced by its congener, *S. degenhardtii*. Oviparous.

Key Reference: Wilson and Meyer (1985).

Symphimus mayae (Gaige). Plates 154, 155.

Vernacular Names: Yucatán white-lipped snake, culebra Maya.

Description: A slender, medium to small snake with a long tail; total length approximately 900 mm. Nasal scale entire; loreal single; preoculars 1; postoculars 2; supralabials 5–7, usually 6; infralabials usually 7; dorsal scales smooth with a single apical pit, in 15 rows throughout; ventrals 150–165; anal plate divided; subcaudals 115–146. Dorsum light gray with the anterolateral edges of the dorsal scales a rich orange-yellow, especially in the middorsal region; a broad yellow or whitish vertebral stripe and a narrow, dark, irregular stripe on scale rows 3 and 4 are sometimes present. Head grayish above with the lower edges of the supralabials tinged with white, and occasionally a dark supralabial stripe.

PLATE 154 *Symphimus mayae.* Sarteneja, Corozal District. Photograph by P. Edgar.

PLATE 155 *Symphimus mayae.* Mile 28, Western Highway, Belize District. Photograph by C. Farneti Foster.

Venter white anteriorly, becoming darker posteriorly with pigmentation encroaching from the lateral surfaces.

Habitat: Oak hammocks in savanna formation, and probably semi-evergreen seasonal forest formation; terrestrial and perhaps semiarboreal; sea level to low elevations.

Distribution: Yucatán Peninsula region of Mexico and Belize. In Belize it is known from Corozal, Orange Walk, and Belize Districts.

Similar Species: *Coluber, Dryadophis,* and *Masticophis* are similar in form but have more than 15 rows of dorsal scales at midbody.

Remarks: A little known species, endemic to the Yucatán Peninsula and recently confirmed from Belize (Lee, 1996). Insectivorous in feeding habits; diet includes a wide range of invertebrates including grasshoppers and katydids, mantids, moths (noctuids), and various orthopterans. Diurnal. Oviparous. This snake was previously included in the genus *Opheodrys.*

Key Reference: Rossman and Schaeffer (1974).

Key to the Species of *Tantilla* and *Tantillita* in Belize

1. Nuchal band present 2

   Nuchal band absent. 3

2. Pale lateral stripe present (often indistinct); top of head marked with a dark mottled pattern and pale spot on the snout; subcaudals 48–55 . . . . *Tantilla cuniculator*

   Pale lateral stripe absent; top of head uniformly dark brown without a pale spot on the snout; subcaudals 24–42 . . . . *Tantilla schistosa*

3. Pale middorsal stripe usually present; top of head marked with pale spots; dorsal and ventral color grading into each other; subcaudals 32–44. . . . . *Tantillita canula*

   Middorsal stripe absent; top of head without pale spots; dorsal and ventral color sharply demarcated; subcaudals 43–56. . . . *Tantillita lintoni*

Tantilla cuniculator Smith. Plates 156, 157.

Vernacular Names: Yucatán centipede snake, culebra cienpiés de Yucatán.

Description: An exceptionally small snake; total length approximately 160 mm. Head only slightly distinct from neck. Nasal scale divided; loreal absent; preoculars 1; postoculars 2; supralabials 6 or 7, usually 7, with third and fourth entering orbit; infralabials 6 or 7, usually 6; dorsal scales smooth, in 15 rows throughout and without apical pits; ventrals 139–154; anal plate divided; subcaudals 48–55. Dorsum dark

PLATE 156   Adult *Tantilla cuniculator*. Sarteneja, Corozal District. Photograph by P. Edgar.

PLATE 157 Head detail of *Tantilla cuniculator.* Sarteneja, Corozal District. Photograph by P. Edgar.

brown, paling to a lighter shade of brown on the first two scale rows, with a barely discernible pale lateral stripe on adjacent halves of scale rows 3 and 4, extending length of body and tail; head mottled dark brown above with a pale yellow-orange spot on the upper surface of the rostral, internasals, and prefrontals, and a complete pale yellow-orange nuchal collar extending for 2 to 2 1/2 scales from the posterior edge of the parietals. Venter uniform reddish orange or creamish in color.

Habitat: Semi-evergreen seasonal forest formation and possibly savanna formation; terrestrial and semifossorial; sea level to 50 m.

Distribution: Yucatán Peninsula region of Mexico, northern Guatemala and Belize. In Belize it is known from Corozal and Orange Walk Districts; possibly also occurs in Belize and northern Cayo Districts.

Similar Species: *Tantillita canula* and *T. lintoni* both lack a nuchal collar and have fewer than 117 ventral scales (117 or more in *Tantilla*); *T. canula* also has a pale middorsal stripe. *Tantilla schistosa* lacks lateral stripes, has a less prominent nuchal band, and no pale spot on the snout. *Adelphicos* and *Ninia* both have a loreal scale; *Adelphicos* also lacks a nuchal band and often has a heavily marked venter; *Ninia* has strongly keeled dorsal scales (smooth in *Tantilla*).

Remarks: Opisthoglyphous, although mouth too small to be capable of biting and envenomating humans. Inoffensive. A little known species, endemic to the Yucatán Peninsula. Nocturnal in habits, inhabiting leaf litter and occasionally observed abroad on the surface at night. The specimen illustrated (Plates 156 and 157) was found in the decaying stump of a coconut palm. Feeds on centipedes, beetle larvae, and other soft-bodied invertebrates. Oviparous.

Key Reference: Wilson (1982).

Tantilla schistosa (Bocourt). Fig. 25.
Vernacular Names: Red earth centipede snake, culebrita de tierra roja.

FIGURE 25   Head of *Tantilla schistosa* (BMNH 95.4.29.9; Matagalpa, Nicaragua) in lateral view. Scale bar = 5 mm.

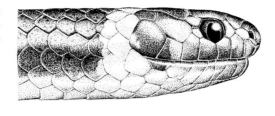

Description: A very small snake; total length approximately 290 mm. Head only slightly distinct from neck. Nasal scale divided; loreal absent; preocular 1; postoculars 1 or 2; supralabials 7, with third and fourth entering orbit; infralabials 5 or 6; dorsal scales smooth, in 15 rows throughout and without apical pits; ventrals 117–147; anal plate divided; subcaudals 24–42. Dorsum of head and body uniform dark brown with a pink or yellowish nuchal collar. Venter cream, or pale pink anteriorly, grading to salmon-pink or red-orange posteriorly.

Habitat: Evergreen broadleaf forest, semi-evergreen seasonal forest, subtropical evergreen forest, savanna, and highland pine savanna formations, and cleared forest; terrestrial and semifossorial; 50–600 m.

Distribution: Southern Mexico to Panama. In Belize it is found countrywide in appropriate habitat.

Similar Species: *Tantillita canula* and *T. lintoni* both lack a nuchal collar and have fewer than 117 ventral scales (117 or more in *Tantilla*); *T. canula* also has a pale middorsal stripe or row of spots. *Tantilla cuniculator* has a brighter, more prominent nuchal collar, an indistinct lateral stripe, and a pale spot on the snout. *Adelphicos* and *Ninia* both have a loreal scale; *Adelphicos* also lacks a nuchal band and often has a heavily marked venter; *Ninia* has strongly keeled dorsal scales (smooth in *Tantilla*). A third species of *Tantilla*, *T. moesta*, although currently known only from areas surrounding Belize, also has a pale nuchal collar; this species, however, is larger (up to 600 mm) and is uniformly dark brown or black both above and beneath (venter pale cream or pinkish orange in *T. schistosa* contrasting sharply with dark-colored dorsum).

Remarks: Opisthoglyphous, although mouth too small to be capable of biting and envenomating humans. Inoffensive. Most frequently found under logs or among leaf litter on the forest floor. Feeds on centipedes, beetle larvae, and similar soft-bodied invertebrates. Chiefly crepuscular and nocturnal. Oviparous.

Key Reference: Wilson (1982).

Tantillita canula (Cope). Plate 158.

Vernacular Names: Yucatán dwarf short-tailed snake, culebrita enano de Yucatán.

Description: A very small snake; total length approximately 185 mm. Head somewhat pointed and only slightly distinct from the neck. Nasal scale divided; loreal absent; preoculars 1; postoculars 2; supralabials 6 or 7, usually 7, with third and fourth entering orbit; infralabials 6; dorsal scales smooth, in 15 rows throughout and without apical pits; ventrals 103–114; anal plate divided; subcaudals 32–44. Dorsum tan to dark brown, palest on the lower sides and grading into ventral color, usually with a thin pale middorsal stripe or line of discrete spots, often more distinct on the tail; head darker brown above with variously sized pale spots on the snout and parietals. Venter immaculate cream.

Habitat: Evergreen broadleaf forest, semi-evergreen seasonal forest, and perhaps savanna formations, also cleared land and agricultural pasture; terrestrial and semifossorial; sea level to 450 m.

Distribution: Yucatán Peninsula region of Mexico, northern Guatemala and Belize. In Belize it probably occurs countrywide, in appropriate habitat.

Similar Species: Most easily confused with *Tantillita lintoni*, from which it can be distinguished by the presence of a pale middorsal stripe, or line of spots, and pale spots on the head; the ventral and dorsal color are

PLATE 158 Adult *Tantillita canula*. Sarteneja, Corozal District. Photograph by P. Edgar.

sharply demarcated in *Tantillita lintoni* but blend gradually with each other in *T. canula*. *Tantillita canula* also has a more slender body shape than *T. lintoni*, a more pointed head, and a shorter tail with fewer subcaudals. *Tantilla schistosa* and *T. cuniculator* both lack a middorsal stripe, have a nuchal collar, and have more than 115 ventrals. *Adelphicos* and *Ninia* both have a loreal scale; *Adelphicos* also has a heavily marked venter and striped dorsal pattern (sometimes inconspicuous); *Ninia* has strongly keeled dorsal scales (smooth in *Tantillita*).

Remarks: An opisthoglyphous though inoffensive snake; mouth too small to be capable of biting and envenomating humans. Most frequently found beneath logs or among leaf litter on the forest floor. Feeds on soft-bodied invertebrates. Chiefly nocturnal. Oviparous. In the wetter forest formations this species may be ecologically replaced by its congener, *T. lintoni*.

Key Reference: Wilson (1982).

Tantillita lintoni (Smith). Plate 159.

Vernacular Names: Linton's dwarf short-tailed snake, culebrita enano de Linton.

PLATE 159   Adult *Tantillita lintoni*. Las Cuevas, Chiquibul Forest, Cayo District.

Description: A very small snake; total length approximately 210 mm. Head relatively broad compared with *Tantilla* though not distinctly wider than neck. Nasal scale divided; loreal absent; preoculars 1; postoculars 2; supralabials 6 or 7, usually 7, with third and fourth entering orbit; infralabials 6; dorsal scales smooth, in 15 rows throughout and without apical pits; ventrals 103–115; anal plate usually divided; subcaudals 43–56. Dorsum uniformly brown to dark brown, sharply demarcated from ventral coloration. Venter immaculate yellowish cream or pinkish orange.

Habitat: Evergreen broadleaf forest and possibly subtropical evergreen forest formation; terrestrial and semifossorial; sea level to 500 m.

Distribution: Southern Mexico to Honduras. In Belize it is known from Belize, Cayo, and Toledo Districts.

Similar Species: Most easily confused with *Tantillita canula*, from which it can be distinguished by the absence of a pale middorsal stripe and lack of pale spots on the head; coloration of the dorsum and venter are sharply demarcated in *Tantillita lintoni* but blend gradually with each other in *T. canula. Tantillita canula* also has a more slender body shape than *T. lintoni*, a more pointed head, and a shorter tail with fewer subcaudals (32–44). *Adelphicos* and *Ninia* both have a loreal scale; *Adelphicos* also has a heavily marked venter and striped dorsal pattern (sometimes inconspicuous); *Ninia* has strongly keeled dorsal scales (smooth in *Tantillita*)

Remarks: Opisthoglyphous, although mouth too small to be capable of biting and envenomating humans. Inoffensive. Chiefly crepuscular and nocturnal. A secretive species, most frequently found under logs, among leaf litter on the forest floor, or crossing trails at night. The dietary habits of this diminutive snake are unknown but it presumably feeds on small invertebrates, as does *T. canula*. Oviparous.

Key Reference: Wilson (1988).

Key to the Species of *Thamnophis* in Belize

Supralabials below eye marked with vertical black bars; dorsum typically spotted or checked; paired occipital blotches present; venter with distinct patterning . . . . *T. marcianus*

Supralabials without black markings; dorsum pattern typically of three pale longitudinal stripes; occipital blotches absent; venter usually immaculate . . . . *T. proximus*

Thamnophis marcianus (Baird and Girard). Fig. 26; Plate 160.
Vernacular Names: *Pine ridge tommygoff,* checkered garter snake, sochuate.

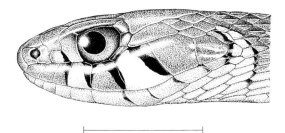

FIGURE 26 Head of *Thamnophis marcianus* (BMNH 1978.1999; northern Belize) in lateral view, showing characteristic supralabial markings. Scale bar = 1 cm.

Description: A medium to medium small snake; total length approximately 1000 mm. Nasal scale divided; loreal single; preoculars usually 1; postoculars 2–5, usually 3 or 4; supralabials 6–9, usually 8, with fourth and fifth entering orbit; infralabials 8–12, usually 10; dorsal scales keeled, in 19 rows at midbody and without apical pits; ventrals 134–173; anal plate entire; subcaudals 56–83. Dorsum brownish or olive, with three rows of darker, alternating black blotches (markings frequently indistinct in aging specimens) either side of the vertebral line and usually a broad, pale vertebral stripe; interstitial skin light orange to reddish. Head with a large postoccipital black blotch, a pale, black-outlined preorbital and postorbital blotch, and bold black edging to the supralabials beneath the orbit. Venter pale cream with or without dark pigment at the anterior edge of each ventral, or two rows of small rounded dots.

PLATE 160 *Thamnophis marcianus.* Quintana Roo, Mexico. Photograph by J.R. McCranie.

Habitat: Near water in semi-evergreen seasonal forest, savanna, and interior wetlands formations; brackish water among mangroves in coastal lagoons and marshes formation; terrestrial and semiaquatic; sea level to 100 m.

Distribution: Southwestern United States to Costa Rica. In Belize it is known from Orange Walk, Belize, and northern Cayo Districts.

Similar Species: *T. proximus* differs in having unmarked supralabials and a dorsal pattern consisting of stripes only rather than a vertebral stripe and lateral blotches; the middorsal stripe in *T. marcianus* is also broader than in *T. proximus.*

Remarks: An alert, diurnal snake, usually observed hunting for small fish and amphibians (including tadpoles and eggs) in and around water. Viviparous; in Belize newborn young have been found in July and August (Lee, 1996).

Key Reference: Rossman (1971).

Thamnophis proximus (Say). Plate 161.

Vernacular Names: Gulf Coast ribbon snake, Central American ribbon snake, culebra aquática.

Description: A medium-large snake; maximum total length approximately 1240 mm. Nasal scale divided; loreal single; preoculars 1; post-

PLATE 161 *Thamnophis proximus.* Gold Button Creek area, Orange Walk District. Photograph by S. Von Peltz.

oculars usually 3; supralabials 6–9, usually 8, with fourth and fifth entering orbit; infralabials 8–11, usually 10; dorsal scales keeled, in 19 rows at midbody and without apical pits; ventrals 141–181; anal plate usually entire; subcaudals 82–131. Dorsum olive-gray or olive-brown to black, with a narrow grayish, yellow-gold, orange, or red middorsal stripe and usually a yellowish lateral stripe on scale rows 3 and 4; head usually with a pair of light spots on the parietals (occasionally fused), pale orange, unmarked supralabials, a light postocular and a dark postorbital blotch. Venter uniform pale olive, or pale yellow at neck becoming greenish posteriorly.

Habitat: Near water in semi-evergreen seasonal forest, savanna, and interior wetlands formations, and cleared land; brackish water among mangroves in coastal lagoons and marshes formation; terrestrial and semi-aquatic; sea level to 100 m.

Distribution: Central United States to Costa Rica. In Belize it is known from Corozal, Orange Walk, Belize, Stann Creek, and Toledo Districts, and probably occurs countrywide.

Similar Species: *T. marcianus* has a unique head pattern with distinct black markings on the supralabials, and a dorsal pattern consisting of a broad dorsal stripe and lateral blotches rather than stripes alone.

Remarks: An alert, diurnal snake, usually observed hunting for small fishes and amphibians (including tadpoles and eggs) in and around marshes, ponds, lakes, and other bodies of water. Lee (1996) reported finding specimens coiled in emergent vegetation half a meter above the surface of the water. Viviparous; in Belize newborn young have been found in July (Neill, 1962).

Key Reference: Rossman (1963).

Tretanorhinus nigroluteus Cope. Plate 162.
Vernacular Names: *Cativo, river snake,* orange-bellied swamp snake, black water snake, buceadora.
Description: A medium-sized snake; maximum total length approximately 880 mm, although usually less than 500 mm. Head relatively long and elongate, with the small eyes and nostrils in an elevated dorsolateral position. Nasal scale divided or semidivided; loreal single or divided; preoculars 1–3, usually 2; postoculars 2; supralabials 7–9, with fourth or fifth entering orbit; infralabials 9–11; dorsal scales keeled, without apical pits, in 21 rows at midbody; ventrals 127–151; anal plate divided; subcaudals 56–82. Dorsum variable, usually pale brown or olive-brown to black, uniform or with a double series of paravertebral and dorsolateral blotches, or a reddish lateral stripe involving the third and fourth scale rows; paravertebral blotches sometimes fused into an irregular stripe,

PLATE 162 *Tretanorhinus nigroluteus.* Izabal, Guatemala. Photograph by J.A. Campbell, courtesy of the University of Texas at Arlington.

either broken in places or coursing the whole length of the body. Venter scarlet red to light tan, with or without midventral black mottling.

Habitat: Slow-flowing rivers, freshwater pools, swamps, and drainage channels in evergreen broadleaf forest, semi-evergreen seasonal forest, savanna, and interior wetlands formations; brackish water in coastal lagoons and marshes formation; aquatic; sea level to 100 m.

Distribution: Southern Mexico to northern South America. In Belize it occurs countrywide, including the Turneffe group of islands and some of the larger cayes.

Similar Species: None.

Remarks: A nocturnal, thoroughly aquatic snake. May be observed among floating plants, anchored to submerged vegetation, or crawling along the bottom in shallow water at night. Feeds on small fish and amphibians. Adult males develop breeding tubercles seasonally, especially pronounced on the infralabials and scales of the chin and throat. Oviparous.

Key Reference: Henderson (1979).

Urotheca elapoides (Cope). Plate 163.

Vernacular Names: *Coral, bead-and-coral,* false coral snake, imitacoral; probably other local names applied generally to coral snake look-a-likes.

Description: A medium-small snake; total length approximately 660 mm with an exceptionally long tail (unbroken tail 35–50% of total length).

PLATE 163   *Urotheca elapoides.* Honduras. Photograph by J.R. McCranie.

Nasal scale divided; loreal single; preoculars 2; postoculars 2; supralabials 7–9, with fourth and fifth entering orbit; infralabials 8–10; dorsal scales smooth, without apical pits, in 17 rows throughout; ventrals 122–144; anal plate divided; subcaudals 85–115. Dorsum (including tail) and venter red with approximately 10–20 black rings, usually flanked by cream or yellow rings; red bands present on the tail, often darker at the edges and with some or all scales tipped with black; black rings may or may not completely encircle the body (open dorsally or on the venter). Head with broad cream or yellowish band.

Habitat: Evergreen broadleaf forest, karst hills forest, subtropical evergreen forest, and highland pine savanna formations, and citrus grove; terrestrial; 200–700 m.

Distribution: Central Mexico to western Honduras and El Salvador. In Belize it is known from Cayo, Stann Creek, and Toledo Districts.

Similar Species: Remarkably similar to the coral snakes (*Micrurus* spp.), particularly *M. diastema*, from which it can be distinguished by the presence of red bands on the tail (tails of *Micrurus* spp. in Belize have black and yellow bands only), a loreal scale, and dorsal scales in 17 rows (15 rows in *Micrurus*).

Remarks: An almost perfect mimic of the venomous coral snakes, which it emulates in both color and behavior. Aglyphous, although bite has been known to produce mild poisoning effects in humans (Seib, 1980). Tail loss is well developed; the long and fragile tail may be an adaptation to facilitate a number of tail breaks, allowing the snake more than one chance of escape in encounters with predators. Essentially diurnal in habits. The diet consists largely of salamanders. Oviparous. In a recent review of this highly variable species, Smith and Chiszar (1996) distinguished between several geographic forms and retained the former generic name *Pliocercus.*

Key Reference: Wilson and Meyer (1985).

Xenodon rabdocephalus (Wied). Plate 164.

Vernacular Names: *Boba,* false fer-de-lance, falso terciopelo.

Description: A medium-sized, moderately stout snake; total length approximately 800 mm. Head moderately broad with blunt snout and relatively large eye. Nasal scale divided; loreal single; preoculars 1; postoculars 2–4, usually 2 or 3; supralabials 7–9, with fourth and fifth entering orbit; infralabials 9–12; dorsal scales smooth, with a single apical pit, in 19 rows at midbody; ventrals 124–153; anal plate entire; subcaudals 35–52. The scales on the tip of the tail are swollen and knob-like in juveniles less than 15 cm in length (Garth Underwood, personal communication). Dorsum brown or grayish (pale yellow-brown or pinkish in juveniles) with a series of approximately 14 hourglass-shaped blotches extending laterally to the ventral edge; blotches darker at the margins

PLATE 164 Adult *Xenodon rabdocephalus* showing expanded dorsoventral hood. Sibun and Mullins River area, Belize District. Photograph by C. Farneti Foster.

and outlined with whitish flecks; head brown or grayish above with a nape blotch extending onto the neck; iris of eye bronze. Venter cream with reddish brown blotches and stippling, or black crossbands.

Habitat: Typically near water in evergreen broadleaf forest, semi-evergreen seasonal forest, and highland pine savanna formations; terrestrial; sea level to 600 m.

Distribution: Southern Mexico to Amazonian South America. In Belize it occurs countrywide.

Similar Species: The dorsal color pattern is very similar to that of *Bothrops asper,* but the head is typically colubrid-like and quite different in shape, with a round eye pupil. *Bothrops* also has keeled dorsal scales in 25–29 rows at midbody and a distinct loreal pit.

Remarks: An aggressive, opisthoglyphous snake that flattens its head and body when provoked and strikes repeatedly, although it tends to refrain from outright biting. Diurnal. The diet consists largely of toads and other amphibians. Most commonly observed foraging near water, or on the forest floor, especially after rain. Oviparous.

Key Reference: Wilson and Meyer (1985).

CORAL SNAKES (FAMILY ELAPIDAE)

This family of venomous snakes embraces approximately 250 species, characterized by nonerectile, partially grooved fangs in the front of the mouth (proteroglyphous). Many have the appearance of harmless colubrids. Elapid snakes occur mainly in tropical and subtropical regions of both the Old and New Worlds. The family includes such dangerously venomous species as the cobras, kraits, mambas, sea snakes, and taipans, which are responsible for a large proportion of human snake bite fatalities in other parts of the world. The only elapids in the New World are the coral snakes (*Leptomicrurus, Micruroides,* and *Micrurus*), represented in Belize by three species of the genus *Micrurus;* all are brightly colored, patterned with alternating bands of red, yellow, and black. There are also two questionable records of the sea snake, *Pelamis platurus,* from the waters of the Caribbean.

Elapid venom is strongly neurotoxic, attacking nerve tissues and interfering with the transmission of nerve impulses. For information concerning coral snake bites see the chapter appendix "Features and Treatment of Snake Bites in Belize."

In Belize there are a number of harmless snakes that imitate coral snakes with varying degrees of likeness: *Lampropeltis* is well known as a mimic but is a larger snake with the colored bands arranged in a different sequence (red flanked by black rather than red next to yellow); *Oxyrhopus* has broad red and black bands or blotches (not triads) that never encircle the body completely; *Sibon sartorii* also has red (or whitish) and black bands only, with dorsal scales arranged in 17 rows throughout (15 rows in *Micrurus*); *Dipsas brevifacies*, in common with *Micrurus*, has 15 rows of dorsal scales at midbody, but the dorsum is banded with black and red (or whitish in juveniles) only, and it is also a conspicuously more elongate, arboreal snake. *Urotheca* is the most comparable species with red, yellow, and black bands arranged in the same sequence as *Micrurus*, although it also has red bands present on the tail (tails of *Micrurus* in Belize have black and yellow bands only); *Scaphiodontophis* has bands only on the anterior part of its body. Two other snakes, although not banded, are conspicuously red and black: juvenile *Clelia* are red or orange with a pale nuchal collar and black head; *Ninia sebae* is also reddish, either unicolor or with a dorsal pattern of spots rather than bands. In Belize there appears to be little discrimination between the harmless coral snake mimics and the true coral snakes, all of which are collectively referred to as either "bead-and-coral," "coral," or "corallilo." The main visible character that distinguishes the true coral snakes from mimic species is the absence of red bands on the tail. The tail end of the body is rather flattened and when danger threatens may be turned upward and waved about to distract attention away from the head, a habit also adopted by several mimic species.

Key to the Species of *Micrurus* in Belize

1. Snout entirely black (sometimes with pale spot at tip); black body rings usually complete dorsally; red dorsal scales usually black-tipped or with irregular black blotches. 2

   Snout frequently marked with a pale band across the tip (occasionally entirely black); black rings on body often not complete dorsally; red dorsal scales sometimes darker at edges but not conspicuously marked with black . . . . *M. hippocrepis*

2. Usually more than 20 black body bands; usually more than 30% of subcaudals entire; red dorsals not uniformly tipped with black; males without supraanal tubercles . . . . *M. diastema*

   Usually fewer than 20 black body bands; none or very few subcaudals entire; red dorsals uniformly tipped with black; supraanal tubercles present in males . . . . *M. nigrocinctus*

Micrurus diastema (Duméril, Bibron, and Duméril). Plates 165, 166, 167, 168.
Vernacular Names: *Coral, bead-and-coral, corallilo,* variable coral snake, coral variable.

PLATE 165 *Micrurus diastema.* Sarteneja, Corozal District. Photograph by P. Edgar.

PLATE 166 *Micrurus diastema.* Las Cuevas, Chiquibul Forest, Cayo District.

PLATE 167 Head of *Micrurus diastema,* showing details of scalation. Mile 29, Western Highway, Belize District. Photograph by C. Farneti Foster.

PLATE 168 A suspected intergrade *Micrurus diastema x hippocrepis.* Cuxta Bani, upper Raspaculo River, Cayo District. The tail is coiled upward in a typical defensive posture.

264

Description: A medium-small snake; total length approximately 850 mm. Head only slightly wider than neck; eye small and completely black, with vertically oriented subcircular pupil. Nasal scale divided; loreal absent; preoculars 1; postoculars 2; supralabials 7, with third and fourth entering orbit; infralabials 7; dorsal scales smooth, without apical pits, in 15 rows throughout; ventrals 189–228; anal plate divided; subcaudals 28–62, usually more than 30% entire. Coloration variable; dorsum and venter (excluding tail) red with usually more than 20 black rings, flanked by relatively narrow yellow rings (1/2–1 scale wide); the first black ring (nuchal) is usually incomplete ventrally, and the red bands may be suffused with a variable amount of black pigment. Snout black, the black pigment extending posteriorly to, but not usually encroaching on, the parietals; tip of snout usually pale. The black nuchal ring frequently involves the posterior edges of the parietals and may be several scales broader than the other black body rings. Tail yellow with 0–16 (typically 6–9) black rings that may be more or less the same width as or up to two times wider than the yellow interspaces. Completely red snakes that have a black head, yellow nuchal collar, and rings only on the tail are also known.

Habitat: Evergreen broadleaf forest, semi-evergreen seasonal forest, karst hills forest, subtropical evergreen forest, savanna, and highland pine savanna formations, and edificarian situations; terrestrial; sea level to 700 m.

Distribution: Southern Mexico to western Honduras. In Belize it is found countrywide.

Similar Species: *M. hippocrepis* has fewer black body rings that are often irregular and incomplete dorsally, fewer black tail rings (typically 4–5 vs. 6–9 in *M. diastema*), and no or little black pigment on the red scales; in *M. hippocrepis* the tip of the snout may also be marked with a broad yellow band. *M. nigrocinctus* in Belize typically has fewer black body rings than *M. diastema* and subcaudal scales that are mostly divided (typically more than 30% entire in *M. diastema*); in *M. nigrocinctus* the red dorsal scales are also uniformly and usually more boldly marked with black, the snout is invariably black, and supraanal tubercles are present in males. Also coral snake mimics (see Coral Snakes section above and *Lampropeltis, Oxyrhopus, Scaphiodontophis, Sibon sartorii,* and *Urotheca*).

Remarks: Venomous. Usually observed foraging for small lizards and snakes in leaf litter, especially after rain. May occasionally be found in gardens. Nocturnal and diurnal; the authors have found the species active at night just after dark, during the cooler times of the day, and also very early in the morning before sunrise. Oviparous. *Micrurus diastema* appears to be the most common and widespread of the three species of coral snake in Belize.

Key Reference: Roze (1996)

Micrurus hippocrepis (Peters). Fig. 27; Plates 168, 169.

Vernacular Names: *Coral, bead-and-coral, corallilo,* Maya coral snake, coral Maya.

Description: A small- to medium-sized snake; total length approximately 850 mm in females. Head only slightly wider than neck; eye small and completely black, with vertically oriented subcircular pupil. Nasal scale divided; loreal absent; preoculars 1; postoculars 2; supralabials 7, with third and fourth entering orbit; infralabials 7; dorsal scales smooth, without apical pits, in 15 rows throughout; ventrals 199–226; anal plate divided; subcaudals 37–57, mostly divided. Coloration variable; dorsum and venter (excluding tail) red with 3–17 black rings, often not complete, flanked by narrow yellow rings (1–1 1/2 scales wide); the first black ring (nuchal) is usually incomplete ventrally. The red bands may be dusky or edged with black, but are not usually marked heavily with black. The tip of the snout may be completely black or more frequently marked with a broad yellow band involving the rostral, internasals, and prefrontal region, which is usually, although not always, followed by a black band. Tail yellow with 4–7 (usually 4–5) black rings, each approximately the same width as or slightly wider than the yellow interspaces.

Habitat: Evergreen broadleaf forest and highland pine savanna formations; terrestrial; 50 to 600 m.

Distribution: Eastern Guatemala and Belize. In Belize it is known from Cayo, Stann Creek, and Toledo Districts.

Similar Species: *M. diastema* and *M. nigrocinctus* tend to have more black body rings that are mostly if not entirely complete dorsally, at least some black pigmentation on the red dorsal scales, and invariably a black snout (snout of *M. diastema* sometimes marked with a pale spot

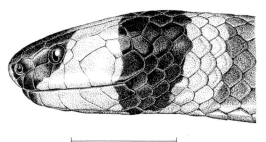

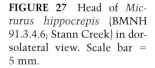

FIGURE 27 Head of *Micrurus hippocrepis* (BMNH 91.3.4.6; Stann Creek) in dorsolateral view. Scale bar = 5 mm.

PLATE 169   *Micrurus hippocrepis.* Izabal, Guatemala. Photograph by J.A. Campbell, courtesy of the University of Texas at Arlington.

but never a distinct yellow band). Males of *M. nigrocinctus* also have supraanal tubercles, and *M. diastema* frequently has more black tail rings (typically 6–9 vs. 4–5 in *M. hippocrepis*) that may be up two times the width of the yellow interspaces (width of black and yellow rings usually subequal in *M. hippocrepis*). Also coral snake mimics (see Coral Snakes section above and *Lampropeltis, Oxyrhopus, Scaphiodontophis, Sibon sartorii,* and *Urotheca*).

Remarks: Venomous. Typically observed foraging among leaf litter, probably for small lizards and snakes. Nocturnal and diurnal; Campbell and Lamar (1989) reported finding specimens active during the cooler times of the day (early morning and late afternoon), as well as after dark. Oviparous. *M. hippocrepis* exhibits much of the same color and pattern variation as seen in *M. diastema,* and the two species may be easily confused. Females appear to grow larger than males (Campbell and Lamar, 1989).

Key Reference: Roze (1996).

Micrurus nigrocinctus (Girard). Figs. 28, 29.

Vernacular Names: *Coral, bead-and-coral, corallilo,* Central American coral snake, coral gargantilla.

Description: A medium-sized snake; total length approximately 1070 mm. Head somewhat rounded in dorsal view, only slightly wider than neck; eye small and completely black, with a vertically oriented subcircular

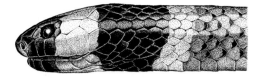

FIGURE 28 Head of *Micrurus nigrocinctus* (FMNH 16120; Guaymas District, Depto. Atlántida, Honduras) in lateral view. Scale bar = 2 cm.

pupil. Nasal scale divided; loreal absent; preoculars 1; postoculars 2; supralabials 7, with third and fourth entering orbit; infralabials 7; dorsal scales smooth except for supraanal tubercles in males, in 15 rows throughout and without apical pits; ventrals 180–230; anal plate divided; subcaudals 31–56, mostly divided. Dorsum and venter (excluding tail) red with 10–29 (usually fewer than 20) black rings, flanked by yellow rings (up to 2 scales wide and occasionally absent). In most snakes the red scales are heavily marked with black; in some specimens the red scales are dusky or uniformly tipped with tiny black dots. Snout entirely black, typically involving the rostral, internasals, prefrontals, and supraoculars, sometimes extending laterally to include the first four supralabials; the chin and anterior infralabials may also be black. Tail yellow with 3–8 broad black rings.

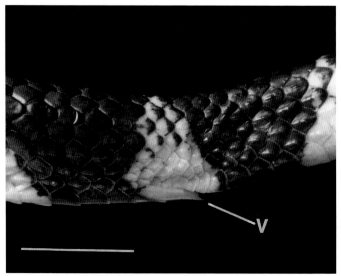

FIGURE 29 Detail of lower body and base of tail in a male *Micrurus nigrocinctus* showing supraanal tubercles. V = vent. Scale bar = 1 cm. Photograph by P. Hurst.

Habitat: Evergreen broadleaf forest, semi-evergreen seasonal forest, high-land pine savanna, and possibly subtropical evergreen forest formations; terrestrial; sea level to 450 m.

Distribution: Southern Mexico to northern South America. In Belize it has been recorded from Orange Walk, Belize, Stann Creek, and Toledo Districts.

Similar Species: In *M. diastema* the red scales are not uniformly tipped with black, or the black pigment is concentrated into irregular blotches (in *M. nigrocinctus* the red scales are uniformly and often boldly marked with black); *M. diastema* also usually has more than 20 black body rings, a pale spot on the snout, no supraanal tubercles in males, and subcaudal scales that are mostly entire (largely divided in *M. nigrocinctus*). From *M. hippocrepis* it is distinguished by the presence of an entirely black snout (frequently pale yellowish in *M. hippocrepis*) and the presence of supraanal tubercles in males. Also coral snake mimics (see Coral Snakes section above and *Lampropeltis, Oxyrhopus, Scaphiodontophis, and Urotheca*).

Remarks: Venomous. Typically observed foraging among leaf litter for small lizards and snakes, although has been found crawling through low vegetation 3 m above ground (Smith, 1943). Principally nocturnal, although may also be encountered by day. Oviparous. The few museum specimens of *Micrurus nigrocinctus* known to have definitely come from Belize appear to represent *M. diastema* and *M. hippocrepis*, and the status of this species in the region is uncertain.

Key Reference: Roze (1996).

PITVIPERS AND RATTLESNAKES (FAMILY VIPERIDAE)

This family of highly venomous snakes has a worldwide distribution. Viperids appear to be the most highly evolved of all snakes; unlike the elapids and rear-fanged colubrids, the poison fang canal is almost completely closed, with only a vestigial groove on the surface indicating its presence beneath. The fangs themselves are not fixed in place but hinged at the point of attachment to the maxillary bone and are capable of being pivoted independently of one another (solenoglyphous). Normally, they are kept folded back along the roof of the mouth, encased in a protective sheath, but are rotated outward as the mouth is opened to strike.

Viperid snakes in the Americas all belong to the subfamily Crotalinae, which have a heat-sensitive pit (loreal pit) on each side of the face between the eye and nostril, an adaptation for detecting warm-blooded prey. The dorsal scales are invariably keeled, with or without apical pits. Ventral scales are as wide as the body, and the subcaudals may be divided or undivided. Six species occur in Belize; there is a single ambiguous record of a seventh, *Porthidium yucatanicum*, from Benque Viejo in Cayo, but this is widely believed to have been mistaken for *P. nasutum*, a close relative. The eyes of all pitvipers have vertically elliptic pupils. In Belize they are predominantly crepuscular and nocturnal snakes, although *Atropoides nummifer* may be frequently observed by day.

The venom of viperid snakes is essentially antihemostatic in nature, directed toward the blood and circulatory system, although that of *Crotalus durissus* differs in also having a neurotoxic fraction. From a human health risk and mortality viewpoint, *Bothrops asper* and *Crotalus durissus* are the most important species in Belize (see the chapter "Features and Treatment of Snake Bites in Belize" in this volume).

Key to the Genera and Species of the Family Viperidae in Belize

1. Tail terminating in a rattle (or button in small juveniles) . . . .
. . . . *Crotalus durissus*

    Rattle or button absent 2

2. Dorsum of head with usually 9 enlarged symmetrical plates . . . .
. . . . *Agkistrodon bilineatus*

    Dorsum of head with more than 9 and usually numerous small, irregularly arranged scales. 3

3. Two or three pointed scales above the eye; arboreal with prehensile tail
. . . . *Bothriechis schlegelii*

    No such scales above the eye; terrestrial with nonprehensile tail . . . 4

4. Snout with strongly upturned rostral scale giving horned appearance; dorsal pattern bisected by a pale vertebral line . . *Porthidium nasutum*

    Snout not or only slightly upturned; dorsal pattern not bisected by a vertebral line. 5

5. Supraoculars large, broad, and conspicuous; subcaudals mostly paired; dorsal body scales keeled but not knob-like. . . . . *Bothrops asper*

    Supraoculars small, narrow, and elongate or divided into small scales; subcaudals mostly entire; dorsal body scales strongly keeled and knoblike . . . . *Atropoides nummifer*

Agkistrodon bilineatus (Günther). Fig. 30; Plate 170.
Vernacular Names: *Tommygoff*(?), *Wolpoch* or *uol-poch* (Yucatec Maya), cantil, tropical moccasin, vibora de freno.

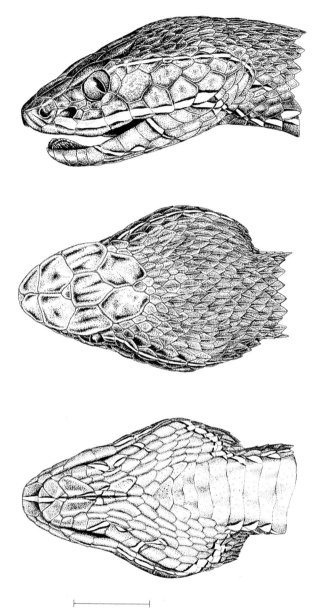

FIGURE 30 Head detail of *Agkistrodon bilineatus* (BMNH 75.4.30.1; Belize). Lateral (top), dorsal (middle), and ventral (bottom) aspects. The provenance of this specimen has been questioned by Gloyd (1972). Scale bar = 1 cm.

PLATE 170 *Agkistrodon bilineatus* from Costa Rica. Photograph by S. Von Peltz.

Description: A stout, medium-sized snake with a nonprehensile tail; total length approximately 1050 mm. Head broadly triangular and distinctly wider than neck. Top of head with 9 symmetrical enlarged plates; nasal scale divided; loreal single; preoculars 2 or 3, the lower or middle one forming the upper and posterior border of the pit; post/suboculars 3–5; supralabials 8, the upper portion of the second forming the anterior border of the pit; lower margin of pit formed by a single subfoveal; infralabials 11 or 12; dorsal scales keeled, except for lowermost 1 or 2 rows, with 2 apical pits, in 23 rows at midbody; ventrals 129–144; anal plate entire; subcaudals 46–68, divided and undivided. Dorsum tan, reddish brown, or gray with 12 to 25 (usually 14–16) broad, darker crossbands, each outlined with a narrow pale border or irregular whitish spots; tip of tail usually paler with faint narrow crossbands. Head dark with a contrasting whitish stripe that extends obliquely downward through the supralabials, breaking into a series of spots on the lateral gulars, and another pale line at the level of the eye; the rostral and mental are each marked with a similar whitish bar. Venter pinkish gray, heavily flecked with small white marks outlined with black.

Habitat: Near water in semi-evergreen seasonal forest formation, possibly interior wetlands formation and along streams in savanna formation; terrestrial and semiaquatic; sea level to 50 m.

Distribution: Northern Mexico to Costa Rica. In Belize it is known only from Corozal and northern Belize Districts; possibly also occurs in northern Orange Walk District.

Similar Species: *Atropoides nummifer* is similar in size and form but has numerous small, heavily keeled scales on the top of the head; in *Agkistrodon* the dorsal head scales are large, smooth, and arranged in a symmetrical pattern.

Remarks: Venomous. A rare snake apparently restricted to the seasonally dry forests of northern and eastern Belize, where it has also been found in wet areas around sugarcane fields (Hoevers and Henderson, 1974). The tip of the tail is paler than the dorsum, and in juveniles is used as a lure to attract prey. Nocturnal. Viviparous. Snakes from Belize have been assigned to the subspecies *A. b. russeolus* Gloyd, endemic to the Yucatán Peninsula.

Key Reference: Gloyd and Conant (1990).

Atropoides nummifer (Rüpell). See Fig. 18; Plates 171, 172, 173, 174.

Vernacular Names: *Jumping tommygoff, chehpat,* jumping pitviper, nauyaca saltadora, mano de metate.

PLATE 171 Adult *Atropoides nummifer*. Cuxta Bani, upper Raspaculo River, Cayo District.

PLATE 172 Juvenile *Atropoides nummifer*. Cuxta Bani, upper Raspaculo River, Cayo District.

PLATE 173 *Atropoides nummifer*. Juvenile. Yellow color variant. Bladen Nature Reserve, Toledo District. Photograph by C. Farneti Foster.

PLATE 174 *Atropoides nummifer.* Gray variant. Cuxta Bani, upper Raspaculo River, Cayo District.

Description: An exceptionally thick-bodied, medium-sized snake with a prominent spinal ridge and a nonprehensile tail; total length approximately 800 mm. Head large, broadly triangular and distinctly wider than neck. Top of head covered with small, keeled scales; loreal single; lacunals 3; foveals 3–4; preoculars 1; postoculars 1–4; supralabials 9–12; infralabials 10–14; dorsal scales strongly keeled, knob-like, in 23–31 rows at midbody and without apical pits; ventrals 114–135; anal plate entire; subcaudals 22–39, undivided. Dorsum yellowish brown, reddish brown, or grayish with 15–24 dark brown to black rhomboid-shaped dorsal blotches, often fused posteriorly to form a partial zig–zag stripe, connecting with or separate from a series of lateral blotches. Head pale brown or grayish with dark stripe extending from behind the eye to the angle of the jaw. Venter usually mottled or with dark squarish blotches.

Habitat: Evergreen broadleaf forest, edges of highland pine savanna, and possibly subtropical evergreen forest formations; terrestrial; 100 to 700 m.

Distribution: Central Mexico to Panama. In Belize it is known from Cayo, Stann Creek, and Toledo Districts; possibly also occurs in western parts of Orange Walk District.

Similar Species: Other terrestrial pitvipers: *Agkistrodon* is similar in size and form but has a symmetrical arrangement of large, smooth, well-defined scales on top of the head. *Bothrops asper* is more slender, with a pattern consisting of triangular blotches oriented laterally. *Porthidium nasutum* has a distinctive rostral horn with a pattern of dorsal blotches bisected by a pale vertebral line.

Remarks: Venomous. Widely believed to be capable of launching itself into the air when striking, as insinuated by its vernacular name, but in truth not able to jump much more than two-thirds of its length. Nocturnal and, in the dry season at least, also diurnal. Typically encountered basking on forest trails or coiled among leaf litter; if provoked will often form a circular coil with the head in the center and mouth widely agape. Adults feed largely on lizards and small mammals; juveniles may also prey on invertebrates. Viviparous.

Key Reference: Wilson and Meyer (1985).

Bothriechis schlegelii (Berthold). Fig. 31; Plates 175, 176.

Vernacular Names: *Green tommygoff*, eyelash palm pitviper, nauyaca de pestañas.

Description: A medium-sized pitviper with a prehensile tail; maximum total length approximately 800 mm, although more commonly less than 600 mm. All scales on top of head keeled except for canthals; internasals, and supraoculars; loreal divided; lacunals 3; foveals 4–10; preoculars 1; suboculars 1–2; postoculars 2 or 3; supraoculars bordered laterally by a row of tiny scales and 1–3 projecting, elongate, pointed scales; supralabials 7–10; infralabials 8–12; dorsal scales keeled except for outermost row, in 21–25 rows at midbody and without apical pits; ventrals

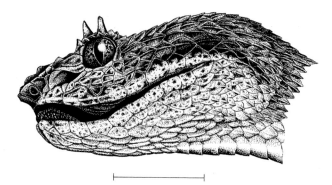

FIGURE 31 Head of *Bothriechis schlegelii* (BMNH 1956.1.15.96, near Millionario, Cayo District) in lateral view, illustrating eyelash-like character of supercilliary scales. Scale bar = 1 cm.

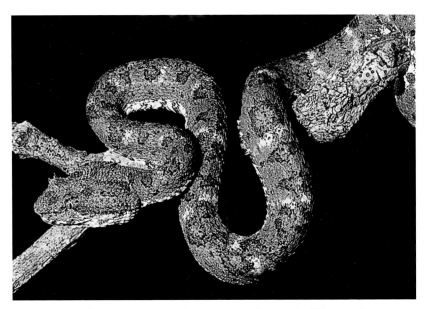

PLATE 175   Adult *Bothriechis schlegelii*. Cerro Cacao, Cordillera de Guanacaste, Costa Rica.

PLATE 176   Juvenile *Bothriechis schlegelii*. Grano de Oro, Chiquibul Forest, Cayo District. Photograph by T. King.

SNAKES

140–169; anal plate entire; subcaudals 43–62, mostly undivided. Dorsum a dull shade of green, olive-green, gray, or gray-brown stippled with black, usually with a broken zig–zag stripe of brown or rust dorsal markings, and a series of brownish, yellow, or pinkish paravertebral blotches arranged either opposite or alternate to one another. A further series of small dark lateral spots is normally present. Venter yellowish anteriorly, with darker ventrolateral blotches posteriorly.

Habitat: Evergreen broadleaf forest formation. The species may also occur in the narrow belts of broadleaf woodland along some of the streams bordering Mountain Pine Ridge (highland pine savanna formation); arboreal; 100 to 500 m.

Distribution: Southern Mexico to Colombia, Ecuador, and northwestern Venezuela. In Belize it is known from Western Orange Walk, Cayo, Stann Creek, and Toledo Districts.

Similar Species: Inasmuch as *B. schlegelii* is the only snake in Belize with pointed scales above the eye, it is unlikely to be confused with any other species. No other pitviper is habitually arboreal, although juveniles of *Bothrops asper* may occasionally be found in low bushes.

Remarks: Venomous; may draw the body into a defensive coil and hold its mouth agape if disturbed. A highly camouflaged arboreal species, characterized by the presence of small raised, pointed scales above the eye, giving the appearance of eyelashes. Typically found perched on low branches, or in the leaf axils of heliconias (*Heliconia* spp.), cohunes (*Attalea cohune*), dwarf palms, etc.; also occasionally found in the roofs of old forest buildings and palm-thatched shelters. Principally nocturnal. Viviparous.

Key Reference: Wilson and Meyer (1985).

Bothrops asper (Garman). Plates 177, 178.

Vernacular Names: *Yellow jaw tommygoff*, terciopelo, fer-de-lance, barba amarilla, cuatro narices.

Description: A very large snake with a nonprehensile tail; total length approximately 2460 mm. All scales on top of head keeled except for canthals, supraoculars, and usually internasals; loreal single; lacunals 1; foveals 4–7; preoculars 2; suboculars 1–3; postoculars 2–4; supralabials 7–8, large; infralabials 8–12; dorsal scales keeled, in 23–33 (usually 25–29) rows at midbody; ventrals 161–240; anal plate entire; subcaudals 46–81, divided. Dorsum brown or olive-brown with large diamond-shaped blotches demarcated by darker, triangular-shaped lateral blotches extending from the venter to the middorsal line, where they may fuse to give an hourglass-like shape; some lateral blotches offset from those on opposite flank to give an undulating zig-zag effect. Dorsum of head dark olive-brown; supralabial area and lower jaw yellow or cream with a dark

278

PLATE 177 Adult *Bothrops asper*. Sibun Hills area, Belize District. Photograph by S. Von Peltz, courtesy of the Belize Zoo.

PLATE 178 Juvenile *Bothrops asper*. Las Cuevas, Chiquibul Forest, Cayo District.

stripe extending from posterior edge of eye to angle of jaw. Venter cream with diffuse pale brown blotches medially and bolder markings laterally.

Habitat: Evergreen broadleaf forest, semi-evergreen seasonal forest, karst hills forest, near water in savanna, and highland pine savanna formations, and among mangroves in coastal lagoons and marshes formation; terrestrial (juveniles also semiarboreal); sea level to 700 m.

Distribution: Central Mexico to Colombia, Ecuador, and Venezuela. In Belize it occurs countrywide.

Similar Species: *Xenodon rabdocephalus* is strikingly similar in color and pattern, but can be distinguished by its typical colubrid-shaped head with a rounded eye pupil, and smooth dorsal scales in fewer rows (19). *Atropoides nummifer* is a more stoutly proportioned snake with darker, bolder, triangular markings on the dorsum, and a broader head; *P. nasutum* has a thin pale middorsal line and a prominently upturned snout. *Boa constrictor* is a similarly sized snake and has elliptical eye pupils, but is otherwise incomparable.

Remarks: Highly irascible and dangerously venomous. A well-camouflaged, rather slender pitviper capable of unprecedented agility and speed. When disturbed usually moves away into thick cover, but may turn back on itself to face aggressor if pursued; defends itself vigorously if cornered. Chiefly nocturnal; may be encountered by day coiled at the bases of large trees and also frequently found along streams. Viviparous. This snake is also known under the name *Bothrops atrox asper.*

Key Reference: Villa (1984).

Crotalus durissus Linnaeus. Plates 179, 180.

Vernacular Names: *Rattlesnake,* Yucatán rattlesnake, tzab-can, cascabel, cascavel.

Description: A large, heavily built snake distinguished by a rattle (or button in small juveniles) on the end of the tail; total length approximately 1800 mm. Adults have a conspicuous spinal ridge. Head broad and distinctly wider than neck. Top of head covered with small, smooth plates anteriorly, and keeled scales posteriorly; loreal divided; foveals 5–16; preoculars 2, the lower forming the dorsal edge of loreal pit; suboculars 2–4; postoculars 1–3; supralabials usually 13–16; infralabials usually 14–17; dorsal scales strongly keeled and knob-like, usually in 25–33 rows at midbody and without apical pits; ventrals 155–195; anal plate entire; subcaudals 18–34, up to 10 (usually 1 or 2) of which may be divided. Dorsum usually a pale shade of gray, blue-gray, brownish, straw-yellow, or reddish, with a pair of dark, longitudinal paravertebral stripes on the head and neck, replaced by a series of 18–35, darker rhombic or diamond-shaped blotches. Below the dorsal blotches near the lateral edge of the ventrals are a similar number of smaller blotches. Dorsum of head often

PLATE 179 *Crotalus durissus.* Mile 29, Western Highway, Belize District. Photograph by C. Farneti Foster.

PLATE 180 Head detail of *Crotalus durissus.* Mile 30, Western Highway, Belize District. Photographed at the Belize Zoo, courtesy of Sharon Matola and Tony Garel.

with a dark transverse bar between the eyes. Venter yellowish and usually immaculate.

Habitat: Semi-evergreen seasonal forest, savanna, and highland pine savanna formations; terrestrial; sea level to 600 m.

Distribution: Central Mexico to Argentina. In Belize it occurs countrywide, but in Toledo District only on the coast.

Similar Species: No other snake in Belize has a rattle on the end of the tail.

Remarks: Highly irascible and dangerously venomous. When alarmed this snake elevates its head and anterior part of the body high off the ground with the neck bent like a shepherd's crook, facing source of threat and rattling its tail; the tongue is also protruded and withdrawn in a slow, controlled manner. Nocturnal and diurnal. Viviparous. The form occurring in Belize and the Yucatán Peninsula in general is known under the subspecific name *C. d. tzabcan* Klauber.

Key Reference: Villa (1984).

Porthidium nasutum (Bocourt). Plate 181.

Vernacular Names: *Hognosed tommygoff,* rainforest hognosed pitviper, chalpate, nauyaca chatilla.

Description: A small- to medium-sized snake; total length approximately 630 mm but generally less than 400 mm. All scales on top of head keeled except canthals, internasals, and supraoculars; rostral projecting above snout, giving horned appearance, bordered laterally by anterior edge of nasal and first supralabial; internasals elongate, bent up at the middle forming lateral edges of horn; loreal single; lacunals 2–3; foveals 3–26; preoculars 2–4, usually 3; suboculars 1–4; postoculars 1–4, usually 3; supralabials 8–11; infralabials 10–13; dorsal scales keeled, in 21–27 rows at midbody; ventrals 123–145; anal plate entire; subcaudals 24–41, undivided. Dorsum yellowish brown, reddish brown, pale brown, or grayish, with a series of 13–23 dark triangular blotches outlined with white, arranged either alternately or opposite each other; there is usually a pale orange-tan or yellowish middorsal line coursing the length of the body. Venter heavily mottled with brown.

Habitat: Evergreen broadleaf forest, highland pine savanna, and possibly subtropical evergreen forest formations; terrestrial; 100 to 600 m.

Distribution: Southern Mexico to Colombia and Ecuador. In Belize it is known only from Cayo District, although may also occur in Stann Creek and Toledo Districts.

Similar Species: Other terrestrial pitvipers: *Atropoides nummifer* does not have a distinctive rostral horn and is much stouter, with a pattern of dorsal blotches not bisected by a pale vertebral line; *Bothrops asper* also lacks a rostral horn and has a different pattern of triangular lateral blotches without a pale vertebral line. The colubrid species *Ficimia pub-*

PLATE 181 *Porthidium nasutum.* Caracol, Cayo District. Photograph by C.M. Miller.

lia has a similarly upturned, pointed snout, but has a round pupil, smooth dorsal scales; and a markedly different color pattern.

Remarks: Venomous. A small, well-camouflaged forest pitviper, characterized by a projecting, upturned rostral scale giving the snout a horned appearance. Nocturnal and diurnal. Usually observed foraging in leaf litter after rain. Adults feed largely on small mammals and lizards; the diet of juveniles includes earthworms and possibly other invertebrates. Viviparous.

Key Reference: Porras *et al.* (1981).

FEATURES AND TREATMENT OF SNAKE BITES IN BELIZE

David A. Warrell
Centre for Tropical Medicine, University of Oxford,
John Radcliffe Hospital, Oxford OX3 9DU, United Kingdom

The diverse venomous snake fauna of Belize, the nature of the terrain, and the rural activities of a large proportion of the population should create a high risk of snake bite, especially among those who hunt or work on farms or plantations in forest, swamp, and savanna areas. The only published study of the incidence of snake bites in Belize was based mainly on hospital records of 57 bites and 8 deaths from 1980 to 1985, an incidence of bites of only 1–10 per 100,000 population per year (Martin, 1988, 1989). However, in most parts of the country, it is not hospital doctors, but the traditional village "snake doctors" who see and treat most cases of snake bite. Unreported fatal cases, especially those following bites by *Bothrops asper* (yellow jaw tommygoff, terciopelo, fer-de-lance, barba amarilla, cuatro narices; page 278), occur in the forest (Byron Foster, personal communication, 1995).

Clinical Features of Snake Bites

Bites by venomous snakes, even when the presence of fang marks indicates that the skin has been punctured, do not inevitably lead to injection of venom and the development of local and systemic envenoming. Based on studies of proven bites by particular species, the ratio of bites to envenoming is usually about 2:1. In Belize, when envenoming has occurred, one of four different syndromes (complexes of symptoms and signs) may be expected:

1. **Bothrops Syndrome:** There is severe local envenoming [swelling, bruising, inflammation, bacterial infection, and necrosis (gangrene)] with or without shock, spontaneous systemic bleeding, defective blood clotting, and acute kidney failure. The most common cause of this type of envenoming is *B. asper* (page 278), but the other species of Crotalinae (pitvipers) might also be responsible, especially *Agkistrodon bilineatus* (cantil, tropical moccasin, víbora de freno, page 270). The smaller species such as *Atropoides nummifer* (jumping tommygoff, chehpat, jumping pitviper, nauyaca saltadora, mano de piedra, braza de piedra; page 273), *Bothriechis schlegelii* (green tommygoff, eyelash palm pitviper, nauyaca de pestañas; page 276), and *Porthidium nasutum* (hognosed tommygoff, rainforest hognosed pitviper, chalpate, nauyaca chatilla; page 282) are more likely to cause mild or moderate local envenoming without systemic symptoms. The clinical features of *B. asper* envenoming have been reviewed recently by Hardy (1994a,b). Early symptoms include severe local pain, nausea, vomiting, diarrhea, and fainting. Swelling and bruising spread rapidly up the bitten limb with tender enlargement of local lymph nodes draining the bitten area. Blisters may appear within 12–24 hr and signs of local abscess formation and necrosis may develop in the next few days. Signs of severe systemic envenoming include shock (low blood pressure with impaired circulation), spontaneous bleeding from the gums, nose, lungs, stomach, and bowels, and blood-stained urine. Bleeding into the brain can cause death rapidly. Diminishing urine output suggests acute kidney failure.

Up to 7% of cases of *B. asper* envenoming are fatal (Bolaños, 1984), whereas mortality among victims of bites by *Atropoides, Bothriechis,* and *Porthidium* species is negligible.

2. **Rattlesnake Syndrome:** Local envenoming is mild (pain, swelling, and redness without blistering and necrosis), but there is paralysis of muscles innervated by the cranial nerves (drooping of the eyelids, inability to speak or swallow, etc.), generalized damage to skeletal muscle resulting in painful, aching, or tender muscles all over the body, and the passage of dark (Coca Cola-colored) urine containing muscle pigment (myoglobin) with or without mild bleeding and clotting disorders, shock, and acute kidney failure. The cause is envenoming by *Crotalus durissus tzabcan* (Yucatán rattlesnake, tzab-can, cascabel/cascavel; page 280). Early symptoms resemble those of *Bothrops* envenoming—nausea, vomiting, and diarrhea—but the progressive paralysis and myoglobinuria are distinctive.

3. **Coral Snake Syndrome:** Symptoms and signs of local envenoming are negligible but there is progressive paralysis, starting with the eyelids, which may not start until 6–9 hr after the bite. The cause is envenoming by coral snakes or bead-and-corals (*Micrurus diastema, M. hippocrepis,* and *M. nigrocinctus;* pages 261–269). The appearance and behavior of the biting snake, the mildness of local symptoms and signs, the severity of neurotoxicity, and the absence of symptoms or signs of skeletal muscle breakdown distinguish this clinical picture from that of rattlesnake syndrome.

4. **Colubrid Syndrome:** There is mild local pain or paresthesia ("pins and needles"), swelling, and bruising following bites by colubrid snakes [for example, of the genera *Coniophanes* (pages 188–195), *Conophis* (pages 195–196), *Leptodeira* (page 213–217), *Leptophis* (pages 217–221), *Oxybelis* (pages 225–227), *Urotheca* (pages 258–260), and perhaps other opisthoglyphous species]. Severe or life-threatening envenoming has not been attributed to any of these snakes.

Treatment of Snake Bites

First Aid

Most traditional first-aid treatments for snake bite, such as excision, suction, and tourniquets, are time-wasting, useless, and harmful. They should not be used!

The principles of modern first aid for snake bite are:

1. **Delivery** of the victim as quickly as possible to a place where he or she can be treated by medically trained staff;

2. **Delay** of evolution of life-threatening envenoming at least until the victim is in the hands of medically trained staff;
3. **Alleviation** of severe and potentially life-threatening early symptoms of envenoming.

First aid must be initiated by the person who has been bitten or by anyone else who is around at the time of a bite, using materials that are immediately available.

1. **Reassure** the victim or **keep calm** if you are the victim. Many bites by venomous snakes do not result in envenoming (see above) and, even if there is envenoming, progression to death is rare and usually takes many hours after coral snake bites and several days after pitviper bites.
2. **Remove** rings, bracelets, and tight-fitting clothing from the bitten limb (which may swell rapidly).
3. **Immobilize** the bitten limb. Muscle contraction in the limb will increase systemic absorption of venom. Immobilization can be achieved with a splint or sling. **Pressure immobilization** (Sutherland *et al.*, 1979) is the most effective way to immobilize the limb and also compresses superficial veins and lymphatics, retarding absorption of venom. A very long stretchy (crepe) bandage, about 10 cm wide and preferably at least 3 m long, should be bound around the entire bitten limb, starting over the bite site itself. The bandage should be applied as firmly as for a sprained ankle, but not so tightly that (1) a finger cannot be introduced easily between its layers; (2) the peripheral pulse (at the wrist or on the foot and ankle) is occluded and cannot be felt; or (3) the hand or foot becomes blue and ischemic.

   Pressure immobilization should be employed where possible after coral snake bites and is probably safe in the case of rattlesnake bites. However, with other pitviper bites, the benefit of delaying systemic venom absorption must be balanced against the risk of increasing local tissue destruction. The pressure bandage will increase intracompartmental pressure in the limb and so may impair the blood supply to swollen envenomed muscles within tight connective tissue compartments. The bitten limb should *not* be raised above the level of the heart, even though it may feel more comfortable in that position.
4. **Transport** the snake bite victim as quickly but as passively as possible to the nearest place where he or she can be treated by a medically trained person. A **stretcher** is ideal or the victim can be carried on a bicycle or on someone's back to the nearest vehicle or boat.
5. **Treat** pain with paracetamol (acetaminophen) or codeine but **not** with aspirin or other nonsteroidal anti-inflammatory agents (such as ibuprofen and diclofenac), which may cause bleeding from the stomach.

6. **Do not** tamper with the wound in any way. **Do not** use traditional first-aid methods such as local cauterization; incision; excision; amputation; suction by mouth, vacuum pump, or syringe; injection or instillation of compounds such as potassium permanganate; electric shocks; or ice packs. **Do not** pursue and kill the snake responsible for the bite as this may risk further accidents. However, if the snake has been killed or captured, try to take it (safely!) with the patient for identification.

On the Way to the Hospital

The journey to hospital may take many hours or, in exceptional cases, days. Life-threatening envenoming may develop. Ideally, the patient should lie on his or her side (recovery position) to maintain a clear airway and reduce the risk of inhaling any vomitus into the lungs. Persistent vomiting can be treated with chlorpromazine (adult dose 10–25 mg every 4–6 hr by mouth, 25 mg by intramuscular injection, or 100 mg every 6–8 hr by rectal suppository). Patients with incoagulable blood (for example after *Bothrops* bites) will bleed locally after intramuscular or subcutaneous injections and so the intravenous route should be used whenever possible. A firm pressure dressing should be applied to all venepuncture sites. Neurotoxic envenoming (coral snakes and rattlesnakes) may impair the victim's ability to cough and clear saliva and other secretions from the throat and windpipe. Eventually, the breathing muscles may become paralyzed. A clear airway should be established and maintained. Oxygen should be given if available and mouth-to-mouth artificial ventilation may be required. If the patient is unconscious and no femoral (in the groin) or carotid (in the neck) pulse can be felt, cardiopulmonary resuscitation should be started immediately. Patients who feel faint or are obviously in shock must always be laid flat.

Hospital Treatment

Snake Bite: Hospital Treatment

(Resuscitation)
Clinical assessment
Species diagnosis
?Antivenom treatment
Ancillary treatment
Clinical monitoring
Treatment of complications
Rehabilitation

Clinical Assessment. Ideally, snake-bitten patients should be kept under medical observation for at least 24 hr. Local swelling usually appears within 15 min of a pitviper bite and within 2 hr of bites by other snakes (except coral snakes), if significant envenoming has occurred. Absence of visible fang marks does not exclude the risk of significant envenoming. Pain and tender enlargement of lymph nodes draining the bitten area (for example, in the groin in bites on the lower limb, at the elbow or in the armpit after bites on the hand) is an early sign of envenoming by pitvipers and, rarely, by coral snakes. The gums should be examined carefully as they are usually the first site of bleeding caused by circulating venom. Other common sites are nose, skin, gastrointestinal tract, urogenital tract, and eyes. Persistent bleeding from the fang marks, injection and venepuncture sites, and other wounds suggests that the blood is incoagulable. Hypotension and shock are important signs of reduced circulating blood volume (hypovolemia) or damage to the heart muscle, and are seen particularly in victims of bites by *Bothrops* and rattlesnakes. Inability to raise the eyelids fully when looking upward (ptosis) is the earliest sign of neurotoxic envenoming. If an antihemostatic venom is suspected (*Bothrops*, rattlesnake), blood clotting should be checked at the bedside, using the simple 20-min whole blood clotting test (see below).

Investigations   A useful test requiring no apparatus except a new, clean, dry, glass test tube is the 20-minute whole blood clotting test.

20-Minute Whole Blood Clotting Test

A few milliliters of venous blood is placed in a new, clean, dry, glass test tube and left to stand vertically at ambient temperature for 20 min. At the end of this time, the tube is tipped: if the blood is still liquid and runs out, the patient has venom-induced coagulopathy, an indication for antivenom treatment.

Other tests of blood clotting that may be available in some laboratories are prothrombin time, partial thromboplastin time, INR, and fibrin(ogen) degradation products.

Other useful investigations are:

1. Full blood count: the hemoglobin or hematocrit (PCV) may be raised initially from hemoconcentration but later will fall if there is bleeding. The platelet count may be reduced in *Bothrops* victims. Systemic envenoming may be associated with a neutrophil leukocytosis.
2. If there is extensive tissue damage at the site of the bite, or generalized skeletal muscle breakdown (for example, in rattlesnake envenoming), serum concentrations of creatine kinase and aspartate aminotransferase may be elevated.
3. Serum creatinine, blood urea, and plasma potassium concentrations are increased in patients with kidney failure.
4. Stix testing of urine may reveal blood/hemoglobin/myoglobin.

Examination of the urine under the microscope may detect red blood corpuscles (hematuria).

5. ECG/EKG may show evidence of myocardial damage (ST segment/T wave changes, arrhythmia) and in patients with acute kidney failure, may indicate a high plasma potassium concentration.

Clinical Monitoring in the Hospital   Blood pressure, pulse rate, respiratory rate, level of consciousness, presence or absence of ptosis, extent of local swelling, and appearance of any new symptoms must be recorded every 30–60 min while the patient is under observation in the hospital.

Antivenom Treatment

Antivenom is the only specific antidote to snake venom.

In patients with systemic or severe local envenoming, the benefits of antivenom treatment far outweigh the risks of antivenom reactions.

Indications for Antivenom Treatment

Systemic envenoming
  Shock, abnormal heart rhythm, or ECG/EKG abnormality
  Paralysis
  Systemic bleeding (e.g., from the gums)
  Incoagulable blood
  Dark (red/black) urine (myoglobinuria/hemoglobinuria)
  Abnormal laboratory tests:
    Peripheral neutrophil leukocytosis ($>15,000/\mu l$)
    Elevated serum creatine kinase or aminotransferases
    Hemoconcentration, anemia, hypoxemia, or acidosis
Severe local envenoming
  Rapid progression of swelling   } necrotic venom
  Bite on a finger   }
  Swelling of more than half the bitten limb within 24 hr of the bite

Rules for Antivenom Treatment

1. An antivenom should be chosen whose stated range of specificity includes the species thought to be responsible for the bite (see Table 6 and rules 2–8).
2. Liquid or reconstituted freeze-dried (lyophilized) antivenoms should not contain visible particles, which would suggest precipitation of protein and indicate loss of activity and increased risk of reactions.
3. Skin or conjunctival hypersensitivity tests do not predict antivenom reactions and should not be used.

TABLE 6 Antivenoms Claimed to Neutralize Venoms of Species Found in Belize

Manufacturer	Antivenom	Range of specificity against species found in Belize
Costa Rica		
1. Instituto Clodomiro Picado[a]	Polyvalent antivenom	B. asper, C. d. durissus, B. schlegelii, P. nasutum, A. bilineatus
2. Instituto Clodomiro Picado	Anti-coral (polyvalent)	M. nigrocinctus
3. Instituto Clodomiro Picado	Pan-American serum; anti-coral polyvalent serum	M. nigrocinctus
Mexico		
4. Gerencia General de Biologicos y Reactivos[b]	Anti-Crotalus	C. durissus
5. Gerencia General de Biologicos y Reactivos	Anti-Bothrops	A. bilineatus, B. asper
6. Gerencia General de Biologicos y Reactivos (?formerly Grupo Pharma)	Suero antiofidico	B. atrox, C. d. terrificus
	Export lyophilized	Mexican and South American Bothrops and Crotalus species
7. Laboratorios Bioclon[c]	Snake antivenin	A. bilineatus, B. asper, A. nummifer, C. durrissus
8. Laboratorios Bioclon	Monovalent Bothrops	B. asper
9. Laboratorios Bioclon	Polyvalent Crotalus	C. d. terrificus
10. Laboratorios Bioclon	Polyvalent Mexico	B. asper, C. d. terrificus
11. Laboratorios "Myn"[d]	Snake antivenin	B. asper, C. d. tzabcan, A. bilineatus and all other Mexican crotalids
12. Laboratorios "Myn"	Monovalent Bothrops	B. asper
13. Laboratorios "Myn"	Polyvalent Crotalus	C. d. terrificus
14. Laboratorios "Myn"	Polyvalent Mexico	B. asper, C. d. terrificus
United States		
15. Wyeth-Ayerst[e]	Wyeth antivenin	Agkistrodon species, B. atrox
	(Crotalidae) polyvalent	C. d. terrificus

[a] Instituto Clodomiro Picado, Facultad de Microbiologia, Universidad de Costa Rica, Ciudad Universitaria, Rodrigo Facio, San José, Costa Rica (Tels) ++506 2290344/2293135; (Fax) ++506 2920485; E-mail: icpucr@cariari.ucr.ac.cr. Website available at http://www.icp.ucr.ac.cr/index.shtml
[b] Gerencia General de Biologicos y Reactivos, Ministerio de Salud, M. Escobado 20, CP 11400 Mexico, DF, Mexico (Tel) ++52 5276127/7368; (Fax) ++52 5276693.
[c] Laboratorios Bioclon, Calzada de Tlalpan 4687, CP14050 Mexico, DF, Mexico (Tel) ++52 6654111/4317/4309; (Fax) ++52 6661036.
[d] Laboratorios "Myn," SA Av Coyoacan 1707, Mexico 12 DF, Mexico.
[e] Wyeth-Ayerst Laboratories, PO Box 8299, Philadelphia, PA 19101-8299, U.S.A. (Tels) ++(1) 800 9345556, Option 4 (product information); ++(1) 800 6667247 (ordering).

4. Antivenom treatment is potentially useful as long as signs of systemic envenoming persist, which may be for several days, but, ideally, it should be given as soon as possible after these signs appear.
5. The intravenous route is the most effective. Push injections of undiluted antivenom at the rate of about 4 ml per minute and infusions diluted in approximately 5 ml of isotonic fluid per kilogram body weight are associated with the same incidence and severity of antivenom reactions.
6. The initial dose of antivenom depends partly on clinical assessment of the severity of envenoming and partly on the particular type of antivenom. The dose is rarely less than 4–5 ampoules/vials.
7. Patients should be observed closely for signs of early (anaphylactic) antivenom reactions for at least 1 hr after the dose has been injected/infused.
8. The clinical response should be checked. In the case of *Bothrops* envenoming, the 20-min whole blood clotting test should be repeated 6 hr after antivenom treatment. If the blood is still incoagulable, a second dose should be given. In the case of neurotoxic envenoming (coral snakes, rattlesnakes), the clinical response may be slow or uncertain. The dose of antivenom should be repeated if there is further deterioration after 1–2 hr. Severely envenomed patients should be observed in the hospital for several days as there may be recurrence of signs of systemic envenoming after the initial response to antivenom.

Choice of Antivenom for Snake Bites in Belize   Wyeth antivenin (Crotalidae) polyvalent has been the antivenom available in Belize in the past (Martin, 1988, 1989). However, it seems unlikely that it would be very effective against local venoms. From a geographical point of view, antivenoms manufactured in Mexico, especially those covering venoms of Mexican species found in the Yucatán Peninsula (for example, *C. d. tzabcan*, *B. asper*, and *A. bilineatus*) might have the best chance of efficacy against the venom of species in Belize. However, the laboratory and clinical efficacy of the antivenoms manufactured in Mexico has not been studied. Instituto Clodomiro Picado in Costa Rica produces good antivenoms with a reasonable chance of efficacy in Belize. Until more information is available, Instituto Clodomiro Picado antivenoms are recommended.

Antivenom Reactions   Early anaphylactic reactions usually develop within 1 hr of antivenom treatment. Symptoms include itching, urticaria (nettle rash/hives), angioedema (swelling of lips, tongue, and face), cough, wheezing (asthma), nausea, vomiting, fever, tachycardia, and shock. Pyrogenic reactions (fever and shivering alone) may develop later. Serum sickness begins about 7 days after antivenom treatment. The symptoms include fever, itching, urticaria, joint pains, swelling around the joints, enlargement of lymph nodes, and rarely neurological abnormalities.

Prevention of Antivenom Reactions   Adrenaline (epinephrine) given by subcutaneous injection before antivenom treatment (adult dose 0.25 mg of 0.1% soln.) reduces the incidence of reactions, but the antihistamine promethazine given by intramuscular injection is not effective.

Treatment of Antivenom Reactions Adrenaline (epinephrine) is the most effective treatment for early reactions; the adult dose is 0.5–1.0 ml of 0.1% (1 in 1000, 1 mg/ml) adrenaline given by subcutaneous or intramuscular injection at the first signs of a reaction. This dose may be repeated after 10–15 min if the reaction is not controlled. An antihistamine such as chlorpheniramine maleate (adult dose 10 mg) and hydrocortisone (100 mg) should also be given intravenously. Pyrogenic reactions are treated by cooling the patient and giving antipyretic drugs such as paracetamol. Late serum sickness reactions respond to antihistamine tablets such as chlorpheniramine (adult dose 2 mg every 6 hr) or to prednisolone tablets (adult dose 5 mg every 6 hr).

Use of Antivenom in the Field People living and working in remote areas of Belize might be bitten many hours or even days away from the nearest medical help. Bites by large pitvipers (especially *Bothrops asper* and *Crotalus durissus*) and coral snakes may be life-threatening and, in the case of *B. asper*, can cause severe local tissue destruction sometimes requiring amputation. In these cases, early treatment with antivenom, administered in the field and by people without medical training, may be justified. In a study of 10 field workers in Middle America bitten by *B. asper*, seven were given intramuscular antivenom under these conditions (Hardy *et al.*, 1994). Although its efficacy is uncertain, this treatment is recommended when the snake involved is a large *B. asper* or rattlesnake or coral snake. Ideally, self-injectable epinephrine (adrenaline) (e.g., "EpiPen" or "AnaPen") delivering 0.3 mg of 0.1% solution intramuscularly, and an injectable antihistamine, should be available to deal with antivenom reactions (see above). Four ampoules of antivenom are reconstituted and given by deep intramuscular injection (1 1/2'' 21 gauge needle) at 4 or more different sites in the lateral parts of both thighs. The antivenom should not be injected into the gluteal region (buttocks) as absorption is particularly poor from this fatty area. Firm pressure should be applied over the injection sites, particularly in patients who have bleeding problems and would almost certainly develop large hematomas (bruises).

Supportive Treatment

Neurotoxic (Paralytic) Envenoming Paralysis of swallowing and breathing muscles may lead to aspiration of vomit, airway obstruction, and respiratory failure. A clear airway must be maintained and, if secretions begin to pool in the back of the throat or breathing difficulties develop, a cuffed endotracheal tube should be inserted or a tracheostomy performed. Antivenom may not produce rapid or dramatic improvement of paralysis. However, anticholinesterase drugs may produce obvious improvement within 5–20 min in patients envenomed by some species of coral snake (Vital Brazil and Pellegrini Filho, 1978). **When possible, the tensilon test should be done in all cases of severe neurotoxic envenoming:** Atropine sulfate (adult dose 0.6 mg) is given by intravenous injection followed by edrophonium chloride (adult dose 10 mg) or another anticholinesterase drug, such as neostigmine. If there is a convincing response (for example, recovery of ptosis, improved strength of neck flexor muscles), treatment can be continued with neostigmine methylsulfate and atropine, given every 4 hr or by continuous intravenous infusion.

Shock and Low Blood Pressure The major cause of shock and low blood pressure is decreased circulating blood volume resulting from leakage of blood and plasma into a massively swollen limb (*Bothrops* envenoming). This hypovolemia should be corrected, preferably by transfusing fresh whole blood, fresh frozen plasma, or some other plasma expander such as Haemacell, Gelofusine, or dextran. If there is persistent or profound hypotension despite antivenom treatment and volume replacement, a vasopressor drug, such as dopamine, should be used.

Decreased Urine Output (Oliguria/Anuria) and Kidney Failure Victims of *Bothrops* and rattlesnake may develop acute renal failure. The warning signs are decreasing urine output and rising serum creatinine, urea, and plasma potassium concentrations. If cautious rehydration, diuretics (for example intravenous frusemide up to 1000 mg), and dopamine are ineffective in increasing urine output, the patient should be put on strict fluid balance and the feasibility of peritoneal hemodialysis or hemofiltration should be considered.

Local Infection at the Site of the Bite Bites by *Bothrops* species seem particularly likely to introduce bacterial flora from the snake's venom or oral cavity into the wound. These organisms include Enterobacteriaecae, *Pseudomonas*, *Clostridia*, and other anaerobic bacteria. Fluctuant swellings in the region of the site of the bite should be aspirated and, if possible, the pus should be cultured. Otherwise empirical broad spectrum antimicrobial treatment should be given (for example, chloramphenicol or benzyl penicillin plus a single dose of gentamicin). Routine chemoprophylaxis of *Bothrops* bites may be justified. A booster dose of tetanus toxoid (or, where indicated, antitetanus serum) should be given, especially in the case of necrotic wounds that have been incised or tampered with in any way.

Local Necrosis (Gangrene) of the Bitten Limb This effect of bites by *Bothrops* should be treated by early surgical débridement, followed by application of split skin grafts. A cold, tense, cyanosed, swollen, and apparently pulseless limb may suggest the need for fasciotomy, but this should not be performed unless there is convincing objective or clinical evidence of greatly increased intracompartmental pressure and blood coagulability has been restored with antivenom.

Appendix 1

ECOLOGICAL SUMMARY

The following table includes ecological information drawn from observations in Belize and various published sources (table structure adapted from Rand and Myers, 1990).

Explanatory notes:

Apr. (appearance): con = constant, meaning little variation in adult color pattern ([sd] = adults sexually dimorphic; [yng] = juvenile color pattern markedly different); var = noticeably variable or polymorphic color patterns not explained by sex or age.

Abun. (abundance): C = common, many individuals can be found; U = usual, individuals can be found if searched for in appropriate habitat and season; I = infrequent, not predictable; R = rarely seen.

Habitat: EBF = evergreen broadleaf forest; SSF = semi-evergreen seasonal forest; KHF = karst hills forest; SEF =subtropical evergreen forest; Elf = elfin forest; S = savanna [H = wooded hammocks]; HPS = highland pine savanna; IW = interior wetlands; CLM = coastal lagoons and marshes, mangrove swamp; SSC = sand strand and cocotal; Agr = agricultural land [F = fruit orchards, banana groves, etc.; S = sugarcane plantations]; Edif = edificarian; Fw = freshwater; Bw = brackish water, estuarine; M = marine.

Adap. Zone (adaptive zone): Aq = aquatic; AqMrg = aquatic margin, riparian; Arb = arboreal (C = tree canopy; B = tree limbs, branches, lower canopy; T = tree trunk; U = bush and/or forest understory); Fos = fossorial, subterranean; Gnd = ground and leaf litter, terrestrial; SAq = semiaquatic. First listed indicates adaptive zone with which species is most usually associated.

Elev. Range (elevational range [meters]): SL = coastal and/or island distribution at sea level only. The distributions of species above 600 m are poorly known, and ranges may be greater than indicated.

Diel: D = diurnal; N = nocturnal, crepuscular; ND = active during night or day, no clearcut pattern of activity.

Food: B = birds and nestlings; C = caecilians; E = bird eggs; F = frogs and tadpoles; H = herbivorous; I = invertebrates (A = arachnids; Cr = crustaceans; G = gastropods; In = insects in general; T = ants, termites, and pupae); L = lizards; M = mammals; O = omnivorous; P = fish; S = snakes; Td = toads; Tr = turtles; U = salamanders. Range of food taken by many snakes is probably greater than indicated.

Rep. Mode (reproductive mode): O = oviparous; P = parthenogenetic; V = viviparous.

Mimic: coral = coral snake pattern; viper = resembles viperid snake (* indicates true coral snake or viperid).

Ecological Summary[a]

Species	Apr.	Abun.	Habitat	Elev. range	Adap. zone	Diel	Food	Rep. mode	Mimic
Crocodylidae									
Crocodylus acutus	con	I	Bw₁[CLM], M	SL	Aq	D	P	O	
Crocodylus moreletii	con	U	Fw[EBF,SSF,S,IW], Bw[CLM]	0–450	Aq	D	M,Tr, I[Cr,In], P	O	
Cheloniidae									
Caretta caretta	con	I	M	SL	Aq	D	O	O	
Chelonia mydas	con	I	M	SL	Aq	D	O	O	
Eretmochelys imbricata	con	I	M	SL	Aq	D	O	O	
Dermochelyidae									
Dermochelys coriacea	con	R	M	SL	Aq	D	O	O	
Dermatydidae									
Dermatemys mawii	con	U	Fw₁[EBF,SSF,S,IW], Bw[CLM]	0–200	Aq	N	H	O	
Chelydridae									
Chelydra serpentina	con	R	Fw[EBF,SSF] Bw[CLM]	0–100	Aq	ND	O	O	
Kinosternidae									
Claudius angustatus	con	I	Fw[SSF,S]	0–200	Aq	ND	F, I[Cr,In], P	O	
Kinosternon acutum	con	I	Fw[EBF,SSF,S,IW]	0–300	Aq	ND	O	O	
Kinosternon leucostomum	con	U	Fw[EBF,SSF,S,HPS,IW]	0–600	Aq	ND	O	O	
Kinosternon scorpioides	con	U	Fw[SSF,S,IW]	0–450	Aq	ND	O	O	
Staurotypus triporcatus	con	I	Fw[SSF,S,IW]	0–200	Aq	ND	O	O	
Emydidae									
Rhinoclemmys areolata	con[yng]	U	EBF, SSF, S, HPS	0–600	Gnd, SAq	D	O	O	
Trachemys scripta	con[yng]	U	Fw[EBF,SSF,S,IW]	0–200	Aq	D	O	O	
Eublepharidae									
Coleonyx elegans	con[yng]	U	EBF, SSF, KHF, HPS	0–600	Gnd	N	I[A,In]	O	

(continues)

Ecological Summary—*Continued*

Species	Apr.	Abun.	Habitat	Elev. range	Adap. zone	Diel	Food	Rep. mode	Mimic
Gekkonidae									
Aristelliger georgeensis	con[yng]	U	SSC, Edif	SL	Arb[T], Gnd	ND	I[A,In], L	O	
Gonatodes albogularis	con[sd]	U	Edif	SL	Arb[T]	D	I[A,In]	O	
Hemidactylus frenatus	con	C	Edif	SL	Arb[T]	N	I[A,In]	O	
Phyllodactylus insularis	con	I	SSC	SL	Arb[T], Gnd	N	I[A,In]	O	
Phyllodactylus tuberculosus	con	U	CLM, SSC, Edif	SL	Arb, Gnd	N	I[A,In]	O	
Sphaerodactylus glaucus	var[yng]	U	EBF, SSF, KHF, S, HPS, SSC, Edif, Agr[F]	0–600	Arb[T], Gnd	D	I[A,In]	O	
Sphaerodactylus millepunctatus	var[yng]	I	EBF, SSF, KHF, SEF, S, HPS, Agr[F]	0–1000	Arb[T], Gnd	D	I[A,In]	O	
Thecadactylus rapicauda	con	I	EBF, SSF, KHF, SEF, HPS, Agr[F]	0–750	Arb[T], Gnd	N	I[A,In]	O	
Corytophanidae									
Basiliscus vittatus	con[sd]	C	EBF, SSF, KHF, S, HPS, IW, CLM, Edif, Agr	0–600	Arb[B,U], AqMrg, Gnd	D	I[A,In]	O	
Corytophanes cristatus	con	I	EBF, SSF, KHF, HPS?	0–600	Arb[B,T,U]	D	I[A,In], L	O	
Corytophanes hernandezii	con	I	EBF, SSF, KHF	0–300	Arb[B,T,U]	D	I[A,In]	O	
Laemanctus longipes	con	I	EBF, SSF, KHF	0–600	Arb[B,C], Gnd	D	I[A,G?,In], L?	O	
Laemanctus serratus	con	R	SSF	0–100	Arb[B,C], Gnd	D	I[A,G,In], L	O	
Iguanidae									
Ctenosaura similis	con[yng]	C	SSF, S, HPS, CLM, SSC, Edif, Agr	0–600	Arb[B,T,U], Gnd	D	O	O	
Iguana iguana	con	U	EBF, SSF, HPS, CLM, SSC	0–600	Arb[B,C,T], AqMrg	D	O	O	
Phrynosomatidae									
Sceloporus chrysostictus	con[sd]	U	S, SSF, HPS	0–600	Gnd	D	I[A,In]	O	
Sceloporus lundelli	con[sd]	I	SSF, HPS	0–600	Arb[B,T]	D	I[A,In]	V	

Sceloporus serrifer	con[sd]	R	SSF, HPS	0–600	Gnd	D	I[A,In]	V
Sceloporus variabilis	con[sd]	U	SSF, S, HPS, Agr, Edif	0–600	Gnd	D	I[A,In]	O
Polychrotidae								
Anolis allisoni	con[sd]	U	SSC	SL	Arb[B,C,T]	D	I[A,In]	O
Anolis carolinensis	con[sd]	?	SSC	SL	Arb	D	I[A,In]	O
Anolis biporcatus	con[sd]	I	EBF, SSF, KHF, HPS	0–600	Arb[B,C,T]	D	I[A,In], L	O
Norops capito	var[sd]	I	EBF, SSF, KHF, HPS?	0–600	Arb[T,U]	D	I[A,In], L	O
Norops lemurinus	var[sd]	U	EBF, SSF, KHF, HPS, CLM, SSC	0–600	Arb[T,U], Gnd	D	I[A,In]	O
Norops pentaprion	con[sd]	R	EBF, SSF	0–300	Arb[T]	D	I[A,In]	O
Norops rodriguezii	var[sd]	U	EBF, SSF, KHF, SEF, HPS, SSC, Agr[F], Edif	0–1000	Arb[U], Gnd	D	I[A,In]	O
Norops sagrei	var[sd]	C	CLM, SSC, Edif	0–75	Arb[B,T,U]	D	I[A,In]	O
Norops sericeus	var[sd]	U	EBF, SSF, KHF, S, HPS	0–600	Arb[U], Gnd	D	I[A,In]	O
Norops tropidonotus	var[sd]	U	EBF, SSF, KHF, HPS	0–600	Arb[T], Gnd	D	I[A,In]	O
Norops uniformis	var[sd]	U	EBF, SSF, KHF, SEF, HPS	0–1000	Arb[T], Gnd	D	I[A,In]	O
Scincidae								
Eumeces schwartzei	con[yng]	I	EBF, SSF, KHF	0–200	Gnd	D	I[A,In]	O
Eumeces sumichrasti	con[yng]	I	EBF, SSF, KHF, HPS?	0–600	Gnd	D	I[A,In], L	O
Mabuya unimarginata	con	U	EBF, SSF, KHF, S, HPS, SSC, Agr, Edif	0–600	Gnd, Arb[T]	D	I[A,In]	V
Sphenomorphus cherriei	con	U	EBF, SSF, KHF, SEF, S, HPS	0–1000	Gnd	D	I[A,In]	O
Gymnophthalmidae								
Gymnophthalmus speciosus	con	R	SSF, S	0–100	Gnd	D	I[A,In]	O
Teiidae								
Ameiva festiva	con[yng]	U	EBF, SSF, KHF, SEF, HPS	0–800	Gnd	D	I[A,In]	O
Ameiva undulata	con[sd,yng]	U	EBF, SSF, KHF, S, HPS, SSC, Agr, Edif	0–600	Gnd	D	I[A,In]	O
Cnemidophorus angusticeps	con[sd]	U	S	0–50	Gnd	D	I[A,In]	O
Cnemidophorus lemniscatus	con[sd]	I	SSC	SL	Gnd	D	I[A,In]	O
Cnemidophorus maslini	con	U	SSF, S	0–50	Gnd	D	I[A,In]	P

(continues)

Ecological Summary—Continued

Species	Apr.	Abun.	Habitat	Elev. range	Adap. zone	Diel	Food	Rep. mode	Mimic
Xantusiidae									
Lepidophyma flavimaculatum	con	I	EBF, SSF, KHF, HPS	0–600	Gnd	ND	I[A,In]	V	
Lepidophyma mayae	con	R	EBF, SEF	700–800	Gnd	ND	I[A,In]	V	
Anguidae									
Diploglossus rozellae	con[yng]	R	EBF, HPS	100–600	Arb, Gnd?	D	I[A,In]	V	
Typhlopidae									
Typhlops microstomus	con	R	SSF?, S	0–50	Fos	N?	I[T]	O	
Leptotyphlopidae									
Leptotyphlops goudotii	con	R	SSF, S?	0–50	Fos	ND	I[T]	O	
Boidae									
Boa constrictor	con	I	EBF, SSF, KHF, SEF, S, HPS, CLM, Agr	0–700	Gnd, Arb	ND	M, B, L	V	
Colubridae									
Adelphicos quadrivirgatus	con	R	EBF, HPS?	50–600	Fos	N?	I	O	
Amastridium veliferum	con	R	EBF, Agr[F]	100–500	Gnd	D	F?	?	
Clelia clelia	con[yng]	I	EBF, KHF, SEF	0–1000	Gnd	ND	F?, L, M, S	O	
Clelia scytalina	con[yng]	?	SSF	0–50	Gnd	ND	F?, L, M, S	O	
Coluber constrictor	con	R	S, HPS	100–600	Gnd	D	L, M	O	
Coniophanes bipunctatus	con	I	EBF, SSF, IW, Agr[F]	0–300	Gnd, Aq Mrg, SAq	ND	F, P?, U	O	
Coniophanes fissidens	con	U	EBF, SEF, HPS	100–700	Gnd	D	F, I, L, S, U	O	
Coniophanes imperialis	con	U	EBF, SSF, KHF, S, HPS, Agr	0–600	Gnd, Fos	D	F, I[In], L	O	
Coniophanes schmidti	con	R	EBF, HPS	0–600	Gnd	D	F?, L?	O	
Conophis lineatus	con	I	SSF, S, HPS	0–600	Gnd	D	L, S	O	
Dendrophidion nuchale	con	R	EBF, SEF?, Agr[F]	200–700	Gnd	D	F, L	O	
Dendrophidion vinitor	con	R	SEF, EBF?	700–800	Gnd	D	F, L?	O	
Dipsas brevifacies	con	U	SSF?, S[H]	0–100	Arb	N	I[G]	O	
Dryadophis melanolomus	con	U	EBF, SSF, KHF, SEF, S, HPS	50–800	Gnd	D	F, L, M, S	O	

300

Drymarchon corais	con	I	EBF, SSF, KHF, S, HPS, CLM, Agr	0–700	Gnd	D	B, E?; F, L, M, S	O	
Drymobius margaritiferus	con	U	EBF, SSF, KHF, SEF?, S, HPS, IW, CLM, Agr	0–600	Gnd, AqMrg	D	F, Td, U?	O	
Elaphe flavirufa	con	R	EBF, SSF, HPS	0–600	Arb, Gnd	N	B, M, L!	O	
Ficimia publia	con	I	EBF, SSF, Agr	0–200	Gnd, Fos	ND	I	O	
Imantodes cenchoa	con	U	EBF, SSF, KHF, SEF, HPS, Agr[F]	0–700	Arb[B,U]	N	F, L	O	
Lampropeltis triangulum	con	I	EBF, SSF, KHF, SEF, S, HPS, Agr	0–600	Gnd	ND	F, L, M, S	O	coral
Leptodeira frenata	con	U	EBF, SSF, S, Agr, Edif	0–300	Arb[B,U], Gnd	N	F, L, S	O	
Leptodeira septentrionalis	con	I	EBF, SSF, KHF, HPS, IW?, Agr[F], Edif	0–650	Arb[B,U]	N	F, L	O	
Leptophis ahaetulla	con	I	EBF, SSF, KHF, SEF?, S[H], HPS, Agr[F]	0–600	Arb[B]	D	B, E, F, L	O	
Leptophis mexicanus	var	U	EBF, SSF, KHF, S, HPS, CLM, SSC, Agr[F], Edif	0–700	Arb[B,U], Gnd	D	F, L	O	
Masticophis mentovarius	con	I	SSF, S, HPS, CLM, Agr	0–600	Gnd	D	L, M, S	O	
Ninia diademata	con	R	EBF, SEF?	50–500	Gnd, Fos	N	I[G]	O	
Ninia sebae	con	U	EBF, SSF, KHF, S, HPS, Agr, Edif	0–600	Gnd, Fos	N	I[G]	O	coral
Oxybelis aeneus	con	I	EBF, SSF, KHF, S, HPS, CLM, Agr[F]	0–600	Arb[B,U]	D	B, F, L	O	
Oxybelis fulgidus	con	I	EBF, SSF, KHF, HPS, Agr[F]	0–600	Arb[B,C,U]	D	B, F, L	O	
Oxyrhopus petola	con	I	EBF, SSF, KHF, SEF?, HPS	0–600	Gnd	N	L, M	O	coral
Pseustes poecilonotus	var[yng]	I	EBF, SSF, S[H], KHF, HPS	0–600	Arb[B,U], Gnd	D	B, E, M	O	
Rhadinaea decorata	con	R	EBF, SSF?	0–100	Gnd	D	F, U	O	
Scaphiodontophis annulatus	con	I	EBF, SSF, KHF, S, HPS, Agr[F]	50–600	Gnd, Fos	D	L	O	coral
Senticolis triaspis	var[yng]	I	EBF, SSF, KHF, SEF?	50–500	Gnd	N	B, M	O	
Sibon dimidiata	con	I	EBF	100	Arb	N	I[G]	O	
Sibon nebulata	con	I	EBF, SSF, Agr[F]	100–700	Arb, Gnd	N	I[G]	O	
Sibon sanniola	var	I	EBF, SSF, HPS	0–600	Arb, Gnd	N	I[G]	O	

(continues)

Ecological Summary—Continued

Species	Apr.	Abun.	Habitat	Elev. range	Adap. zone	Diel	Food	Rep. mode	Mimic
Sibon sartorii	con	I	EBF, SSF, Agr[F]	0–200	Gnd	N	I[G]	O	coral
Spilotes pullatus	var	I	EBF, SSF, KHF, S, HPS, CLM, Agr, Edif	0–600	Arb[B], Gnd	D	B, E, F, L, M	O	
Stenorrhina degenhardtii	con?[yng]	I	EBF, SEF?	450–700	Gnd, Fos	D	I[A]	O	
Stenorrhina freminvillii	var	I	SSF, S, HPS	0–600	Gnd, Fos	D	I[A]	O	
Symphimus mayae	con	I	SSF?, S[H]	0–50	Gnd, Arb?	D	I	O	
Tantilla cuniculator	con	R	SSF, S?	0–50	Gnd, Fos	N	I	O	
Tantilla schistosa	con	I	EBF, SSF, SEF, S, HPS	50–600	Gnd, Fos	N	I	O	
Tantillita canula	con	I	EBF, SSF, S?, Agr	0–450	Gnd, Fos	N	I	O	
Tantillita lintoni	con	I	EBF, SEF?	0–500	Gnd, Fos	N	I	O?	
Thamnophis marcianus	con	I	SSF, S, IW, CLM	0–100	SAq, AqMrg	D	I[Cr?], F, P	V	
Thamnophis proximus	con	I	SSF, S, IW, CLM	0–100	SAq, AqMrg	D	F, P	V	
Tretanorhinus nigroluteus	var	I	Fw[EBF,SSF,S,IW], Bw[CLM]	0–100	Aq	N	P	O	
Urotheca elapoides	con	I	EBF, KHF, SEF, HPS, Agr[F]	200–700	Gnd	D	F, U	O	coral
Xenodon rabdocephalus	con	I	EBF, SSF, HPS	0–600	Gnd	D	F, Td	O	viper
Elapidae									
Micrurus diastema	con	U	EBF, SSF, KHF, SEF, S, HPS, Edif	0–700	Gnd	ND	C?, L, S	O	coral*
Micrurus hippocrepis	var	I	EBF, HPS	50–600	Gnd	ND	C?, L?, S?	O	coral*
Micrurus nigrocinctus	con	I	EBF, SSF, SEF?, HPS	0–450	Gnd	ND	C, S, L	O	coral*
Viperidae									
Agkistrodon bilineatus	con	R	SSF, S?, IW?, AGR[S]	0–50	Gnd, AqMrg	N	F, M	V	viper*
Atropoides nummifer	con	I	EBF, SEF?, HPS	100–700	Gnd	ND	L, M	V	viper*
Bothriechis schlegelii	con?	R	EBF	100–500	Arb[B,T,U]	ND	B, F, L, M	V	viper*
Bothrops asper	con	I	EBF, SSF, KHF, S, HPS, CLM	0–700	Gnd	N	F, L, M	V	viper*
Crotalus durissus	con	I	SSF, S, HPS	0–600	Gnd	ND	L, M	V	viper*
Porthidium nasutum	con	R	EBF, SEF?, HPS	100–600	Gnd	ND	F?, I, L, M	V	viper*

[a]Table structure adapted from Rand and Myers (1990).

Appendix 2

DISTRIBUTIONAL SUMMARY

The gazetteer represents sites of selected museum reptile collections (AMNH, BMNH, CM, FMNH, LSUMZ, MPM, MZUM, UKMNH, UMIAM, USNM, UTA), literature citations, field observations, and photographs of specimens verified by the authors. Coordinates are approximate and based on 1:250,000 scale maps, series D.O.S.649/1 (Edition 2-O.S. 1991). The number in brackets following each grid reference corresponds to the map localities given in Fig. A-1. Principal sources: Allen and Neill (1959), Edgar (1997), Fugler (1960), Henderson (1976a, 1978), Henderson and Hoevers (1975, 1977a), Hoevers and Henderson (1974), Iremonger and Sayre (1994), Lee (1996), McCoy (1970, 1990), McCoy et al. (1986), Meerman (1992, 1993, 1995, 1996a,b, personal communications), Meyer (personal observations), Moll (1985, 1986), Neill (1965), Neill and Allen (1959b,c, 1960, 1961a,b), Parker et al. (1993), Platt (1995a, personal communication), R.P. Reynolds and J.F. Jacobs collection (USNM), Rogers et al. (1994), Schmidt (1941), Stafford (1991, 1994, personal observations).

GAZETTEER

AHa: Altun Ha, Belize District; archaeological site, embracing Rockstone Pond, in cleared semi-evergreen seasonal forest formation and agricultural land. 17°46′N 88°21′W [1].

Air: Airport Camp, Belize District; military encampment at Philip Goldson International Airport. 17°32′N 88°18′W [2].

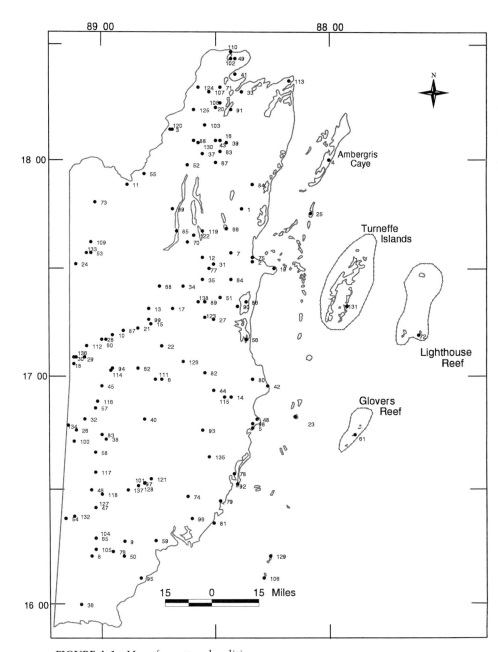

FIGURE A-1 Map of gazetteer localities.

Abn: Albion Island, Orange Walk District; island with limestone quarry between branches of Rio Hondo. 18°08'N 88°41'W [3].

Amb: Ambergris Caye, centered at Laguna de Mato; a large caye with sand strand and cocotal vegetation and mangrove approx. 25 km off the coast of Corozal District, extending northward to the Mexican state of Quintana Roo. 17°58'N 87°54'W [4].

APi: All Pines, Stann Creek District; a settlement on the coast in cleared savanna formation. 16°47'N 88°18'W [5].

Bal: Baldy Sibun, Cayo District; a settlement near Baldy Beacon hill. 17°00'N 88°43'W [6].

BBm: Burrell Boom, Belize District (including Mussell Creek area); a town on the Belize River surrounded largely by agricultural land. 17°34'N 88°24'W [7].

BCr: Blue Creek, Toledo District; a small settlement and minor archaeological site on Blue Creek. 16°12'N 89°03'W [8].

BDN: Bladen Branch, Toledo District; a protected area (Nature Reserve) centered around the Bladen branch of the Monkey River on the eastern flank of the Maya Mountains, covering 99,678 acres (40,370 hectares). Vegetation falls mostly within the evergreen broadleaf forest formation. 16°30'N 88°53'W.

BgF: Big Fall, Toledo District; a settlement on the Southern Highway and bridge over the Rio Grande. 16°15'N 88°53'W [9].

BkP: Baking Pot, Cayo District; a settlement and archaeological site. 17°12'N 88°57'W [10].

Blu: Blue Creek, Orange Walk District; a settlement in semi-evergreen seasonal forest formation near the Mexican border. See also Blue Creek, Toledo District (BCr). 17°53'N 88°53'W [11].

Bmd: Bermudian Landing, Belize District; a town on the Belize River in a protected area (Community Baboon Sanctuary), a Private Reserve embracing 12,980 acres (5257 ha). 17°33'N 88°32'W [12].

Bna: Banana Bank, Cayo District; a settlement on the Belize River in agricultural pasture. 17°19'N 88°47'W [13].

Bok: Bokawina, Stann Creek District; a hill on the eastern flank of the Maya Mountains. 16°55'N 88°24'W [14].

Bpn: Belmopan area, Cayo District; capital of Belize surrounded largely by cleared land. 17°15'N 88°46'W [15].

BRD: Burdon Canal, Belize District; a protected area (Private Nature Reserve) to the south of Belize City, covering 5255 acres (2130 ha). Vegetation consists largely of mangrove forest and falls within the coastal marshes and lagoons formation. 17°28'N 88°15'W.

But: Button Lagoon, Orange Walk District; inland lagoon connecting with Freshwater Creek in coastal lagoons and marshes formation. 18°05'N 88°27'W [16].

BvD: Beaver Dam Creek, Cayo District; a rocky tributary of Labouring Creek. 17°19'N 88°40'W [17].

Bvj: Benque Viejo Del Carmen, Cayo District (including San Jose Succoths area); a largely Mayan community on the Belize river near the Guatemalan border. 17°04'N 89°08'W [18].

BzC: Belize City area, Belize District; the principal city of Belize, surrounded by coastal lagoons and marshes vegetation. 17°30'N 88°12'W [19].

BzR: Belize River; the principal river of Belize draining in an easterly direction. See Fig. 1.

Cal: Caledonia, Corozal District (including lagoon area); a settlement on the New River amid interior wetlands and mangrove vegetation. 18°14'N 88°28'W [20].

Cam: Camelot, Cayo District; a small settlement on the Western Highway. 17°14'N 88°50'W [21].

Cav: Cave's Branch, Cayo District; a tributary of the Sibun River. 17°09'N 88°43'W [22].

Cbw: Carrie Bow Caye; a small caye off the coast of Stann Creek District and site of marine research station. 16°48'N 88°04'W [23].

CCh: Chan Chich, Orange Walk District; a lodge and ecotourist center near Chan Chich Creek. 17°31'N 89°07'W [24].

CCk: Caye Caulker, a caye off the coast of Belize District, largely given to sand strand and cocotal vegetation. 17°45'N 88°02'W [25].

Ccl: Caracol, Cayo District; a major archaeological site in evergreen broadleaf forest formation. 16°46'N 89°07'W [26].

CCr: Cornhouse Creek, Belize District; a freshwater stream draining eastward into the Southern Lagoon through coastal lagoons and marshes vegetation. 17°16'N 88°29'W [27].

CFm: Central Farm, Cayo District; an agricultural station. 17°11'N 89°00'W [28].

CFR: Columbia River, Toledo District; a protected area (Forest Reserve), centered around the upper reaches of the Rio Grande and covering 102,940 acres (41,690 ha). Vegetation falls mostly within the evergreen broadleaf forest formation, with karst hills forest vegetation predominating in the southern foothills. 16°20'N 89°58'W.

Cha: Chaa Creek, Cayo District (including Ix Chel Farm); a lodge and tropical education center on the Mopan River. 17°06'N 89°05'W [29].

Chi: Chial, Cayo District; a settlement on the Western Highway. 17°06'N 89°07'W [30].

CkL: Cooks Lagoon, Belize District; a brackish lagoon amid mangrove vegetation and savanna formation. 17°31'N 88°29'W [31].

CMB: Cockscomb Basin, Stann Creek District; a protected area (Wildlife Sanctuary) totalling 86,929 acres (35,210 ha) centered around the Sittee River, South Stann Creek River, and Swasey Branch watersheds, and embracing Victoria Peak. Vegetation falls mostly within the evergreen broadleaf forest formation, with subtropical evergreen and elfin forest formations on the higher slopes. 16°47'N 88°29'W.

CnR: Cohune Ridge, Cayo District; a settlement in evergreen broadleaf forest formation dominated by corozo palms. 16°49'N 89°05'W [32].

Cnx: Chunox, Corozal District; a settlement on the southern shore of Laguna Seca. 18°18'N 88°21'W [33].

Coq: Coquericot, Cayo District; a settlement on the Belize River. 17°25'N 88°37'W [34].

Cox: Cox Lagoon, Belize District; an alluvial freshwater lagoon in savanna formation. 17°27'N 88°32'W [35].

CQB: Chiquibul Forest, Cayo District; a protected area (National Park), comprising 286,289 acres (115,950 ha) centered around the Chiquibul River drainage. Vegetation falls mostly within the evergreen broadleaf forest and semi-evergreen seasonal forest formations. The reserve includes areas of limestone with extensive underground cave systems. 16°45'N 89°00'W.

CqS: Crique Sacro, Toledo District; a settlement on the Temash River. 15°59'N 89°06'W [36].

Crm: Carmelita, Orange Walk District; a settlement on the Northern Highway. 18°01'N 88°32'W [37].

CRT: Crooked Tree, Belize District; a protected area (Wildlife Sanctuary), comprising 41,297 acres (16,725 ha) based around Crooked Tree village and covering several freshwater lagoons. The site is characterized by interior wetlands vegetation and has extensive areas of logwood (*Haematoxylon campechianum*) swamp. 17°45'N 88°32'W.

Cvs: Las Cuevas, Cayo District; site of limestone caves and research station in evergreen broadleaf forest formation. 16°44'N 88°59'W [38].

Cwa: Chiwa Lagoon, Orange Walk District; a shallow freshwater lagoon in interior wetlands formation surrounded by semi-evergreen seasonal forest formation. 18°04'N 88°25'W [39].

CxB: Cuxta Bani, Cayo District; camp of the Joint Services Scientific Expeditions to the upper Raspaculo River basin, in evergreen broadleaf forest formation. 16°49'N 88°48'W [40].

Czl: Corozal Town, Corozal District; principal town of the district. 18°23'N 88°23'W [41].

Dan: Dangriga, Stann Creek District (formerly Stann Creek Town); principal town of the district with extensive citrus agriculture. 16°58'N 88°14'W [42].

Dbl: Doubloon Bank Lagoon, Orange Walk District; a freshwater lagoon in interior wetland formation surrounded by semi-evergreen seasonal forest formation. 18°05'N 88°28'W [43].

DFl: Davis Falls, Stann Creek District; the likely site of an early herpetological collection made by I.T. Sanderson, previously understood to have originated from Double Falls (16°42'N 88°38'W), a locality near the boundary with Toledo. 16°57'N 88°29'W [44].

DPR: Deep River, Toledo District; a protected area (Forest Reserve) located at the foot of the Maya Mountains around the headwaters of the Deep River, comprising 78,574 acres (31,820 ha). 16°27'N 88°48'W.

DSv: Douglas D'Silva (formerly Augustine), Cayo District; settlement and district forestry headquarters in highland pine savanna formation of Mountain Pine Ridge. 16°58'N 89°00'W [45].

DyD: Doyles Delight, Cayo District; an expedition camp site in subtropical evergreen forest formation, centered at 16°30'N 89°03'W [46].

Eza: Esperanza, Toledo District; a camp near Little Quartz Ridge in evergreen broadleaf forest formation. 16°25'N 89°02'W [47].

FCR: Freshwater Creek, Corozal District; a protected area (Forest Reserve) covering 60,177 acres (24,370 ha). Vegetation falls mostly within the interior wetlands and savanna formations. 18°05'N 88°22'W.

Fre: Freetown, Sittee River, Stann Creek District; a settlement on the Sittee River. 16°49'N 88°17'W [48].

FmL: Four Mile Lagoon, Corozal District; a lagoon on the western shore of Corozal Bay. 18°27'N 88°23'W [49].

FSt: Fallen Stones, Toledo District; a butterfly ranch in an area of mixed agriculture and remnant forest. 16°12'N 88°54'W [50].

Gcy: Gracy Rock, Belize District; a limestone promontory near the Sibun River in karst hills formation. 17°22'N 88°27'W [51].

Ggs: Guinea Grass area, Orange Walk District; a settlement near the New
        River in interior wetlands formation. 17°58'N 88°36'W [52].

GJg: Gallon Jug, Orange Walk District; a settlement and former logging center
        surrounded by agricultural pasture and semi-evergreen seasonal forest
        formation. 17°34'N 89°03'W [53].

Gla: Gloria Camp, Toledo District; a camp at Gloria Spring in evergreen
        broadleaf forest formation. 16°22'N 89°10'W [54].

Gld: Gold Button Creek area, Orange Walk District; a ranch with freshwater
        lagoons, agricultural pasture, and semi-evergreen seasonal forest forma-
        tion, near the Mexican border. 17°56'N 88°48'W [55].

Gls: Gales Point, Belize District; a peninsular with coastal lagoons and
        marshes vegetation on the southern edge of Southern Lagoon. 17°11'N
        88°20'W [56].

Gmo: Guacamallo Bridge, Cayo District; a crossing on the Macal River, bor-
        dered to the north by highland pine savanna vegetation and to the south
        by evergreen broadleaf forest formation. 16°52'N 89°02'W [57].

GOr: Grano de Oro, Cayo District; a camp on the Vaca Plateau in evergreen
        broadleaf forest formation. 16°40'N 89°02'W [58].

GSt: Golden Stream, Toledo District. 16°16'N 88°45'W [59].

Gvl: Georgeville, Cayo District; a settlement on the Western Highway.
        17°11'N 88°59'W [60].

GvR: Glovers Reef; a group of cayes off the coast of Stann Creek District,
        centered at Long Caye. 16°45'N 87°47'W [61].

GWK: Grant's Works, Stann Creek District; a protected area (Forest Reserve)
        covering 7906 acres (3200 ha) based around the Mullins River drainage.
        Vegetation falls mostly within the karst hills forest formation. 17°05'N
        88°20'W.

HiV: Hidden Valley and Thousand Foot Falls, Cayo District; a rocky gorge and
        precipitous water fall feature in Mountain Pine Ridge. 17°03'N 88°50'W
        [62].

Hon: Honey Camp, Orange Walk District; a camp on the southwestern edge of
        Honey Camp Lagoon in savanna and interior wetlands formation.
        18°02'N 88°27'W [63].

Hvl: Hattieville area, Belize District; a settlement on the Western Highway in
        savanna formation. 17°27'N 88°24'W [64].

Jmy: Jimmy Cut, Toledo District; a locality in the southwestern foothills of the
        Maya Mountains in evergreen broadleaf forest formation. 16°17'N
        89°02'W [65].

JnL: Jones Lagoon, Belize District; a very shallow lake bordered by mangrove
        and reed swamp. 17°41'N 88°25'W [66].

KtL: Kate's Lagoon, Orange Walk District, a lake and marshland area in
        interior wetlands formation. 17°59'N 88°28'W [67].

Lam: Lamanai, Orange Walk District; a major archaeological site and field
        station near Indian Church on New River Lagoon. 17°46'N 88°40'W
        [69].

LbC: Labouring Creek area; a freshwater stream that runs along the boundary
        between southern Orange Walk and northern Cayo districts. 17°25'N
        88°44'W [68].

Lem: Lemonal, Belize District; a settlement on Spanish Creek surrounded by
        savanna and interior wetlands vegetation. 17°37'N 88°36'W [70].

LHR: Lighthouse Reef; an outlying group of cayes and protected area (Natural

Monument) off the coast of Belize District, centered at Half Moon Caye. 17°12′N 87°32′W [72].

Lib: Libertad, Corozal district; a settlement on the Northern Highway. 18°19′N 88°27′W [71].

LMp: La Milpa, Orange Walk District; a major archaeological site and biological field station. 17°48′N 89°02′W [73].

Lom: Last Lomitas, Toledo District; a locality on the coastal plain surrounded largely by savanna formation. 16°28′N 88°36′W [74].

LQr: Little Quartz Ridge, Toledo District; an upland area of evergreen broadleaf and subtropical evergreen forest formations in the southern Maya Mountains. 16°24′N 89°05′W. See Fig. 1.

Lvl: Ladyville area, Belize District; a settlement on the Northern Highway near the international airport. 17°33′N 88°88′W [75].

Mac: Macal River, Cayo district; a large river fed by tributaries draining the northwestern slopes of the Maya Mountains and flowing north into the Belize River. See Fig. 1.

Maf: Mafredi, Toledo District; an agricultural station. 16°13′N 88°57′W [76].

MAN: Manatee, Belize District; a protected area (Forest Reserve) centered around the Manatee River drainage in the border region of southern Belize and northern Stann Creek Districts. 17°09′N 88°29′W.

Mck: Mucklehenny Lagoon, Belize District; an alluvial lake in savanna formation. 17°30′N 88°30′W [77].

MCr: Mango Creek, Stann Creek District; a settlement on Mango Creek on the coastal plain. 16°32′N 88°23′W [78].

Med: Medina Bank, Toledo District; a settlement on the Southern Highway. 16°27′N 88°45′W [79].

Mel: Melinda; a forestry camp in the lower Stann Creek valley. 17°00′N 88°18′W [80].

Mid: Middlesex, Stann Creek District; a settlement on the Hummingbird Highway in a valley with extensive citrus cultivation. 17°02′N 88°31′W [82].

Mil: Millionario, Cayo District; an abandoned forestry camp in evergreen broadleaf forest formation. 16°45′N 89°00′W [83].

MKB: Monkey Bay, boundary of western Belize and northeastern Cayo Districts; a protected area (National Park) covering 1799 acres (730 ha). 17°28′N 88°37′W.

MkR: Monkey River Town, Toledo District; a town at the mouth of the Monkey River. 16°21′N 88°29′W [81].

MM: Maya Mountains; a protected area (Forest Reserve) of two parts on the eastern slopes of the Maya Mountains, totalling 128,111 acres (51,885 ha). Vegetation falls mostly within the evergreen broadleaf forest formations. The southern reserve is centered at approximately 16°22′N 88°55′W, and the northern reserve at 16°36′N 88°41′W.

MPR: Mountain Pine Ridge, Cayo District; a protected area (Forest Reserve) comprising 126,825 acres (51,360 ha), embracing Hidden Valley and Thousand Foot Falls. The reserve is characterized by extensive upland pine forests and also includes areas of broadleaf woodland rich in lime-loving species. 17°03′N 88°50′W.

Msk: Maskall, Belize District; a town on the Northern River. 17°53′N 88°18′W [84].

New: New River Lagoon, Orange Walk District; a long, narrow lake at the base of the New River drainage with semi-evergreen seasonal forest formation on the western shore and interior wetlands vegetation with relictual mangrove on the eastern shore. 17°40'N 88°39'W [85].

NnL: Northern Lagoon, Belize District; a large freshwater lake in the northwestern section near Crooked Tree. (Note: a coastal lagoon with the same name is located in southern Belize District.) 17°21'N 88°20'W [86].

NwR: New River, Orange Walk District; a river flowing in a more or less northerly direction and emptying into Corozal Bay. See Fig. 1.

Ont: Ontario, Cayo District; a village on the Western Highway. 17°13'N 88°54'W [87].

OrW: Orange Walk Town, Orange Walk District (including Otro Benque); a town on the New River surrounded by extensive sugarcane plantations. 18°05'N 88°34'W [88].

PaW: Parrot's Wood, Belize District; an area of wooded savanna vegetation and site of a biological station. 17°21'N 88°31'W [89].

PeH: Peccary Hills, Belize District; an area of rocky promontories in karst hills forest formation, centered at 17°20'N 88°22'W [90].

PgL: Progresso Lagoon, Corozal District; a lake surrounded by savanna and interior wetlands vegetation. 18°13'N 88°24'W [91].

PlL: Placentia Lagoon, Stann Creek District; a coastal lagoon surrounded largely by mangrove. 16°32'N 88°23'W [92].

Prc: Pearce Camp, Stann Creek District; a camp in the eastern foothills of the Maya Mountains. 16°46'N 88°32'W [93].

Prv: Privassion Creek, Cayo District; a rocky stream and site of camp in highland pine savanna vegetation. 17°03'N 88°57'W [94].

PuG: Punta Gorda, Toledo District; the principal town of Toledo District on the Gulf of Honduras. 16°06'N 88°49'W [95].

PyC: Paynes Creek, Toledo District; a stream on the coastal plain in savanna formation. 16°22'N 88°35'W [96].

QOr: Quebrada de Oro Camp, Toledo District; a camp on the eastern versant of the Maya Mountains in evergreen broadleaf forest formation. 16°32'N 88°48'W [97].

RBR: Rio Bravo Conservation and Management Area, Orange Walk District; a protected area (Private Reserve), comprising approximately 245,822 acres (99,560 ha), including extensive areas of savanna and semi-evergreen seasonal forest formations. 17°35'N 89°05'W.

Reg: Regalia, Stann Creek District; a settlement on the coastal plain. 16°48'N 88°18'W [98].

RiC: Richardson Creek Camp, Toledo District; a camp in evergreen broadleaf forest formation on the southern slopes of Richardson's Peak. 16°32'N 88°48'W [101].

Rmt: Remate, Corozal District; a settlement on the northern Highway near the border with Quintana Roo. 18°27'N 88°24'W [102].

RoC: Roaring Creek, Cayo District; a settlement on the Western Highway in the vicinity of Belmopan. 17°16'N 88°47'W [99].

Rto: Retiro Camp, Cayo District; an abandoned camp near the Guatemalan border in evergreen broadleaf forest formation. 16°43'N 89°08'W [100].

SaE: San Estevan, Orange Walk District; an archaeological site and settlement on the Northern Highway. 18°09'N 88°31'W [103].

Sal: Salamanca, Toledo District; a forestry camp at the foot of the southern slopes of the Maya Mountains. 16°17'N 89°02'W [104].

San: San Antonio, Toledo District; a settlement in the southern foothills of the Maya Mountains. 16°14'N 89°02'W [105].

Sap: Sapodilla Cayes; a group of cayes in the Gulf of Honduras at the southern limit of the barrier reef, centered at Hunting Caye. 16°06'N 88°15'W [106].

SBN: Sibun, Belize District; a protected area (Forest Reserve) of karst topography covering some 11825 acres (4790 ha) centered around the Sibun River valley. Vegetation falls within the karst hills forest and semi-evergreen seasonal forest formations. 17°22'N 88°25'W.

SCl: Santa Clara, Corozal District; a settlement in interior wetlands formation near the Northern Highway. 18°18'N 88°30'W [107].

SCz: Santa Cruz, Corozal District; a small settlement on the New River. 18°15'N 88°27'W [108].

Sec: Laguna Seca, Orange Walk District; a freshwater lake and marsh (interior wetlands formation) in an area of semi-evergreen seasonal forest formation. 17°37'N 89°03'W [109].

SEl: Santa Elena, Corozal District; a border post at the crossing point of the Northern Highway and Rio Hondo. 18°29'N 88°24'W [110].

Sib: Sibun Hill, Cayo District; a promontory and broadcasting relay station in the Mountain Pine Ridge area. 17°00'N 88°45'W [111].

SIg: San Ignacio (formerly El Cayo), Cayo District; a large town on the Western Highway near the Guatemalan border. 17°09'N 89°04'W [112].

SIT: Sittee River, Stann Creek District; a protected area (Forest Reserve) covering approximately 94,156 acres (38,130 ha) centered around the Sittee River drainage. 16°50'N 88°24'W.

Sja: Sarteneja, Corozal District; a coastal settlement in Bahia Chetumal. 18°21'N 88°08'W [113].

SlC: Slate Creek area, Cayo District; a protected area (Private Reserve) covering 3700 acres (1500 ha) of broadleaf Forest bordering Mountain Pine Ridge. 17°03'N 88°57'W [114].

Slk: Silk Grass Hill, Stann Creek District; the site of an early herpetological collection made by I.T. Sanderson, some specimens of which may originate instead from Silk Grass village (16°53'N 88°20'W). 16°55'N 88°26'W [115].

SLu: San Luis, Cayo District; an abandoned saw mill in Mountain Pine Ridge. 16°54'N 89°01'W [116].

Smk: Smokey River Camp, Cayo district; a mineral exploration site in evergreen broadleaf forest formation on the eastern branch of the Chiquibul River. 16°35'N 89°02'W [117].

SnC: Snake Creek, Toledo District; a stream in evergreen broadleaf forest formation on the southern slopes of the Maya Mountains. 16°29'N 89°00'W [118].

SnL: Southern Lagoon, Belize District; a large freshwater lake in the northern section near the boundary with Orange Walk. (Note: a coastal lagoon with the same name is located in southern Belize District.) 17°40'N 88°32'W [119].

SNR: Shipstern Nature Reserve, Corozal District; a protected area (Private Reserve), covering 18,841 acres (7,630 ha) centered around Shipstern Lagoon (saltwater) and embracing Shipstern Caye. The reserve includes areas of coastal marshes and lagoons, semi-evergreen seasonal forest, and savanna vegetation. 18°16'N 88°10'W.

Snt: San Antonio, Orange Walk District; a village at the edge of Albion Island on a tributary of the Rio Hondo. 18°08'N 88°40'W [120].

Sol: Solomon Camp, Toledo District; a camp on the Bladen Branch of the Monkey River. 16°33'N 88°46'W [121].

SpC: Spanish Creek, Belize District; a freshwater stream near the boundary with Orange Walk District, centered at Caesar Cato. 17°39'N 88°34'W [122].

SPd: Sally's Pond, Belize District; a shallow freshwater lagoon surrounded by savanna vegetation. 17°17'N 88°31'W [123].

SpL: Sapote Lagoon, Corozal District; a freshwater lake in interior wetlands formation near the Mexican border. 18°19'N 88°33'W [124].

SPo: San Pablo, Orange Walk District; a settlement on the Northern Highway near the boundary with Corozal District. 18°13'N 88°34'W [125].

SRT: Sarstoon-Temash, Toledo District; a protected area (National Park) of marshland and swamp forest centered around the Sarstoon and Temash Rivers, covering 41,898 acres (16,970 ha). 15°57'N 89°04'W.

Svr: Silver Creek, Cayo District; a rocky tributary of the Sibun River in evergreen broadleaf forest formation at the entrance to Sibun Gorge. 17°05'N 88°37'W [126].

SWB: Swasey-Bladen, Toledo District; a protected area (Forest Reserve) of two parts comprising 14,779 acres (5985 ha) centered around the Swasey Branch of the Monkey River. 18°36'N 88°35'W.

Tgr: El Tigre Camp, Toledo District; a camp on the Central River in the Columbia River Forest Reserve. 16°25'N 89°02'W [127].

Tkl: Teakettle Camp, Toledo District; a camp on the Bladen Branch of the Monkey River. 16°31'N 88°50'W [128].

Tom: Tom Owen's Caye; a small caye in the Gulf of Honduras at the southern point of the barrier reef. 16°12'N 88°13'W [129].

Tow: Tower Hill, Orange Walk District; a settlement and sugarcane processing center on the New River. 18°04'N 88°33'W [130].

Tur: Turneffe Islands; a large group of cayes off the coast of Belize District, centered at Calabash Caye, site of a marine research station. 17°17'N 87°49'W [131].

UnC: Union Camp, Toledo District; a camp in evergreen broadleaf forest formation in the Little Quartz Ridge area of the Maya Mountains. 16°23'N 89°08'W [132].

VAC: Vaca, Cayo District; a protected area (Forest Reserve) of 52,352 acres (21,200 ha) in the northern sector of the Vaca Plateau. 16°50'N 89°06'W.

Ver: Laguna Verde, Orange Walk District; a nonalluvial freshwater lake and marshland area. 17°34'N 89°04'W [133].

Vtn: Valentin, Cayo District; a camp near the Guatemalan border in evergreen broadleaf forest formation. 16°46'N 89°10'W [134].

Wah: Waha Leaf Creek, Stann Creek District; a tributary of the Bladen Branch of the Monkey River on the coastal plain, centered at 16°39'N 88°30'W [135].

Xun: Xunantunich, Cayo District; a major archaeological site overlooking the Belize River. 17°06'N 89°08'W [136].

Xux: Ek Xux Camp, Toledo District; a camp on the Bladen branch of the
        Monkey River. 16°30′N 88°53′W [137].
Zoo: Belize Zoo, Belize District (includes site of the old zoo at Mile 29,
        Western Highway); located in an area of savanna vegetation. 17°21′N
        88°33′W [138].

DISTRIBUTION TABLE

Locality records are given in abbreviated form as listed in the gazetteer. Place names given in block capitals represent protected areas (Forest Reserve, Nature Reserve, Wildlife Sanctuary, National Park, Private Reserve, or Natural Monument). The information is presented for the purpose of giving an overall picture of distribution patterns as currently known, and should not be regarded as complete, or necessarily as a measure of abundance. Some of the museum records are included on an unverified basis and may represent misidentified animals (e.g., *Tantillita lintoni* mistaken for *Tantillita canula*), although an attempt has been made to exclude as far as possible erroneous records and other information of a potentially ambiguous nature.

Note: (C) = coastal area only; O = oceanic; ? = questionable occurrence; # = confirmed from District but specific locality(s) unknown.

Distribution Table

Species	District						
	Corozal	Orange Walk	Belize	Cayo	Stann Creek	Toledo	Cayes
Crocodylidae							
Crocodylus acutus	Cnx, SNR		BzC, MAN		PlL	PyC	Amb, Cbw, CCk, LHR, Tur
Crocodylus moreletii	Cal, Cnx, SNR, SpL	But, CCh, Cwa, Dbl, GJg, Gld, KtL, New, NwR, OrW, Sec, Tow, Ver	AHa, BBm, BRD, BzR, Cox, JnL, MAN, Mck, SBN, SPd, Zoo	Bna, BkP, Bpn, Coq, CxB, Mac	#	BDN, MkR	
Dermatydidae							
Dermatemys mawii	Czl, FCR, FmL, PgL, SEl	Blu, Gld, Hon, Lam, LbC, OrW, New, NwR, RBR	BBm, BzR, CkL, CRT, Gls, Hvl, JnL, NnL, SBN, SnL, SpC	Bpn, Mac, Xun	?	PuG, SRT	
Chelydridae							
Chelydra serpentina						Maf, Sal	
Kinosternidae							
Claudius angustatus		Gld, LMp, RBR	AHa, BBm, Hvl, Zoo	BvD	Mid		
Kinosternon acutum	SNR?	GJg, Gld, OrW, RBR	BBm, BzC, MAN, Zoo	Ccl, HiV, Prv, SlC	CMB, LQz, Mid		
Kinosternon leucostomum	SNR	CCh, GJg, Gld, RBR	BBm, BzC, Lem, MAN, Zoo	Bpn, CFm, CnR, Cvs, CxB, DSv, Gmo, Mil, Prv, Smk, Vtn	APi, Bok, CMB, DFl, Mid, Slk, Wah	BgF, Sal, SWB	
Kinosternon scorpioides	SNR	GJg, Gld, Lam, OrW	BBm, BzC, CCr, CRT, Hvl, PaW, Zoo	CxB	MCr	BDN, SPe	
Staurotypus triporcatus	#	CCh, GJg, Gld, Lam, OrW, RBR	BBm, BzC, SPd	CFm	#	BgF, Maf, PuG	

Emydidae							
Rhinoclemmys areolata	SNR, SPo	CCh, Glg, Gld, OrW, RBR	BBm, BzC, Hvl, Zoo	Bpn, DSv, HiV	Fre, Slk	#	Amb, Tur
Trachemys scripta	SNR	CCh, Glg, Gld, KtL, OrW, RBR, Tow	AHa, BzC, Msk, Zoo	Gvl, RoC	Mid, Wah	Maf, SPe	Amb
Eublepharidae							
Coleonyx elegans	Czl, SNR	CCh, Lam, OrW, Tow	AHa, BBm, BzC, MAN, Msk	BkP, Bpn, Bvi, Cam, CFm, Chi, Cvs, CxB, DSv, Gvl, MPR, Slg, SLu, Xun	CMB, Prc, Slk	BDN, BgF, CFR, Sal, San, SPe	
Gekkonidae							
Aristelliger georgeensis	(C)		MAN, (C)		(C?)	(C?)	Amb, CCk, Sap, Tom, Tur
Gonatodes albogularis			BzC				
Hemidactylus frenatus	Czl		Air, BzC	Bpn	Dan		
Phyllodactylus insularis							GvR, LHR
Phyllodactylus tuberculosus	SNR, (C)		AHa, BBm, BzC, (C)		(C)	(C)	CCk, GvR, LHR
Sphaerodactylus glaucus	Czl, SNR	CCh, Glg, OrW, Tow	AHa, BBm, BzC, Gcy, Lem, Lvl, MAN	Bpn, Ccl, DSv, Ont, Slg, SlC, Xun	APi, CMB, Dan, Mid, Slk	BCr, BgF, CFR, CqS, FSt, SPe	Amb, CCK, Tur
Sphaerodactylus millepunctatus			BBm, PaW	DyD, Vtn	APi, CMB, Slk	BDN, GSt, Tkl	
Thecadactylus rapicauda	SNR	Lam	BBm	CQB, HiV	CMB, Prc	BDN, CFR, CqS, Gla, FSt, SlC, SPe	
Cortyophanidae							
Basiliscus vittatus	Czl, SNR	CCh, Glg, Gld, KtL, OrW, RBR, Tow	AHa, BBm, BzC, Hvl, Lvl, MAN, Msk	Bpn, Bvi, Ccl, CFm, Cha, Cys, CxB, DSv, Gvl, HiV, MPR, Prv, Slg, SlC, Xun	APi, Bok, CMB, Dan, GWK, MCr, Mid, Prc, Slk	BCr, BDN, BgF, CFR, GSt, Lom, MkR, San, SPe, SWB	Amb, Tur

(continues)

Distribution Table—*Continued*

Species	District						
	Corozal	Orange Walk	Belize	Cayo	Stann Creek	Toledo	Cayes
Corytophanes cristatus		CCh, Glg	MAN	Bpn, Ccl, CnR, CxB, SlC, Svr, Sib, SlC	CMB, Prc, Slk	BDN, BgF, MkR, PuG, SPe, Tkl	Amb, CCk, GvR, LHR, Tur
Corytophanes hernandezii	SNR	CCh, Glg			Slk	Sol	CCk, LHR
Laemanctus longipes	SNR?	CCh, Glg	MAN	Ccl, CQB, CxB, SlC, Smk	CMB, Mid	Sal, SPe	
Laemanctus serratus	Czl, Sar, SEl, SNR						
Iguanidae							
Ctenosaura similis	SNR	Ggs, Tow	Air, BBm, BzC, Hvl, Lvl, MAN, Zoo	Bpn, Cog, DSv, Slg	Dan, MCr	(C)	
Iguana iguana		Gld, OrW	AHa, BBm, BzC, Zoo	Bna, Bpn, Bvi, Cha, CxB, GOr, Slg, Xun	CMB	CFR, Lom, MkR, SPe	
Phrynosomatidae							
Sceloporus chrysostictus	SNR	Hon, KtL, Lam, OrW, Tow	BzC, Lvl, Msk, AHa	Bpn, DSv, Gvl, Prv, Slg, SlC			Amb
Sceloporus lundelli	SNR			CnR, DSv, Slg		CFR, SlC	
Sceloporus serrifer				HiV			
Sceloporus variabilis	SNR	OrW, Tow	AHa, BBm, Gls, Zoo	BkP, Cam, Cha, Ccl, DSv, Gvl, HiV, MPR, Prv, Slg, SLu, Xun	MCr, Slk	CRF, SWB	
Polychrotidae							
Anolis allisoni							LHR

						LHR
Anolis carolinensis						
Norops biporcatus	SNR?	CCh, Glg, LMp		Bpn, Cav, Ccl, CnR, CQB, CxB, DSv, Prv, SlC, Vtn	Bok, DFl, Slk	BDN, BgF, Sal, SPe	
Norops capito		CCh, LMp	MAN	Ccl, CQB, Cvs, DSv, GOr, Vtn, Slg, Xun	Bok, CMB, Dan, Slk	BDN, CFR, Gla, Tkl	
Norops pentaprion							
Norops lemurinus	SNR	CCh, Ggs, Glg, Hon, KtL, LMp, OrW, PgL, Tow	AHa, BBm, BzC, Lem, MAN	BkP, Bpn, BvD, Ccl, Cha, CnR, Coq, CQB, Cvs, CxB, DSv, Gmo, Gvl, Prv, SlC, Vtn, Xun	Bok, CMB, Dan, DFl, GWK, Mid, Prc, Slk	BCr, BDN, BgF, CFR, CqS, FSt, GSt, MkR, PuG, Sal, SnC, SPe, Tkl, UnC	
Norops rodriguezii	Czl, PgL, SNR	OrW, Tow	BBm, Zoo	Bpn, Ccl, Cvs, CxB, HiV, Prv, Vtn, SlC	Dan, DFl, Slk	BDN, CRF, FSt, Sal, SPe	CCk
Norops sagrei	Czl, SNR	Gld, OrW, Tow	BBm, BRD, BzC, MAN	Bpn	Dan, GWK, MCr	MkR, PuG	Amb, Cbw, CCk, GvR, LHR, Tom, Tur
Norops sericeus	SNR	Ggs, NwR, OrW, Tow	BzC, Zoo	Bvj, Ccl, DSv, Gvl	CMB, Slk	BDN, CRF, PuG, Sal, Tkl	
Norops tropidonotus		Glg, LMp	MAN	Ccl, CnR, CQB, Cvs, DSv, Mil, Slg, Xun		CFR	
Norops uniformis		#	Gls?	Bpn, Bvi, Ccl, CQB, Cvs, CxB, DyD, GOr, Prv, Slg, Vtn, Xun	Bok, CMB, DFl, Mid, Prc, Slk	BCr, BDN, BgF, CFR, Gla, GSt, MkR, Sal, SPe, Tgr	
Scincidae							
Eumeces schwartzei	Sia, SNR	CCh, Glg, Gld, LMp		Bpn, Ccl	#		
Eumeces sumichrasti	SNR			Ccl, CnR, CxB, Rto		BDN, Tkl	

(continues)

Distribution Table—*Continued*

				District			
Species	**Corozal**	**Orange Walk**	**Belize**	**Cayo**	**Stann Creek**	**Toledo**	**Cayes**
Mabuya unimarginata	Lib, Sia, SNR	CCh, GIg, Gld, LMp, OrW, RBR, Tow	AHa, BBm, BzC, Lvl, MAN, PaW, Zoo	Bpn, DSv, Gvl, HiV, Slg, Xun	CMB, Dan, DFl, Mid, Slk	BgF, CFR	Tur
Sphenomorphus cherriei	Sia, SNR	CCh, GIg, Hon, Lam, LMp, OrW	BzC, Zoo	CxB, DSv, DyD, GOr, HiV, Prv, Svr, Xun	Bok, CMB, Dan, DFl, Mid, Prc, Slk	BCr, BDN, CFR, Tkl	
Gymnophthalmidae							
Gymnophthalmus speciosus		Crm					
Teiidae							
Ameiva festiva			BBm, MAN	Cvs, CxB, Vtn	Bok, DFl, CMB, Mid, Prc, Slk	BCr, BDN, CFR, SWB, Tkl	
Ameiva undulata	Czl, PgL, Rmt, Sia, SNR	GIg, Gld, KtL, OrW, Snt, Two	AHa, BBm, Bvi, BzC, CRT, Lvl, MAN, Msk, Zoo	BkP, Bpn, Cam, Cha, DSv, Gmo, Gvl, MPR, Prv, Slg, SlC, Xun	CMB, Dan, MCr, Mid, Slk	BCr, CFR, Med, SWB	Amb
Cnemidophorus angusticeps	?	?	BBm, BzC, Lvl, Msk, PaW, Zoo		#		
Cnemidophorus maslini	#?	Ggs, Tow	MAN			Lom, SWB	CCk?
Cnemidophorus lemniscatus						MkR	
Xantusiidae							
Lepidophyma flavimaculatum			PeH	BkP, Ccl, GOr, Gvl, Ont, Prv, Slg, SlC, Xun	Bok, CMB, DFl, Mid, Slk	BCr, BDN, CFR, Eza	
Lepidophyma mayae						Lqr	

Anguidae							
Diploglossus rozellae				CxB, Vtn	Bok, CMB, Prc, Slk	#	Amb, CCk, Tur
Typhlopidae							
Typhlops microstomus	Sja, SNR		AHa				
Leptotyphlopidae							
Leptotyphlops goudotii	Cnx						
Boidae							
Boa constrictor	Czl, FCR, SNR	CCh, Glg, Gld, OrW, Tow	AHa, BBm, BzC, CRT, Gcy, Zoo	Bna, Ccl, Cvs, Coq, CQB, CxB, DSv, MPR, Prv, Slg, SlC, Xun	Dan, Mid	CR, MkR	
Colubridae							
Adelphicos quadrivirgatus		CCh, Glg		CxB, MPR?	Dan, Slk	#	
Amastridium veliferum				Bpn, SlC	Mid	Jmy, Lqr, Med, SnC	
Clelia clelia				Bpn, CQB, CxB, DyD, Smk	Dan, Mid	BDN, CFR	
Clelia scytalina	Czl, SNR, SPo	OrW, Tow		DSv, HiV, MPR			
Coluber constrictor constrictor							
Coniophanes bipunctatus	FCR, SNR?	CCh, Glg, OrW, Sec, Tow	BBm, BzC	Bpn, CFm, Gvl	CMB, Dan, Mid	CFR	
Coniophanes fissidens	SNR?		MAN	Cvs, CxB	Bok, DFl, Mid, Slk	CFR, QOr, UnC	
Coniophanes imperialis	Czl, SNR, SPo	CCh, Glg, Gld, KtL, OrW, Tow	AHa, BBm, BzC, MAN, Msk, Zoo	Bna, BkP, Cha, CnR, DSv	Dan, Mid	CFR	
Coniophanes schmidti	Sja, SNR			DSv, Gmo, SlC	Dan, Mid	FSt	

(continues)

Distribution Table—*Continued*

				District			
Species	**Corozal**	**Orange Walk**	**Belize**	**Cayo**	**Stann Creek**	**Toledo**	**Cayes**
Conophis lineatus	SNR		Hvl, MAN	DSv, Prv, SlC			
Dendrophidion nuchale				Bal, CxB, Cvs, Sib	Mid	BDN, SnC	
Dendrophidion vinitor						Lqr	
Dipsas brevifacies	FCR, Sia, SNR		BzC				
Dryadophis melanolomus	Czl, FCR, PgL, SNR	OrW, Tow	AHa, Zoo	BkP, Ccl, Cvs, CQB, CxB, DSv, Gvl, MPR, Prv, Slg, SlC	Bok, Mid, Slk	BgF, CFR	
Drymarchon corais	Czl, FCR, SCz, SNR	CCh, Gld, LMp, OrW, Tow	BBm, BzC, SPd, Zoo	Chi, Cvs, DSv, MPR, Prv, SlC	Bok, CMB, Dan, Fre, Mid, Slk	#	CCk?
Drymobius margaritiferus	Czl, FCR, SNR, SPo	Blu, CCh, Gld, Glg, LMp, OrW, RBR, Tow	BBm, BzC, Lem, MAN, Zoo	BkP, Bvj, Ccl, Chi, Coq, Cvs, CxB, DSv, MPR, Prv, Slg, SlC, Xun	Dan, Mid	CFR, Eza	
Elaphe flavirufa	FCR, SNR	OrW		BkP, Ccl, CFm, DSv	#	BDN, CFR, Tkl	
Ficimia publia	Czl, FCR, Lib	CCh, Glg		BkP, Bpn, Slg	#	CFR	
Imantodes cenchoa	Czl, FCR, SNR	CCh, Glg	BBm, Hvl	CxB, DSv, Gvl, Prv, SlC	CMB, Dan, DFl, Mid, Prc, Slk	BgF, CR, FSt, SnC, UnC, Xux	
Lampropeltis triangulum	FCR, Sia, SNR	LMp, RBR	#	Ccl, Cha, CxB, DSv	Mid, Reg, Slk	BCr	
Leptodeira frenata	Czl, FCR, SNR	KtL, OrW, RBR, Tow	AHa, BBm, BzC, Lem, MAN	Slg	CMB, DFl	MkR	
Leptodeira septentrionalis	FCR, Czl, SNR	CCh, Glg, OrW, Tow	BBm, BzC, Gcy, MAN, SpC	BkP, Bpn, Ccl, CnR, Cvs, DSv, MPR, Prv, SlC, Smk	CMB, Dan, GWK, Mid	BCr, BDN, BgF, CFR	

Species							
Leptophis ahaetulla	SNR	CCh, OrW, Tow	AHa, BBm, MAN, Zoo	BkP, Ccl, CnR, Coq, DSv, Gvl, HiV, Prv, SIC, Smk	Dan, CMB, Mid	BCr, BDN, BgF, CFR, Tkl, Xux	Amb, Tur
Leptophis mexicanus	FCR, SNR	CCh, Glg, OrW, Tow	BBm, BzC, Lem, MAN, Zoo	CnR, DSv, HiV, Prv, SIC	CMB, Dan, Mid, Prc	FSt	
Masticophis mentovarius	FCR, SNR	OrW, Tow	AHa, BBm, BzC, Hvl, Msk	DSv, MPR			
Ninia diademata				CxB	#?	GSt	?
Ninia sebae	Czl, FCR, SCz	CCh, Ggs, Gld, OrW, Tow	BBm, BzC, MAN, Zoo	BkP, Ccl, Cha, Chi, CxB, DSv, Gvl, MPR, Slg, Xun	Bok, CMB, Dan, DFl, GWK, Mid, Slk	Ant, BDN, BgF, CFR, SPe, SWB	
Oxybelis aeneus	FCR, SNR	CCh, LMp	BBm, BzC, Lvl, MAN	BkP, Ccl, CnR, Cvs, DSv, MPR, Prv, Slg	CMB, Mid	BDN, CFR, MkR, PuG, SPe, Tkl	
Oxybelis fulgidus	FCR, SNR	OrW, Tow	BBm, Hvl, MAN	Cha, DSv, HiV, SIC	CMB, Dan, Slk	BDN, CRF, Tkl	
Oxyrhopus petola		RBR	PaW	BkP, Bpn, CQB, Cvs, CxB, DSv	Fre	CFR	
Pseustes poecilonotus	Cnx, Sia, SNR	CCh, Glg	AHa, BzC, Lvl, Msk	BvD, Cvs, DSv, Gmo, HiV, MPR, Prv, SIC, Vtn	CMB, Mid	CFR	
Rhadinaea decorata						BgF	
Scaphiodontophis annulatus	Sia, SNR	OrW, Tow	BzC, Zoo	BkP, Bpn, Cav, CxB, DSv, MPR, Slg, Xun	Mid, Slk	#	
Senticolis triaspis	SNR?		Gcy	Slg		BCr, BDN BCr	
Sibon diadematum							
Sibon nebulata	FCR	CCh, Lam	MKB	BkP, Bpn, CFm, Cha, Gvl, Slg, SlC	CMB, Mid	CFR, Eza, UnC	
Sibon sanniola	Czl, SNR	CCh, Glg	BzC	Cha, DSv, Xun		CFR	
Sibon sartorii	Czl, FCR, SNR, SPo	CCh, Glg, Lam, LMp, OrW, RBR, Tow		BkP, CFm, Slg	Mid	CFR	

(continues)

Distribution Table—*Continued*

Species	District						
	Corozal	Orange Walk	Belize	Cayo	Stann Creek	Toledo	Cayes
Spilotes pullatus	FCR, Sia, SNR	CCh, Glg, Gld, KtL, LMp, OrW, Tow	Air, AHa, BBm, BzC, Lvl, Zoo	BkP, Bvi, Ccl, Cfm, Coq, Cvs, CxB, DSv, HiV, Gmo, Prv, SlC Cvs, CxB	CMB, Dan, Mid, Prc	BCt, CFR, MkR, SPe	Amb?
Stenorrhina degenhardtii					?	Lqr	
Stenorrhina freminvillii	Czl, FCR, Lib, SCl, SCz, SPo	#		Chi, DSv, Gvl	#	CFR	
Symphimus mayae	SNR	LMp	Zoo				
Tantilla cuniculator	Sia	OrW, Tow					
Tantilla schistosa	SNR?	OrW, Tow	BBm, Hvl, Lem	CxB, DSv, Slg	#	CFR	
Tantillita canula	SNR	Lam	AHa	CxB	#	#	
Tantillita lintoni		Gld	#	Ccl, Cvs, CxB Bpn			
Thamnophis marcianus			Air, BBm, BzC, Hvl, Zoo				
Thamnophis proximus	FCR, SNR	OrW, SaE, Tow	BBm, Bmd, BzC, Msk, Zoo		APi, MCr, Slk	BDN, DPR	
Tetanorhinus nigroluteus	Czl, SNR?	Lam, OrW, Tow	Air, BBm, BzC, Lem	Bna, Slg	Mid	MkR	Tur
Urotheca elapoides				Ccl, CxB, DSv, Gmo, Smk	DFl, Mid	BDN, CFR, Eza, SPe, UnC	
Xenodon rabdocephalus	FCR	CCh, Glg, KtL, Tow	BzC	BkP, CQB, Cvs, CxB, Sib, Smk	Mid, Slk	CFR, Lqr, Xux	

322

Elapidae						
Micrurus diastema	Czl, FCR, SNR	OrW, Tow	Air, BBm, BzC, Zoo	Bal, Bpn, Ccl, Chi, Coq, Cvs, CxB, DSv, Gmo, GOr, Gvl, MPR, Slg, Vtn	CMB, Dan, Slk	BgF, CFR
Micrurus hippocrepis				BkP, CxB, DSv	CMB, Mid	CFR, RiC, SWB
Micrurus nigrocinctus	SNR?	GJg, Ggs	#	Bna, Ccl, CxB	Dan	SWB, Xux
Viperidae						
Agkistrodon bilineatus	SCz	OrW	BBm			
Atropoides nummifer				BkP, Ccl, CnR, CQB, Cvs, CxB, DSv, MPR, Rto, Smk, Vtn	DFl	BDN, CFR, Sal
Bothriechis schlegelii		GJg		CQB, GOr, Mil, Vtn	#	SnC
Bothrops asper	Czl, FCR, SCz, SNR	CCh, GJg, KtL, LMp, OrW, RBR, SaE, Tow	AHa, BBm, MAN, Zoo	BkP, Bpn, Bvj, Ccl, Cvs, CxB, DSv, Gmo, Mac, Prv, Sib, Slg, SlC, Vtn, Xun	Bok, CMB, Dan, DFl, Mid, Prc, Slk	BCr, BDN, CFR, Eza, MkR, Xux
Crotalus durissus	Czl, FCR, SNR	Ggs, Gld, OrW, Tow	BBm, Hvl, Zoo	DSv, HiV, MPR	#	(C)
Porthidium masutum				Bvj, Ccl, Xun	?	?

Glossary

Abdominal

pertaining to the undersurface of the body, exclusive of the head and tail.

Adaptive zone

the particular environment with which a species is typically associated (e.g., terrestrial, arboreal, fossorial, aquatic), and to which it may be specifically adapted.

Adpress

to press flat against the body, with the forelimbs directed backward and the hind limbs directed forward.

Aglyphous

a term applied to snakes with unmodified teeth (used in the context of venom delivery).

Anal plate

an enlarged scale that covers the cloacal opening in snakes.

Apical pit

a microscopic depression (often paired) at the tips of the dorsal scales of some snakes; function not clear although possibly involved in the skin-shedding process.

Aposematic coloration

color and patterning designed to advertize the toxic or noxious character of an animal.

Arboreal

tree-dwelling.

Autotomy

a term used to describe a form of urotomy (tail loss) for species having intravertebral breakage, spontaneous separation, and tail regeneration. Applies to most lizards.

Axilla

pertaining to the area of the body directly behind the insertion of the forelimb (generally used in reference to lizards).

Barbel

a fleshy, pointed outgrowth on the chin or throat of some turtles (e.g., *Chelydra* and *Staurotypus*).

Bridge
section of the shell in turtles connecting the carapace and plastron.

Canthus (rostralis)
pertaining to the ridged contour of the snout formed between the top and side of the head in certain lizards and snakes.

Carapace
the dorsal shell of turtles.

Carinate
ridged; usually pertains to the longitudinal keels on the carapace of some turtles. The carapace may be **unicarinate,** with a single medial keel, or **tricarinate,** with three keels.

Casque
a helmet-like extension of the head in some lizards (e.g., *Laemanctus*).

Caudal
of or pertaining to the tail.

Cephalic
of or pertaining to the head.

Cloaca
common opening of the reproductive and digestive tracts, viewed externally as the vent.

Congener
a member of the same genus.

Crepuscular
active at dusk or dawn.

Cruciform
cross-shaped; used in the context of plastron shape in certain turtles.

Cryptic coloration
color and patterning designed to conceal an animal in its natural environment.

Cryptozoic
a secretive existence; living hidden underground, beneath leaves, etc.

Dewlap
an extendible throat fan, especially well developed in anoline lizards (family Polychrotidae).

Dichromatic
a term applied to species in which the sexes are differently colored.

Diel
pertaining to the 24-hr cycle of daylight and darkness.

Diurnal
active during the day.

Dorsal
pertaining to the upper surface of the body (or part thereof).

Dorsolateral
a position on the body intermediate between the dorsum and sides.

Dorsum
the upper surface of the body (or part thereof).

Endemic
restricted in distribution to a particular, usually small geographical area.

Estivation
a condition of dormancy during periods of heat and drought.

Femoral pore
one of a linear series of small, specialized glandular scales beneath the posterior edge of the thighs in some lizards. These are typically better developed in males.

Fossorial
the habit of burrowing; generally

used in reference to a species' adaptive zone.

Gular flap
a pendulous throat fan in some lizards (e.g., *Iguana iguana*).

Herbivorous
feeding on plant material.

Imbricate
overlapping; used in the context of scale configuration.

Infraspecific
pertaining to a taxonomic category below species level (i.e., subspecies).

Insular
pertaining to islands, and species whose distribution is restricted to islands.

Intercalary
inserted; usually used in the context of lateral body markings placed between and below uppermost dorsal markings.

Interorbital
pertaining to the area between the eyes on the upper surface of the head.

Interstitial skin
area of skin between scales; usually used in reference to dorsal color.

Lamella (*pl. lamellae*)
one of a series of expanded transverse scales on the undersurface of the digits in some families of lizards (e.g., Gekkonidae and Polychrotidae).

Lateral
pertaining to the side of the body.

Loreal pit
heat-detecting cavity between the eye and naris of certain snakes.

Medial
of or pertaining to the middle.

Mental groove
a medial, lengthwise cleft in the lower jaw of most snakes.

Mesic
moist, humid.

Middorsal
of or pertaining to the center of the dorsal surface (vertebral line).

Monotypic
a term normally used to describe a genus represented by only a single species.

Mucronate
a term used in reference to scales that narrow abruptly with a projecting spine at the tip.

Naris (*pl. nares*)
external opening of the nasal passage.

Neonate
newly born or hatched.

Nocturnal
active at night.

Nominate
a term used to distinguish a subspecies representing the population on which the species description was based, and bearing the same name; for example, *Masticophis mentovarius mentovarius* is the nominate subspecific form of *Masticophis mentovarius*.

Nuchal
pertaining to the nape, or upper surface of the neck.

Nuptial
sexually active; usually used in the context of breeding coloration.

Ocellus (*pl. ocelli*)
a rounded, eye-like spot; usually used in the context of color pattern.

Occipital
pertaining to the area at the base of the head.

Ocular
of or pertaining to the eye.

Omnivorous
feeding on both plant and animal matter.

Ophiophagous
snake-eating; a species whose diet consists largely or entirely of snakes.

Opisthoglyphous
a term applied to snakes possessing fixed, nonerectile fangs (with external venom grooves) in the back of the mouth (syn. rear-fanged).

Orbit(al)
of or pertaining to the outline of the eye socket.

Osteoderm
bony plate.

Oviparous
egg-laying; applied to species that produce partially developed young in an egg that hatches outside of the body, normally some time after it has been laid.

Oviposition
the physical act of laying eggs.

Paravertebral
adjacent to the vertebral line.

Parthenogenetic
capable of reproducing without males; female produces genetically identical young from unfertilized ova.

Parturition
the act of giving birth.

Pelagic
inhabiting the open ocean.

Phalanx (*pl. phalanges*)
one of several bones linking the joints of the fingers and toes.

Plastral hinge
a transverse articulation on the plastron in certain turtles that allows movement of one or both of the adjacent lobes. In some species with a fixed middle lobe (e.g., certain kinosternid turtles) there are two hinges allowing movement of both the anterior and posterior lobes.

Plastron (*pl. plastra*)
the abdominal shell of turtles.

Postfemoral dermal pocket
a small, elongate invagination directly behind the insertion of the hind limb in some lizards (e.g., *Sceloporus variabilis*).

Preanal pore
one of a series of small, specialized glandular scales preceding the vent in some lizards. These are typically better developed in males. In some species (e.g., *Hemidactylus frenatus*) they may fuse with the femoral pores forming a continuous series across the posterior underside of the thighs and lower abdomen (**preanofemoral pores**).

Preorbital ridge
a hump-like swelling on the medial part of the upper mandible in some crocodiles (e.g., *Crocodylus acutus*); this appears to develop with age and may be a sex-specific character.

Proteroglyphous
a term applied to snakes possessing fixed, nonerectile fangs (with partially enclosed venom canals) in the front of the mouth.

Pseudautotomy
a term used to describe a form of urotomy for species having a high incidence of tail loss and intervertebral breakage with no capacity for spontaneous separation or tail regeneration. Applies to snakes and some lizards.

Rear-fanged
see **Opisthoglyphous**.

Riparian
pertaining to the margins of rivers and other water courses.

Rugose
a term applied to scales characterized by an irregularly carinate surface rather than a regular, single medial keel (e.g., head scales of some sceloporine lizards).

Saurophagous
lizard-eating; a species whose diet consists largely or entirely of lizards.

Sceloporine
of or pertaining to lizards of the genus *Sceloporus.*

Scutes
bony, plate-like scales comprising the shell of turtles and tortoises.

Solenoglyphous
a term applied to snakes possessing hinged, erectile fangs (with enclosed, internal venom canals) in the front of the mouth.

Subcaudal
of or pertaining to the undersurface of the tail.

Subdigital
of or pertaining to the undersurface of a finger or toe.

Supra-anal
pertaining to the upper lateral edge of the vent.

Sympatric
occurring in the same area; used in the context of species with overlapping geographic distributions.

Temporal
pertaining to the area of the head above and behind the eye.

Terrestrial
ground-dwelling.

Urotomy
a general term used to describe all kinds of tail breakage. Tail loss presumably functions as an anti-predator defense mechanism.

Venter
undersurface of body.

Ventrolateral
pertaining to the outside edge of the venter and adjoining lower sides of the body.

Viviparous
live-bearing; applied to species in which the female retains the eggs internally so that parturition takes place only when the young are fully developed; neonates are born encased in a membranous sack.

Xeric
arid; usually used in the context of a dry environment.

References & Further Reading

Abercrombie, C.L., D. Davidson, C.A. Hope, and D.E. Scott. (1980). Status of Morelet's crocodile, *Crocodylus moreleti*, in Belize. *Biol. Conserv.* **17**(2), 103–113.

Allen, R., and W.T. Neill. (1959). Doubtful locality records in British Honduras. *Herpetologica* **15**(4), 227–233.

Alvarez del Toro, M. (1982). "Los Reptiles de Chiapas," 3rd ed. Publicación del Instituto de Historia Natural, Tuxtla Guttiérez, Chiapas, Mexico.

Andrews, R.M., and A.S. Rand. (1974). Reproductive effort in anoline lizards. *Ecology* **55**, 1317–1327.

Arnold, E.N. (1986). Mite pockets of lizards, a possible means of reducing damage by ectoparasites. *Biol. J. Linn. Soc.* **29**, 1–21.

Bailey, J.R. (1939). A systematic study of the snakes of the genus *Coniophanes. Pap. Mich. Acad. Sci., Arts Lett.* **24**, 1–48.

Bateson, J.H., and I.H.S. Hall. (1977). The geology of the Maya Mountains, Belize. *Overseas Mem.—Inst. Geol. Sci. (G.B.)* **3**.

Bauer, A.M., and A.P. Russell. (1993). *Aristelliger georgeensis. Cat. Am. Amphib. Reptiles* **568**, 1–568.2.

Beargie, K., and C.J. McCoy. (1964). Variation and relationships of the teiid lizard *Cnemidophorus angusticeps. Copeia* No. 3, pp. 561–570.

Beebe, W. (1944). Field notes on the lizards of Kartabo, British Guiana, and Caripito, Venezuela. Part 1. Gekkonidae. *Zoologica (N.Y.)* **29**, 145–160.

Bezy, R.L. (1973). A new species of the genus *Lepidophyma* (Reptilia: Xantusiidae) from Guatemala. *Contrib. Sci. Los Angeles Co. Mus.* **239**, 1–7.

Bezy, R.L. (1989). Morphological differentiation in unisexual and bisexual lizards of the genus *Lepidophyma* in Central America. *Herpetol. Monogr.* **3**, 61–80.

Blaney, R.M., and P.K. Blaney. (1978). Additional specimens of *Amastridium veliferum* Cope (Serpentes: Colubridae) from Chiapas, Mexico. *Southwest. Nat.* **23**, 692.

Bock, B.C. (1987). *Corytophanes cristatus:* Nesting. *Herpetol. Rev.* **18**, 35.

Bohuslavek, J. (1996). *Ninia sebae sebae:* Reproduction. *Herpetol. Rev.* **27**(3), 146.

Bolaños, R. (1984). "Serpientes, Venenos y Ofidismo en Centroamérica." Ciudad Universitaria, Costa Rica, Universidad de Costa Rica, San José.

Campbell, J.A. (1998). "The Amphibians and Reptiles of Tikal-Flores and Adjacent Regions of Guatemala and Belize." Oklahoma University Press, Norman (in press).

Campbell, J.A., and R.J. Camarillo. (1994). A new lizard of the genus *Diploglossus* (Anguidae: Diploglossinae) from Mexico, with a review of the Mexican and northern Central American species. *Herpetologica* **50**(2), 193–209.

Campbell, J.A., and W.W. Lamar. (1989). "The Venomous Reptiles of Latin America." Cornell University Press, Ithaca, NY.

Campbell, J.A., and J.P. Vannini. (1989). Distribution of amphibians and reptiles in Guatemala and Belize. *Proc. West. Found. Vertebr. Zool.* **4**(1), 1–21.

Censky, E.J., and C.J. McCoy. (1988). Female reproductive cycles of five species of snakes from the Yucatán Peninsula. *Biotropica* **20**, 326–333.

Conant, R., and J. Collins. (1991). "A Field Guide to Reptiles and Amphibians of Eastern and Central North America." Peterson Field Guides, Houghton Mifflin, New York.

Cooper, W.E., and L.J. Vitt. (1985). Blue tails and autotomy: Enhancement of predation avoidance in juvenile skinks. *Z. Tierpsychol.* **70**(4), 265–276.

Dixon, J.R. (1960). The discovery of *Phyllodactylus tuberculosus* (Reptilia: Sauria) in Central America, the resurrection of *P. xanti,* and a description of a new gecko from British Honduras. *Herpetologica* **16**(1), 1–11.

Dixon, J.R. (1964). The systematics and distribution of lizards of the genus *Phyllodactylus* in North and Central America. *Sci. Bull. N.M. State Univ. Res. Cent. No.* **64**(1), 1–139.

Dixon, J.R., and F.S. Hendricks. (1979). The worm snakes (Family Typhlopidae) of the neotropics, exclusive of the Antilles. *Zool. Verh., Leiden* **173**, 1–39.

Dodd, C.K., Jr. (1978). A note on the defensive posturing of turtles from Belize, Central America. *Herpetol. Rev.* **9**, 11–12.

Dowling, H.G. (1952). A taxonomic study of the ratsnakes, genus *Elaphe* Fitzinger. II. The subspecies of *Elaphe flavirufa* (Cope). *Occas. Pap. Mus. Zool., Univ. Mich.* **540**, 1–14.

Dowling, H.G. (1960). A taxonomic study of the ratsnakes, genus *Elaphe* Fitzinger. VII. The *triaspis* section. *Zoologica (N.Y.)* **45**, 53–80.

Duellman, W.E. (1958). A monographic study of the colubrid snake genus *Leptodeira. Bull. Am. Mus. Nat. Hist.* **114**, 1–152.

Duellman, W.E. (1963). Amphibians and reptiles of the rainforests of southern El Petén, Guatemala. *Publ. Mus. Nat. Hist. Univ. Kans.* **15**, 205–249.

Duellman, W.E. (1965). Amphibians and reptiles from the Yucatán Peninsula, Mexico. *Publ. Mus. Nat. Hist. Univ. Kans.* **15**(12), 577–614.

Dundee, H.A., D.A. White, and V. Rico-Gray. (1986). Observations on the distribution and biology of some Yucatán Peninsula amphibians and reptiles. *Bull. Md. Herpetol. Soc.* **22**, 37–50.

Echternacht, A.C. (1968). Distributional and ecological notes on some reptiles from northern Honduras. *Herpetologica* **24**(2), 151–158.

Echternacht, A.C. (1971). Middle American lizards of the genus *Ameiva* (Teiidae) with emphasis on geographic variation. *Publ. Mus. Nat. Hist., Misc., Univ. Kans.* **55**, 1–86.

Edgar, P. (1997). Notes on the snakes of north east Belize. *The Rephiberary* **32**, 8–13.

Ernst, C., and R. Barbour. (1989). "Turtles of the World." Smithsonian Institution Press, Washington, DC.

Fitch, H.S. (1970). Reproductive cycles in lizards and snakes. *Publ. Mus. Nat. Hist., Misc., Univ. Kans.* **52**, 1–247.

Fitch, H.S. (1973). A field study of Costa Rican lizards. *Univ. Kans. Sci. Bull.* **50**, 39–126.

Fritts, T.H. (1969). The systematics of the *Cnemidophorus cozumela* complex. *Copeia* No. 3, 519–535.

Frost, D.R., and R.E. Etheridge. (1989). A phylogenetic analysis and taxonomy of Iguanian lizards (Reptilia: Squamata). *Publ. Mus. Nat. Hist. Misc., Univ. Kans.* **81**, 1–65.

Fugler, C.M. (1960). New herpetological records for British Honduras. *Tex. J. Sci.* **12**(1–2), 8–13.

Garel, T., and S. Matola. (1996). "A Field Guide to the Snakes of Belize." Corporación Gráfica, Costa Rica.

Gehlbach, F.R., J.F. Watkins, II, and H.W. Reno. (1968). Blind snake defensive behavior elicited by ant attacks. *BioScience* **18**, 784–785.

Gloyd, H.K. (1972). A subspecies of *Agkistrodon bilineatus* (Serpentes: Crotalidae) from the Yucatán Peninsula, Mexico. *Proc. Biol. Soc. Wash.* **84**(40), 327–334.

Gloyd, H.K., and R. Conant. (1990). "Snakes of the *Agkistrodon* complex: A Monographic Review." Society for the Study of Amphibians and Reptiles, Oxford, OH.

Gray, J.E. (1845). Description of a new genus of night lizards from Belize. *Ann. Mag. Nat. Hist.* **16**, 162–163.

Greene, H.W. (1973). Defensive tail display by snakes and amphisbaenians. *J. Herpetol.* **7**, 143–161.

Greene, H.W. (1975). Ecological observations on the red coffee snake, *Ninia sebae*, in southern Veracruz, Mexico. *Am. Mid. Nat.* **93**, 478–484.

Gutiérrez, J.M. (1995). Clinical toxicology of snake bite in Central American. *In* "Handbook of Clinical Toxicology of Animal Venoms and Poisons" (J. Meier and J. White, eds.), pp. 645–665. CRC Press, Boca Raton, FL.

Guyer, C., and M.S. Laska. (1996). *Coluber (= Masticophis) mentovarius* (Neotropical whipsnake): Predation. *Herpetol. Rev.* **27**(4), 203.

Guyer, C., and J.M. Savage. (1986). Cladistic relationships among anoles (Sauria: Iguanidae). *Syst. Zool.* **35**, 509–531.

Hardy, D.L. (1994a). *Bothrops asper* (Viperidae) snakebite and field researchers in Middle America. *Biotropica* **26**(2), 198–207.

Hardy, D.L. (1994b). Snakebite and field biologists in México and Central America: Report on ten cases with recommendations for field management. *Herpetol. Nat. Hist.* **2**(2), 67–82.

Hardy, L.M. (1975). A systematic revision of the colubrid snake genus *Ficimia. J. Herpetol.* **9**, 133–168.

Harris, D., and A. Kluge. (1984). The *Sphaerodactylus* (Sauria: Gekkonidae) of Middle America. *Occas. Pap. Mus. Zool., Univ. Mich.* **706**, 1–59.

Harrison, C.R. (1993). A taxonomic revision of the *Coniophanes piceivittis* species group. M.S. Thesis, University of Texas, El Paso.

Hartshorn, G.S., L. Nicolait, L. Hartshorn, G. Bevier, R. Brightman, J. Cal, A. Cawich, W. Davidson, R. Dubois, C. Dyer, J. Gibson, W. Hawley, J. Leonard, R. Nicolait, D. Weyer, H. White, and C. Wright (1984). "Belize: Country Environmental Profile; A Field Study." Robert Nicolait Associates Ltd., Belize City, Belize.

Henderson, R.W. (1973). Ethoecological observations of *Ctenosaura similis* (Sauria, Iguanidae) in British Honduras. *J. Herpetol.* **7**(1), 27–32.

Henderson, R.W. (1974a). Aspects of the ecology of the Neotropical vine snake, *Oxybelis aeneus* Wagler. *Herpetologica* **30**, 19–24.

Henderson, R.W. (1974b). Aspects of the ecology of the juvenile common iguana *(Iguana iguana)*. *Herpetologica* **30**, 327–332.

Henderson, R.W. (1976a). Notes on reptiles in the Belize City area, Belize. *J. Herpetol.* **10**(2), 143–146.

Henderson, R.W. (1976b). A new insular subspecies of the colubrid snake *Leptophis mexicanus* (Reptilia, Serpentes, Colubridae). *J. Herpetol.* **12**, 412–413.

Henderson, R.W. (1978). Notes on *Agkistrodon bilineatus* (Reptilia, Serpentes, Viperidae) in Belize. *J. Herpetol.* **12**, 412–413.

Henderson, R.W. (1979). Variation in the snake *Tretanorhinus nigroluteus lateralis* in Belize with notes on breeding tubercles. *Herpetologica* **35**, 245–248.

Henderson, R.W., and L.G. Hoevers. (1975). A checklist and key to the amphibians and reptiles of Belize, Central America. *Milw. Publ. Mus. Contrib. Biol. Geol.* **5**, 1–63.

Henderson, R.W., and L.G. Hoevers. (1977a). The seasonal incidence of snakes at a locality in northern Belize. *Copeia* No. 2, 349–355.

Henderson, R.W., and L.G. Hoevers. (1977b). The head-neck display of *Ninia s. sebae* (Reptilia, Serpentes, Colubridae) in northern Belize. *J. Herpetol.* **11**, 106–108.

Henderson, R.W., L.G. Hoevers, and L.D. Wilson. (1977). A new species of *Sibon* (Reptile, Serpentes, Colubridae) from Belize, Central America. *J. Herpetol.* **11**(1), 77–79.

Hoevers, L.G., and R.W. Henderson. (1974). Additions to the herpetofauna of Belize (British Honduras). *Milw. Publ. Mus. Contrib. Biol. Geol.* **2**, 1–16.

Holdridge, L.R. (1967). "Life Zone Ecology." Tropical Science Center, San José, Costa Rica.

Horwich, R.H., and J. Lyon. (1990). "A Belizean Rainforest; The Community Baboon Sanctuary." Orang-Utan Press, Wisconsin.

Iremonger, S., and N.V.L. Brokaw. (1995). Vegetation classification for Belize. *In* "Towards a National Protected Area Systems Plan for Belize," Appendix 1. Prepared by Programme for Belize, in collaboration with the Inter-American Development Bank, for the Natural Resources Project (USAID), Belize.

Iremonger, S., and R. Sayre. (1994). "Bladen Nature Reserve, Toledo District, Belize: Rapid Ecological Assessment." The Nature Conservancy, Arlington, Virginia.

Iverson, J.B. (1976). The genus *Kinosternon* in Belize. *Herpetologica* **32**, 258–262.

Johnson, J.D. (1977). The taxonomy and distribution of the Neotropical whipsnake *Masticophis mentovarius* (Reptilia, Serpentes, Colubridae). *J. Herpetol.* **11**(3), 287–309.

Johnson, J.D. (1982). *Masticophis mentovarius. Cat. Am. Amphib. Reptiles* **295**, 1–295.4.

Johnson, J.D. (1989). A biogeographic analysis of the herpetofauna of northwestern Nuclear Central America. *Milw. Pub. Mus. Contrib. Biol. Geol.* **76**, 1–66.

Junghanss, T., and M. Bodio. (1996). "Notfall-handbuch gifttiere." Thieme, Stuttgart.

Keiser, E.D., Jr. (1974). A systematic study of the neotropical vine snake, *Oxybelis aeneus* (Wagler). *Bull. Tex. Mem. Mus.* **22**, 1–51.

Klauber, L. (1945). The geckos of the genus *Coleonyx* with descriptions of new subspecies. *Trans. San Diego Soc. Nat. Hist.* **10**(11), 133–216.

Kofron, C.P. (1983). Female reproductive cycle of the Neotropical snail-eating snake *Sibon sanniola* in northern Yucatán, Mexico. *Copeia* No. 4, 963–969.

Lang, M. (1989). Phylogenetic and biogeographic patterns of basiliscine iguanians (Reptilia: Squamata: 'Iguanidae'). *Bonn. Zool. Monogr.* **28**, 1–172.

Lazcano-Barrero, M.A., and E. Gongóra-Arones. (1993). Observation and review of the nesting and egg-laying of *Corytophanes cristatus* (Iguanidae). *Bull. Md. Herpetol. Soc.* **29**, 67–75.

Lee, J.C. (1980). An ecogeographical analysis of the herpetofauna of the Yucatán Peninsula, Guatemala, Belize and Mexico. *Publ. Mus. Nat. Hist., Misc., Univ. Kans.* **67**, 1–75.

Lee, J.C. (1996). "The Amphibians and Reptiles of the Yucatán Peninsula." Cornell University Press, Ithaca, NY.

Lieb, C.S. (1988). Systematic status of the Neotropical snakes *Dendrophidion dendrophis* and *D. nuchalis* (Colubridae). *Herpetologica* **44**, 162–175.

Liner, E.A. (1994). "Scientific and Common Names for the Amphibians and Reptiles of Mexico in English and Spanish," Society for the Study of Amphibians and Reptiles, Oxford, OH. Herpetol. Circ. No. 23.

List, J.C. (1966). Comparative osteology of the snake families Typhlopidae and Leptotyphlopidae. *Ill. Biol. Mongr.* **36**, 1–112.

Loveridge, A. (1947). Revision of the African lizards of the family Gekkonidae. *Bull. Mus. Comp. Zool.* **98**(1), 133–216.

Marcellini, D.L. (1974). Acoustic behaviour of the gekkonid lizard *Hemidactylus frenatus. Herpetologica* **30**, 44–52.

Marlin, J.A., K.K. Marlin, and S.G. Platt. (1995). A documented case of an attack by Morelet's crocodile *(Crocodylus moreletii)* on man. *Bull. Chicago Herpetol. Soc.* **30**(8), 165–167.

Martin, P.S. (1955). Herpetological records from the Gómez Farías region of southwestern Tamaulipas, Mexico. *Copeia* No. 3, 173–180.

Martin, P.S. (1958). A biogeography of amphibians and reptiles in the Gómez Farías region, Tamaulipas, Mexico. *Misc. Publ. Mus. Zool., Univ. Mich.* **101**, 1–102.

Martin, T.E. (1988). Snake bite injury in Belize (its incidence and how best to manage it). *Med. Corps Int.* **6**, 11–16.

Martin, T.E. (1989). Snake bite injury in Belize (its incidence and how best to manage it). *Med. Corps Int.* **7**, 60–70.

Maslin, T.P. (1963). Notes on a collection of herpetozoa from the Yucatán Peninsula of Mexico. *Univ. Colo. Stud., Ser. Biol.* **9**, 1–20.

McCarthy, T.J. (1982). A note on reproduction in *Laemanctus longipes* in Belize (Sauria: Iguanidae). *Caribb. J. Sci.* **18**(1–4), 133.

McCoy, C.J. (1968). A review of the genus *Laemanctus* (Reptilia: Iguanidae). *Copeia,* No. 4, 665–678.

McCoy, C.J. (1970). The snake fauna of Middlesex, British Honduras. *J. Herpetol.* **4,** 135–140.

McCoy, C.J. (1986). Results of the Carnegie Museum of Natural History expeditions to Belize. 1. Systematic status and geographic distribution of *Sibon neilli* (Reptilia: Serpentes). *Ann. Carnegie Mus.* **55,** 117–123.

McCoy, C.J. (1990). Additions to the herpetofauna of Belize, Central America. *Caribb. J. Sci.* **26**(3–4), 164–166.

McCoy, C.J., E.J. Censky, and R.W. Van Devender. (1986). Distribution records for amphibians and reptiles in Belize, Central America. *Herpetol. Rev.* **17,** 28.

Meerman, J.C. (1992). A new snake for Belize. *Occas. Pap. Belize Nat. Hist. Soc.* **1**(1–4), 26–27.

Meerman, J.C. (1993). Checklist of the reptiles and amphibians of the Shipstern Nature Reserve. *Occas. Pap. Belize Nat. Hist. Soc.* **2**(1–11), 65–69.

Meerman, J.C., ed. (1995). Monkey River special development area, Toledo District, Belize. Vol. 2. Biodiversity study 1995. Appendices. *Belize Trop. For. Stud. Publ.* No. 5.

Meerman, J.C. (1996a). Slate Creek Preserve, checklist of reptiles. *In* "Rapid Environmental Assessment, San Antonio, Cayo District, Belize" (J.C. Meerman and T. Boomsma, eds.). Belize Environmental Consultancies Ltd., Belmopan, Belize.

Meerman, J.C. (1996b). Half Moon Caye: Terrestrial survey results and management implications. Unpublished report to Belize Audubon Society.

Meerman, J.C., and G. Williams. (1995). Maya Mountains traverse expedition, January 16–February 4, 1995. Biological Report. *Belize Trop. For. Stud. Publ.* No. 3, 1–45.

Meier, J., and J. White, eds. (1995). "Handbook of Clinical Toxicology of Animal Venoms and Poisons." CRC Press, Boca Raton, FL.

Mendelson, J.R. (1992). Frequency of tail breakage in *Coniophanes fissidens* (Serpentes: Colubridae). *Herpetologica* **48,** 448–455.

Meyer, J.R. (1966). Records and observations on some amphibians and reptiles from Honduras. *Herpetologica* **22,** 172–181.

Meyer, J.R. (1969). A biogeographic study of the amphibians and reptiles of Honduras. Ph.D. Thesis, University of Southern California, Los Angeles.

Meyer, J.R., and C. Farneti Foster. (1996). "A Guide to the Frogs and Toads of Belize." Krieger Publ. Co., Melbourne, FL.

Meyer, J.R., and L.D. Wilson. (1971). A distributional checklist of the amphibians of Honduras. *Contrib. Sci. Los Angeles Co. Mus.* **218,** 1–47.

Meyer, J.R., and L.D. Wilson. (1973). A distributional checklist of the turtles, crocodilians and lizards of Honduras. *Contrib. Sci. Los Angeles Co. Mus.* **244,** 1–39.

Moll, D. (1985). The marine turtles of Belize. *Oryx* **19**, 144–157.

Moll, D. (1986). The distribution, status, and level of exploitation of the freshwater turtle *Dermatemys mawei* in Belize, Central America. *Biol. Conserv.* **35**, 87–96.

Moll, E.O., and J.M. Legler. (1971). The life history of the neotropical slider turtle, *Pseudemys scripta* (Shoepff), in Panama. *Bull. Los Angeles Co. Mus. Nat. Hist.* **11**, 1–102.

Moritz, C., J.W. Wright, V. Singh, and W. Brown. (1992). Mitochondrial DNA analyses and the origin and relative age of parthenogenetic *Cnemidophorus.* V. The *cozumela* species group. *Herpetologica* **48**(4), 417–414.

Myers, C.W. (1971). Central American lizards related to *Anolis pentaprion:* Two new species from the Cordillera de Talamanca. *Am. Mus. Novit.* **2471**, 1–40.

Myers, C.W. (1974). The systematics of *Rhadinea* (Colubirdae), a genus of New World snakes. *Bull. Amer. Mus. Nat. Hist.* **153**, 1–262.

Neill, W.T. (1960). Nature and man in British Honduras. *Md. Natur.* **30**(1–4), 2–14.

Neill, W.T. (1962). The reproductive cycle of snakes in a tropical region, British Honduras. *Q. J. Fla. Acad. Sci.* **25**(3), 234–253.

Neill, W.T. (1965). New and noteworthy amphibians and reptiles from British Honduras. *Bull. Fla. State Mus.* **9**(3), 77–130.

Neill, W.T., and R. Allen. (1959a). The rediscovery of *Thamnophis praeocularis* (Bocourt) in British Honduras. *Herpetologica* **15**(4), 223–227.

Neill, W.T., and R. Allen. (1959b). Studies on the amphibians and reptiles of British Honduras. *Publ. Res. Div., Ross Allen's Reptile Inst.* **2**(1), 1–76.

Neill, W.T., and R. Allen. (1959c). Additions to the British Honduras hepetofaunal list. *Hepetologica* **15**(4), 235–240.

Neill, W.T., and R. Allen. (1960). Noteworthy snakes from British Honduras. *Herpetologica* **16**(3), 145–162.

Neill, W.T., and R. Allen. (1961a). Further studies on the herpetology of British Honduras. *Herpetologica* **17**(1), 37–52.

Neill, W.T., and R. Allen. (1961b). Colubrid snakes *(Tantilla, Thamnophis, Tropidodipsas)* from British Honduras and nearby areas. *Herpetologica* **17**(2), 90–98.

Neill, W.T., and R. Allen. (1962). Reptiles of the Cambridge Expedition to British Honduras, 1959–1960. *Herpetologica* **18**(2), 80–91.

Parker, T., B. Holst, L. Emmons, and J. Meyer. (1993). "A Biological Assessment of the Columbia River Forest Reserve, Toledo District, Belize," RAP Working Papers No. 3. Conservation International, Washington, DC.

Pérez-Higareda, G., and H.M. Smith. (1988). Courtship behavior in *Rhinoclemmys areolata* from western Tabasco, Mexico (Testudines; Emydidae). *Great Basin Nat.* **48**(2), 263–266.

Pérez-Higareda, G., and H.M. Smith. (1989). Termite nest incubation of the eggs of the Mexican snake *Adelphicos quadrivirgatus. Herpetol. Rev.* **20,** 5–6.

Pérez-Higareda, G., A. Rangel-Rangel, and H.M. Smith. (1990). Maximum sizes of Morelet's and American crocodiles. *Bull. Md. Herpetol. Soc.* **27**(1), 34–37.

Peters, J.A. (1960). The snakes of the subfamily Dipsadinae. *Misc. Publ. Mus. Zool. Univ. Mich.* **114,** 1–224.

Platt, S.G. (1993). The natural history of the Mexican giant musk turtle *(Staurotypus triporcatus)* in Belize. *Vivarium* **5,** 26–27, 35.

Platt, S.G. (1994). *Dermatemys mawei:* (Central American river turtle). Geographic distribution. *Herpetol. Rev.* **25**(2), 75.

Platt, S.G. (1995a). Wildlife survey of Gold Button Ranch, Belize (1992–1995). Unpublished report.

Platt, S.G. (1995b). Preliminary assessment of the status of the American crocodile *(Crocodylus acutus)* in the Turneffe Atoll, Belize. Unpublished report.

Platt, S.G. (1996). The ecology and status of Morelet's crocodile in Belize. Ph.D. Dissertation, Clemson University, Clemson, SC.

Polisar, J. (1994). New legislation for the protection and management of *Dermatemys mawii* in Belize, Central America. *Herpetol. Rev.* **25**(2), 47–49.

Polisar, J., and R.H. Horwich. (1994). Conservation of the large, economically important river turtle *Dermatemys mawii* in Belize. *Biol. Conserv.* **8**(2), 338–342.

Porras, L., J.R. McCranie, and L.D. Wilson. (1981). The systematics and distribution of the hognose viper *Bothrops nasuta* Bocourt (Serpentes: Viperidae). *Tulane Stud. Zool. Bot.* **22,** 85–107.

Rabinowitz, A. (1987). "Jaguar: One Man's Struggle to Save Jaguars in the Wild." Collins, London.

Rand, A.S., and C.W. Myers. (1990). The herpetofauna of Barro Colorado Island, Panama; an ecological summary. *In* "Four Neotropical Rainforests" (A.H. Gentry, ed.), pp. 386–409. Yale University Press, New Haven, CT.

Rand, A.S., and E.P. Ortleb. (1969). Defensive display in the colubrid snake *Pseustes poecilonotus shropshirei. Herpetologica* **25,** 46–48.

Rogers, A.D.F., D.A. Sutton, and P.J. Stafford, eds. (1994). "Report of the 1993 Joint Services Scientific Expedition to the Upper Raspaculo River, Belize, Central America, April-June 1993." Natural History Museum and H.M. Stationery Office, London.

Ross, C., ed. (1989). "Crocodiles and Alligators." Facts on File, New York.

Ross, F.D., and G.C. Mayer. (1983). On the dorsal armor of the Crocodilia. *In* "Advances in Herpetology and Evolutionary Biology: Essays in Honor of Ernest E. Williams" (A.G.J. Rhodin and K. Miyata, eds.), pp. 305–331. Harvard University Press, Cambridge, MA.

Rossman, D.A. (1963). The colubrid snake genus *Thamnophis:* A revision of the *Sauritus* group. *Bull. Fla. State Mus.* **7,** 99–178.

Rossman, D.A. (1971). Systematics of the Neotropical populations of *Thamnophis marcianus* (Serpentes: Colubridae). *Occas. Pap. Mus. Zool. La State Univ.* **41,** 1–13.

Rossman, D.A., and G.C. Schaeffer. (1974). Generic status of *Opheodrys mayae,* a colubrid snake endemic to the Yucatán Peninsula. *Occas. Pap. Mus. Zool., La State Univ.* **45,** 1–12.

Roze, J.A. (1996). "Coral Snakes of the Americas: Biology, Identification, and Venoms." Krieger Publ. Co., Melbourne, FL.

Ruibal, R., and E. Williams. (1961). Two sympatric Cuban anoles of the *carolinensis* group. *Bull. Mus. Comp. Zool.* **125**(7), 183–208.

Russell, S.M. (1964). "A Distributional Study of the Birds of British Honduras," *Ornithol. Monogr. No. 1.* American Ornithologists' Union.

Sanderson, I.T. (1941). "Living Treasure." Viking Press, New York.

Savage, J.M. (1982). The enigma of the Central American herpetofauna: Dispersals or vicariance. *Ann. Mo. Bot. Gard.* **69,** 464–547.

Savage, J.M., and J.B. Slowinski. (1996). Evolution of coloration, urotomy and coral snake mimicry in the snake genus *Scaphiodontophis* (Serpentes, Colubridae). *Biol. J. Linn. Soc.* **57**(2), 129–194.

Schmidt, K.P. (1924). Notes on Central American crocodiles. *Field Mus. Nat. Hist. Publ. Zool. Ser.* **12**(6), 77–92.

Schmidt, K.P. (1941). The amphibians and reptiles of British Honduras. *Field Mus. Nat. Hist. Publ., Zool. Ser.* **22**(8), 475–510.

Schwartz, A., and R.W. Henderson. (1991). "Amphibians and Reptiles of the West Indies." University Presses of Florida, Gainesville.

Seib, R.L. (1980). Human envenomation from the bite of an aglyphous false coral snake *Pliocercus elapoides* (Serpentes: Colubridae). *Toxicon* **18,** 399–401.

Sexton, O.J., and H.M. Brown. (1977). The reproductive cycle of an iguanid lizard, *Anolis sagrei* from Belize. *J. Nat. Hist.* **11,** 241–250.

Sites, J.W., Jr., and J.R. Dixon. (1982). Geographic variation in *Sceloporus variabilis* and its relationship to *S. teapensis* (Sauria: Iguanidae). *Copeia* No. 1, 14–27.

Slowinski, J.B., and J. Savage. (1995). Urotomy in *Scaphiodontophis:* Evidence for the multiple tail break hypothesis in snakes. *Herpetologica* **5**(3), 338–341.

Smith, E.N., and M.E. Acevedo. (1997). The northernmost distribution of *Corallus annulatus* (Boidae), with comments on its natural history. *Southwest. Nat.* **42**(3), 347–349.

Smith, E.N., and J.A. Campbell. (1994). A new species of *Rhadinaea* (Colubridae) from the Caribbean versant of Guatemala. *Occas. Pap. Mus. Nat. Hist. Univ. Kansas* **167,** 1–9.

Smith, G.W. (1992). Hawksbill turtle nesting at Manatee Bar, Belize, 1991. *Mar. Turtle Newsl.* **57,** 1–5.

Smith, G.W., K.L. Eckert, and J.P. Gibson. (1992). "WIDECAST Sea Turtle Recovery Action Plan for Belize," CEP Tech. Rep. No. 18. UNEP Caribbean Environment Programme, Kingston, Jamaica.

Smith, H.M. (1939). The Mexican and Central American lizards of the genus *Sceloporus. Field Mus. Nat. Hist. Publ., Zool. Ser.* **12**(6), 79–92.

Smith, H.M. (1941a). A review of the subspecies of the indigo snake *(Drymarchon corais). J. Wash. Acad. Sci.* **31,** 466–481.

Smith, H.M. (1941b). A new name for the Mexican snakes of the genus *Dendrophidion. Proc. Biol. Soc. Wash.* **54,** 73–76.

Smith, H.M. (1942). Mexican herpetological miscellany. *Proc. U.S. Natl. Mus.* **92,** 349–395.

Smith, H.M. (1943). Summary of the collections of snakes and crocodilians made in Mexico under the Walter Rathbone Bacon Traveling Scholarship. *Proc. U.S. Natl. Mus.* **93,** 393–504.

Smith, H.M. (1973). A tentative arrangement of the lizards of the genus *Lepidophyma. J. Herpetol.* **7,** 109–123.

Smith, H.M., and D. Chiszar. (1996). Species-group taxa of the false coral snake genus *Pliocercus.* Ramus Publishing Inc., PA.

Smith, H.M., and T.H. Fritts. (1969). Cannibalism in the lizard *Sceloporus chrysostictus. J. Herpetol.* **3**(3–4), 182–183.

Stafford, P.J. (1991). Amphibians and reptiles of the Joint Services Scientific Expedition to the upper Raspaculo, Belize. *Bri. Herpetol. Soc. Bull.* **38,** 10–17.

Stafford, P.J. (1994). Amphibians and reptiles of the upper Raspaculo river basin, Maya Mountains, Belize. *Bri. Herpetol. Soc. Bull.* **47,** 23–29.

Stafford, P.J. (1996). *Stennorhina degenhardtii* (Degenhardt's scorpion-eating snake): Geographic distribution. *Herpetol. Rev.* **27**(4), 214.

Stuart, L.C. (1935). A contribution to the knowledge of the herpetology of a portion of the savanna region of central Petén, Guatemala. *Misc. Publ. Mus. Zool., Univ. Mich.* No. 29, pp. 1–56.

Stuart, L.C. (1937). Some further notes on the amphibians and reptiles of the Petén forest of northern Guatemala. *Copeia* No. 1, 67–70.

Stuart, L.C. (1939). Studies of neotropical Colubrinae. VIII. A revision of the genus *Dryadophis* Stuart, 1939. *Misc. Publ. Mus. Zool., Univ. Mich.* **49,** 1–106.

Stuart, L.C. (1948). The amphibians and reptiles of Alta Verapaz, Guatemala. *Misc. Publ. Mus. Zool., Univ. Mich.* **69,** 1–109.

Stuart, L.C. (1950). A geographic study of the herpetofauna of Alta Verapaz, Guatemala. *Contrib. Lab. Vertebr. Biol. Univ. Mich.* **45,** 1–77.

Stuart, L.C. (1951). The herpetofauna of the Guatemalan Plateau, with special reference to its distribution on the southwestern highlands. *Contrib. Lab. Vertebr. Biol. Univ. Mich.* **49,** 1–71.

Stuart, L.C. (1954). Herpetofauna of the southeastern highlands of Guatemala. *Contrib. Lab. Vertebr. Biol. Univ. Mich.* **68,** 1–65.

Stuart, L.C. (1955). A brief review of the Guatemalan lizards of the genus *Anolis. Misc. Publ. Mus. Zool., Univ. Mich.* **91,** 1–31.

Stuart, L.C. (1958). A study of the herpetofauna of the Uaxactun-Tikal area of northern El Petén, Guatemala. *Contrib. Lab. Vertebr. Biol. Univ. Mich.* **75,** 1–30.

Stuart, L.C. (1963). A checklist of the herpetofauna of Guatemala. *Misc. Publ. Mus. Zool., Univ. Mich.* **122,** 1–150.

Sutherland, S.K., A.R. Coulter, and R.D. Harris. (1979). Rationalisation of first-aid measures for elapid snakebite. *Lancet* **1,** 183–186.

Taylor, E.H. (1935). A taxonomic study of the cosmopolitan scincoid lizards of the genus *Eumeces* with an account of the distribution and relationships of its species. *Univ. Kans. Sci. Bull.* **23**(1), 1–643.

Taylor, E.H. (1941). Herpetological miscellany, No. II. *Univ. Kans. Sci. Bull.* **27**(7), 105–139.

Taylor, E.H. (1956). A review of the lizards of Costa Rica. *Univ. Kans. Sci. Bull.* **38**(1), 3–322.

Taylor, H., and C. Cooley. (1995a). A multivariate analysis of morphological variation among parthenogenetic teiid lizards of the *Cnemidophorus cozumela* complex. *Herpetologica* **51**(1), 67–76.

Taylor, H., and C. Cooley. (1995b). Patterns of meristic variation among parthenogenetic teiid lizards (Genus *Cnemidophorus*) of the Yucatán Peninsula and their progenitor species, *C. angusticeps* and *C. deppei. J. Herpetol.* **29**(4), 583–592.

Underwood, G. (1993). A new snake from St. Lucia, West Indies. *Bull. Nat. Hist. Mus. (Zool.).* **59**(1), 1–9.

Villa, J. (1984). The venomous snakes of Nicaragua. *Milw. Publ. Mus. Contrib. Biol. Geol.* **59,** 1–41.

Villa, J., L.D. Wilson, and J.D. Johnson. (1988). "Middle American Herpetology: A Bibliographic Checklist." University of Missouri Press, Columbia.

Vital Brazil, O., and A. Pellegrini Filho. (1978). The antagonistic effect produced by neostigmine upon the paralysis caused by *Micrurus frontalis* venom (Film). *In* "Toxins: Animal, Plant and Microbial" (P. Rosenberg, ed.), p. 437. Pergamon, Oxford.

Vital Brazil, O., A. Pellegrini Filho, and M. Diasfontana. (1978). Antagonism of *Micrurus frontalis* venom by neostigmine. Treatment of experimental envenomation (abstract). *In* "Toxins: Animal, Plant and Microbial" (P. Rosenberg, ed.), pp. 437–438. Pergamon, Oxford.

Vitt, L.J., and P.A. Zani. (1997). Ecology of the nocturnal lizard

Thecadactylus rapicauda (Sauria: Gekkonidae) in the Amazon region. *Herpetologica* **53**(2), 165–179.

Walker, S.H. (1973). "Summary of Climatic Records for Belize." Land Res. Div., Surbiton, Surrey, UK.

Warrell, D.A. (1995). Animal toxins. *In* "Manson's Tropical Diseases" (G.C. Cook, ed.), 20th ed., Chapter 22, pp. 468–515. Saunders, London.

Warrell, D.A. (1996). Injuries, envenoming, poisoning and allergic reactions caused by animals. *In* "Oxford Textbook of Medicine" (D.J. Weatherall, J.G.G. Ledingham, and D.A. Warrell, eds.), 3rd ed., Chapter 8.4.1, pp. 1124–1151. Oxford University Press, Oxford.

Wellman, J. (1963). A revision of the snakes of the genus *Conophis. Publ. Mus. Nat. Hist., Univ. Kans.* **15**, 251–295.

Weyer, D. (1990). "Snakes of Belize." Belize Audubon Society, Belize.

Williams, K.L. (1988). "Systematics and Natural History of the American Milk Snake *Lampropeltis triangulum*," 2nd ed. Milw. Public Museum, Milwaukee, WI.

Wilson, L.D. (1966). *Dendrophidion vinitor*: An addition to the snake fauna of British Honduras. *J. Ohio Herpetol. Soc.* **5**(3), 103.

Wilson, L.D. (1978). *Coluber constrictor. Cat. Am. Amphib. Reptiles* **218**, 1–218.4.

Wilson, L.D. (1982). A review of the colubrid snakes of the genus *Tantilla* of Central America. *Milw. Publ. Mus. Contrib. Biol. Geol.* **52**, 1–77.

Wilson, L.D. (1988). *Tantillita, T. brevissima, T. lintoni. Cat. Am. Amphib. Reptiles* **455**, 1–455.2.

Wilson, L.D., and D. Hahn. (1973). The herpetofauna of the Islas de La Bahia, Honduras. *Bull. Fla. State Mus.* **17**(2), 93–150.

Wilson, L.D., and J.R. Meyer. (1985). "The Snakes of Honduras," 2nd ed. Milw. Public Museum, Milwaukee, WI.

Wright, A.C.S., D.H. Romney, R.H. Arbuckle, and V.E. Vial. (1959). "Land in British Honduras: A Report of the British Honduras Land Use Survey Team," Colonial Res. Publ. No. 24. H.M. Stationery Office, London.

Zaher, H. (1996). A new genus and species of pseudoboine snake, with a revision of the genus *Clelia* (Serpentes, Xenodontinae). *Boll. Mus. Reg. Sci. Nat. Torino* **14**(2), 289–337.

Zisman, S. (1996). "The Directory of Belizean Protected Areas and Sites of Nature Conservation Interest," 2nd ed. Government of Belize/USAID/WWF, Belmopan, Belize.

Index

This index includes scientific names, commonly used Belizean, English, and Spanish names, and references to general subject matter. Page numbers in boldface type indicate the location of the principal species account; pages on which associated figures, maps, and color plates appear are denoted by *.